MONASTIC ICELAND

This book provides an overview of medieval monasticism in Iceland, from its dawn to its downfall during the Reformation.

Blending the evidence from material remains and written documents, *Monastic Iceland* highlights the realities of everyday life in the male and female monasteries operated in Iceland. The book describes the incorporation of monasticism into the Icelandic society, the alleged land of the Vikings, and thus how the monasteries coexisted with the natural and social environments on the island while keeping their general aims and objectives. The book shows that large social systems, such as monasticism, can cross social and natural borders without necessitating fundamental changes apart from those triggered by the constant coexistence of nature and culture inside the environment they exist within. The evidence provided debunks the myth that Icelandic monasteries, male or female, were isolated, silent places or simple cells functioning principally as retirement homes for aristocrats. To be a member of an ecclesiastical institution did not mean a quiet, secluded life without any outside interaction, but rather active participation in the surrounding community.

The book is for researchers in archaeology, osteology, and medieval history, in addition to all those interested in monasticism and the medieval history of northern Europe.

Steinunn Kristjánsdóttir is Professor of Archaeology at the University of Iceland. Her main interests lie in the field of medieval monasticism, feminism, and gender archaeology. Steinunn has published two monographs in Icelandic. Both books were nominated for the Icelandic Literature Prize. Steinunn was the head of Department of Philosophy, History and Archaeology, University of Iceland, from 2018 to 2022.

MONASTIC ICELAND

Steinunn Kristjánsdóttir

Routledge
Taylor & Francis Group
LONDON AND NEW YORK

Designed cover image: A cornerstone from the monastic building in Hítardalur (National Museum of Iceland_Mýra-006)

First published 2023
by Routledge
4 Park Square, Milton Park, Abingdon, Oxon OX14 4RN

and by Routledge
605 Third Avenue, New York, NY 10158

Routledge is an imprint of the Taylor & Francis Group, an informa business

British Library Cataloguing-in-Publication Data
A catalogue record for this book is available from the British Library

ISBN: 978-1-032-42071-4 (hbk)
ISBN: 978-1-032-42072-1 (pbk)
ISBN: 978-1-003-36107-7 (ebk)

DOI: 10.4324/9781003361077

Typeset in Bembo
by Apex CoVantage, LLC

CONTENTS

FIGURES

TABLES

ACKNOWLEDGEMENTS

It was by an incident that I participated as an archaeology student in an excavation on the monastic site in Viðey in 1990. I continued working there for some seasons. In 2000, I was invited to chair an excavation on another monastic site, Skriðuklaustur. The excavation there lasted for ten seasons but during the excavation, my sincere interest awakened in investigating all the monastic houses run in Iceland. I have been working on the topic ever since and I hope I will have the opportunity to continue to do so.

I would like to thank Skúli Björn Gunnarsson, director at Gunnarsstofnun in Skriðuklaustur for committing me the task to investigate Skriðuklaustur. I also want to thank Agnes S. Arnórsdóttir for reading so carefully over my manuscript, which here is published, even Þórhallur Þráinsson for such thorough comments and reflections on it, but likewise Ásdís Egilsdóttir, Gunnar F. Guðmundsson, and James Clark for reading the manuscript too. I also want to thank Gavin Lucas for encouraging words during the writing of the book, John Luke Murphy for translations of the names of ecclesiastical items, and both Sarah Thomas and Sigrún Hannesdóttir for proofreading the manuscript in its early stage. Last but not least, I want to thank Anna Benassi for making the text readable in English but even for her patience throughout the work.

I am also grateful for inspiring and lively discussion on monastic Iceland, during the last years, months, or weeks, with Andri Kristjánsson, Gísli Kristjánsson, Guðjón Þór Erlendsson, Gottskálk Jensson, the participants in the project *Gendering the Nordic Past* at University of Oslo, and again Þórhallur Þráinsson. Thank you all and I hope that we will continue our discussion because this book should not be observed as any kind of an end product on monastic Iceland. The discussion must continue; there is so much to learn and absorb, not at least due to potentially new theoretical approaching in the near future.

Finally, I want to thank Matthew Gibbons and Sharma Herranshi at Routledge not only for their prompt assistance with the publication process of this book, but also for trusting me for the task of writing a book on monastic Iceland.

The research behind this book was made possible through funding from The Icelandic Research Fund (IRF) and The University of Iceland Research Fund.

SPECIFIC NOTES

Following Icelandic convention, Icelandic authors without surnames are referred to by given name in the general text. The manuscript includes also the Icelandic letters ð and þ. Besides this, historical names of people and places are written in the modern Icelandic form (-ur; e.g. Unnur instead of Unnr, Reynistaður instead of Reynistaðr).

1

INTRODUCTION

Monastic houses were some of the leading institutions of medieval Europe. They shared a collective consciousness and ideology as places of prayer, charity, learning, production, power, and economical wealth, which materialized through different religious orders and communities but were nevertheless grounded in their environment – social and natural. Importantly, the monastic houses were self-sufficient communities containing their means of subsistence within. In the book, the dynamic incorporation of Christian celibacy and monasticism into Icelandic society is examined and described from its dawn to its downfall during the Reformation. Fourteen monastic houses of either Benedictine or Augustinian orders operated there for shorter or longer periods during the Middle Ages. Besides this, at least thirteen hermits and anchorites[1] appear to have lived on the island from the tenth century until the thirteenth century. The origins of the work lie in the field of historical archaeology, which aims to intertwine the evidence preserved in material remains and written documents. The work is otherwise based on materials gained from two recently finished projects and whose objectives were to explore monasticism in medieval Iceland. Both projects prompted the writing of this book; these are an excavation of the ruins of the monastery Skriðuklaustur in eastern Iceland, which took place between 2000 and 2012, and a research project entitled *Mapping Monasticism in Iceland*,[2] which lasted from 2013 to 2017. The aim was to explore the diverse ways in which the monastic houses in Iceland synchronized with their surrounding environment while keeping their dedication to their orders and ideology. The main discoveries made during both projects are covered thoroughly in this book, embedded in a general discussion of medieval monastic Iceland. Some recurring themes concern not only the significance of gender in the operation of the monastic houses but also the ways in which the religious houses responded to periods of prosperity and hardship, such as those caused by the plague, social conflicts, or the Reformation. Overall, the results indicated that large systems of

DOI: 10.4324/9781003361077-1

social networks, such as monasticism, can cross social and natural borders without necessitating fundamental changes apart from amendments triggered by the coexistence of nature and culture inside the environment within which they existed. Thus, Iceland's monastic history, while unique, is certainly a part of pan-European monastic history. In fact, all monastic houses have their own history and distinctive characteristics, owing to the wide range of societal developments, unforeseen occurrences, or even single events, which affected them in various ways. This is what makes their stories so varied but still so alike.

The Background in Brief

By and large, the monastic houses established in Iceland are thought to have been proportionately fewer than in other medieval Christian societies. Additionally, it is particularly noteworthy that the early representatives of celibate life, eremitism and anchoritism, have barely been mentioned in Icelandic historical overviews, albeit with a few exceptions.[3] Most commonly, these individuals are observed as fictional figures, sometimes as odd outlaws or, in the case of the females, identified only as old church women.[4] In fact, the discrepancy in the number of monastic houses and the absence of early eremitic or anchoritic representatives in historical overviews can be explained in part by a general lack of systematic investigation of monasticism in Iceland. The MMI research project showed that all these monastic institutions and religious celibate individuals influenced the making and development of the Icelandic society in past and present times. All of them are therefore included in this synopsis of monastic Iceland.

The fourteen monastic houses that were established in Iceland during the Middle Ages were Bæjarklaustur (1030–1049), Þingeyraklaustur (1133[5]–1551), Munkaþverárklaustur (1155–1551), Hítardalsklaustur (1166–1207), Þykkvabæjarklaustur (1168–1548), Flateyjarklaustur (1172–1184), Helgafellsklaustur (1184–1544), Kirkjubæjarklaustur (1186–1543), Keldnaklaustur (1193–1222), Saurbæjarklaustur (1200–1224), Viðeyjarklaustur (1226–1539), Reynistaðarklaustur (1295–1551), Möðruvallaklaustur (1296–1551), and Skriðuklaustur (1493–1554).[6] Two monasteries were for women (Kirkjubæjarklaustur and Reynistaðarklaustur) but all the other were for men. Some of these monastic institutions were short-lived, such as the first one established at Bær, while others survived for centuries and had long and largely successful histories. One of these short-lived monasteries was Flateyjarklaustur, which was moved to the mainland only twelve years after its establishment on Flatey island. It was consequently renamed Helgafellsklaustur, after the farm to which it moved, Helgafell (Figure 1.1). Five of the monastic houses were run in accordance with the Augustinian Order, or the suborder of St. Victor, and five belonged to the Benedictine Order; in four cases, however, the order is not known for certain. The thirteen Christian hermits and anchorites who appear to have lived in Iceland from the initial settlement there in the ninth century to the end of the thirteenth century were Ketill (*c.* 900), Ásólfur (*c.* 900), Jörundur (*c.* 900), Máni (*c.* 980), Guðrún (*c.* 1000), Guðríður (*c.* 1000),

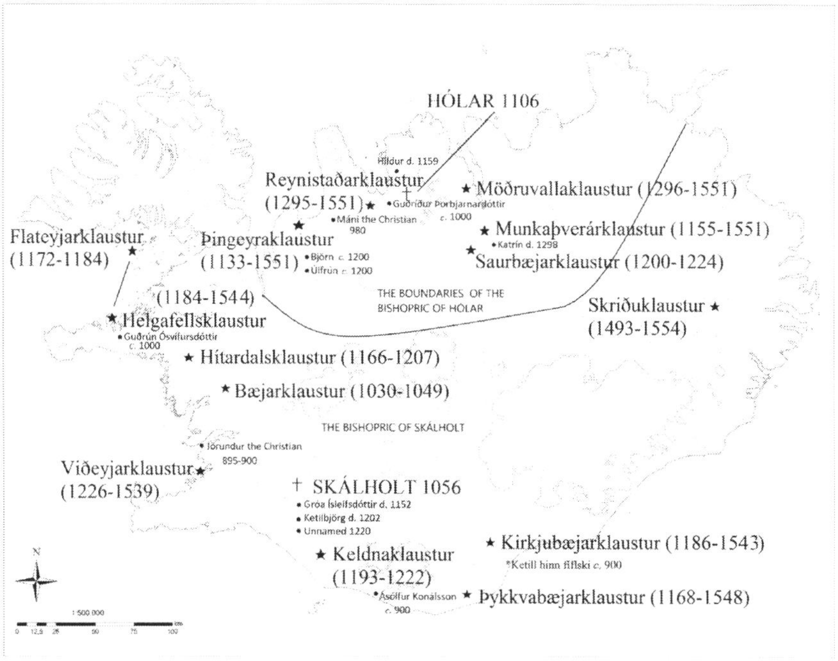

FIGURE 1.1 The location and dates of activity of hermits, anchorites, male and female monasteries, and bishoprics in Iceland during the Middle Ages.

Gróa (*d.* 1152), Hildur (*d.* 1159), Úlfrún (*c.* 1200), Björn (*c.* 1200), Ketilbjörg (*d.* 1201), an unnamed anchoress (*c.* 1210), and Katrín (*d.* 1299) (Figure 1.1). This form of monasticism disappeared in Iceland when the last one. Katrín, moved into the female convent Reynistaðarklaustur.[7]

The significant number of monastic houses operating in Iceland from 1030 to 1554 (in addition to the Christian hermits and anchorites) is indeed noteworthy, given the sparse population of the country. On the basis of the number of farmers listed in *Landnámabók* (the Book of Settlements), there were around 40,000 people living in Iceland during the Middle Ages.[8] This fact alone points to the considerable influence of Christian celibacy and monasticism in wider Icelandic society from the settlement in the ninth century until the Reformation in the mid-sixteenth century, when the last operating monastic institutions were permanently closed all at once.

Yet, the number of the monastic houses established in Iceland before the Reformation is not exclusively disputed among Icelandic scholars. Generally, the monastic houses are considered as having been operated in accordance with Icelandic demands rather than on the premises of the Roman Catholic Church, with only a few religious residents. Thus, as we will see in Chapter 2, containing the historiography of monastic studies in Iceland, the overall belief among scholars is that

Iceland's monastic houses were not involved with the wider society, or open to all those who wished to reside and work inside them as lay brothers and sisters (*oblates*[9]). Nor are the monastic houses believed to have provided customary service to the general public, such as caring for invalids, the poor, and the homeless, or even traveling pilgrims.[10] Rather, they have been observed as functioning principally as retirement homes for male aristocrats. Accordingly, because of their supposed privateness and isolation from the rest of the society, Iceland's monastic institutions are commonly thought not to have been involved in internal political struggles between secular and ecclesiastical powers, such as those occurring during the so-called Staðamál,[11] which lasted intermittently from approximately 1193 to 1297. This approach implies that the monastic houses were somehow a separate niche within Icelandic society rather than a part of a wider network of monasticism and Catholic ideology. Icelanders were indeed devoted followers of Roman Catholic doctrine throughout the Middle Ages, wherein the monastic houses – as well as all the other ecclesiastical institutions operating wherever located geographically in Northwest Europe – played an active role.[12]

A brief perusal of the history of Northwest Europe during the Middle Ages reveals in fact the close internal ties between the societies living there, indicating a shared worldview.[13] This begs the question of why the monasteries, male and female, to the exclusion of other ecclesiastical institutions, were run differently in Iceland. After having mainly practiced the Old Norse religion, which an unknown portion of the settlers brought with them to the island, Icelanders formally adopted Christianity around the year 1000. At that occasion, Iceland became a member of the Nordic archdiocese at Bremen in Germany. This arrangement continued unchanged until 1104, when the Church in Iceland was transferred to the archdiocese at Lund in Scania (present-day Sweden) and remained there for nearly half a century. From 1152/1153 to 1537, the Church in Iceland was under the jurisdiction of the archbishopric at Niðarós (Trondheim), together with Norway, the Faeroe Islands, Greenland, Shetland, Orkney, the Hebrides, and the Isle of Man. At this point in time, there were ten bishoprics belonging to the Niðarós archdiocese, two of them in Iceland: Skálholt, established in 1056, and Hólar, established in 1106 (see Figure 1.1). The archbishopric at Niðarós was dissolved during the Reformation in Norway in 1537 but had already been reduced in size in the fourteenth century, when the Norse settlements along the southwestern coast of Greenland disappeared. In the fifteenth century, it was reduced again when the Scottish islands officially left the archbishopric with the formation of the archbishopric of St. Andrews.[14] In Iceland, the Reformation occurred in Skálholt diocese in 1541, when the Lutheran Church ordinance of King Christian III was passed by the country's general assembly, *Alþingi*. However, Iceland remained semi-Catholic and semi-Lutheran from 1541 to 1550 because the bishop of Hólar diocese, Jón Arason, refused to accept the Lutheran Church ordinance and remained as the representative of Catholics until he was forcibly removed from his post and executed late in 1550. The execution of Bishop Jón Arason marked Iceland's ultimate shift from Catholicism to Lutheranism (see Chapter 9).[15]

With regard to the secular realm, the settlers of Iceland and their descendants soon formed their own system of government based on chieftaincies, codified by the establishment of *Alþingi* in 930. This epoch in the history of Iceland, the so-called Commonwealth or Icelandic Free State, lasted until 1262/1264, when Icelanders swore allegiance to the Norwegian crown. In 1397, more than a century later, the kingdoms of Norway, Sweden, and Denmark were ultimately united under a single monarch in the Kalmar Union. Inevitably, the union included Norway's dependencies, one of which was Iceland, but with the break-up of the Union in 1521/1523, Iceland became a Danish province. Norway remained under the Union until 1537 when the country became a hereditary kingdom in union with Denmark. In 1874, Denmark granted Iceland a constitution, followed by home rule in 1904, and in 1918 Iceland was recognized as a sovereign state, although it remained a domain of the Danish crown until 1944, when Icelanders voted to become a fully independent republic.[16] The historical background of medieval Iceland will be discussed further in Chapter 3.

Skriðuklaustur – Above and Beyond

Skriðuklaustur is the only site of a monastic house that has been excavated in its entirety in Iceland. However, the sites of Viðeyjarklaustur[17] and Kirkjubæjarklaustur[18] have also been partly excavated in recent years, wherefrom data was similarly used during the writing of this book. Still, the results from the Skriðuklaustur excavation became indicative of the subsequent search for the other monastic houses established in Iceland during the Middle Ages and the MMI project emerged. The reasons behind this are numerous. Traditionally, Skriðuklaustur was supposed to have been a closed community with only a few canons resident as the only inhabitants, but the excavation showed that there was a hospital in operation. The monastery housed a number of people seeking social service or accommodation as pilgrims and occasional guests, besides lodging the canons and the serving laity.[19] In this manner, the material structure of Skriðuklaustur revealed a microcosm of the ideal monastic universe, although hybridized in accordance with its contextual meaning. The excavation demonstrated, accordingly, that Skriðuklaustur's location on the outskirts of medieval Christian Europe did not prevent the monastery from fulfilling the requirements of monasticism.

Skriðuklaustur monastery was established in 1493 on the farm Skriða, located in the inland valley of Fljótsdalur in eastern Iceland. This last monastery to be founded in Iceland during the Middle Ages was run according to the Rule of the Augustinian Order until the Reformation in the mid-sixteenth century. Skriðuklaustur appears to have stopped functioning as a monastery when the new Lutheran ordinance was instituted in Skálholt diocese in 1541, although the last prior there did not leave his institution until 1552. This last serving monastic settlement in Iceland was formally taken over by the Danish king in 1554.[20] The excavation at Skriðuklaustur showed that the monastic building and the adjoining church, both partially two stories, occupied an area of just over 1,500 square meters. In contrast, the living quarters of a typical medieval Icelandic farm was 150 square meters, on average.[21] The monastic church was divided into four zones: a chancel, a nave, a narthex with a sacrarium, and finally a chapel. The rooms of the monastic complex included the dormitory, refectory, kitchen, chapterhouse, infirmary hall, heating room, brewery, and night stairs leading from the dormitory to the church. There were three entrances: one leading to the narthex of the church, another functioning as the gate to the monastic garden and the infirmary, and a third located between the refectory and the kitchen. The night stairs, meant only for the canons, led from the dormitory to the church's nave and chancel (Figure 1.2).

Moreover, a total of 298 graves were found in the monastic cemetery, some inside the church and in the rooms in close proximity to the church. This was a surprisingly large number of burials, since the graveyard was only in use during the monastic period that lasted only around sixty years.[22] The graves revealed clearly that a multitude of people lived and died at the monastery, including people who

FIGURE 1.2 The ground plan of Skriðuklaustur.

obviously sought aid there because they suffered from a wide range of afflictions: diseases, injuries, occupational stress, and birth defects. Furthermore, the cemetery itself was divided into four hierarchical areas, each serving a different group of residents: patients, lay people, canons, and benefactors. According to this division, 150 were patients, 130 were lay people or/and occasional residents, and up to twenty were benefactors, patrons, or canons.[23] The artifacts and plants found at the monastery indicated even that attempts were made to provide medical treatment for the patients. Instruments such as lancets, scalpels, and needles were among the finds, and there was evidence of non-native medicinal plants growing at the monastery. Imported mercury was also used for healing.[24]

The building complex and the traces of human habitation from Skriðuklaustur are similarly all indicative of the extensive activities at the monastery, which was stocked with supplies from all over eastern Iceland and even from beyond Iceland's shores. In addition to the mercury, imported healing plants, and surgical equipment, bones of seabirds and sharks caught in the waters off Iceland's eastern coast were found at the site, as were fragments of pottery and an abbey token from the south of France. A figurine made in the Netherlands of St. Barbara, one of the fourteen saints venerated as holy helpers, stood in the church. A horn for calling the canons to services was also imported from the Netherlands; it was found broken in the monastic ruins, as was the figurine of St. Barbara.[25] A gold ring was discovered in a grave located east of the church, indicating that one of the two priors who died in service, Þorvarður or Jón, was buried there.[26] The canons even owned poodles.[27] Furthermore, the inhabitants of the monastery ate meat from domestic animals raised on the inland farms of eastern Iceland, fish from their local farms along the shoreline in the east and south, turnips and fresh vegetables from the garden, and imported dried wild apples.[28] These results were supported by isotope analysis showing that a mixed marine and terrestrial diet with freshwater fish input was consumed by those buried at Skriðuklaustur. Isotope analyses conducted to investigate the geographic provenance of the people buried at Skriðuklaustur showed however that they were mostly locals, coming from the southeastern quarter of the country.[29]

The Agents of Monasticism

The discoveries from the excavation on the ruins of Skriðuklaustur were a revelation and changed the view on the operation of monastic houses in Iceland. In fact, the excavated material from Skriðuklaustur provided a perfect example on how culture constantly interacts with natural surroundings. Written documents also contributed vastly to the research on the monastery in question and on the thirteen other ones established in medieval Iceland, but notwithstanding, intertwined with the archaeological material. During the research for the MMI project, the widest possible range of material and textual data was collected to explore the framework of medieval monasticism in Iceland, observed as being designed in the flux relationship of humans and non-human (or other-than-human) agents. Nothing was left outside the framework of monastic Iceland. No stone was left unturned, and nothing was excluded or ruled out, under the mindset that all human and non-human materials were considered to be of equal importance. This approach provided an opportunity to explore the names of specific rooms in the monastic houses, their interiors and relics and even the titles of professionals or social practices appearing in the medieval official charters, inventories, and letters of the kind preserved, for example, in the *Diplomatarium Islandicum (DI)*.[30] Mentions of individuals, buildings, rooms, incidents, or ideas beside preserved or excavated portable and non-portable objects, illustrations, manuscripts, textiles, and ruins were accordingly observed as agentive material in the search for the Icelandic monastic houses. Current residents at the monastic settlements were even interviewed, geophysical surveying undertaken, and test trenches dug.[31] Medieval monasticism in Iceland had not been researched under the frame of historical archaeology before or under new materialism. The argument of historical archaeology is that when material and written sources are considered together, such residues embrace better the realities of everyday life, which are often absent in historical metanarratives but are highly worthy of being given a public voice. As is shown in this book, monasticism in Iceland encompasses one of the realities that deserve inclusion and historical contextualization.

Certainly, written and oral sources provided valuable insight into elements that could not be determined at the monastic sites themselves, although all sets of data were observed as valid views of the past. At the same time, it was essential to focus on cultural exchange across spatial and temporal boundaries and to view narratives on the settlement of Iceland or the initial development of monasticism as verbal *reflections* of cultural and social realities. These narratives included accounts presented in *Landnámabók* (the Book of Settlements), *Íslendingabók* (the Book of Icelanders), the Icelandic Sagas, *Sturlunga saga*, the bishop's sagas,[32] and even vernacular chivalric sagas. Surely, all kinds of sources are unavoidably imprecise and contain biases, whether they are contemporary or not, by not being the events themselves but only what is memorialized about them or even fabricated. On each occasion, these sources recorded not only the establishment of the monastic houses, their possessions, and their interiors but also their involvement in wider economic and political affairs within and beyond Icelandic society.

These varied materials and data provided useful information, not only about the specialized work carried out in the monastic houses, such as the manuscript and textile making, but also about their individual roles and activities. These included information on how the fasting periods affected the choice of diet or how saintly devotion mirrored interchangeably their needs and objectives during times of prosperity and crisis – to mention some aspects presented in this book. The names of rooms – such as chapterhouses, sacristies, abbots' lodgings, bishops' lodgings, dormitories, refectories, schoolrooms, corrodians' quarters, corrodians' houses, and living rooms – emphasized that the monastic buildings in Iceland were accommodative in a manner to be expected of such a house in a pan-European context. The same applies to the descriptions of the churches, which according to the documents were generally divided into chapels, choirs, naves, narthexes, and aisles, besides being furnished with a freestanding steeple. In written documents, there are also references to the domestic buildings, such as a grinding house, storage rooms, smithies, sheds, pantries, kitchens, and even outdoor kitchens, emphasizing the typical household or farm work taking place in the monastic houses, as will be shown later in this book. Furthermore, the religious roles mentioned in these documents are no less important. They certainly sound familiar in the context of monasticism, but these included abbots, abbesses, monks, nuns, sacristans, novices, students, priests, and deacons, while the other professions ranged from smiths, brewers, stewards, and cook maids to teachers, weavers, and writers, to mention a few.[33] Concurrently with the MMI project, and under its aegis, research was also conducted on some other specific aspects of monastic activity in Iceland, such as the underground passages at the monastic sites were examined, as were the associated place names, the family relationships of monastery residents, folklore about the monasteries, their geographic position in relation to the main travel routes, the use of water from rivers and wells for both secular and sacred purposes, and finally, the lives of hermits and anchorites in Icelandic society during the Middle Ages.[34] Pollen samples were collected from test pits, enabling research on gardening and the use of plants in the monastic houses.[35]

Each and every human and non-human material of the monastic activities discovered during the writing of this book was observed and understood as an agent of pan-European medieval monasticism. The search for the tiniest glimpses of people's lives ultimately delivered a more holistic view of monastic Iceland than had been expected, and at any rate, the monastic houses appear to have thrived finely in Icelandic society, but inevitably, there as everywhere else, they became hybrid versions of their desired form.

Present and Absent-Present

None of Iceland's monastic buildings are visible anymore above ground, but some of their interiors and objects are and, likewise, their stories that they embrace through their absence. By the end of the MMI project, the ruins of at least eight of the fourteen monastic institutions had been identified with a reasonable degree of certainty, but the ruins have often more or less vanished from the surface, as they have from people's minds. In addition to the excavated sites at Skriðuklaustur, Viðeyjarklaustur, and Kirkjubæjarklaustur, five other monastic sites – those of Bæjarklaustur, Þingeyraklaustur, Munkaþverárklaustur, Þykkvabæjarklaustur, and Reynistaðarklaustur – can be included in this list. Even so, while some information was found about the fourteen Icelandic monasteries in written documents, much less is known about the housing of the hermits and anchorites living in Iceland from the settlement of the island until the Middle Ages. Though, as will be discussed, a number of seals still hang under various kinds of written documents from the monastic institutions, occasionally displaying images that could give some hints about their housings. Yet, it is also theorized later in this book that the famous carved door from Valþjófsstaður in Fljótsdalur valley, in eastern Iceland, could originally have stood for the entrance to the monastery at Keldur (see Figure 9.1). The door is now kept in the National Museum of Iceland and is one of its most renowned artifacts on display. It might be the only complete piece preserved of a monastic house in Iceland.

The very few tangible interiors and objects that came into light during the search undertaken within the framework of the MMI project were, for example, a carved cornerstone from an ecclesiastical building was unearthed in Bær, where Bæjarklaustur was located. One other carved cornerstone is preserved above ground at another monastic site in Iceland; specifically, in Hítardalur (see the cover image). Furthermore, a brief excavation carried out at Þingeyraklaustur revealed a liturgical bronze comb from the ruins of the monastery.[36] Other surviving items include a church bell from Bæjarklaustur – the oldest one preserved in Iceland, dating to the eleventh century[37] – a chasuble from Þingeyraklaustur, parts of a processional cross from Þykkvabæjarklaustur, a vestment from Reynistaðarklaustur, a candlestick from Möðruvallaklaustur, and a gilded ornamental chain with the small locket from Skriðuklaustur. Two gold rings from each monastery at Skriðuklaustur and Viðeyjarklaustur must also be mentioned here, as well as four chalice and paten sets, all of which are relics from the Icelandic monasteries, one each from Kirkjubæjarklaustur, Helgafellsklaustur, and Reynistaðarklaustur, as well as one set from Skriðuklaustur.

This is not much but, perhaps, the likenesses and images of earthly saints[38] fared the worst when the monastic houses in Iceland were closed down during the Reformation because they, more than many other objects, symbolized the Roman Catholic faith. The likenesses of heavenly saints[39] were more likely to survive the ongoing iconoclasm during the Reformation because they were still used in the Lutheran teaching. Medieval inventories from the Icelandic monasteries list, for example, ninety-four likenesses (statues, figurines, or other saintly images), depicting a total of thirty different saints.[40] Unfortunately, only five of them are preserved. Roman Catholic likenesses and images were regularly and purposefully destroyed during the Reformation, as they were connected to idolatry and thus not favorable to the Protestants, but some were destroyed in fires or storms.[41] Möðruvallaklaustur burnt down in its entirety in 1316, as did Munkaþverárklaustur in a deadly fire in 1429. Moreover, the monastic churches at Þingeyraklaustur and Viðeyjarklaustur were also damaged by fires in 1157 and *c.* 1480, respectively. Finally, Möðruvallaklaustur church broke into pieces in a storm in 1421 (see Chapter 7).[42]

One of the preserved likenesses is from Möðruvallaklaustur, and it depicts the Virgin Mary and Jesus Christ. The right hand of the likeness is broken off, but in the left hand, the Virgin holds her child.[43] The other four likenesses have been discovered either during archaeological excavations or by chance at three monastic sites in Iceland. One is of St. Dorothy and was found during a construction work in Viðey – the site of Viðeyjarklaustur. Another, of St. Andrew, was found during groundwork on the island of Flatey, but it may be from a church pre-dating the monastery there. The remaining two were found at Skriðuklaustur. These are the figurine of St. Barbara, identified during the archaeological excavations there, and the effigy of Virgin Mary, discovered approximately a century ago hidden in the wall of a barn at the farm where Skriðuklaustur was located.[44] The heads of both the figurines of St. Barbara and St. Dorothy had been broken off, showing evidence of deliberate desecration.[45] Additionally, according to the surviving inventories, the Icelandic monasteries owned at least eight such shrines, but all are lost. There is, however, one shrine preserved from the monastic site Keldur and it might thus be from the monastery there.[46] Besides this, three English alabaster altarpieces displaying saintly images have been preserved from all three monasteries in the north of Iceland: Þingeyraklaustur, Munkaþverárklaustur, and Reynistaðarklaustur. The altarpieces were imported from Nottingham in England and date back to the fifteenth century, but two of them appear to have been a subject to iconoclasm. Still, the cult of saints is indeed apparent not only in preserved likenesses or sculptures but also in hagiographies and textiles. In fact, the MMI project showed that the monastic houses owned hagiographies of sixty-six saints, some in multiple copies. Moreover, several cloths (such as antependia, tapestries, wall-hangings, and burses) embroidered with images of saints, biblical events, or historical scenes, mixed with both sacred and secular motifs, are preserved today from Iceland, but most of them are believed to have been made in the Icelandic female convents, Kirkjubæjarklaustur and Reynistaðarklaustur (see Figures 4.1 and 7.1).[47]

The monasteries' property and possessions were, however, not lost only through iconoclasm or disasters, and thus, the general absence of identifiable portable artifacts from the monastic sites could be explained in part by the fact that many such items were transferred to Denmark during the Reformation. At the time, Iceland was under the control of the Danish king, and this was done on his command. As is discussed further in the last chapter of this book, Chapter 9, all silver was collected from ecclesiastical institutions in the Skálholt bishopric and had already been transported to Copenhagen in 1541. Lists of ship cargoes from the bishopric of Hólar likewise note that silver artifacts, relics, altarpieces, and effigies largely ended up in Copenhagen in 1551. The loot was explicitly said to come from the three monasteries in that diocese: Þingeyraklaustur, Munkaþverárklaustur, and Möðruvallaklaustur.[48] After the transport of monastic goods from Iceland on the order of the Danish king, coins and silver objects were melted down in order to make equipment for his army. The monastic churches were also refurnished and reconstructed on the orders of the Danish king after the Reformation (in Iceland and Denmark), as he considered them too costly to operate.[49] This certainly happened at Þingeyraklaustur, Þykkvabæjarklaustur, Reynistaðarklaustur, and Skriðuklaustur, but the fate of the churches at other monastic sites is still uncertain. The monastic building of Viðeyjarklaustur was also deliberately torn down by the king's men in 1539 and new ones built on their foundations for his representatives in Iceland. With this act the dissolution of monastic Iceland started. Fifteen years later, all the monastic houses had been closed for good and gradually all the human and non-human agents of monasticism in Iceland were wiped out.

The search for the Icelandic monastic houses, their buildings, relics, and interiors, under the auspices of the MMI project, was concluded in 2017. The project showed that a great deal of information about them had disappeared during their dissolution and the overall Reformation in Iceland, but as we will see, their history has never been lost.

Notes

1 1 An anchoress is the female equivalent to an anchorite. In the book, 'anchorite' will be used as a general term for both male and female anchorite life, except when the discussion is specifically directed at anchoresses.
2 Referred to hereafter using the initials MMI.
3 See Arnórsdóttir, *Konur og vígamenn*, pp. 135–136; Egilsdóttir, 'Skjaldmær drottins', pp. 29–42; Þorsteinsson, *Íslensk miðaldasaga*, p. 125; Cormack, 'Monastic Foundations and Foundation Legends', pp. 60–79; Skórzewska, *Constructing a Cult*, pp. 82, 152–153.
4 In Icelandic: *kirkjukerling*. Hugason, 'Frumkristni og upphaf kirkju', p. 353; Kristjánsdóttir, 'A Nocturnal Wake at Hólar', pp. 225–228. See also Jakobsson and Egilsdóttir, 'Abbadísin sem hvarf', pp. 7–9.
5 Þingeyraklaustur was established in 1112 but did not begin operation until 1133.
6 Kristjánsdóttir, *Leitin að klaustrunum*, pp. 57–63.
7 Kristjánsdóttir, 'Ankorítar og hermítar á Íslandi', pp. 46–69; Kristjánsdóttir, *Leitin að klaustrunum*, pp. 79–83.
8 Karlsson, *Iceland's 1100 Years*, pp. 14–15, 35; *Landnámabók*, pp. 1–20.
9 Individuals who are not professed monks or nuns but affiliated with a monastic community of their choice as lay servants or clerics.
10 See, for example, Þorsteinsson and Grímsdóttir, 'Enska öldin', pp. 152–155; Harðardóttir, 'Vangaveltur um íslensk klausturhús – íslenskun erlendra áhrifa'; Karlsson, *Iceland's 1100 Years*, pp. 44–51; Þorláksson, 'Þjóðhagir og samfélagshópar', pp. 124–129; Sigurðsson, *Det norrøne samfunnet*, pp. 158–160; Jónsson, 'Áhrif klaustranna á Íslandi', pp. 283–298; Guttormsson and Kjartansson, 'Siðaskiptin og fátækraframfærsla', pp. 11–43; Patzuk-Russell, *The Development of Education*, p. 69; Sigurdson, *The Church in Fourteenth Century Iceland*, p. 17.
11 In short, the term *Staðamál* refers specifically to the conflict (persisting on and off until 1297) between ecclesiastical authorities and the Icelandic chieftains about the operation and investiture of churches that the chieftains had built on their estates. These estates were entitled *staðir*, or *beneficia*, as they were named in canon law. However, in accordance with amendments made to canon law, starting on the Continent in the eleventh century, laymen were prohibited from interfering in ecclesiastical matters, including the running of churches. These amendments considerably curtailed the chieftains' previous authority over the *beneficia*, causing the abovementioned conflict. In this book, *staðir* are referred to henceforth as *beneficia* (the plural form of *beneficium*).
12 This matter is discussed in Hreinsson, *Force of Words*. See also, Sharp, 'Bishops, Canon Law, and the Religious, c. 1140–1350', pp. 193–194.
13 See, for example, Walaker Nordeide, *The Viking Age as a Period of Religious Transformation*, pp. 79–83.
14 Karlsson, *Iceland's 1100 Years*, pp. 38–43; Sigurðsson, 'Samskipti íslenskra biskupa', pp. 508–515; Nyberg, *Monasticism in North-Western Europe*, pp. 20–22; Woolf, 'The Diocese of Sudreyar'; Thomas, 'The Diocese of Sodor', p. 35.
15 See, for example, Karlsson, *Iceland's 1100 Years*, pp. 132–133; Lausten, *Luther og Danmark i 500 år*, pp. 69–70; Ísleifsdóttir, *Byltingin að ofan*, pp. 86–103, 219–261.
16 Karlsson, *Iceland's 1100 Years*, pp. 267–272, 280–284.
17 Hallgrímsdóttir, 'Rannsóknir í Viðey', pp. 99–102, 129; Hallgrímsdóttir, *Fornleifarannsókn í Viðey 1987*; Hallgrímsdóttir, *Viðey. Fornleifarannsóknir 1988–1989*; Hallgrímsdóttir,

Viðey. Fornleifarannsóknir 1989–1990; Hallgrímsdóttir, *Húsakostur Viðeyjarklausturs*; Kristjánsdóttir, 'Klaustureyjan á Sundum'; Kristjánsdóttir, *Heiðnar og helgar minjar í Viðey*; Kristjánsdóttir, 'Viðey – trúarheimar mætast'.

18 Einarsson, *Kirkjubær. Klaustur og umhverfisaðstæður*; Mímisson and Einarsson, *Rannsókn á rústum nunnuklaustursins á Kirkjubæ*; Mímisson and Einarsson, 'Klausturlíf kvenna í Skaftárþingi. Fornleifarannsóknir á Kirkjubæjarklaustri 1995–2006'; Mímisson and Einarsson, ' "*Ora et labora*". Efnisveruleiki klausturlífs á Kirkjubæjarklaustri', pp. 151–177.

19 Steinsson, *Munklífi á Skriðu*; Steinsson, 'Jarðir Skriðuklausturs og efnahagur', pp. 74–103.

20 Jónsson, 'Um klaustrin á Íslandi', pp. 264–265; Steinsson, *Munklífi á Skriðu*; Steinsson, 'Jarðir Skriðuklausturs og efnahagur', pp. 74–103.

21 Kristjánsdóttir, *Sagan af klaustrinu á Skriðu*, pp. 64–65.

22 It is unlikely that those residing in the monastery's care would have been sent away immediately after the closing in 1541. Burials may thus have taken place there at least until 1552, when the last prior there left Skriðuklaustur permanently, and even longer but these burials are not many.

23 Kristjánsdóttir, 'The Tip of the Iceberg', pp. 54–58; Kristjánsdóttir, 'No Society Is an Island', pp. 166–167.

24 Kristjánsdóttir, *Sagan af klaustrinu á Skriðu*, pp. 277–283; Kristjánsdóttir et al., 'The Icelandic Medieval Monastic Garden'; Walser III et al., 'Volcanoes, Medicine, and Monasticism', pp. 48–61.

25 Mehler et al., 'The Sound of Silence', pp. 551–560.

26 Kristjánsdóttir, *Sagan af klaustrinu á Skriðu*, pp. 155–158.

27 Hamilton-Dyer, 'Skriðuklaustur Monastery – Animal Bones 2003–2007', p. 29; Kristjánsdóttir, *Sagan af klaustrinu á Skriðu*, pp. 98–100.

28 Hamilton-Dyer, 'Skriðuklaustur Monastery – Animal Bones 2003–2007'; Kristjánsdóttir, 'Lost Paths', pp. 1–8.

29 Walser III et al., 'At the World's Edges', pp. 142–163.

30 Hereafter *DI*.

31 Reports can be downloaded from the project's website here: https://steinunn.hi.is/is/rannsoknirresearch/kortlagning-klaustra-islandi.

32 The bishops' sagas are a special genre of the Icelandic medieval sagas. Several of them tell the lives of saintly bishops (called a *vita* in Latin), but generally, these contain sacred biographies of the Icelandic bishops. See Egilsdóttir, 'Biskupasögur', pp. 45–46; Egilsdóttir, 'Biskupasögur og helgar ævisögur', pp. xiv–xviii.

33 See discussion on lay brothers and sisters in Cassidy-Welch, 'Lay Brothers and Sisters', pp. 1028–1037.

34 Jónsdóttir, 'Þjóðleiðir við klaustrin á kaþólskum tíma'; Jónsdóttir and Kristjánsdóttir, 'Tengsl fólks í miðaldaklaustrunum á Íslandi'; Jónsdóttir and Kristjánsdóttir, 'Þjóðleiðir við klausturstaði á kaþólskum tíma'; Hjartarson, 'Lífsins vatn'; Hjartarson and Kristjánsdóttir, 'Rannsókn á örnefnum um klaustur á Íslandi'; Hjartarson and Kristjánsdóttir, 'Jarðgöng frá fornri tíð á Íslandi'; Gunnarsdóttir and Kristjánsdóttir, 'Varðveittir gripir'.

35 Riddel, 'Flotation Sampling Procedure'; Riddel and Erlendsson, 'Viðey Pollen Analysis'; Riddel and Erlendsson, 'Bær in Borgarfjörður. Rapid Scanning for Cereals in Sample KLI-2014–51–11'; Riddel and Erlendsson, 'Helgafell Pollen Analysis'; Riddel and Erlendsson, 'Reynistaðir Pollen Analysis'; Riddel and Erlendsson, 'Trumbsvalir (Þingeyrar)'; Riddel and Erlendsson, 'Þingeyrar soil sampling'; Riddell et al., 'Pollen, Plague and Protestants'.

36 Kristjánsdóttir, 'Þingeyraverkefnið. Áfangaskýrsla 2018', pp. 10–11.

37 Kristjánsdóttir, *Leitin að klaustrunum*, p. 19.

38 People once living but sanctified by papal authorities after their death.

39 The biblical figures.

40 Agatha, Agnes, Andrew, Anne, Anthony, Augustine, Barbara, Bartholomew, Benedict, Bonaventura, Cecilia, Clement, Catherine, Clare, Lucy, Magnus Earl of Orkney, the Virgin Mary, Martin, Matthew, Michael, Nicholas, Olaf King of Norway, Paul, Peter,

Roch, Dionysius, Egidius, Zita, Hallvard, Stephen, James, Thomas, Jesus Christ, the Trinity, John, John the Baptist, Veronica, and the bishops Þorlákur Þórhallsson and Jón Ögmundsson.

41 Aston, 'Public Worship and Iconoclasm', pp. 9–28; Graves, 'From an Archaeology of Iconoclasm', pp. 35–47; Spicer, 'Iconoclasm and Adaptation', pp. 29–43; Tarlow, 'Reformation and Transformation', pp. 110–112.

42 Harðardóttir, 'Nokkrar kynslóðir kirkna', pp. 14–15; Kristjánsdóttir, *Leitin að klaustrunum*, pp. 98, 137, 335, 392–394.

43 Gunnarsdóttir and Kristjánsdóttir, 'Varðveittir gripir', pp. 27–28.

44 Kristjánsdóttir, *Sagan af klaustrinu á Skriðu*, pp. 97–100.

45 Kristjánsdóttir, *Leitin að klaustrunum*, p. 445. See also Cormack, 'Voru helgimyndir eyðilagðar á Íslandi?' p. 246.

46 Cormack, 'Voru helgimyndir eyðilagðar á Íslandi?' pp. 247–248; Harðardóttir, 'Innanbúnaður kirkna', p. 206.

47 See for example, Guðjónsson, '. . . "slitur úr eldgömlu húss-tjaldi"', pp. 9–10; Guðjónsson, 'Íslensk kirkjuklæði á miðöldum', pp. 85–89; Eldjárn, *Hundrað ár í Þjóðminjasafni*, nr. 18 and 32; Jónsdóttir, 'Gömul krossfestingarmynd', pp. 134–145; Wandel, 'Íslenzk altarisklæði', pp. 51–54.

48 *Kancelliets brevbøger vedrørende Danmarks indre forhold 1551–1555*, pp. 31–32; see also *Kancelliets brevbøger vedrørende Danmarks indre forhold 1561–1565*; *Kancelliets brevbøger vedrørende Danmarks indre forhold 1571–1575*; *Kancelliets brevbøger vedrørende Danmarks indre forhold 1576–1579*.

49 DI XIII, pp. 480–481; Seesko, 'Between King and Congregation', p. 277.

2

THE HISTORIOGRAPHY OF MEDIEVAL MONASTICISM IN ICELAND

One of the questions dealt with in this book is why the monastic houses have generally been observed as insignificant and powerless institutions in Iceland, despite obviously being the agents of the larger worldview of Christian Europe. The book aims to present an alternative to that theory. The narrow view of monasticism is evident not only in overviews of Icelandic history, but it is also apparent in some academic work in Iceland's neighboring countries, such as Norway, Denmark, and Ireland – perhaps wider.[1] The history of monasticism in Norway has in fact been disapproved for having largely been written from a Protestant perspective, thereby providing a skewed view of the general history of Norwegian monasticism. The only comprehensive overview on medieval monasticism in Norway is still the one that historian and archivist, Christian Lange, wrote in 1847.[2] In Denmark, the discussion has centered on how anti-Catholicism has influenced Danish society and research on monasticism during the last two centuries.[3] The Reformation in Denmark has even in recent years been observed as having been accomplished a return to the original Christendom, based on the appeal to end the ongoing abuse of the Roman Catholic Church.[4] Henceforth, examining the historiography of monasticism in Iceland reveals clearly that it has been influenced by the same political and theoretical movements, much like all other academic work is. This is outlined further in the following sections, while a critical overview of the historiography of monastic research in Iceland is provided through Protestantism, nationalism, new social history, feminism, and historical archaeology.

Protestantism and Nationalism

A recurring theme in the research undertaken on monasticism in Iceland during the nineteenth and most of the twentieth century is that the Roman Catholic

DOI: 10.4324/9781003361077-2

Church was morally corrupt and politically incompetent, and that Protestantism was a desirable power. This perspective should hardly come as a surprise in societies that banned Catholic Christianity after the Reformation, as Iceland, Norway, and Denmark did. In Iceland, religious freedom was not reinstated until 1874, when Denmark granted Iceland its own constitution. Similarly, it was not until 1843 that the Norwegian Parliament passed a limited religious freedom act, which permitted legal non-Lutheran public religious services for the first time since the Reformation. The ban on non-Lutheran religious activity was finally lifted in Denmark in 1849 and in Norway in 1897.[5]

The influences of Protestantism were in fact already visible in scholarly work shortly after Martin Luther published his ninety-five theses in Germany in 1517. Since then, Protestantism has inevitably undergone several periods of reawakening, with many notable peaks; for example, during the eighteenth and mid-nineteenth centuries, although a prejudice against Roman Catholicism seems to have been evident for quite a long time after the Reformation in Denmark, Norway, and Iceland, compared to how it was later in these countries.[6] In Iceland, Protestantism appears to have had its influence from the early eighteenth century. For example, when the great manuscript collector Árni Magnússon (1663–1730) initiated a search for empirical evidence of the past in Iceland, he mostly collected manuscripts written in the native language, Icelandic, rather than texts written in the language of the Church, Latin.[7] He appears even to have neglected ecclesiastical textiles in his search for antiques in Iceland. Still, in the early Protestant era of Árni's youth, liturgical books and artifacts were considered rubbish that deserved to be burnt – and most likely even medieval wall hangings and tapestries, embroidered with stories and Catholic ornaments.[8] It must be noted, however, that Árni was following the footsteps of Danish Renaissance men, such as the famous antiquarian Ole Worm (1588–1654), who had a keen interest in Nordic antiquity and wanted to collect Icelandic sagas rather than popish literature.[9] It is true that Icelandic monks (and perhaps nuns, too, although they are rarely mentioned in this context) wrote, translated, and recorded both secular and sacred books in their native Old Norse/Icelandic, not just in ecclesiastical Latin. This custom is discussed further later in the book, but many of the manuscripts Árni collected came from these medieval Icelandic monks. The writing and linguistic customs prevailing in Icelandic monastic houses have nevertheless been interpreted as evidence that the monks needed no language other than their native Icelandic to communicate and that consequently, the official language of the Church did not interest them.[10]

Still, while monasteries are rarely discussed in overviews of the history of medieval Iceland, there are cases where they are described as either overly authoritarian or totally passive. In fact, there is often an inconsistency in the characterization of Icelandic monasteries, with scholars referencing their limited impact while – virtually in the same breath – emphasizing their enormous wealth and greed for valuable possessions such as the farms owned by common Icelanders.[11] Despite this paradox, it is generally acknowledged that by the time of the Reformation, the monastic houses owned 13% of all farms in Iceland.[12] How they succeeded in acquiring all of these properties, often valuable farms, given their small number and lack of social connections has on the other hand rarely been questioned. The reality is that historical research on the settlement, the Commonwealth period, and the Middle Ages in Iceland has focused primarily on the viewpoint of the Icelandic chieftains and on aspects of the society traditionally classified as Icelandic. Meanwhile, the monastic houses – as much as the Roman Catholic Church – have been considered foreign entities and insignificant participants in Icelandic society, despite being active there for more than 500 years.[13] Also evident in this context is the scant interest shown to date in studying the leaders of the monastic houses, either abbots or abbesses, whereas secular chiefs, both men and women, from the sagas or written documents have been etched indelibly into the history of medieval Iceland. The abbesses, who for decades managed the largest female institutions that have ever existed in Iceland, are barely mentioned in historical overviews – not until vaguely during second- or third-wave feminism, when emphasis was placed on 'writing women into history'. The same can be said about the abbots. The names of church leaders, male and female, have certainly been listed in historical publications,[14] but only in contexts where the monastic houses are presented as a separate, isolated niche within Icelandic society.

A condemnatory approach to papal interference in local governmental affairs in Iceland, as upheld through the episcopal see in Niðarós, has in this manner long been prominent in research on medieval Icelandic church history. To complicate matters, studies are even strongly influenced by another international movement: nationalism. The influence of nationalism appears in various ways, often entwined with Protestantism, in scholarly work from the second half of the nineteenth century through the end of the twentieth century. One influential scholar from the early twentieth century claimed that international monasticism failed to succeed in integrating itself into medieval Icelandic culture because Icelanders were too independent and 'racially strong' for it.[15] However, the most notable and influential idea to be found in research done by Icelandic scholars during the first half of the twentieth century was that Icelanders did not need advice from abroad, from either the papacy or its subordinate archbishoprics, about how to run their ecclesiastical institutions, so they did not take any.[16] Meanwhile, the same scholars generally accepted that after the Reformation, Icelanders followed Lutheran ordinances and subsequent regulations from Danish authorities, without any noticeable resistance. Moreover, the most frequently raised research questions of the last century have centered on how the ideology of monasticism could have survived in Iceland's harsh and remote environment and how the monasteries that did survive managed to assimilate and become 'Icelandic' in terms of both building design and activities.[17] This implied that because Icelanders had limited access to a wide variety of building resources (other than turf and stone), they were hardly capable of fulfilling the requirements of monasticism. It was also assumed that growing medicinal plants and vegetables in monastic gardens was made impossible by Iceland's inclement weather, as compared with more favorable conditions in mainland Europe.

In fact, it may come as no surprise that research on monasticism in Iceland was heavily influenced by the nationalist movement, which was one of the most significant political and social forces in recent history – and in academic research – from the nineteenth century until long after the World War II. When Icelanders began to demand independence from Denmark during the second half of the nineteenth century, their efforts were built upon the international movement of nationalism, which by then had become highly popular, both on the Continent and in the United States. The core belief was that each nation should govern itself, free of outside interference, including from the papacy.[18] The Icelandic independence movement soon turned into a collective effort that lasted until the twentieth century, but it was initially led by a few Icelandic-born, Danish-educated male intellectuals. These leaders introduced the idea of a national consciousness to other Icelandic scholars, and soon nationalism became as fashionable in Iceland as it was elsewhere in the Western world. This surfaced not least in historical and scientific eugenics research during the twentieth century. The extensive archaeological excavations in Þjórsárdalur valley in southern Iceland, undertaken by major Nordic archaeologists in 1939, offer an example of such research. The excavation was meant to identify morphologically the origin and prototypes of the Nordic, or Aryan race, but during the excavation, six medieval farms were dug up, in addition to one cemetery.[19]

As a result, during the nineteenth and much of the twentieth centuries, historical research in Iceland was inevitably colored by Protestantism and nationalism as much as the Icelandic fight for independence was.[20] In the prevailing interpretation, the period from 1262/1264 up to 1874, when the first phase of the Icelandic fight for independence came to an end, was considered as the worst in Iceland's history – sometimes referred to as the dark ages in the history of Iceland. Meanwhile, the period from the settlement until the end of the Commonwealth period has been glorified as one in which Icelanders were successfully governed by their own native chieftains until they lost their independence to Norway. The generally held view is that this loss of independence ushered in a long period of decline characterized by foreign dominance until Iceland regained its independence in the twentieth century. This interpretation is, however, supported neither by documentary nor by archaeological evidence – rather the contrary.[21]

Still, monasticism has been present in people's minds throughout the ages, but mainly through folklore and legends. Most of these stories were recorded in later times, long after the Reformation. They usually portray the religious inhabitants as greedy and even treacherous, and the monks and nuns are depicted as either helpful or selfish, in accordance with current Protestant views on monasticism and Roman Catholic Christianity. Revelry and a life of luxury at the expense of the common people are also typical motifs. For example, a canon from Helgafellsklaustur was said to have swum in Helgafellsvatn, confronting all the bones of the unwanted children he had disposed of there; an abbess from Kirkjubæjarklaustur was said to have been seen with male underpants on her head instead of a scapular after a visit to the monks at Þykkvabæjarklaustur; another story tells of monks, who simply died of obesity in their monastery. Many of the stories also describe how the monks managed to acquire the assets of dying people on their deathbed. Moreover, the anchorites and hermits in the stories are said to be thievish but at the same time provident.[22] Even though these are legendary stories, they would nonetheless have influenced people's general opinion of monasticism – and they still do. While collecting sources for the MMI project, the researchers were constantly reminded of these old stories.

It is clear from the historiography of monasticism in Iceland that Icelandic scholars have been primarily interested in monasticism within its national rather than transnational context. However, as the coming sections illustrate, there have been scholars from the mid-twentieth century until the present day, who have nevertheless studied monasticism in Iceland as an essential part of medieval Christian society in Iceland. Despite this, the belief that monasteries were an outlandish or undesirable addition to Icelandic society has been the most persistent and prominent one in grand narratives of medieval Iceland from the late nineteenth century onwards.

Grand Narratives

One of the early scholars interested in the monastic history was the Rev. Finnur Jónsson, bishop of Skálholt, who wrote his four-volume *Church History of Iceland* during the last quarter of the eighteenth century. In the fourth volume, published in 1778, he describes the monasteries in detail but, however, without characterizing them as foreign or unwanted institutions, as many scholars did later.[23] Bishop Finnur's overview of monasticism in Iceland is the first thorough study of the topic, but the second one was written a century later by the Rev. Janus Jónsson and published as an article in 1887.[24] This was notably at the time when Catholicism was regaining strength in Iceland after religious freedom was guaranteed in 1874, often appearing in controversial views on monasticism. Just as Bishop Finnur did, Janus listed not only the names of the medieval Icelandic monasteries but also the names of their abbots and abbesses, in addition to briefly summarizing their history, starting with the foundation of the earliest monastery in 1030. Furthermore, both scholars listed most of the hermits and anchorites who had lived in Iceland during the early medieval ages, but Rev. Finnur recorded even the farms owned by monasteries at the time of their dissolution during the Reformation.

It appears that after Janus Jónsson published his article, scholars assigned monasticism an increasingly smaller and more negative place in their overviews of the history of Iceland. The next scholar to publish research on monasticism in Iceland was the Rev. Magnús Jónsson, who wrote a detailed article on the subject in 1914. His article can be interpreted as a kind of a critical response to the writings of his colleague Janus, but in it Magnús describes the 'spiritual death' of the monasteries, as being non-functional institutions. He believed that the monastic life did not fit with the Icelandic temperament and claimed that the Icelandic nation lacked what he termed 'monastic thinking', which was necessary for monastic institutions to survive in Iceland. According to him, Icelanders were too phlegmatic and wise to follow religious orders that were, to his mind, based on pagan ideologies. Magnús was also one of the scholars who first stated that monasteries in Iceland were much smaller and more influenced by national circumstances than those in neighboring countries.[25] It is noteworthy that he made no mention of nuns or female convents in his overview, only of male monasteries and monks. This is, however, in line with studies in medieval monasticism at that time, where female monasteries commonly seem to have had a lower status than the male ones and been regarded as less important for the study of monasticism.[26] It is particularly notable that Janus, unlike his colleague Magnús, made no judgements about the monasteries, male or female, or about whether monastic life was bad or good.

Historian Páll Eggert Ólason's four-volume work on the Reformation, published in 1919–1926, displays further the ongoing debate on medieval monasticism in Iceland, a debate that had in fact started with Janus Jónsson's publication in 1887. Although the first volume was based on his doctoral thesis, Páll Eggert differs from Rev. Magnús in that all four volumes depict monastic houses as important institutions that significantly influenced Icelandic society, especially at the peak of the Catholic era during the late Middle Ages.[27] Apparently, though, Páll Eggert Ólason's publication did not appeal to other scholars of the time or to the general public, except to a limited extent. It is, at least, barely cited by other scholars. On the contrary, Magnús' writings had a major influence on the formation of new ideas on medieval monasticism and how monastic institutions functioned in Iceland. Magnús, who was a Lutheran writer, a parliamentarian, and a professor of theology, obviously expressed his negative views on monasticism in his writings. Until his retirement in 1952, he was a tutor to generations of priests who, like Magnús himself, were raised within both the Protestant and the nationalistic mindset. Magnús' emphasis can even be seen in the repeated weight he put on the fact that the monks had placed greater importance on writing books in their native language, Icelandic, than on writing in the international language of the medieval Church, Latin.[28] Similar criticism can also be noticed in politics and scholarly work in Denmark after religious freedom was permitted there again in 1849. By then, Catholicism was observed as a foreign religion in the Danish society, along with Judaism, and dangerous to what was identified as Danishness. This statement appears in scholarly work of the Danish professor of theology, Hans Lassen Martensen, in 1873. The ties between nationalism and Protestantism even appear to have become stronger as time passed, at least has Lutheranism for long been an integral part of Danish identity.[29]

The next scholars to contribute to the study of Icelandic history were the historians Björn Þorsteinsson, Jón Jóhannesson, and Magnús Stefánsson. Their extensive overviews on the history of Iceland were published around the middle of the twentieth century. In these publications, the Icelandic male and female monasteries are only listed briefly in a separate chapter. All these three scholars emphasized that monasticism should be approached as part of an international movement, although they all agreed that the monastic houses run in Iceland were different by being nationalistic in nature but without discussing this point further.[30]

The monasteries were in this way presented as a distinct and foreign niche within the Icelandic medieval society, and no attempt was made whatsoever to contextualize them. Historian Magnús Stefánsson is best known, however, for his research on the *Staðamál* and consequent disputes, wherefrom he in fact excluded the monastic institutions – as other scholars have done since – because he saw them as being so isolated and disciplined in their devotion that such conflicts stood outside their scope and interests.[31] Nevertheless, both Jón Jóhannesson and Magnús Stefánsson underlined that the Icelandic monasteries were important cultural institutions for ecclesiastical writing and teaching, but even so isolated from the rest of the Icelandic society, just as the Rev. Magnús Jónsson had stated.[32]

It is thus very plausible that the writings of the Rev. Magnús Jónsson set the stage for how monastic institutions would be viewed in the future: as imports that failed to integrate into Icelandic society. Still, in contrast to both Jón Jóhannesson and Magnús Stefánsson, Björn Þorsteinsson claimed that the Icelandic monastic houses became extremely wealthy as time went by. He emphatically did not see this as a positive development, though, and he maintained that through their acquisition of the possessions of ordinary people in Iceland, particularly those whom the Church had excommunicated, the monasteries had decreased their quality of life. In Björn's view, the regular clergy had thus become a pest for Icelanders by suspiciously claiming to be working in the name of God. He stated furthermore that the monastic institutions supported Iceland's churchly leaders by providing them with all the resources that they selfishly managed to acquire from ordinary people. Björn claimed thus that they became the country's wealthiest institutions – in the name of God.[33]

The Church's control over the general public was certainly great, and it grew significantly until the Reformation. For example, the Church had the power to place obligations on tenants living on its farms or to get common people to work in its own interest. But it is far from true that ecclesiastical institutions weakened the condition of the public or the poor: quite the contrary, in fact. Ecclesiastical institutions such as monasteries were open to all those who needed shelter.[34] There are no examples of people having been forced to work for the monastic houses or of laymen permanently moving into them, except certainly in cases of obligations that the Church could impose on people in the name of absolution – a matter that later became the core of criticism of the Roman Catholic Church during the Reformation. Gradually, the monastic houses in Iceland became popular cultural institutions, educational centers, hospitals, retirement homes, and workplaces for the rich as well as the poor who wanted to contribute to the improvement of society or themselves. Consequently, the monastic institutions were important for the development and growth of Icelandic medieval society and were not meant to serve the ecclesiastical upper echelons alone. They were an inseparable part of society, no less than they were elsewhere in medieval Europe or the Latin West.

Historian Jón Jóhannesson also gave voice to the persistent idea that the monastic houses had functioned first and foremost as retirement homes for rich and powerful chieftains during their old age but only until the end of Commonwealth period. Jón underlined, however, that he doubted that the chieftains had changed their mindset by moving into a monastery.[35] It is not clear what Jón meant with this statement, but by being member of a Christian society, all Icelanders – the chieftains and the clergy, as much as the general public – followed Catholic teachings devotedly throughout the Middle Ages, for better or worse. The wide assortment of resources presented in the following chapters demonstrates that. Furthermore, it became particularly popular *after* the Commonwealth period to make a corrody agreement with the monastic houses. The Icelandic corrodians, who are discussed in detail in Chapter 8, could be of all classes, genders, and ages. Moreover, most of the monasteries were run by native Icelanders: people who were in charge of them for considerable periods of time, in some cases for more than half a century. This applies to both abbots and abbesses but apparently this was their profession. Those who held their posts for the longest time, fifty-two years, were Abbess Halldóra Sigvaldadóttir of Kirkjubæjarklaustur, Abbot Jón Gamlason of Þingeyraklaustur, and Abbot Einar Ísleifsson of Munkaþverárklaustur. Next on the list is Abbess Sólveig Hrafnsdóttir, who spent fifty years of her life serving as an abbess in Reynistaðarklaustur. In this context, it is worth mentioning the three clerics who were all educated at Þykkvabæjarklaustur at the same time during the mid-thirteenth century and later served as abbots, each for a long period, in the largest monasteries in the diocese of Skálholt. They were Runólfur Ólafsson, abbot of Viðeyjarklaustur for forty-nine years; Ólafur Hjörleifsson, abbot of Helgafellsklaustur for forty-four years; and Runólfur Sigmundsson, abbot of Þykkvabæjarklaustur for forty-two years. More examples can be found. Nevertheless, there are certainly examples of chieftains who chose celibacy in their old age and established their own monasteries, but they were few. The monasteries concerned were Keldnaklaustur, Saurbæjarklaustur, and Viðeyjarklaustur, all of which were established by the most renowned secular chiefs in Iceland during the era of the *Staðamál*.[36] However, it is difficult to comprehend how the monastic institutions could have been unaffected by the *Staðamál* conflicts – as historian Magnús Stefánsson claimed – since the issue regarded their control through the Church, bishops, abbots, and abbesses, including the operation of ecclesiastical institutions. The MMI project showed at least that during the thirteenth century, while the conflicts were at their peak, all the male monasteries and the only active female convent at the time were confronted with these defensive struggles. Most, although not all, of the monastic houses survived when these long-standing conflicts ended in 1297 with a virtually complete victory by the Church.

Soon after the four scholars – the Rev. Magnús Jónsson and the historians Björn Þorsteinsson, Jón Jóhannesson, and Magnús Stefánsson – published their influential works on the history of medieval Iceland, monasteries almost completely disappeared from general overviews of Icelandic history. It may be concluded that they had been written off as foreign institutions that did not conform to the Icelanders' way of life. As late as 1990, historian Björn Þorsteinsson and medievalist Guðrún Ása Grímsdóttir claimed that almost no documents were preserved on the activities of the monastic houses in Iceland and that this proved their inactivity and limited influences in the country. Furthermore, Björn and Guðrún Ása argued that the monasteries had probably been so undermanned that they had all eventually been closed down long before the Reformation.[37] Historian Orri Vésteinsson made an argument similar to that presented by Björn Þorsteinsson and Guðrún Ása Grímsdóttir in his doctoral thesis from 2000 on the Christianization of Iceland from 1000 to 1300. He writes:

> It is unusual that very little information is preserved about the religious houses or monastic life [in Iceland]; even though a number of works are known by the hands of monks . . . they deal mostly with the outside world and give only a limited insight into monastic attitudes and none into the size or condition of these establishments. What can be said about the religious houses is that they are conspicuously private in origin, that they were all very small and that their principal function was to be retirement homes for aristocrats.[38]

However, Orri did not go as far as to claim, as Björn and Guðrún Ása had done, that the monasteries might have been closed down long before the Reformation. Nevertheless, this long-held view that the monastic houses were tiny and uninfluential institutions can in fact still be seen in recent works, such as those of historian Jón Viðar Sigurðsson, published in 2008, and medievalists Erica Sigurdson and Ryder Patzuk-Russell, both works published in 2016.[39]

New Social History and Feminism

A flurry of interest in writing the histories of specific monasteries appeared briefly around the mid-twentieth century. Thus, while the monasteries had been written off in historical overviews, the history of some of them suddenly became a subject of interest and was subsequently recorded. However, as before, these writings mostly did not locate the monastic houses within the framework of the general history of Iceland. On the other hand, this sudden attention, which aimed to depict daily life inside selected monasteries, may be understood as the outcome of the growth of so-called New social history or New archaeology in academic research. In history, this field seeks to approach the ordinary lives of people, often with an emphasis on a certain ethnic group, gender, labor, or family, but within the framework of wider society. In theology, the emphasis was on examining how churchly organizations were run.[40]

During the last decades of the twentieth century, there also emerged, for the first time, an interest within research on medieval Icelandic history in investigating the design of single monastic houses in Iceland and their dissolution during the Reformation. Concurrent with this growing interest in writing complete monographs and essays on selected monasteries, a series of monthly articles on all of the monastic institutions was published in 1966 and 1967 in Iceland's largest newspaper.[41] It was historian Jónas Guðlaugsson who summarized the history of each monastery, not unlike what the Rev. Janus Jónsson had done a little less than a century beforehand and Finnur Jónsson long before. Two monographs published during the mid-nineteenth century were academic theses that focused solely on Möðruvallaklaustur. The first was written by the Rev. Ágúst Sigurðsson for a degree in theology at the University of Iceland in 1965, and the second by Eiríkur Þormóðsson for a degree in history in 1966. In 1965, another theology thesis, this one on Skriðuklaustur, was written by the Rev. Heimir Steinsson. In addition to these three academic theses, historian Hermann Pálsson published a monograph on Helgafellsklaustur in 1967, while historian Árni Óla wrote about Viðeyjarklaustur in 1969.[42] All of these publications reflect the scale and scope of the activities of these four monasteries and their involvement in spiritual affairs in Iceland. Each thesis even presents the complete history of the monastery in question and sheds new light on their daily activities and inner workings. Both Ágúst and Eiríkur claim, however, that there were very few clerics at Möðruvallaklaustur, in harmony with the earlier historiography.[43] This may have been true, since Möðruvallaklaustur was always run as a school for Augustinian canons in the Hólar bishopric, and not strictly as a monastery, like the other Augustinian institutions. In contrast, both Hermann Pálsson and Árni Óla emphasized the complex and multifaceted lives in Helgafellsklaustur and Viðeyjarklaustur.

Furthermore, in 1988, historian Anna Sigurðardóttir published a detailed study of the two female convents run in Iceland, Kirkjubæjarklaustur and Reynistaðarklaustur.[44] This was during the second wave of feminism, which aimed to draw attention to the work of women in the past as well as the present.[45] Anna Sigurðardóttir highlights the valuable work of the nuns, especially regarding the production of textiles. As is noted earlier, before Anna's publication, nuns and female convents had barely been mentioned in studies on the medieval monastic houses. Importantly, in accordance with her feminist approach, Anna pointed out that the nuns of Iceland had been no less influential than the monks – not at least through their making of ecclesiastical clothes. Very few scholars had paid attention to the manufacturing of textiles in the female convents before. Even the post-Reformation antiquarians, such as Árni Magnússon, seem not have observed cloths and fabrics as antiques worth collecting, although these portrayed stories in images and words just as the manuscripts and rune stones. The truth is that the most precious medieval cloths currently preserved from Iceland are those that were sold abroad during the early nineteenth century. Thus, a number of wealthy tourists visiting the island at that time sought out Icelandic manuscripts for purchase and even other antiques, such as textiles.[46] Nevertheless, the nuns' textile work seems to have gradually ended up in the shadow of the manuscripts. At any rate, the very few female scholars, who did after all conduct research on the Icelandic medieval textiles around the mid-twentieth century, never gained the attention they deserved. The history of textile research and female monasticism may therefore be observed as a part of women's history and their combat for being heard. In other respects, though, Anna treated the Icelandic female convents as national institutions, in a manner similar to the approach taken in research on monasticism at that time.

In 1989, the year after Anna Sigurðardóttir's book was published, researcher Hörður Ágústsson made a noteworthy attempt to find out how monasteries were built in Iceland. Still, he based his observations on the approach utilized earlier by the Rev. Magnús Jónsson, Jón Jóhannesson, and Magnús Stefánsson, underlining that the monastic houses were nationalistic in nature and character.[47] When Hörður undertook his research, no remains of a monastic building had ever been excavated in Iceland. Using inventories to get an idea of what they might have looked like was both imaginative and different from what had been done before. The problem is that Hörður relied mainly on descriptions of houses that had been built on the monastic sites long after the monasteries had been deserted. As a result, the research was observed as having confirmed his own hypothesis and those of other scholars: that the Icelandic monasteries had operated in buildings of a purely vernacular type, like larger farms built of turf and stone.[48]

Hörður Ágústsson's study had a major impact on the attitude prevailing even in later years, when monasteries were – as never before – viewed as national institutions that functioned differently from monastic institutions in Christian countries in Scandinavia and on the Continent. Historian Guðrún Harðardóttir is one of the scholars who later continued Hörður's work, albeit mostly after his death. She has somewhat revivified his ideas that the monasteries in Iceland were built in accordance with vernacular building traditions. Nonetheless, she placed special emphasis on examining how international monastic characteristics blended with those that are often considered uniquely Icelandic. Guðrún claimed thus that the monastic houses, with respect to their operation and lodgings, were made Icelandic to fit into the society there.[49] Moreover, Hörður Ágústsson's research had a significant impact on excavations on the island of Viðey, where Viðeyjarklaustur had stood. As a rescue excavation, which lasted from 1987 to 1995, it was not directly intended to investigate the monastic ruins. It focused instead on the old farm mound there, which was directly at risk from the restoration of the houses standing nearby. Archaeologist Margrét Hallgrímsdóttir, one of the excavation's directors, inevitably used Hörður Ágústsson's methods, based on written documents, to interpret the ruins as those belonging to the monastery. Her conclusion was that the monastic building of Viðeyjarklaustur had to have been of a vernacular type, where the rooms were arranged in a manner similar to that which was common in the living quarters of the larger farmhouses in Iceland.[50] Later on, it became clear that these remains were not those of the monastery, but rather those of the post-monastic farm, which had been constructed immediately after the monastery had been closed, as the inventories Hörður used for his interpretation.[51]

Still, in 1997, historian Vilborg Auður Ísleifsdóttir approached monasticism in Iceland in a completely new way in her book[52] (which was republished in 2013[53]) based on her doctoral studies on the Reformation in Iceland. She argued that the monasteries were very influential, internationally orientated institutions that were important to the public wherever they were run, in Iceland and elsewhere.[54] In her publications, Vilborg Auður underlines the charity and educational work undertaken in monastic houses, and she argues that their closure during the Reformation caused Iceland's social system to collapse. This collapse, she argues, stemmed from the fact that the sick and the poor lost their access to secure shelter in the monastic houses as a result of the Reformation.[55] With her approach, she was one of the first scholars to discuss the monastic houses as an integral part of Icelandic medieval society and not as a separate niche within it, working outside the scope of internal political conflicts. Still, although Vilborg Auður Ísleifsdóttir's view of monasticism in Iceland was very different from that of her fellow historians, her approach was somewhat similar to Páll Eggert Ólason's work a century earlier. Both have also been criticized – and often renounced – for their views on monasticism in Iceland.[56] Even though her research has been generally denied or neglected by Icelandic scholars, Vilborg Auður's approach was partly followed up by historian Gunnar F. Guðmundsson in his extensive overview of Christianity during the Middle Ages in Iceland, published in 2000. However, Gunnar concluded in his overview that the monasteries might have had a practical role in assisting the homeless, the poor, and the old, but not much more than that. He even highlighted that the monastic institutions were more or less closed to the general public and were intended primarily to serve men and women who had taken their vows with the aim of seeking contemplation and shelter from the outer world.[57]

Historical Archaeology

The antiquarian and manuscript collector Árni Magnússon was, in fact, the first scholar to systematically undertake research on medieval Icelandic monasteries by surveying their ruins around 1700.[58] However, Árni is mostly famous for his passion for collecting manuscripts; he managed to treasure the largest number of medieval manuscripts and documents ever gathered in Iceland. Complete books or parts of them he collected number nearly 2,000, beside several official letters, mainly written in old Norse.[59] Many more have been collected or registered since then. The manuscripts and documents, mainly those that Árni treasured, became vital for the writing of this book, because quite a large portion of them relate to the monastic houses in one or another way. Even the field work, which Árni documented mainly in diary notes, proved to be highly valuable, providing an important window into monasticism in Iceland so soon after it had become history. It may thus be fairly stated that Árni Magnússon fertilized the soil that historical archaeology grew from more than three centuries later.

For quite long time after Árni's days, however, written documents have generally been viewed as the most ideal sources for undertaking research on historical periods. This, in turn, situated archaeology as a sub-discipline or handmaiden to history, in which material remains were observed as merely providing complementary data to confirm the messages from written sources or serving as colorful illustrations in historical overviews. It wasn't until the rise of the study of material culture, enhanced by the theoretical movement of post-structuralism and post-processualism[60] in the 1980s and 1990s, that archaeology gained a deep theoretical basis for the first time in Northwest Europe, the United States, and gradually also in Iceland.[61] As known, this shifted the status of the discipline towards dealing first and foremost with material remains, and consequently, with material culture and its all-embracing materiality. In accordance with studies on material culture, material remains – whether found in the ground or written down in documents – should be regarded as equal bearers of their social contexts and fully valid sources in their own right.[62] Henceforth, it soon thereafter became academically accepted that archaeological residues, small and large, could provide equally reliable, although often alternative, views of the past to written sources. Intertwining archaeological remains and written documents, as here is done, allow thus for a more holistic view of the past than can be obtained if the two types of sources are considered separately. After this shift, medieval and post-medieval archaeology, as sub-disciplines of historical archaeology, became increasingly appealing to scholars.[63] The historiography of monasticism in Iceland reveals such developments, but the theoretical shift in archaeology seems moreover to have changed the understanding of Iceland's medieval and contemporary past.[64]

Indeed, in recent years, there has been a significant increase in interest in studying medieval monasticism in Iceland through archaeological research as well as through a re-examination of written documents, indicating at the same time a general reawakening in monastic studies. As a result of the recent excavations in Viðey, where Viðeyjarklaustur was located (1987–1995), Skriðuklaustur (2000–2012), and Kirkjubæjarklaustur (2002–2006), a number of students have chosen monasticism as a subject for their undergraduate and postgraduate dissertations at the University of Iceland during the last two decades.[65] Moreover, during the winter of 2013–2014, the University of Iceland's Centre for Medieval Studies held a multidisciplinary seminar on monastic culture in Iceland, underlining further the general interest in the topic. A number of specially selected lectures from the seminar were published in one volume in 2016. The articles cover topics such as the monastic orders present in medieval Iceland, the saints of the monasteries, the closure of Helgafellsklaustur, the monasteries as sanctuaries, and the culture of writing in the monasteries, to mention but a few.[66] In 2014, historian Árni Daníel Júlíusson also gathered together and published, in one volume, the enormous assets of the monasteries and bishoprics in Iceland from 1000 to 1550.[67] New research interests even include studying the changes that the Reformation had on the rhythm of poetry, and the recording of ecclesiastical psalms.[68] Experts have likewise analyzed and catalogued plant remains from most of the monastic sites in Iceland a few years ago.[69] Haraldur Hreinsson's dissertation in theology from 2020 is similarly worth highlighting. In it, he provides a critical examination of Iceland's earliest ecclesiastical discourse, shedding new and innovative light on medieval Christianity, including monasticism, and how it must be observed as an inseparable entity in the lives of medieval Icelanders.[70]

In many of the more recent publications, it is argued that the history of monasticism in Iceland should be revisited and revised. That is precisely the ambition of this book. By intertwining written documents and material remains, it became clear that the successful monastic houses in Iceland gradually became well-staffed with both religious and lay members. They also came to be wealthy landholders who owned a number of valuable farms. In addition, female and male monasteries alike successfully ran large cattle and sheep ranches, manufactured manuscripts and textiles of various kinds, and provided a broad range of social services to their local communities. Some of the monastic houses took care of the sick, the poor, and the elderly; one even ran a proper hospital, while the other provided the healthy and rich a comfortable life as corrodians, lay sisters and brothers, occasional or permanent workers, trained future canons, and educated girls and boys, as they did elsewhere in medieval Europe.

Notes

1 See Bitel, 'Monastic Identity in Early Medieval Ireland', p. 297; Grell, 'The Catholic Church and its Leadership', pp. 70–113.
2 See, for example, Ekroll, 'Thrown to the Wolves?' footnote 1; Haug, 'Challenges in Research of Norwegian Monastic History', pp. 64–96.
3 Møller and Østergård, 'Lutheran Orthodoxy', pp. 165–189.
4 Gregersen and Bach-Nielsen, 'Reformationen som kirkeligt og kulturelt Program', pp. 15–16.
5 Møller and Østergård, 'Lutheran Orthodoxy', pp. 165–189; Kærgård, 'Det danske samfund', p. 464; Steinersen and Libaek, *The History of Norway*, pp. 80–96.
6 Møller and Østergård, 'Lutheran Orthodoxy', pp. 176–180.
7 Jensson, 'Latin Hagiography in Medieval Iceland', p. 880.
8 Jónsson, 'Íslensk bókasöfn fyrir siðabyltinguna', p. 77; Helgason, *Handritaspjall,* p. 38; Þorkelsson, *Digtningen paa Island*, p. 13.
9 See, for example, Romero-Raverón and Arráes-Abyar, 'Ole Worm (1588–1654)', pp. 300–301.
10 Jónsson, 'Áhrif klaustranna á Íslandi', pp. 285–288.
11 See, for example, Þorsteinsson, *Íslenska þjóðveldið*, pp. 217–226; Þorsteinsson, *Íslensk miðaldasaga*, p. 336; Jónsson, 'Íslensk bókasöfn fyrir siðabyltinguna', p. 77; Jóhannesson, *Íslendinga saga I,* pp. 235–236; Sigurðsson, *Det norrøne samfunnet*, pp. 158–159; Þorkelsson, *Digtningen paa Island*, pp. 10–15; Jónsson, 'Áhrif klaustranna á Íslandi', pp. 283–284; Stefánsson, 'Kirkjuvald eflist', pp. 81–85.
12 See, for example, Júlíusson, *Jarðeignir kirkjunnar,* pp. 242–244; Jónsson, *Historia ecclesiastica Islandiæ IV*, pp. 15–121; Patzuk-Russell, *The Development of Education*, p. 69; Sigurdson, *The Church in Fourteenth Century Iceland*, p. 17; Ísleifsdóttir, *Byltingin að ofan*, p. 98.
13 See, for example, Harðardóttir, 'Vangaveltur um íslensk klausturhús', pp. 108–113; Ágústsson, 'Húsagerð á síðmiðöldum', pp. 292–293; Jónsson, 'Áhrif klaustranna á Íslandi', pp. 283–284.
14 Sigurðardóttir, *Allt hafði annan róm áður í páfadóm*; Jónsson, *Historia ecclesiastica Islandiæ IV*, pp. 15–121; Jónsson, *Um klaustrin á Íslandi.*
15 Jónsson, 'Áhrif klaustranna á Íslandi', p. 286.
16 Jónsson, 'Áhrif klaustranna á Íslandi', pp. 283, 289, 292.
17 Þorsteinsson and Grímsdóttir, 'Enska öldin', pp. 152–155; Harðardóttir, 'Vangaveltur um íslensk klausturhús', pp. 108–113; Ágústsson, 'Húsagerð á síðmiðöldum', pp. 292–293.
18 See, for example, Finlayson, 'Nationalism', pp. 100–102.

19 The results were published in the monograph, *Forntida gårdar i Island: meddelanden från den nordiska arkeologiska undersökningin i Island sommaren 1939*, ed. by Mårten Stenberger, Aage Roussell, and Jón Steffenesen.
20 Hálfdanarson, 'Severing the Ties', pp. 237–254; Hálfdanarson, 'Iceland: A Peaceful Secession', pp. 87–100; Jakobsson, 'Defining a Nation', pp. 91–101.
21 See, for example, Kristinsson, *Hnignun, hvaða hnignun?* pp. 27–37; Hálfdanarson, 'Sagan og sjálfsmynd(ir) íslenskrar þjóðar', pp. 113–135; Gardiner and Mehler, 'Introduction: German trade in the North Atlantic', pp. 9–24; Jónsson, *Pots, Pipes, and Plates*; Lucas and Hreiðarsdóttir, 'The Archaeology of Capitalism in Iceland', pp. 604–621.
22 See, for example, Skúlason, *Um eyjar og annes*, pp. 44–45; *Íslenskar þjóðsögur og ævintýri*, vol. i, pp. 75–78; *Íslenskar þjóðsögur og sagnir*, vol. i, pp. 9–11; *Íslenskar þjóðsögur og sagnir*, vol. vii, p. 193; *Íslenskar þjóðsögur og sagnir*, vol. x, pp. 201–202, 264–265.
23 Jónsson, *Historia ecclesiastica Islandiæ IV*, pp. 15–121.
24 Jónsson, *Um klaustrin á Íslandi*, pp. 174–265.
25 See Jónsson, 'Áhrif klaustranna á Íslandi', pp. 283, 289, 292.
26 Gilchrist, *Gender and Material Culture*; Burton and Stöber, 'Introduction', pp. 1–2; Beach and Cochelin, 'General Introduction', pp. 5–7; Collins, *Female Monasticism in Medieval Ireland*.
27 See Ólason, *Menn og menntir siðskipataldarinnar á Íslandi*; Ólason, *Menn og menntir siðaskiptaaldarinnar á Íslandi, Ögmundur Pálsson, Gizur Einarsson og samherjar hans*; Ólason, *Menn og menntir siðaskiptaaldarinnar á Íslandi, Guðbrandur Þorláksson og öld hans*; Ólason, *Menn og menntir siðaskiptaaldarinnar á Íslandi, Rithöfundar*.
28 Jónsson, 'Áhrif klaustranna á Íslandi', p. 286.
29 Møller and Østergård, 'Lutheran Orthodoxy', pp. 181–185.
30 Þorsteinsson, *Íslenska þjóðveldið*, pp. 217–226; Þorsteinsson, *Íslensk miðaldasaga*, pp. 125–128; Jóhannesson, *Íslendinga saga I*, pp. 227–236; Stefánsson, 'Kirkjuvald eflist', pp. 81–85.
31 Stefánsson, 'Kirkjuvald eflist', pp. 81–85. See also Stefánsson, 'Frá goðakirkju til biskupskirkju', pp. 111–257.
32 Jóhannesson, *Íslendinga saga I*, pp. 235–236; Jónsson, 'Áhrif klaustranna á Íslandi', pp. 283–284; Stefánsson, 'Kirkjuvald eflist', pp. 81–85.
33 See Þorsteinsson, *Íslenska þjóðveldið*, pp. 218, 225–226; Þorsteinsson, *Íslensk miðaldasaga*, p. 336.
34 Berman, 'Later Monastic Economies', pp. 836–837; Brenner, 'The Medical Role of Monasteries', pp. 865–880.
35 Jóhannesson, *Íslendinga saga I*, p. 236.
36 Kristjánsdóttir, *Leitin að klaustrunum*, pp. 44–45.
37 Þorsteinsson and Grímsdóttir, 'Enska öldin', p. 153.
38 Vésteinsson, *The Christianization of Iceland*, p. 133.
39 See Sigurðsson, *Det norrøne samfunnet*, pp. 158–159; Patzuk-Russell, *The Development of Education*, p. 69; Sigurdson, *The Church in Fourteenth Century Iceland*, p. 17.
40 Kessler-Harris, *Social History*; Magnússon, *Sjálfssögur. Minni, minningar og saga*, pp. 305–306.
41 Guðlaugsson, 'Þingeyraklaustur'; Guðlaugsson, 'Munkaþverárklaustur'; Guðlaugsson, 'Þykkvabæjarklaustur'; Guðlaugsson, 'Helgafellsklaustur'; Guðlaugsson, 'Kirkjubæjarklaustur'; Guðlaugsson, 'Viðeyjarklaustur'; Guðlaugsson, 'Reynistaðarklaustur'; Guðlaugsson, 'Möðruvallaklaustur'; Guðlaugsson, 'Skriðuklaustur'; Guðlaugsson, 'Klaustur í Bæ, Hítardal, Saurbæ og á Keldum'.
42 See Sigurðsson, 'Drög að sögu Möðruvallaklausturs'; Óla, *Viðeyjarklaustur*; Þormóðsson 'Möðruvallaklaustur'; Steinsson, 'Saga munklífis á Skriðu'; Pálsson, *Helgafell – saga höfuðbóls og klausturs*.
43 Sigurðsson, 'Drög að sögu Möðruvallaklausturs', p. 121; Þormóðsson 'Möðruvallaklaustur', p. 6.
44 Sigurðardóttir, *Allt hafði annan róm áður í páfadóm*.
45 See, for example, Gilchrist, *Gender and Archaeology*, pp. 2–4; Sørensen, *Gender Archaeology*, p. 17.

46 Guðjónsson, 'Íslenzkur dýrgripur í hollenzku safni', pp. 132–134; Wandel, 'Íslenzk altarisklæði', pp. 52–53.

47 Ágústsson, 'Húsagerð á síðmiðöldum', pp. 292–295. See also Jóhannesson, *Íslendinga saga I*, p. 236; Jónsson, 'Áhrif klaustranna á Íslandi', pp. 283, 286; Stefánsson, 'Kirkjuvald eflist', p. 85.

48 Ágústsson, 'Húsagerð á síðmiðöldum', pp. 292–295.

49 Harðardóttir, 'Nokkrar kynslóðir kirkna', pp. 34–37; Harðardóttir, 'Vangaveltur um íslensk klausturhús', pp. 108–113.

50 Hallgrímsdóttir, 'Rannsóknir í Viðey', pp. 99–102, 129; Hallgrímsdóttir, 'Húsakostur Viðeyjarklausturs', pp. 152–158.

51 Kristjánsdóttir, 'Klaustureyjan á Sundum', pp. 44–47.

52 Ísleifsdóttir, *Siðbreytingin á Íslandi 1537–1565*.

53 Ísleifsdóttir, *Byltingin að ofan*.

54 Ísleifsdóttir, *Ný heimsmynd*, pp. 32–34; Ísleifsdóttir, *Byltingin að ofan*, pp. 97–108.

55 See also Ísleifsdóttir, *Ný heimsmynd*, pp. 40–48; Ísleifsdóttir, 'Öreigar og umrenningar', pp. 121–123; Ísleifsdóttir, *Byltingin að ofan*, pp. 298–304.

56 See, for example, Þorláksson, 'Þjóðhagir og samfélagshópar', p. 126; Guttormsson and Kjartansson, 'Siðaskiptin og fátækraframfærsla', pp. 119–143.

57 Guðmundsson, 'Íslenskt samfélag og Rómarkirkja', pp. 212–225.

58 Magnússon, 'Um klaustrin', pp. 32–47; Friðriksson, *Sagas and Popular Antiquarianism*.

59 Jensson, 'Þingeyrar Abbey in Northern Iceland'; Jónsson, *Árni Magnússon*.

60 Broadly equivalent to post-modernism.

61 See, for example, Gerrard, *Medieval Archaeology*; McClain, 'Theory, Disciplinary Perspectives', pp. 131–170; Gilchrist, 'Monastic and Church Archaeology', pp. 235–290.

62 See, for example, Andrén, *Mellan Ting och Text*, pp. 35–45; Deetz, *In Small Things Forgotten*; Deetz, *History and Archaeological Theory*, pp. 13–22; Galloway, 'Material Culture and Text', pp. 42–64; Gilchrist, 'Monastic and Church Archaeology', pp. 235–290; González-Rubial, 'Contemporary Past, Archaeology of the', pp. 1683–1691; Lucas, 'Íslensk fornleifafræði', pp. 11–17; Lucas, *Writing the Past*, pp. 73–80; McClain, 'Theory, Disciplinary Perspectives', pp. 131–170; Olsen, 'Material culture after text: re-membering things', pp. 87–104; Rathje and Murphy, *Rubbish!*; Pétursdóttir, 'Small Things Forgotten Now Included', pp. 577–579, 585–588.

63 See, for example, Gerrard, *Medieval Archaeology*; Gilchrist, 'Monastic and Church Archaeology', pp. 235–290; McClain, 'Theory, Disciplinary Perspectives', pp. 131–170.

64 See discussion on the topic in for example, Friðriksson, 'Sannfræði íslenskra fornleifa', pp. 347–375; Einarsson, 'Íslenskar fornleifar', pp. 376–402; Þórisdóttir, 'Klaustur á Íslandi', pp. 5–11, 25; Þorláksson, 'Deila um gildi fornleifa og ritheimilda', pp. 183–185; Lucas, 'Íslensk fornleifafræði', pp. 11–17.

65 See, for example, Jónsdóttir, 'Þjóðleiðir við klaustrin á kaþólskum tíma?' Magnúsdóttir, 'Bak við veggi klaustursins'; Magnúsdóttir, 'Klaustur á Íslandi'; Traustadóttir, 'Skák og mát'; Halldórsdóttir, 'Viðey – heimsótt á ný'; Wood, 'Charity on the Fringes of the Medieval World'; Stephensen, 'Menntasetur að Viðeyjarklaustri'.

66 Cormack, 'Monastic Foundations and Foundation Legends', pp. 59–82; Jensson, 'Íslenskar klausturreglur', pp. 9–57; Kristjánsdóttir, 'Handritalýsingar í benediktínaklaustrinu á Þingeyrum', pp. 227–311; Harðardóttir, 'Myndefni íslenskra klausturinnsigla', pp. 201–227; Gunnlaugsson, 'Voru scriptoria í íslenskum klaustrum?', pp. 173–200; Harðarson, 'Viktorsklaustrið í París', pp. 119–148; Bernharðsson, 'Kirkja, klaustur og norskublandið ritmálsviðmið', pp. 149–172; Jakobsson, 'Frá Helgafellsklaustri til Stapaumboðs', pp. 83–102; Walgenbach, 'Church Sanctuary in the Contemporary Sagas', pp. 102–117.

67 Júlíusson, *Jarðeignir kirkjunnar*.

68 Ingólfsson, *Tónlist liðinna alda*; Ingólfsdóttir, *Á hverju liggja ekki okkar göfugu kerlingar?*

69 Kristjánsdóttir et al., 'The Icelandic Medieval Monastic Garden?' Åsen, *Norske klosterplanter*.

70 Hreinsson, *Force of Words*.

3

THE MAKING OF ICELANDIC SOCIETY

The exact dating of the colonization of Iceland has long been debated. Most commonly, the initial settlement is associated with a story, recorded in *Landnámabók* (The Book of Settlements), of the first settler, Ingólfur Arnarson, who is said to have arrived on the island in 874 and settled there permanently. *Landnámabók* even describes in detail the course of events during the settlement and lists the names of 435 initial settlers who are claimed to have typically been Pagan Norse Vikings. The fact is that the story of Ingólfur, along with other narratives in *Landnámabók*, have formed the interpretation on the construction of Icelandic society ever since.[1] Thus, the most traditional view has been that the settlers were Vikings, practicing the Old Norse religion, and that religious habits in Iceland shifted rather suddenly from Old Norse religion to Christianity with the Christianization in 999–1000. However, the myth of a cultural unity shared by the Vikings has been rightfully debunked in recent years, and attention has been drawn instead to the heterogeneity of the Iron Age Scandinavian culture, so developments may not have been as clear-cut as they might sound. A homogeneous pre-Christian or Christian faith has never existed because both are non-static hybrid outcomes of their continued evolution.[2] Nowadays, the conversion to Christianity is likewise approached as a political and administrative act rather than as a solely religious or cultural change.[3] In fact, a recent study confirms a complex mix of Old Norse/Pagan and Christian burial customs in Iceland, dating from the initial settlement until after the official Christianization. The same study also identified certain uniformity in Christian burial practices right after the turn of the eleventh century.[4]

The Settlement of Iceland

Much like the arrival of monasticism in Iceland, the timing of the settlement has long been a topic of research, discussion, and debate. Still, research based on the

DOI: 10.4324/9781003361077-3

analysis of a tephra layer, in combination with radiocarbon dates, suggests the years around 870–877, enhancing the credibility of these principal written sources on the earliest settlement. The timing mentioned in *Landnámabók* may thus be true, although the stories in it certainly do not tell the whole truth. It is clear from excavations that people had been in the country some decades prior to that date. The question remains whether their occupation can be identified as a seasonal or permanent settlement with farming and cultivation. Regardless of this, it is undoubtedly the case that most of the earliest archaeological finds and evidence of agricultural land use in Iceland date to the last quarter of the ninth century.[5] Moreover, according to recent studies, people continued to migrate to Iceland until after the Christianization around 999–1000, which shows that the settlement period was a long one.[6] Perhaps it has never ended. Furthermore, genetic studies demonstrate that early Icelanders were a combination of Norse, Gaelic, and other mixed heritage, indicating that most of the people who settled in Iceland during the initial settlement period until after the conversion to Christianity came from western Scandinavia and the British Isles. Specifically, the males in the Icelandic founding population appeared to averagely be of Scandinavian descent, but the majority of the females had Gaelic ancestry.[7] Interestingly enough, the further studies suggested that during the 1,100 years since the settlement, Icelanders have been influenced by an extensive genetic drift much greater than in neighboring countries.[8] Another intriguing study showed that graves identified as those of a Viking most frequently belong to immigrants with close genetic ties to their Scandinavian homeland, while others point towards the British Isles and Ireland.[9] The cultural background of those settling in Iceland from 870 to 1000 must therefore have been combined with different religious views and habits from both Old Norse/Pagan and Christian practices.[10] It should come as no surprise, then, that Gaelic influences are prominent in the Icelandic Sagas and the Skaldic Poetry, as studies on Icelandic Medieval Literature have shown.[11] Moreover, tools used for textile work found in Iceland resemble those found in the British Isles rather than those found in Scandinavian context, indicating that the female settlers brought the knowledge of textile making to Iceland from their homeland.

Notwithstanding, soon after the settlement of Iceland, the colonizers and their descendants started building up their own system of government based on the principles of chieftaincy. This involved no centralized executive authority. Instead, the power was shared by secular chiefs, the so-called chieftains (Icel. sing. *goði*, pl. *goðar*) or their representatives. The main assembly, *Alþingi*, was located at Þingvellir in southern Iceland, established in 930. Around 965, *Alþingi* divided the island into four quarters, providing each quarter a separate judicial court at the main assembly (see Figure 5.1). One chieftain was appointed as president of the assembly, the so-called lawspeaker (Icel. *lögsögumaður*). Each lawspeaker served for three years, with the possibility of re-appointment.[12] Through this system, those who gained the status of chieftains or lawspeakers came to be among the most powerful leaders in Iceland throughout the Commonwealth period, responsible for reviewing and amending the vernacular laws of the land. The chieftains' families soon came to form the country's ruling elite.[13] When the secular governance of the country was taken over by the Norwegian crown in 1262/1264, the model of chieftaincy diminished considerably and vanished quickly. As a result, both the secular and the churchly governance of Iceland were transferred from the hands of Icelanders to the Norwegian king and archbishops. With this shift, the chieftains and their family clans were replaced by rich and powerful landlords – aristocrats and seneschals – who, along with the most powerful clerics, were the elite members of Icelandic society until the Reformation. The role of the lawspeaker was even taken over by a new post, termed lawman (Icel. *lögmaður*), who was the chief jurist in internal legal matters. Unlike the lawspeakers, the number of lawmen was not fixed, although it soon became customary to have two at a time, each serving half of the country.[14] Another result of the transfer of the secular governing of the country to the Norwegian crown, moreover, was that knighthood became popular in Iceland, and at least forty knights served there as elite fighters for the Norwegian king from the mid-thirteenth century until the sixteenth century.

The transfer of the Icelandic society under the Norwegian crown was certainly not a peaceful act, but rather it caused extremely violent and long-lasting domestic conflicts, named the *Sturlungaöld* war. It began around 1220 and was fought among various family clans under the leadership of their chieftains, as will be discussed further later in this chapter.[15] The course of events was that Håkan the Old, King of Norway (r. 1217–1263), had strived from the beginning of his reign to extend his influence in Iceland. Many Icelandic chieftains became his vassals and were thus obliged to do his bidding in the country. The conflict centered on the disputes among the six main family clans[16] in Iceland, some of whom supported Norwegian sovereignty over Iceland, while others refused to accept it.[17] In three battles that were a part of these domestic conflicts, Bishop Guðmundur góði of Hólar was involved. The most historic ones, the Battle of Örlygsstaðir in northern Iceland, took place on 21 August 1238 at Örlygsstaðir in northern Iceland. This great battle was fought between the Sturlungar family clan, on one side, and the Ásbirningar and Haukdælir family clans, on the other. The Ásbirningar and Haukdælir emerged victorious after a short battle in which over fifty men were killed, including some of the most powerful chieftains in Iceland at the time.[18]

The Expansion of Monasticism

With the conversion to Christianity, decided in Alþingi in 999 or 1000, Icelanders agreed to follow dual law, that is, canon law and their own vernacular land laws. The vernacular land laws were later documented in *Grágás*, which even included a specific Christian law section, *Kristinna laga þáttur*. *Grágás* was replaced in 1271 by *Járnsíða*, which contained a revised version of the Christian law section, *Kristinréttur Árna Þorlákssonar*, dating from 1275. These were the first vernacular laws of Iceland after it became part of the Kingdom of Norway. *Járnsíða* was then replaced by *Jónsbók* in 1281, which later included the Christian laws section, but again in a reduced form.[19] Moreover, certain instructions or enactments – *statutes* – were regularly sent out in order to inform recipients about additions or amendments made to canon law or to emphasize specific matters of the Church, old and new. Inevitably, these were also sent to Iceland. The statutes needed to have been recognized in advance at the ecclesiastical councils of the Holy See, such as those held regularly from 1123 in the Lateran Palace in Rome. Archbishops had permission to release statutes – indeed, they were tasked with doing so – but these had to be accepted by local councils held at their episcopal see before being sent out and were therefore valid only within that see.[20] Canon law, along with the statutes, other instructions, and reforms that had to be followed, constantly stimulated people's Christian identity. However, the distribution and observance of Christian doctrine, including the fabrication of new traditions and cults, can be traced to many sources other than various official acts of the Church, such as personal spread through Christian settlers, pilgrimage, trade,[21] and even eremitism and anchoritism (see Chapter 4). Recent studies on the medieval sagas, *Njáls saga* and *Laxdæla saga*, show, for example, that hagiographical motifs frequently appear in them, showing that the actions the persons in them take correspond to Roman Catholic fashions.[22] Furthermore, it is also apparent that the principles of Roman Catholic Christianity continued to circulate and develop throughout the Middle Ages.

It must be taken into consideration that the Norse societies of the Orkney and Faeroe Islands and Norway also officially converted to Christianity around the same time as Iceland. Ireland, Scotland, Wales, England, and Germany had all adopted Christianity some centuries earlier, and Denmark had done so around 965.[23] Notably, these countries were the former homelands of early Icelandic migrants, and, apparently, the cooperation remained intact. Only thirty years after Christianity had been officially accepted at *Alþingi* in 999–1000, the first attempt was made to establish a monastic house in Iceland. This was Bæjarklaustur, located on the farm Bær in Borgarfjörður and founded in 1030. A similar attempt to establish a monastery appears to have been made in Niðarholm in Norway around the same time. It is not known how long this monastery operated, if it ever did. It is said to have been built by the crusader Sigurd Ullstreng in honor of St. Benedict and the martyr Lawrence.[24] The monasteries at Niðarholm and Bær might therefore be the first attested ones founded in northern Europe. The founder of Bæjarklaustur was the missionary Bishop Rudolf, who was sent to Iceland by Archbishop Liavizos of Hamburg-Bremen,[25] most likely to strengthen Christianity in northern Europe, as one of his successors, Archbishop Asser, later tried to do as well. Rudolf left Iceland after living there for approximately two decades, whereupon Bæjarklaustur appears to have been closed. It lacked sufficient support for its operation because no bishopric was then based in Iceland. After Rudolf abandoned Iceland in 1049, he served as the abbot of the famous Abingdon monastery in England until his death four years later.[26]

After that, the reorganization of the Church in northern Europe in the early twelfth century appears to have been minted by Pope Paschal II, who officially sought to strengthen the administrative power of the papacy in his northernmost provinces. He was in office from 1099 to 1118 and began by making changes to the archdiocese of Hamburg-Bremen, notably with the establishment of the archbishopric in Lund in 1104. He even put Asser Thorkilssen[27] (r. 1104–1137) in office there as archbishop, but he had served as a bishop in Lund from 1089. Archbishop Asser, in turn, started immediately to achieve the goals set by the pope. In 1106, he established the bishopric of Hólar and consecrated Jón Ögmundsson (r. 1106–1121) in office as bishop. Shortly thereafter, Archbishop Asser founded a bishopric in Kirkjubær in the Faeroe Islands, and finally, he established a bishopric in Garðar in Greenland in 1124. It was even around this time that Archbishop Asser and Bishop Jón together laid the groundwork for Þingeyraklaustur in 1112, although its first abbot was not consecrated until 1133, twelve years after Bishop Jón's death. Moreover, it was Archbishop Asser who also advocated that church law would be registered for the first time in Iceland. This refers to the lawbook *Grágás*.[28]

Þingeyraklaustur turned out to be the first monastic institution to effectively gain a foothold in Iceland and it operated uninterrupted until 1551, for more than four centuries.[29] Besides being a direct result of the restructuring of ecclesiastical governance across northern Europe, the establishment of Þingeyraklaustur bears witness to the general expansion of the Benedictines during the fourth quarter of the eleventh century and the first quarter of the twelfth century. From around 1088 to 1095, three Benedictine monasteries had also been founded in Denmark, one in Lund *c.* 1100, and three in Norway from *c.* 1100 to 1110.[30] Even in Ireland, monasticism experienced a process of revival, but the early Irish monastic tradition stretches in fact back to the fourth and fifth centuries.[31] During the first decades of the twelfth century, the further growth of monasticism in Iceland was impressive, but from the time Þingeyraklaustur opened in 1133 until the founding of the first female convent at Kirkjubæjarklaustur in 1186, the expansion of monasticism in Iceland seems to have taken place unhindered. By the end of the twelfth century, there were six monastic houses operating in the country. The Augustinians had even appeared there as early as 1168, with the founding of Þykkvabæjarklaustur. The expansion reached other bishoprics in northern Europe, particularly after the establishment of the archdiocese in Niðarós in 1152–1153. Before the end of the twelfth century, a Benedictine female convent had been founded at Siglufjörður in Greenland, perhaps under the same inspiration as the one at Kirkjubær, Iceland.[32] An Augustinian monastery was established at Ketilsfjörður in Greenland at that point, with the first Augustinian monastery having been founded in Stavanger in Norway before 1160 (exact date unknown).[33] However, no monastery was ever established in the Faeroe Islands.

At the same time as the monastic houses were growing in number at an unprecedented pace in Iceland, the internal system of proprietary churches grew significantly in the country. This can mainly be observed through the increased number of farms classified as *beneficia*. The so-called chieftain-priests also grew in number during the first two centuries after the conversion to Christianity, but at this time, it appears to have been customary for secular chiefs to ordain their own priests. The most powerful chieftains thus ran a church on their private lands and treated it as private property. These churches were served by their own priests, who often were educated at the internal chieftains' schools, such as the one at Oddi in Rangárvellir. However, some of the priests were educated in the cathedrals and monasteries (after they were established) or even sought their clerical education abroad, but these priests unquestionably impacted the development of the medieval Church in Iceland the most, as is further discussed in the following section.[34]

The Roman Catholic Church continued to seek greater influence in Europe throughout the Middle Ages. One of the most powerful actions in this sense was to make the pope a representative of God on Earth. Only by the power of the pope was it possible to bless and thereby acknowledge the divine right of kings or secular chiefs to use power. The kings were crowned by the pope or his representatives. All Catholic Europeans, including Icelanders, gradually became active participants in this worldview of the medieval society because, truly, the matter did not concern a struggle between secular and sacred realms but rather the financial and political governing of the country. Bishops, abbesses, and abbots came from the nobility – in Iceland as elsewhere in Europe – and worked secretly and openly on the issues of their family clans, from the first decades after the conversion to Christianity and, in fact, until the Reformation.[35]

These often blurry boundaries between ecclesiastical and secular power, *regnum and sacerdotium*, inevitably influenced the development and operation of the Church in Iceland, as they did on the mainland Europe. Indeed, this situation became the focal point of the *Staðamál* disputes. Yet, because of their prominent position as the country's main ecclesiastical institutions, Iceland's monastic houses were all dragged into these disputes. Their administrators – abbesses and abbots – became the chief churchly leaders in the country, second only to the bishops, so it mattered greatly who oversaw the monastic houses at any given time. These particular institutions, along with the bishoprics, held the rights to the largest number of estates with churches in Iceland (the *beneficia*), as was common in most societies in Europe by the twelfth century.[36] In any case, after the *Staðamál* were finally settled, a new epoch started in the history of monasticism in Iceland wherein the monastic houses blossomed. The chieftains retained some power but had much less influence over ecclesiastical affairs than before.

The Chieftains and the Church

The *Staðamál* are analogous to the so-called Investiture Controversy, which initially arose on mainland Europe as the result of Pope Gregory VII's (r. 1073–1085) reorganization of the Church, known as the Gregorian reforms. The Investiture Controversy began in earnest as a power struggle between Pope Gregory VII and Emperor Henry IV in 1076. Later, other popes and European kings were involved, eventually including even Magnús Erlingsson, King of Norway (r. 1161–1184). The central aim of these reforms was to create an administrative differentiation between royal and ecclesiastical powers. As a result, they shattered the balance of power between the secular and religious realms and brought about a significant undercutting of imperial power.[37] However, because of how late the Gregorian reforms took effect in northern Europe, the *Staðamál* conflicts in Iceland began much later than conflicts on the mainland and lasted, all in all, for a much longer period. Though the conflicts were settled on the mainland in 1122, they had not yet started in Iceland. The mainland conflicts were settled with the alliance the Concordat of Worms, which saw the victory of the Church, although the aristocrats did retain power over some ecclesiastical matters.[38]

It was only with the establishment of the archdiocese in Niðarós in 1152–1153, though, that efforts to differentiate between royal and ecclesiastical powers were made in this northernmost episcopal see of the Church: Iceland. Before the founding, a special assembly was held in Niðarós with key representatives, both secular and ecclesiastical, from Norway, Greenland, the Faeroe Islands, the Northern Isles, the Hebrides, the Isle of Man, and Iceland. During the meeting, it was decided to base the new archiepiscopal see at Niðarós. Moreover, it was agreed that secular leaders should no longer be involved in the election of bishops or in any other ecclesiastical matters. The Church also claimed full rights over the churches that common landlords had built on their private property.[39] The decisions made in Niðarós were clearly framed in the spirit of the Gregorian reforms, but the resulting conflicts that arose in Iceland centered mainly on these two issues. In claiming the full right to appoint church officials, the Church considerably reduced aristocrats' power to interfere in ecclesiastical affairs, thereby enforcing an even stricter level of control over ecclesiastical institutions, which was its aim. As was also expected, the reforms markedly affected the system of proprietary churches (*beneficia*) by preventing the landlords from operating churches on their private property and retaining investiture of them.[40]

Nevertheless, it was not until after Þorlákur Þórhallsson became bishop of Skálholt in 1178 that the reforms came into action in Iceland and the events of the *Staðamál* started unfolding. Þorlákur was elected bishop at the Icelandic parliamentary assembly in 1174, but his predecessor, Bishop Klængur Þorsteinsson (r. 1152–1176), had remained in his seat for another two years, despite weakness and old age but he also appears to have neglected to follow the new churchly reforms formulated concurrent with the establishment of the archbishopric in Niðarós. Despite that, he supported Þorlákur and was involved in his election.[41] In fact, Bishop Klængur knew Þorlákur quite well, having previously appointed him to an important post in Skálholt diocese: the post of abbot of Þykkvabæjarklaustur, which was the first Augustinian monastery established in Iceland. After returning to Iceland from clerical studies abroad, Þorlákur, refused to marry into the Oddaverjar family clan, as he was required to do by chieftain Jón Loftsson. Instead, he lived with another man, Bjarnhéðinn, in some kind of celibate relationship in Kirkjubær on Síða until he was appointed as the abbot of Þykkvabæjarklaustur in 1168. However, Þorlákur turned even out to be the first abbot in Iceland to be subsequently elected bishop. Oddly enough, one of his first acts as the Bishop Skálholt was to establish Iceland's first female convent at Kirkjubær, that is Kirkjubæjarklaustur, where he had earlier on lived with his fellow friend, Bjarnhéðinn.[42]

Bishop Þorlákur was a distinguished priest who had initially received his clerical education at one of the main chieftains' residence and school, Oddi in Rangárvellir. He later went abroad and studied in Lincoln and at the famous Abbey of Saint Victor in Paris.[43] This widely known school of piety and learning was for a long time the main center of clerical education in Europe, attracting intelligent and promising students, scholars, and intellectuals from all over the medieval European world. It was part of the Augustinian Order and was where the customs of the order of St. Victor were composed.[44] Influenced by his foreign education, Bishop Þorlákur worked in accordance with the Gregorian reforms, with firm support from the archbishop of Niðarós, Eysteinn Erlendsson, unlike his predecessor Klængur. From his first day in office, he appears to have aimed to build up the Church in Iceland in line with the obligations set out by the papal curia and accepted in Niðarós in 1152–1153. Perhaps unsurprisingly, Bishop Þorlákur, according to his bishop's saga and *vita*, faced constant and intense resistance from the Icelandic chieftains throughout his term in office, which lasted from 1176–1178 to 1193. It was, specifically, this resistance that launched the first phase of the *Staðamál*.[45] And with the death of Bishop Þorlákur in 1193, the chieftains in southern Iceland used the opportunity to elect his successor for the episcopal see of Skálholt, in outright defiance of the decision made at Niðarós. They decided to appoint their own representative, and the candidate they chose was none other than Páll Jónsson (r. 1195–1222), one of the illegitimate sons of Jón Loftsson, the chief of the Oddaverjar family clan and a supporter of the internally run Church.[46] Chieftain Jón even used this moment to establish his own monastery, Keldnaklaustur, against all odds. Bishop Þorlákur was, nevertheless, sanctified by popular devotion in 1198 for his work for the Church in Iceland.[47] His earthly remains were at this point dug up and placed in a shrine that stood above the high altar in Skálholt Cathedral until the Reformation (see Chapter 9). Þorlákur's sanctification so soon after his death may certainly sound odd in the light of the resistance that he got from his contemporaries during his period in office in Skálholt. It is noticeable, however, that this was done one year after the death of Jón Loftsson and – unsurprisingly – on the initiative of monks in Þingeyraklaustur, located in Hólar bishopric.[48]

By the time Jón Loftsson founded his monastic cell, Bishop Þorlákur had in fact already excommunicated him for having disrespected the sacrament of matrimony and for having officially criticized the pope and papal authorities in general.[49] He had also predicted that Jón's plans for establishing his own monastery would fail.[50] In the northern diocese of Hólar, the situation was not much different. The bishop of Hólar, Brandur Sæmundarson (r. 1163–1201), clearly decided to follow the chieftains in their resistance against papal interference in the internal matters of the Church in Iceland. It seems that he ignored important ecclesiastical issues, as happened in the province of Skálholt. He failed to attend to the affairs of Munkaþverárklaustur, allowed its monastic building to collapse, and neglected to appoint a new abbot upon the death of Abbot Einar Másson in 1196. Moreover, when Munkaþverárklaustur was about to close, he established and approved the chieftain's monastery in the north, Saurbæjarklaustur.[51]

The bishops of both dioceses in Iceland, Páll and Brandur, should have been very familiar with the new regulations that were accepted in Niðarós at the time of its establishing, because on 17 March 1196, Pope Celestine III sent an enactment, or statute, directed at all clerics serving for the archbishopric of Niðarós, including Iceland. In it he reminded them that the chieftains were prohibited from interfering in ecclesiastical affairs, as in fact had already been decided. The letter declared firmly that landlords were not allowed to keep proprietary churches – or monasteries – on their estates within the provinces of the archdiocese of Niðarós.[52] The letter appeared later in canon law, when the most significant sources of juristic documents from the papal curia (*corpus juris canonici*) were collected and systematically organized in the beginning of the thirteenth century.[53]

Sometimes it is hard to identify, however, who chose to follow the chieftains in their desire to run the Church internally and who supported that it was centrally run through the Holy See. Perhaps nobody knew what was best for their own interest. For example, prior to his election, Guðmundur góði, Brandur Sæmundarson's successor in Hólar from 1203, served as chieftain-priest of the Ásbirningar family clan that founded Saurbæjarklaustur in 1200. Thus, when they nominated him for election as bishop, they thought they had reinforced their position as domestic keepers of the Church, neglecting the requirements of the papal curia that were particularly meant to reduce the ability of the secular leaders to install high ecclesiastical officials through investiture. However, Guðmundur góði seems to have changed his mind because soon after he came into office, he started to observe the decisions made in Niðarós.[54] One of his first tasks as bishop of Hólar was to reconstruct the monastic building of Munkaþverárklaustur and to appoint an abbot to the post held by Einar Másson until his death seven years earlier. Yet, this was what Bishop Brandur Sæmundarson had neglected to do.[55] Still, for his actions, principally though those relating to the Church's claim over the *beneficia* but also those pertaining to the elections of ecclesiastical leaders, Bishop Guðmundur góði was hunted by his former friends, the chieftains in northern Iceland. This situation resembled the difficulties faced by his fellow bishop, Þorlákur, some decades earlier in the southern diocese. For a period, Bishop Guðmundur góði even had to flee Iceland and shelter at the Niðarós archbishopric in Norway. He was also challenged by the chieftains of the Ásbirningar family clan, the very men who initially supported his election as bishop, in the deadly battles of the *Sturlungaöld* conflicts, which were – as was explained before – waged by the greatest local chieftains of that time and their family clans. The first battle of three that Bishop Guðmundur góði was involved in was at Víðines in Skagafjörður in 1208, the second at Helgastaðir in Reykjadalur in 1220, and the third and last on Grímsey island in 1222. On Guðmundur's side at the Battle of Víðines were the abbots of both monasteries in Hólar diocese: Þórarinn Sveinsson from Þingeyraklaustur and Ormur Skeggjason from the newly rebuilt monastery at Munkaþverá. Also on the episcopal side were two unnamed monks and forty priests from Hólar diocese.[56] Thus far, it was not until the death of Guðmundur góði in 1237 that both bishoprics were forced to introduce the papacy's reforms into the Church structure in Iceland. This was when Archbishop Sigurður Indriðason of Niðarós (r. 1231–1252) refused to appoint bishops according to the preferences of the secular chiefs in Iceland. Foreign bishops were thus set in office in both episcopal sees in Iceland from 1238, and so the time of nationally chosen bishops ended – for a while, at least. The chieftains' authority over the domestic ecclesiastical institutions was accordingly reduced because this change in appointment policy curtailed their influence on the internal affairs of the Church.[57]

It was not until Bishop Árni Þorláksson was elected bishop of Skálholt in 1269 that ecclesiastical authorities started again to claim episcopal jurisdiction over the *beneficia*. Consequently, with Bishop Árni's assertion and claims, the second phase of the *Staðamál* was awakened, after the first phase of the dispute had remained unresolved since Bishop Þorlákur's death in 1193.[58] The conflicts were finally settled with an official alliance made at Avaldsnes in Norway in 1297, albeit after negotiations between royal and ecclesiastical authorities in Norway that had lasted since 1272. The archbishop of Niðarós, Jón II the Red (r. 1267–1282), and King Magnús Erlingsson (r. 1287–1309) made an alliance for Norway in 1277, but the case was not settled with respect to Iceland until two decades later. The outcome was largely in the Church's favor, as it had been in mainland Europe nearly two centuries earlier. Simultaneously, Bishop Árni established his set of Christian laws, *Kristinréttur Árna Þorlákssonar*, but not with all the requirements he had hoped for. For example, the Church did not gain full rights over all *beneficia*. Instead, it was stipulated in the agreement that in cases where the Church owned half or more of a *beneficium's* land, the landowners could retain their previous rights, but all other *beneficia* fell under the control of the Church. After this, the power of the Church increased at the expense of secular leaders, and over time, more and more *beneficia* became the property of the episcopate. In addition, the Church won the right to install ecclesiastical officials and prevailed in many other matters.[59]

Periodical Struggle of Monasticism

Bishops, as the chief representatives of the Church in each society, were responsible for executing the injunctions issued under canon law.[60] As a result, through sheer inactivity, they could delay or simply hinder important ecclesiastical developments from being introduced wherever they were in charge. The bishops also had the power to implement certain innovations in ecclesiastical matters that attracted them, as we have seen in the cases of the bishops Þorlákur Þórhallsson, Guðmundur góði, and Árni Þorláksson. Consequently, choosing the person to take charge of the monastic houses at any given time became a crucial matter, since these houses were among the most important and influential ecclesiastical institutions in the country. The posts of abbots and abbesses certainly became worth striving for.

As has been demonstrated previously, while the *Staðamál* conflicts were at their peak in Iceland, all the active monasteries and the only female convent in operation at the time were confronted with defensive struggles, which not all of them survived. In such a sparsely populated country, family ties may have been too strong to allow for the separation of secular and churchly powers any earlier, as the Church had long required. However, because the monastic houses were active stakeholders in the dispute, their participation in political conflicts was inescapable. At any rate, changes of emphasis with respect to the establishment of new monastic institutions can be observed in Iceland as early as 1193, when Jón Loftsson, chief of the Oddaverjar family clan, founded his own monastic cell, Keldnaklaustur, the very same year Bishop Þorlákur Þórhallsson died. Thus, it was only seven years later that the chief of the Ásbirningar family clan in northern Iceland, Ólafur Þorsteinsson, played the same game by establishing his own cell, Saurbæjarklaustur. These acts by the main representatives of Iceland's medieval chieftains, in the north and the south, went completely against the principles of the Roman Curia, which worked sedulously to reduce secular authority over ecclesiastical institutions. Nevertheless, Jón Loftsson seems to have served as prior of Keldnaklaustur until his death in 1197. Ólafur Þorsteinsson, on the other hand, became a canon in his monastery after he had hired a chieftain-priest, Þorkell Skúmsson, to lead it.[61] Moreover, this was done with the firm support of the serving bishops in both bishoprics – Páll Jónsson (r. 1195–1211) of Skálholt diocese, notably the illegitimate son of Jón Loftsson himself, and Brandur Sæmundarson (r. 1163–1201) of Hólar diocese.

Around this time, the chieftains even gradually managed to take over all of the monastic institutions in Iceland by replacing the monasteries' abbots with their own supporters and permanently closing one monastery: Hítardalsklaustur, which had been established in 1166 but stopped functioning as a proper monastery in 1201. Its closure can hardly have been the fault of its abbots, as it was taken over by an experienced abbot from Þingeyraklaustur, Hreinn Styrmisson, in 1168. Surely Hreinn knew what the monastery needed in the way of buildings and artifacts, as he came directly from the newly built monastery in the north. After Hreinn's death in 1177, another respected cleric, Hafliði Þorvaldsson, took over, but after Hafliði's death in 1201, no permanent abbots served there.[62] Moreover, as is mentioned earlier, Munkaþverárklaustur nearly closed around this time but was saved by Bishop Guðmundur góði.

This was not all, Bishop Magnús Gissurarson (r. 1216–1237), who took over the bishop's seat after Bishop Páll in Skálholt, used the political struggle to appoint the chieftain Digur-Helgi Þorsteinsson to be the keeper of Kirkjubær, where Kirkjubæjarklaustur was then operated. At that point, Kirkjubæjarklaustur was closed down as a convent and remained closed from 1218 until the *Staðamál* were nearing resolution in 1293.[63] The course of events at Kirkjubæjarklaustur was such that after the death of Abbess Halldóra Eyjólfsdóttir in 1210, only a prioress, Guðrún, was appointed to replace her. After Guðrún's death in 1217, there are no further records of any prioress or abbess at Kirkjubær for decades. Around 1285, a prioress, Þuríður, is briefly mentioned in office there, but no new abbess was appointed until the convent reopened in 1293. Bishop Árni Þorláksson then chose Abbess Agatha to be in charge.[64] In the meantime, Bishop Magnús Gissurarson had appointed two of his own brothers as abbots over all the monasteries in his jurisdiction in 1221, 1224, and 1226. One of them, Hallur Gissurarson, a representative in

Alþingi and a former lawspeaker (in office 1203–1209), became abbot of Þykkvabæjarklaustur and Helgafellsklaustur simultaneously.[65] Bishop Magnús then helped another of his brothers, Þorvaldur Gissurarson, a chieftain who was later educated as a priest, to found Viðeyjarklaustur in 1226, to which he was assigned as an abbot (or possibly only a prior).[66] Bishop Magnús did this in partnership with the great chieftain, author, and then-current lawspeaker (in office 1215–1218, 1222–1231) Snorri Sturluson, who was fostered and educated, from age three or four, at chieftain Jón Loftsson's home at Oddi in Rangárvellir.[67] These three Augustinian monasteries seem not to have operated properly with the two brothers in charge (from *c.* 1220 until 1250) until three professional clerics were appointed to serve there as abbots by the Norwegian bishop of Skálholt, Sigvarður Þéttmarsson. The three new abbots were Runólfur Ólafsson, abbot of Viðeyjarklaustur from 1250 to 1299; Ólafur Hjörleifsson, abbot of Helgafellsklaustur from 1258 to 1302; and Runólfur Sigmundsson, abbot of Þykkvabæjarklaustur from 1264 to 1307. All served in their offices for decades, after having previously received their clerical education at Þykkvabæjarklaustur. After they took office, a long period of significant economic growth began for their monasteries.[68]

As is mentioned earlier, it took Bishop Árni Þorláksson nearly three decades to settle the *Staðamál*. Around that time, the Church finally managed to regain most of its control over ecclesiastical affairs and institutions in Iceland. Through the Church's affiliation in Niðarós and the agreement made in Avaldsnes in 1297, preparation had already begun for the establishment of two new monastic institutions in the Hólar bishopric: the female convent of Reynistaðarklaustur, founded in 1295, and the monastery of Möðruvallaklaustur, founded in 1296. At this point, the female convent of Kirkjubæjarklaustur had been reopened, and Þykkvabæjarklaustur, Helgafellsklaustur, and Munkaþverárklaustur all regained their earlier status. On the other hand, the monasteries established by the chieftains, Keldnaklaustur and Saurbæjarklaustur, did not survive the domestic crisis, and both were closed around 1225.

Challenging Innovations of Christianity

Internationally, research on the conflicts between royal and ecclesiastical powers has long been prominent in studies on early medieval Christianity. Although these conflicts became acrimonious and had a profound impact on political developments in Iceland, as they did elsewhere in medieval Europe, other practices and beliefs in Christian doctrine and laws also challenged peoples' lives to a considerable degree. These practices concerned matters such as of the habits of cohabitation and the Church's amendments of marital laws.

Matrimony was one of the seven sacraments of Roman Catholic Christianity. Holy orders – vowing to serve God as a bishop, abbot, abbess, monk, nun, priest, or deacon – were another. Initially, the Church had little to do with marriage other than sealing the permanent bond between one man and one woman, who consequently agreed to preserve humankind by having and raising children. The sacrament of holy orders, on the other hand, insisted on clerical celibacy, preventing members of the clergy from any marriage other than a symbolic union with the Church.[69] However, one of the Church's earliest interferences in the sacrament of matrimony can be noticed in the so-called Responsa Gregorii, dating back to the sixth century, when marriage within seven degrees of consanguinity was prohibited. Important reforms were later accepted at the Fourth Lateran Council in 1215, where the previous restrictions on relationships were relaxed down to four degrees, thereby banning individuals from marrying their first, second, or third cousins. In addition to being prohibited from marrying other non-blood relatives or brothers- or sisters-in-law, medieval Christians were even forbidden to have children outside marriage. Furthermore, male relatives of unmarried or widowed women – brothers, fathers-in-law, sons, and other male relations – were responsible for arranging the women's marriages, and moreover, only the children of the married couple were considered legitimate, not those born out of wedlock.[70]

People could nevertheless receive papal dispensations in cases of consanguinity or affinity, thus legitimizing their children as their heirs, as would have been possible in the case of an excommunicated woman, Cecilía Þorsteinsdóttir, who gave her farm Skriða to the Church for the establishment of Skriðuklaustur. Cecilía had borne seven children by her first husband, Einar Ormsson, but their marriage was later deemed by the Church to be invalid on grounds of consanguinity because Einar was her second cousin. When Einar died in 1471, the validity of their marriage was called into question as a result of disputes about the children's inheritance, and Cecilía was excommunicated by churchly authorities. The ban extended to all those who might possibly claim that her seven children were legally born, but it must have included her as well.[71] However, graces of this kind were granted only in specific instances, such as when the couple married without being aware of any obstacles to their marriage[72] – which did not apply in Cecilía's case.

The farm at Skriða was the largest gift given to Skriðuklaustur and was donated to the Church at the time of its foundation. Certainly, the donator, Cecilía, appears to have viewed the gift as an act of atonement, although this is not mentioned explicitly in the contract when the gift was finally sealed in 1500, six years after the monastery started to operate.[73] It seems at least that Skriða was donated to the Church in consultation with the bishop in Skálholt, Stefán Jónsson (r. 1491–1518), who established the monastery, and in return for absolution. At that time Cecilía Þorsteinsdóttir had been excommunicated, but the gift was given in consultation with her second husband, Hallsteinn Þorsteinsson. As indicated earlier, the reason Einar and Cecilía did not receive a papal dispensation for their marriage was because it was proved that they knew about their consanguinity before they married – they had sinned premeditatedly. Moreover, absolution, a remission of sin, could be granted solely by churchly authorities and only while the sinners were still alive.[74] Einar was already dead when the invalidity of his marriage became a matter for the Church. Cecilía appears nevertheless to have wished for his salvation, as much as her own and that of their children, and consequently included Einar's name in her donation, although she had remarried by the time Skriða was given to the Church. Einar had initially owned Skriða, but he and Cecilía had shared the property after their marriage.[75]

Cecilía's case is only one of many. In recent decades, scholars have paid increasing attention to the way in which the sacrament of matrimony, and the emendations appearing gradually in canon law, challenged people's traditional way of living. Above all, through matrimony, the Church called on Christians to practice monogamy. However, before their conversion to Christianity, alternative forms of cohabitation such as extra-marital concubinage had long been practiced among Europeans. Indeed, the sacrament of marriage and the marital codes that gradually appeared in canon law proved to be immensely provoking because marriages, as well as concubinage, were considered important economic and political alliances for those involved. This contrasted with the way marriages came to be seen by Roman Catholic Christianity: as amorous or religious contracts sealed by God. The regulations of the Church even challenged traditions of inheritance by insisting that only legitimate children born into marriages accepted by the Church could be legal heirs.[76] In reality, mistresses, concubines, and their children created essential ties between influential families as much as wives did. Both daughters and sons were given away to cement ties and to transfer property and wealth between families. Although this was especially common among the royal elite, it even took place among the clergy, despite their having taken holy orders. Moreover, a number of examples prove that men tended to choose wives from their close kindred, in contravention of canon law, in order to keep their inheritance within their family, but were inclined to keep concubines who could further strengthen their position outside it.[77]

As we will see, members of the clergy, as well as chieftains – and later, wealthy landlords and seneschals – flouted the sacraments of matrimony and holy orders by keeping mistresses and concubines and having children with them. One of them was the great chieftain, deacon, and owner of Keldnaklaustur, Jón Loftsson, who was married to Halldóra Brandsdóttir but had several concubines with whom he had children, all of whom became well known in the political history of Iceland. One of Jón Loftsson's best-known concubines was Ragnheiður Þórhallsdóttir, the sister of Bishop Þorlákur Þórhallsson. Jón had two sons with her, Ormur and Páll.[78] It was Páll who became bishop of Skálholt after Þorlákur's death in 1193. Jón apparently used one of his illegitimate sons to cement his family's ties to the Church. In addition to this, there are numerous examples showing that celibacy was not respected by ecclesiastical leaders. The most famous is perhaps the case of Bishop Jón Arason (r. 1524–1550), the last Catholic bishop serving in Iceland. Jón had nine children with his wife, Helga Sigurðardóttir, who became his mistress after he was made bishop. In line with the common practice of the time, they gave their daughter, Þórunn, in marriage three times. Þórunn was fourteen years old when she was first given in marriage in 1526 to Hrafn Brandsson, the son of Brandur Hrafnsson, prior of Skriðuklaustur (r. 1534–1552). Hrafn was close to Þórunn in age, and the marriage alliance was based on a compromise between the bishop and the prior.[79] Even Bishop Jón's mistress, Helga Sigurðardóttir, was the daughter of a priest, Sigurður

Sveinbjarnarson. Before she became Bishop Jón's mistress, she was the mistress of another priest, Ólafur Daðason, with whom she had a daughter, Þóra. Þóra became the wife, and later the mistress, of the abbot of Munkaþverárklaustur, Tómas Eiríksson, when he acceded to his ecclesiastical post.[80] Among the sons of Bishop Jón Arason and Helga Sigurðardóttir was Björn, who was temporarily placed as abbot of Þingeyraklaustur when the serving abbot there, Helgi Höskuldsson, was sent three times on a pilgrimage to Rome to make amends for having had children out of wedlock. Strangely enough, through this, Helgi was given absolution from his mortal sins, and Bishop Jón Arason granted it without questioning his own sins.[81] It was also common for the sons of monks or abbots to become abbots themselves, even in the same monastery. For example, Finnbogi Einarsson was elected abbot of Munkaþverárklaustur in 1525 after the death of his father, Einar Benediktsson, the previous abbot.[82] Gissur Ísleifsson, bishop of Skálholt from 1042 to 1118, had a son and a daughter with his mistress, as well as four other sons with his concubines. He gave his daughter, Gróa, to Ketill Þorsteinsson, who later became bishop of Hólar (r. 1122–1145).[83] Gróa was one of the Icelandic women who chose a life of celibacy after she was widowed (see Chapter 4).

As these numerous examples show, many members of the clergy – bishops, abbots, or priests – kept mistresses and concubines as though they were still their wives, even fathering children with them, throughout the medieval Christian period in Iceland. In fact, it is difficult to find cases where the clergy refrained from having relationships with women, so accepted was the practice. Meanwhile, there are no examples of abbesses in Icelandic convents having children or male partners. There are, however, two examples of nuns having children, as is discussed later in this book (see Chapter 7). Both instances are from the same year, 1431, and in one of these two cases, the child's father appeared to be the convent's priest. Furthermore, there are sources preserved about dispensations granted to Icelanders by the papacy for a variety of reasons.[84] Jón Ögmundsson needed a dispensation to be elected as the first bishop of Hólar in 1106 because he had been married twice. He went south to Rome to meet Pope Paschal II to have the matter sorted out before he was consecrated by Archbishop Asser Thorkilsen in Lund.[85]

The truth is that Icelanders, at least the serving bishops in Iceland, were well informed about the sacraments of matrimony and holy orders, and they were aware of the amendments the Church gradually made to canon law regarding marital matters. Instructions from papal authorities – even clear statutes – specifically highlighting these sacraments were sent to Iceland at least twice, *c.* 1189 and *c.* 1199. Another such reminder was sent from Archbishop Eysteinn Erlendsson in Niðarós (r. 1161–1188) in 1180, addressed to Bishop Þorlákur, wherein the archbishop expressed his concerns about the behavior of some well-known chieftains whom he identified by name, among them Jón Loftsson and Gissur Hallsson. In his letter, Archbishop Eysteinn requested that Bishop Þorlákur address the situation.[86] In about 1189, Archbishop Eysteinn sent another letter, explicitly entitled a statute, addressed to Bishop Þorlákur in Skálholt, Bishop Brandur in Hólar, and all Icelanders, in which he conveyed the ecclesiastical instructions regarding marital matters, including clerical celibacy.[87] The letter from *c.* 1199 was, on the other hand, sent by the pope himself, Innocent III, but this time it was addressed to bishops Brandur of Hólar and Páll Jónsson of Skálholt, as well as to all clerics serving in Iceland, reminding them to instruct all Icelanders to follow canon law in marital matters.[88] In truth, both bishops then lived with their mistresses and illegitimate children in their respective bishoprics without having been granted either dispensations or absolution from their sins.

Rights and Duties

In the light of what was said earlier about the marital regulations of the Church, it is clear that it was not only the clergy who maintained the system of concubinage in medieval Iceland; the chieftains also did so despite the Church's command that each man could only unite with one woman at a time. It is well known that the famous thirteenth-century author and lawspeaker Snorri Sturluson fathered several children with his concubines and two wives, just as the chieftain and deacon Jón Loftsson and many others did.[89] As was customary, both gave their daughters to men who had the capacity to strengthen their positions, and both were engaged in the establishing of monastic houses.

One of Snorri's daughters was Þórdís, whom he gave to his friend, the chieftain Þorvaldur Snorrason in Vatnsfjörður in northwestern Iceland. Þorvaldur was some decades older than Þórdís, who was a teenager at the time of their marriage. The union between the two was officially meant to strengthen Snorri's political position in the north-west, but Þórdís objected to her father's arrangement and escaped, only to be brought back to Vatnsfjörður. Later, she became one of the most influential women of her time in the west.[90] Interestingly, Snorri gave another of his daughters in marriage in order to seal the foundation of the monastery of Viðeyjarklaustur in 1226. This time he gave his illegitimate daughter Ingibjörg to Gissur, the son of the other founder, Þorvaldur Gissurarson. Both Ingibjörg and Gissur were about fourteen or fifteen years old at that point.[91] Þorvaldur, in turn for Ingibjörg, gave Snorri his daughter-in-law, Hallveig Ormsdóttir. By that time, Hallveig was a widow after the death of Þorvaldur's son, Björn Þorvaldsson, but she was the wealthiest woman in the country after having inherited her husband's properties upon his death in 1221.[92] Jón Loftsson was her grandfather, but both her father, Ormur (son of Jón by his concubine Þóra), and his only brother, Jón, were killed in 1218. According to *Grágás*, the vernacular lawbook of that time, this situation gave Þorvaldur the first legal right to give his widowed daughter-in-law to Snorri.[93] The establishment of Viðeyjarklaustur was therefore based upon the marriage alliances of these two women, Ingibjörg and Hallveig.

Interestingly, recent research has shown that it may have been desirable for a woman to gain status as the mistress or concubine of a respected and highly positioned man in Iceland. In some cases, it appears to have been more attractive to serve as the concubine of a secular or ecclesiastical chief than to be either married or unmarried.[94] This may indicate that concubinage was a generally acknowledged practice maintained jointly by both men and women. Stories set in the initial settlement period nevertheless allow us to imagine the emotional impact of unofficial or forced sexual unions, such as those based on the principles of concubinage – as the case of Þórdís Snorradóttir may show. These stories often express some awareness of the cruelty of the standard marital practices, but they also prove that different forms of extra-marital relationships were habitually practiced in Iceland before the introduction of Christianity. For example, in *Laxdæla saga*, taking place during the mid-tenth century, Jórunn Bjarnadóttir, wife of Höskuldur Dala-Kollsson, became jealous of her husband's concubine Melkorka, whom he had bought from a slave market on the island Brännö in Kattegat while on a trading expedition to Norway. Thus, Melkorka lived in Höskuldur's home along with his wife and his children from both relationships.[95]

However, the story describes Melkorka's traumatic experience when she was captured at the age of fourteen by Vikings in Ireland in order to be sold into sexual slavery. At the market in Brännö, Höskuldur Dala-Kollsson, from western Iceland, pays a low price for her because she is thought to be deaf since she refuses to talk. Höskuldur buys new clothes for her before he sails with her to Iceland. There she gives birth to two sons, although she was already pregnant with the first upon her arrival. One day, Höskuldur hears her speaking to one of their sons and thus discovers that she is not deaf. Melkorka then tells Höskuldur that she is an Irish princess. As a grown man, her son sails to Ireland and finds her family there, where he speaks fluent Gaelic taught to him by his mother.[96]

The evidence from archaeological research has demonstrated that the story of Melkorka may be based on historical fact, as many other Icelandic sagas may also be. Recent research on the remains from a grave dating to the early settlement period, excavated in 1938 in eastern Iceland, revealed that the woman buried there was born by the end of the ninth century. She was brought up somewhere in the British Isles, most likely the western or southern part of England, Ireland, or Wales, but moved to Iceland between the ages of five and ten. There she lived until her death between the ages of seventeen and twenty-five, approximately during the period from 915 to 925.[97] The results, on the basis of isotopic, genetic, and osteological analysis, may indicate female sexual slavery resembling the story of Melkorka. The woman in the grave was – by force or free will – dressed in typical clothes for a Late Iron Age woman, notably with one trefoil brooch and two oval ones. Around her neck she had a necklace of beads. The other finds in the grave included a spindle whorl, a knife, a sharpener, a blue agate stone, and possibly a wooden shrine. Her clothes reflect Nordic and Celtic weaving and spinning techniques, and the artifacts originate from common Vikings' trading areas.[98] It is appropriate recalling that in the story of Melkorka, Höskuldur bought her new clothes in the market before they sailed back to Iceland. Therefore, her clothes do not necessarily indicate that she belonged to a high-status Viking, but rather that she was dressed in accordance with her slaveholder's wishes. Interestingly, one of the statutes sent from Archbishop Eysteinn concerned a ban on female slavery such as Melkorka experienced. This statute was written in 1176 and directed at the Norwegians,[99] but it may have applied to Icelanders as well, since female slavery was a well-known custom among those who initially settled in Iceland.

In addition to the regulations imposed by the Church regarding marital matters, similar instructions appear not only in the earliest Icelandic land laws of the Middle Ages, *Grágás*, but also in younger medieval land laws, *Járnsíða* and *Jónsbók*. Yet according to these vernacular land laws, it was the father and the mother who decided whom their daughters should marry. If both parents were dead, the daughter's male relatives (Icel. *frændur*) had the legal right to give her in marriage. This could happen after the daughter had reached the age of twelve and if the son was fourteen.[100] A number of cases show that daughters could be given repeatedly in marriage throughout their lives, such as when the chieftains Snorri and Þorvaldur sealed a contract between them while establishing Viðeyjarklaustur. Involved in that arrangement were their children of a young age and the former daughter-in-law of Þorvaldur. Written sources, both the sagas and more official documents, show how common it was for men to give away their young children in sexual unions – often when they were only teenagers – and to marry them off to much older partners. It wasn't until Roman Catholic Christianity offered women the option of becoming nuns that they could escape from forced marriage. In *Grágás,* it is stated explicitly that a female, a young girl or an adult woman, who decided not to marry was allowed to *become a nun.*[101] In this context, it is also worth noting that according to *Jónsbók*, which replaced earlier lawbooks in Iceland during the Middle Ages, a girl who refused to marry the man chosen by her male guardian risked being disinherited.[102]

The great number of people who chose to become nuns or monks indicates that such life was a highly desirable choice in monastic Iceland. The reasons for that people decided to take vows may either have been based on sincere religious faith or perhaps done because of pressure from their relatives, but the decision to become a nun or a monk can likewise have been taken in order to avoid being given to marry. It must be stressed here, however, that early eleventh-century English regulations, distinguished between nuns and vowesses; the latter were widows who could take a vow and thus avert the obligation to remarry.[103] This may have been the reason for why some of the Icelandic widows decided to take vows: Guðrún, Guðríður, and Gróa, who all became anchoresses at times when no monastic institution had been established yet in Iceland. Their stories and other representatives of Christian celibacy will be presented here, but they show that it was socially acceptable to choose to withdraw from the world to live there in solitude as hermit or anchorite, just as much as nun or monk. Additionally, the presence of the thirteen hermits and anchorites in the early medieval Icelandic society may certainly be observed as an important part of the informal Christianization of Iceland, along with pilgrimage. This informal and formal spread of Christianity is also discussed further in the following chapter and how it was for the medieval Icelanders to become Christian.

Notes

1 *Landnámabók*, pp. 1–20. See also, for example, Karlsson, *Iceland's 1100 Years*, pp. 10–14; Sigurðsson, *Det norrøne samfunnet*, pp. 12, 42; Winroth, *The Conversion of Scandinavia*, p. 54.
2 See, for example, Abrams, 'Diaspora and Identity in the Viking Age', pp. 17–38; Andrén, Jennbert and Raudvere, 'Old Norse Religion', pp. 11–14; Andrén, *Tracing Old Norse Cosmology*; Walaker Nordeide, *The Viking Age as a Period of Religious Transformation*, pp. 78–82.
3 See, for example, Karlsson, *Iceland's 1100 Years*, pp. 38–39; Hugason, 'Frumkristni og upphaf kirkju', pp. 152–160; Kristjánsdóttir, 'Becoming Christian', pp. 27–45; Jakobsson, 'Conversion and Cultural Memory in Medieval Iceland', pp. 1–26.
4 Vésteinsson et al., 'Dating Religious Change', pp. 175–176.
5 Schmid et al., 'Tephra Isochrons and Chronologies of Colonisation', pp. 56–66.
6 Sveinbjörnsdóttir et al., '^{14}C dating of the Settlement of Iceland', pp. 387–393; Karlsson, *Iceland's 1100 Years*, pp. 9–13; Vésteinsson and Gestsdóttir, 'The colonisation of Iceland'; Ebenesersdóttir et al., 'Ancient Genomes from Iceland', pp. 1028–1032.
7 Helgason, 'Estimating Scandinavian and Gaelic Ancestry', pp. 697–717.
8 Ebenesersdóttir et al., 'Ancient Genomes from Iceland', pp. 1028–1032.
9 Vésteinsson and Gestsdóttir, 'The Colonisation of Iceland', pp. 137–145.
10 See further Guðmundsson, *Um haf innan*.
11 Sigurðsson, *Gaelic Influence in Iceland*.
12 *Grágás*, pp. 459–460; Sigurðsson, *Gaelic Influence in Iceland*, p. xi; Karlsson, *Iceland's 1100 Years*, pp. 20–27; Sigurðsson, *Frá goðorðum til ríkja*, pp. 30–35.
13 See, for example, Karlsson, *Iceland's 1100 Years*, pp. 33–37; Sigurðsson, *Frá goðorðum til ríkja*, pp. 70–80; Einarsdóttir, *Studier i kronologisk metode*, pp. 72–82, 103–104.
14 Karlsson, *Iceland's 1100 Years*, pp. 92–95; Sigurðsson, *Frá goðorðum til ríkja*, pp. 79–80; *Jónsbók*, pp. 81–88.
15 See, for example, Karlsson, *Iceland's 1100 Years*, pp. 79–82.
16 These were the Haukdælir of Árnesþing, the Oddaverjar of Rangárþing, the Ásbirningar of Skagafjörður, the Vatnsfirðingar of Ísafjörður, the Svínfellingar of the Eastern Region, and the Sturlungar of Dalir.
17 Karlsson, *Iceland's 1100 Years*, pp. 72–95.
18 Karlsson, *Iceland's 1100 Years*, pp. 80–81.
19 See *Grágás*, pp. xi–xxxiii; *Járnsíða og Kristinréttur Árna Þorlákssonar*, pp. 13–44; Jónsson, 'Inngangur', pp. 17–18. See also Arnórsdóttir, *Property and Virginity*, pp. 125, 401–402.
20 Clark, *The Benedictines in the Middle Ages*, pp. 53–56; Guðmundsson, *Íslenskt samfélag og Rómarkirkja*, pp. 93–97.
21 On trade as one of the efforts in the spread of Christianity, see Raaijmakers, 'Missions in the Northern and Eastern Frontiers', pp. 486–487.
22 Godlove, 'Iceland's Secular Saints: Hagiographic Motifs in *Njáls saga* and *Laxdæla saga*', pp. 102–115.
23 See, for example, Hugason, 'Frumkristni og upphaf kirkju', pp. 18–30; Sigurðsson, *Det norrøne samfunnet*, pp. 66–77; Kristjánsdóttir, 'Becoming Christian', pp. 27–45; Walaker Nordeide, *The Viking Age as a Period of Religious Transformation*, pp. 79–83; Winroth, *The Conversion of Scandinavia*, pp. 24–40.
24 Haug, 'Augustinian Canons and Benedictine Monks', pp. 206–207; Walaker Nordeide, *The Viking Age as a Period of Religious Transformation*, p. 117.
25 DI I, p. 483; *Hungrvaka*, pp. 11–12.
26 DI I, p. 483; *Hungrvaka*, pp. 11–12. See also Kristjánsdóttir, *Leitin að klaustrunum*, pp. 67–78.
27 Asser Thorkilsen is sometimes referred to as Össur Sveinsson in Icelandic documents. His father was Thorkil Svend.
28 Cariboni, *No One Can Serve Two Masters*, pp. 39–43, 63–66; Karlsson, 'Stofnár Þingeyraklausturs', pp. 159–167; Jensson, 'Íslenskar klausturreglur', pp. 21–22; Þorláksson,

'Þorgils á Þingeyrum. Um upphaf Þingeyraklausturs', pp. 169–180; Madigan, *Medieval Christianity*, pp. 143–144, 157–158; Nyberg, *Monasticism in North-Western Europe 800–1200*, pp. 98–99.

29 Kristjánsdóttir, *Leitin að klaustrunum*, pp. 46–49.

30 Aston, 'The Expansion of the Monastic and Religious Orders', pp. 9–10; Clark, *The Benedictines in the Middle Ages*, pp. 52–56; Clark, 'The Making of Nordic Monasticism', pp. 15–23; Jensson, 'Íslenskar klausturreglur', pp. 20–24; Jakobsen, 'A Brief History of Medieval Monasticism in Denmark', pp. 67–69; Nyberg, *Monasticism in North-Western Europe 800–1200*, pp. 109.

31 Bitel, 'Monastic Identity in Early Medieval Ireland', pp. 297–315; Ó Clabaigh, 'Monasticism, Colonization, and Ethnic Tension', pp. 901–902; Collins, *Female Monasticism in Medieval Ireland*.

32 Nyberg, *Monasticism in North-Western Europe*, pp. 223–224; Kristjánsdóttir, 'Medieval Monasticism in Iceland and Norse Greenland', pp. 56–57.

33 Gunnes, 'Klosteranlegg i Norge. En oversikt', pp. 57, 100; Nyberg, *Monasticism in North-Western Europe*, pp. 222–223; Kristjánsdóttir, 'Medieval Monasticism in Iceland and Norse Greenland', pp. 56–67.

34 Karlsson, *Iceland's 1100 Years*, p. 40; Hugason, 'Frumkristni og upphaf kirkju', pp. 225–230.

35 Lyon, 'Nobility and Monastic Patronage', p. 863.

36 See further Wood, *The Proprietary Church*, pp. 413–418, 680.

37 See, for example, Jensson, 'Íslenskar klausturreglur', pp. 14–20; Karlsson, *Iceland's 1100 Years*, pp. 39–40; Madigan, *Medieval Christianity*, pp. 132–145; Slocum, 'The Investiture Controversy', pp. 170–175; Jakobsson, 'Saints and Politicians', pp. 193–40; Wood, *The Proprietary Church*, pp. 851–864.

38 Madigan, *Medieval Christianity*, pp. 133–145; Slocum, 'The Investiture Controversy', pp. 170–175; Wood, *The Proprietary Church*, p. 884.

39 Guðmundsson, 'Íslenskt samfélag og Rómarkirkja', pp. 18–22, 84–93. Some other decisions, causing debate, were made by then, such as about a certain tax paid yearly by laymen to the pope in Rome (the so-called Péturskattur), the ban for the clergy to carry weapons, changes to judicial matters that limited the secular power's rights to collect penalty fines, and many more.

40 See Wood, *The Proprietary Church*, pp. 851–864.

41 Grímsdóttir, 'Biskupsstóll í Skálholti', pp. 32–33.

42 Jensson, 'Latin Hagiography in Medieval Iceland', pp. 915–918.

43 Also known as the Royal Abbey and School of Saint Victor.

44 Jensson, 'Íslenskar klausturreglur', pp. 9–57; Guðmundsson, 'Íslenskt samfélag og Rómarkirkja', pp. 28–30; Harðarson, 'Viktorsklaustrið í París', pp. 119–148; *Þorláks saga A*, pp. 57–59. See also Nyberg, *Monasticism in North-Western Europe*, p. 223.

45 Egilsdóttir, 'Biskupasögur og helgar ævisögur', pp. v–xxx; Egilsdóttir, 'St Þorlákr of Iceland: The Emergence of a Cult', pp. 121–131; Grímsdóttir, 'Biskupsstóll í Skálholti', p. 33; Karlsson, *Iceland's 1100 Years*, pp. 41–42, 96; Stefánsson, 'Um staði og staðamál', pp. 152–155.

46 Jakobsson, 'Byskupskjör á Íslandi', pp. 177–178; *Páls saga*, p. 299.

47 It must be noted here that Þorlákur was not sanctified by the pope until 1984, but he is the only Icelander that has ever gained the status of a saint.

48 Jensson, 'Latin Hagiography in Medieval Iceland', pp. 913–918; Jensson, '**Revelaciones Thorlaci Episcopi*', pp. 133–172.

49 Jón is claimed to have said: '. . . hvorki páfi né hans kardináli myndi vita betur né vilja en hinir fornu Íslendingar sem unnu þjóðfrelsi sínu og höfðu bæði vilja og góða greind til að gæta þess' ('Neither the pope nor his cardinals would know or wish better than the ancient Icelanders who care about their national freedom and possess both the will and the intellect to take care of it'). See DI I, p. 543.

50 *Þorláks saga B*, pp. 180–181.

51 Kristjánsdóttir, *Leitin að klaustrunum*, pp. 314–316.

52 DI I, pp. 206–207. See also Arnórsdóttir, *Konur og vígamenn*, pp. 108–111.

53 Guðmundsson, 'Íslenskt samfélag og Rómarkirkja', p. 85.
54 Jakobsson, 'Byskupskjör á Íslandi', pp. 171–173; Grímsdóttir, 'Afskipti erkibiskupa af íslenskum málefnum', pp. 28–62.
55 Skórzewska, *Constructing a cult*; Kristjánsdóttir, *Leitin að klaustrunum*, pp. 132–134.
56 Skórzewska, *Constructing a cult*; Kristjánsdóttir, *Leitin að klaustrunum*, pp. 316–317; *Sturlunga saga*, p. 218.
57 See, for example, Arnórsdóttir, *Konur og vígamenn*, pp. 111–115; Guðmundsson, 'Íslenskt samfélag og Rómarkirkja', pp. 84–93; Karlsson, *Iceland's 1100 Years*, pp. 39–40; Stefánsson, 'Um staði og staðamál', pp. 139–166; Skórzewska, *The Church in Fourteenth-Century Iceland*, pp. 22, 25, 100, 103 and 180.
58 Guðmundsson, 'Íslenskt samfélag og Rómarkirkja', pp. 84–101; Karlsson, *Iceland's 1100 Years*, pp. 96–99; *Járnsíða og Kristinréttur Árna Þorlákssonar*, pp. 26–32; Sigurðsson, 'Samskipti íslenskra biskupa', pp. 508–512; Stefánsson, 'Um staði og staðamál', pp. 155–163.
59 Guðmundsson, 'Íslenskt samfélag og Rómarkirkja', pp. 84–101; Karlsson, *Iceland's 1100 Years*, pp. 96–99; Sigurðsson, 'Samskipti íslenskra biskupa', pp. 508–512; *Járnsíða og Kristinréttur Árna Þorlákssonar*, p. 149; Stefánsson, 'Um staði og staðamál', pp. 139–166. See also Madigan, *Medieval Christianity*, pp. 132–145; Slocum, 'The Investiture Controversy', pp. 170–175.
60 Sharp, 'Bishops, Canon Law, and the Religious, c. 1140–1350', p. 1049.
61 Kristjánsdóttir, *Leitin að klaustrunum*, pp. 300–306, 314–321.
62 Kristjánsdóttir, *Leitin að klaustrunum*, p. 167.
63 Sigurðardóttir, *Allt hafði annan róm áður í páfadóm*, pp. 23–28; Júlíusson, *Jarðeignir kirkjunnar*, p. 110; Þorsteinsson, *Íslenska þjóðveldið*, p. 223; Kristjánsdóttir, *Leitin að klaustrunum*, pp. 274–277.
64 Sigurðardóttir, *Allt hafði annan róm áður í páfadóm*, pp. 23–28; Kristjánsdóttir, *Leitin að klaustrunum*, pp. 276–277.
65 Kristjánsdóttir, *Leitin að klaustrunum*, p. 462.
66 Kristjánsdóttir, *Leitin að klaustrunum*, pp. 326–329.
67 Þorláksson, 'Snorri Sturluson the Aristocrat', p. 33; Patzuk-Russell, *The Development of Education*, p. 27.
68 Kristjánsdóttir, *Leitin að klaustrunum*, pp. 195–199.
69 Arnórsdóttir, *Konur og vígamenn*, pp. 108–109; Guðmundsson, 'Íslenskt samfélag og Rómarkirkja', pp. 252–254; Madigan, *Medieval Christianity*, pp. 85–87.
70 See, for example, Arnórsdóttir, *Konur og vígamenn*, pp. 85–90, 118–123; Arnórsdóttir, 'Ægtesengen skal være uden synd', pp. 303–310; Brundage, *Law, Sex, and Christian Society in Medieval Europe*, pp. 124–175; Guðmundsson, 'Íslenskt samfélag og Rómarkirkja', pp. 252–254; Karras, *Unmarriages*, pp. 25–67; Logan, *A History of the Church in the Middle Ages*, pp. 193–197. Identical codes appeared in the Christian law section of *Kristinréttur Árna Þorlákssonar*, pp. 165–172.
71 Arnórsdóttir, *Property and Virginity*, p. 183; DI V, pp. 608–609; Gestsdóttir, 'Cecilía Þorsteinsdóttir', pp. 31–40; Salonen, 'Forbidden Marital Strategies', p. 182; Kristjánsdóttir, *Sagan af klaustrinu á Skriðu*, pp. 267–274; Kristjánsdóttir, *Leitin að klaustrunum*, pp. 434–439.
72 Arnórsdóttir, 'Marriage in the Middle Ages', pp. 214–215; Magnúsardóttir, *Bannfæring*; Salonen, 'Forbidden Marital Strategies', pp. 181–188.
73 DI V, pp. 486–487.
74 Guðmundsson, 'Íslenskt samfélag og Rómarkirkja', pp. 128–137.
75 DI V, pp. 472, 570; Gestsdóttir, 'Cecilía Þorsteinsdóttir', pp. 34–35.
76 Arnórsdóttir, *Property and Virginity*, pp. 157–167; Arnórsdóttir, 'Ægtesengen skal være uden synd', pp. 312–314.
77 See, for example, Arnórsdóttir, *Konur og vígamenn*, pp. 105–123, 168–169; Arnórsdóttir, *Property and Virginity*, pp. 406–418, 424–426; Jakobsson, 'Masculinities and Politics in *Njáls saga*', pp. 204–209; Magnúsdóttir, *Frillor og fruar*, pp. 47–52; van Houts, *Married Life in the Middle Ages, 900–1300*, pp. 173–176, 185–187.
78 See Arnórsdóttir, *Konur og vígamenn*, p. 109; Magnúsdóttir, *Frillor og fruar*, pp. 47–52, 123; *Þorláks saga B*, p. 166.

79 Arnórsdóttir, *Property and Virginity*, pp. 125, 401–402; Magnúsdóttir, *Frillor og fruar*, pp. 129–133; Hákonardóttir, *Fjarri hlýju hjónasængur*, pp. 40–47; Ísleifsdóttir, *Byltingin að ofan*, pp. 258–266.
80 Ísleifsdóttir, *Byltingin að ofan*, p. 91.
81 Kristjánsdóttir, *Leitin að klaustrunum*, pp. 129, 477.
82 Kristjánsdóttir, *Leitin að klaustrunum*, pp. 370–371, 468.
83 *Hungrvaka*, pp. 19–21.
84 See Arnórsdóttir, *Property and Virginity*, pp. 181–182; Jørgensen and Saletnich, *Synder og pavemakt*; Salonen, 'Forbidden Marital Strategies', pp. 181–208.
85 *Jóns saga ins helga*, pp. 191, 198–202.
86 DI I, pp. 260–264.
87 DI I, pp. 284–289. See also Egilsdóttir, 'Hjúskaparmál: Lög og reynd', pp. 257–258.
88 DI I, pp. 298–301. See also Egilsdóttir, 'Páfi sendir Íslendingum bréf', pp. 42–44.
89 Arnórsdóttir, *Konur og vígamenn*, pp. 163–172; Magnúsdóttir, *Frillor og fruar*, pp. 66–70; Jakobsson, *Auðnaróðal, baráttan um Ísland 1096–1281*, p. 160.
90 Arnórsdóttir, *Konur og vígamenn*, pp. 70, 141–142, 168–169; Magnúsdóttir, *Frillor og fruar*, pp. 69–70.
91 DI I, pp. 484–485; Magnúsdóttir, *Frillor og fruar*, pp. 66–68; Kristjánsdóttir, *Leitin að klaustrunum*, pp. 326–327.
92 Arnórsdóttir, *Konur og vígamenn*, pp. 170–172.
93 *Grágás*, pp. 109–110.
94 Magnúsdóttir, *Frillor og fruar*, pp. 88–90.
95 *Laxdæla*, pp. LIX, 86–229.
96 *Laxdæla*, pp. 86–229. See also, Karras, *Unmarriages*, pp. 102–108.
97 Hayeur Smith, 'Dress, Jewellery and Textiles', pp. 25–46; Einarsdóttir, 'The Ketilsstaðir burial', pp. 17–24; Kristjánsdóttir, 'Introduction', pp. 9–13; Walser III, 'Reading the bones', pp. 47–56.
98 Ómarsdóttir and Walser III, 'The grave good', pp. 65–70; Walser III, 'Reading the Bones', pp. 47–56.
99 DI I, pp. 233–235.
100 *Grágás*, p. 109; *Járnsíða og Kristinréttur Árna Þorlákssonar*, pp. 95–96; *Jónsbók*, pp. 121–122.
101 *Grágás*, p. 109.
102 Egilsdóttir, 'Hjúskaparmál: Lög og reynd', pp. 257–264; *Jónsbók*, p. 121.
103 Gilchrist, *Gender and Material Culture*, p. 34.

4

THE CHRISTIANIZATION

How early monasticism arrived in Iceland is open to question. As was discussed in the previous chapter, it may be reasonable, however, to suggest that the history of Christianity in Iceland is almost as long as the history of Icelandic society and that the Christianization did not start merely with the Conversion in 999–1000. Indeed, both historical and archaeological sources prove that the island was safeguarded neither from the Viking migration nor from the spread of Christianity, despite its geographically remote location in northern Europe. Written documents show that Christian people were among the settlers, in addition to suggesting that the two earliest forms of monasticism, eremitism and anchoritism, were present in Iceland from the time of the initial settlement of the island.[1] Some of the hermits and anchorites lived in locations that later became proper monastic settlements, perhaps indicating that their presence gave these places some kind of sanctity.[2] Moreover, the formal enactments and statutes, regularly sent out by the pope or the archbishops to emphasize specific matters of the Church, echo the drive for a pan-European monastic culture, even on its northernmost fringes. As is discussed in the following sections, it is clear that the ecclesiastical requirements were broadly fulfilled in all possible ways in Iceland, either through imports or by using local resources. Notably, both bishoprics had also at least one ship, each of which sailed to mainland Europe once a year.

Christian Settlers and Pilgrimage

As this book has shown, it is conspicuous how little attention Icelandic scholars have paid to early Christian settlers, particularly to formal eremitism and anchoritism, although these well-known forms of solitary life seem to have been familiar to the settlers of Iceland and their descendants. This lack of attention and interest

DOI: 10.4324/9781003361077-4

may be explained by the prevailing view that Iceland was settled mainly by Pagan Norse Vikings. Meanwhile, the accompanying slaves or purely Christian settlers are frequently dismissed as foreigners. For instance, while the stories of the settlement of Iceland presented in *Landnámabók* and *Íslendingabók* are considered to be descriptions of largely true events, the narratives of the Irish monks, or *papar*, found in the very same sources, have frequently been observed as fictional. If the *papar* are mentioned, they are most often said to have been hermits, living alone in their caves and not socializing with other people. Under Protestant and nationalistic influences, these supposed monks are in some cases said to have perished due to their lonely celibate lives, unwanted in Iceland, leaving nothing behind socially or culturally.[3] In fact, the *papar* may have been true Christian pilgrims – or monks – from Ireland.

In Ireland during the mid-ninth century, a pilgrimage route emerged on the basis of the legendary missions of one of Ireland's earliest saints, St. Brendan (b. 484, d. 577). Brendan is said to have traveled around the North Atlantic in a currach-like boat of wattle sometime in the sixth century and to have visited Iceland and the Faeroe Islands. In fact, St. Brendan may never have existed, but he is referred to in the numerous legends about him as the 'voyager' or the 'navigator'. In the late ninth century, there was significant growth in knowledge about travel over open seas such as the North Atlantic. As a result, following in the steps of St. Brendan became a popular pilgrimage route. Indeed, it was through the legendary story of his navigation that Brendan was initially sanctified, and Irish pilgrims began to imitate his travels by following his route in currachs nearly three centuries after his death.[4] In fact, although pilgrimage was typically based on a journey to the shrine of a saint or a site of importance to the pilgrim's beliefs, it could also center on imitating the journey of a worshipped saint.[5] The ninth-century Irish pilgrims – the *papar* – thus tried to emulate St. Brendan's travels, both by following the same routes he took and by traveling in the same small currachs he was thought to have used. Moreover, it is notable that in the descriptions of the *papar* in, for example, *Landnámabók* and *Íslendingabók*, they are said to have brought with them books, staffs, and bells – the standard outfit of pilgrims.[6]

In fact, there are several documents preserved to prove that, early on, Icelanders did not see it as a hindrance to pilgrimage that they lived on an island in the far north of the North Atlantic. This is perhaps because it may have been easier to travel by sea than by land, which entailed crossing major barriers like mountains and rivers.[7] It is appropriate noting that on one occasion around 1100, thirty-nine Icelanders wrote their names in the guestbook of the Benedictine monastery of Reichenau on their pilgrimage to Rome. This Benedictine monastery, located in southern Germany, was a well-known stopover for pilgrims on their way to the holy places of the Mediterranean or to Compostela in Spain. Eleven of the thirty-nine people in the group were women: Vigdís, Vilborg, Kolþerna, Þórríður, Steinríður, Ása, Dalla, Æsa, Þurí, Þórlaug, and Ástríður.[8] Unfortunately, nothing more is known about these women or the men in the group, nor is it known whether they went on a pilgrimage to seek absolution or for other religious reasons.

The people listed at Reichenau were far from being the first or the only Icelanders to travel as pilgrims, however. Preserved sources confirm that Icelanders, both women and men, participated in pilgrimage for various reasons from the time of the settlement and throughout the Middle Ages, as other Christian Europeans did.[9] Pilgrimage could be either enforced by ecclesiastical authorities as a part of absolution or be undertaken by free will, as is shown in examples presented before in this chapter and later in this book. Some of these accounts appear in tenth- and eleventh-century legendary narratives and in the sagas, indicating that medieval writers were quite familiar with pilgrimage and knew what it entailed. For instance, in one of the medieval family sagas, *Grænlendinga Saga*, is a story of a widely traveled Icelandic woman, Guðríður Þorbjarnardóttir, who went on a pilgrimage to Rome around the year 1000. When she returned to Iceland, she decided to become an anchoress, a practice about which she appears to have learned while on her journey south.[10] Other early Icelandic pilgrims appear in the sagas, but Guðríður is specifically listed here because her story is discussed further in the context of anchoritism in the following section.

It is not difficult to imagine the experiences the pilgrims had on their long journeys, gaining new knowledge and even bringing back souvenirs with them to Iceland. Some of these artifacts have been found as stray finds or during excavations, but the knowledge soon rooted in people's minds.[11] However, the mental and ideological influences have not drawn as much attention by scholars as the direct material evidence of pilgrimage, but such journeys must have been edifying for all who experienced them. Certainly, there were not only Icelanders who traveled to holy places, but people from all over Europe as well, mingling with each other.[12] The experience gained was, in fact, based on physical engagement by the pilgrim, for example, if he was seeking a cure through his journey by ingesting blood, bathing in holy water, or sleeping at a saint's tomb.[13] In this context, it is useful to mention one of the most famous Icelandic pilgrims of the Middle Ages: Hrafn Sveinbjarnarson, who became a learned man during his travels to distant lands and served as a physician and healer after returning to Iceland. In addition to Guðríður, he is one of the most widely traveled Icelanders of the Early Middle Ages. Hrafn was born in 1166 and died in 1213. He visited holy places in England, including Canterbury, traveling through Norway. He is said to have donated a walrus tusk to St. Thomas during his visit to Compostela and is even thought to have traveled along the southern border of the mainland through France before arriving in Rome and then returning home via Norway. After that, he settled in Hrafnseyri in the West Fjords, where he treated sick people from all over Iceland.[14]

Other Icelanders are cited later in this book in the context of pilgrimage, but one supposed Icelandic pilgrim must be mentioned here before proceeding: Nikulás Bergsson, often said to have been the first abbot of Munkaþverárklaustur. The story goes that Nikulás went on a pilgrimage to Jerusalem and visited Rome on the same journey, after which he returned to Iceland in 1154. Nikulás is believed to have served as an abbot the following year but died four years later, in 1159.[15] According to further legendary stories about Nikulás, he is mostly known for having written a guidebook, called *Leiðarvísir*, for pilgrims going both to Rome and to Jerusalem. Recent studies, however, show that it is far from certain that Nikulás Bergsson was the author of this guidebook, although most likely he did serve as the first abbot of Munkaþverárklaustur. Written references about him are too vague to ascertain whether the stories about him are true, besides the fact that *Leiðarvísir* was most likely written much later and thus by another author. Even if *Leiðavísir* has only been attributed to Abbot Nikulás Bergsson, its existence nevertheless emphasizes Icelanders' knowledge about medieval pilgrimage. Either way, this extraordinary book – known in Iceland – must have been very useful for all Icelanders planning and undertaking a pilgrimage to Rome and Jerusalem, which preserved documents show that they frequently did. Unfortunately, the guidebook no longer survives, but its existence is beyond doubt, as it is mentioned frequently in other publications, for example, as a copy, translated to Icelandic, in *Narfeyrarbók*, written in 1387.[16]

The tradition of pilgrimage is about as old as the tradition of withdrawing from the outer world as a hermit or anchorite.[17] As is hinted in the following sections, it may be that in Iceland, religious celibacy fueled early on the more advanced monastic enterprise, at least where some of the known hermits and anchorites accommodated within their later precincts.

Hermits and Anchorites in Iceland

Religious celibacy has been practiced in Christianity since the late fourth century, when it was first observed in the western deserts of Egypt. It became more and more institutionalized and widespread, evolving into eremitism, anchoritism, and monasticism, following the disruptions of the Vikings in the ninth century. An individual reclusion, when a man or a woman voluntarily chose to live rest of their life in celibacy, turned out to be a very common type of religious life in medieval Europe. Eremitism and anchoritism became rarer in most areas of the Continent by the end of the Middle Ages, but after the Reformation, reclusion was prohibited, as was monasticism.[18]

Despite being quite different from each other, both eremitism and anchoritism share the same basic aims: to live in solitude as the servants of God, to improve people's lives on Earth through praying, charity, and fasting – but to do all of this on an individual scale, unlike in monasticism.[19] Hermits were both visible and mobile within the community in which they lived, but anchorites and anchoresses lived fully enclosed from society in their own cells, which were most often attached to a church, monastery, or cathedral. However, anchorites and anchoresses were commonly accompanied by servants who helped them with everyday tasks and provided them food and clothing. They also participated in teaching, but only through a small window in their cell.[20] Hermits, on the other hand, provided themselves with their own housing and could live almost anywhere. Usually, they built a house with a chapel to live in during their enclosed life. Some of them even ran their own farms, from which they gave food or clothes to the poor. Conversely, anchorites and anchoresses were dependent on approval for their celibacy from the bishop or another ecclesiastical authority who also had to verify their physical and mental ability to live a life of permanent solitude. Anchorites and anchoresses were therefore supported directly by the Church and were subject to much stricter rules and discipline than hermits, who were free to go wherever they liked. Both men and women could become hermits or anchorites. Usually, women were more attracted to anchorages, and more often, men chose the eremitical life, perhaps because of the possibility of living independently.[21] In medieval England, for example, the gender ratio among anchorites was four women to every man, or 4:1, while hermits were almost exclusively men.[22] The eremitical life was also a much more common form of celibacy, and it was not until the revival of Christianity in the tenth and eleventh centuries that anchorages gained notable popularity. This may be related to the fact that anchorage was subject to the Church or the bishop, who gave permission for this form of living, and that an anchorage needed to be attached to an ecclesiastical institution, but such institutions did not exist in northern Europe until the time of the Christianization and later. It must be noted here that eremitism went through a period of revival just as much as monasticism did around 1100, although at least a century earlier. This late revival involved some changes of the nature of eremitism, such as in regard to visibility and endeavor. The hermits of the so-called new hermitism continued to live in their individual cells but were more concerned with societal matters by focusing more than previously on poverty.[23]

Conforming to other Catholic societies of medieval Europe, Icelandic documents reflect broad diversity among those who chose celibacy as a lifestyle.[24] Among them are, as we will see, young and old, males and females, widows, monks, and nuns. Moreover, all of the hermits and anchorites that appear in Icelandic medieval documents, the sagas, or other medieval fictional stories share the same commonly understood habits, indicating that this traditional life in religious solitude was known in Iceland from early on, just as much as pilgrimage was. The earliest narratives about these two types of religious celibacy in Iceland are found in *Landnámabók* and various Icelandic sagas, such as *Laxdœla saga, Eyrbyggja saga*, and *Grœnlendinga saga*. The oldest surviving copy of *Landnámabók* dates to the second half of the thirteenth century but is thought to have been written in the period 1122–1133 and thus considered to be based on oral tradition.[25] As mentioned before, it describes, in considerable detail, the settlement of Iceland from the late ninth century to the eleventh. On the other hand, *Laxdœla saga, Grœnlendinga saga*, and *Eyrbyggja saga*, like other Icelandic sagas, are prosaic family narratives based on historical events that took place during the ninth, tenth, and early eleventh centuries. However, what is peculiar is that while both eremitism and anchoritism have been significantly neglected, just as the *papar* or other Christian settlers are, the settlement process has certainly been discussed in historical overviews with references to the very same sources. This may be because so few formal documents and letters are preserved on individuals living in celibacy, unlike what is the case for the monastic houses that actively took part in the surrounding society. Something needed to happen and matter for the community for to be recorded. Actually, one interesting incident, where an anchoress was involved, took place in Tuddal in Norway in 1369, but it was documented because of its severity. In the document, the bishop of Hamar, one of Niðarós' bishoprics in Norway, absolves a man, Ketill, from accusations of having burnt down the church in Tuddal. The reason for the burning was that a fire had lit in the cell (*kofi*) attached to the church, wherein the sacred woman, holy (no. *hellige*) Tuve resided. After that, the fire spread to the church.[26] This case of Tuve can certainly be relevant to describe individually based reclusion in Iceland as well, by also being a part of the Archdiocese of Niðarós and, oddly enough, Roman Catholic Europe.

As can be seen in Figure 1.1, the anchorites living in Iceland were all based either at sites where a monastic house already existed or was established later, or at the episcopal seats themselves. This is unlike the practice of hermits, who did not need support from ecclesiastical institutions and were thus spread around the country. This was customary. Twelve of the individuals living in religious solitude in Iceland are mentioned by name in Icelandic documentary sources, but the thirteenth is unnamed. However, some of them may merely have been baptized people who did not live a formal life of religious celibacy but were nonetheless Christians. This is the case for several ninth- and early tenth-century settlers, such as Auður djúpúðga (the Deep-Minded)[27] who had been baptized before her arrival to Iceland but, according to her story, was not an anchoress. She appears mainly in *Laxdæla saga* but even in *Landnámabók*. According to her saga, Auður traveled to the British Isles with her son but, upon her death, was buried in a ship by the foreshore at her farm, Hvammur in Hvammsfjörður, but no church had yet been built in Iceland and no priest was serving there.[28] The Icelandic hermits were all male, but among the anchorites were one man and eight women, including the unnamed one. However, it can sometimes be difficult to distinguish between eremitism and anchoritism because sources are often so sparse. Three of the anchorites lived on monastic sites, four by the cathedrals, and two attached to private churches. The hermits, on the other hand, all resided in cells located on their own lands.

Early Eremitic and Anchoritic Solitude in Iceland

The earliest known hermits from Icelandic narratives are Ketill and the cousins Jörundur Ketilsson and Ásólfur Konálsson. *Landnámabók* tells about Ketill, who arrived in Iceland from the Hebrides during the time of the settlement. He is said to have settled in Kirkjubær, where Kirkjubæjarklaustur was founded nearly two centuries later. The same source claims that the *papar* had been there and thus sanctified the site. In fact, Kirkjubær means 'church farm'. Nothing more is known about Ketill, but interestingly, he is referred to in *Landnámabók* as Ketill hinn fíflski (the foolish),[29] which indicates a negative attitude towards him. Indeed, twelfth- and thirteenth-century Icelandic writers may have tried to emphasize that their country was settled by Norwegians of noble birth rather than by Christians from the British Isles. Still, it is worth recalling at this point that Þorlákur Þórhallsson also lived in some kind of celibacy in Kirkjubær before he was appointed as the abbot of Þykkvabæjarklaustur in 1168.[30]

According to *Landnámabók*, Jörundur Ketilsson and Ásólfur Konálsson were of Irish descent and became hermits in their old age. Jörundur is said to have moved to Iceland around the year 900 along with his father, Ketill, and settled in Garðar at Akranes. Ásólfur, on the other hand, lived in a few places around the Eyjafjöll mountains but later moved to Akranes to join his uncle, Jörundur, and built his cell by a church at Innri-Hólmur.[31] The suggestion that they were hermits is based on narratives in which they are said to be living free lives in their own houses with chapels. Both had sons from their earlier lives, named Kleppur and Sölvi. It was certainly not uncommon for people who chose religious celibacy in their old age to have had children when they were young. In addition, the narratives state that when Ásólfur came to Iceland, he was accompanied by twelve other men who were going to establish a monastery there. However, according to the documentary sources, all of them except Ásólfur died of fever.[32]

Many similar examples of such plans are known from early medieval Europe, where Christians often formed groups and founded a monastery together. A particular example can be found at one of the best-known monasteries in the world: Benedict's monastery of St. Gallen in Switzerland. In order to establish a monastic institution, a group of twelve men was needed. Thus, even if the story of Ásólfur is fictional, the number of monks needed to form a monastery was at least part of the oral tradition. In this manner, the sources record some of the core details of eremitism and show that it was familiar to Icelanders early on.

The third hermit mentioned by name in the narrative sources, Máni hinn kristni (the Christian), dates to the decades before the conversion to Christianity in Iceland around 999–1000. Máni's story is preserved in *Landnámabók*, along with some other contemporary narratives such as *Kristni saga*,[33] which appears in the bishops' sagas. The stories all tell the same basic tale: when Friðrekur, the earliest Christian missionary bishop working in Iceland, came to Iceland in 981, he baptized Máni, who was referred to thereafter as 'the Christian'. Máni lived his cell in Holt in the north-western part of Iceland, built a church there, and dedicated his life to charity work by feeding the hungry and poor with salmon and trout from a river on his land.[34] This farm, Holt in Ásar, is known to have been inhabited from the tenth century onwards, and may initially have been settled by Máni. Nevertheless, the description of his living habits fits perfectly with what hermits are supposed to stand for, particularly though the 'new hermitism', when hermits became more visible in society and in their charity work.[35]

Around the time of the conversion in 999–1000 and shortly afterwards, two anchoresses feature as characters in the Icelandic sagas: Guðrún Ósvífursdóttir and Guðríður Þorbjarnardóttir. The latter is discussed earlier with reference to pilgrimage. In fact, the stories about these two contemporary women are very similar. It is therefore possible that the writers who documented them used well-known motifs regarding the fate of European medieval women. Likewise, their depictions may show how the rights of women compared with the rights of men at that time. Both women had been given in marriage several times, as was the habit of the time, and both chose religious celibacy when widowed in their old age. Their life stories are thus identical to what is known about most other Icelandic upper class women during the settlement, the Commonwealth period, and Middle Ages.

The story of Guðrún Ósvífursdóttir appears in both *Laxdæla saga* and *Eyrbyggja saga*, where she repeatedly casts men into ruin. Guðrún was first married, against her wish, when she was fifteen years old. In fact, it was a marriage that she protested firmly until the couple was divorced. After that, her parents married her off three times. She moved to Helgafell in Helgafellssveit with her fourth and last husband, Þorkell, who drowned shortly afterwards in Breiðafjörður when he was importing wood from Norway to build a church. The church was eventually built, and Guðrún continued living at Helgafell as a widow but became an anchoress after her husband's death.[36] Thus she did not marry again, as she gained immunity through her vow, in accordance with the law. Her vow must have meant a permanent enclosure, in accordance with the general habits of anchoritic solitude.[37] Yet Guðrún Ósvífursdóttir is famous for having said: 'Þeim var ég verst er ég unni mest' (To him I was worst whom I loved most) in *Laxdæla saga*.[38] This was in response to a question from one of her sons concerning which of her husbands she loved the most. With her answer, she implies that she never got to marry the man she really loved, as women were not allowed at that time to decide for themselves whom they might marry. Although Guðrún's story clearly emphasizes her spiritual devotion, she is presented as a woman widely read, intelligent, and wise. This in turn may emphasize her knowledge about how to live life sincerely in religious celibacy.[39] Guðrún died blind at an advanced age around the middle of the eleventh century, after her son had assisted her in her reclusive life, as was customary. Approximately 130 years after Guðrún's death, the monastery of Helgafellsklaustur was established at the farm where her cell and church had been located.[40]

Guðríður Þorbjarnardóttir was given in marriage three times. According to the narratives about her, recorded in *Eyrbyggja saga* and *Grænlendinga saga*, she traveled widely with all her husbands, to America and other places, but finally settled in Glaumbær in Skagafjörður with her third husband. It was after his death that Guðríður went on pilgrimage to Rome. When she came back, her son built her a church, where she lived as a religious recluse for the rest of her life.[41] Serving as an anchoress may thus have been a desirable alternative for widows like her, providing a legal and religious role in society. However, this had to be done in consultation with the prospective anchorite's oldest son or other close male relatives, who legitimately ruled over widowed women.[42] This seems to have been the case in the stories of both Guðrún and Guðríður. Moreover, the accounts of Guðrún and Guðríður strongly indicate that they decided to become anchoresses, living enclosed in their churches in total solitude, unlike Jörundur, Ásólfur, and Máni the Christian, who all took active part in society, as hermits could do. The monastery at Bær was established while Guðrún and Guðríður were still alive, but it was exclusively for men. On the other hand, no female convent or bishopric existed in Iceland during their lifetime, so the options for a life of celibacy limited them to their own homes.

Eremitic and Anchoritic Representatives After the Conversion

It was not until in the early twelfth century that a new example of a religious celibate appears in Icelandic written documents. In this instance, a young girl named Hildur wished to become an anchoress shortly after the establishment of the bishopric of Hólar in 1106. This happened at a time when solitary life in general was regaining popularity in northern Europe and Latin West.[43] The accounts of Hildur, named 'the nun', are the most detailed and credible of all the narratives of individuals who chose a celibate lifestyle during the Middle Ages in Iceland. Hildur was a niece of Hámundur Bjarnason, a priest at Hólar. In her stories, it is said that even from a young age, she requested permission from him and Bishop Jón Ögmundsson to become an anchoress, which they steadfastly rejected. She refused to accept their decision and fled into Kolbeinsdalur, the valley closest to Hjaltadalur, where the bishop's seat was located. She built herself a shed and lived on berries and water until she was found again by her relatives a few months later. The bishop changed his mind and gave her permission to become an anchoress at the cathedral at Hólar, since she had clearly passed the mental and physical test during her stay in Kolbeinsdalur. The bishop, Jón Ögmundsson, built her a little cell attached to the southern wall of the cathedral's choir in Hólar. Hildur kept her vow until her death on 3 March 1159.[44]

Without a doubt, the stories of Hildur describe a real person because it is known that she actually existed. Several accounts are preserved about her, some undoubtedly mythical in nature and others not. All depict her living a typical life as an anchoress. One of them takes place when Hildur was old and could not remain in her cell because it was too cold. She therefore obtained permission to move into a warmer room where she was nonetheless assisted by her maid. Other stories described her teaching other women to read religious texts and teaching a poor young man, Þórólfur, to read and sing.[45] The initial story of Hildur's stay in Kolbeinsdalur has also clear biblical undertones. It resembles well-known accounts of holy men surviving a hard life in the desert, such as tales of John the Baptist. However, all the other accounts strongly suggest that Hildur was an anchoress who received permission from the bishop for her enclosure and that the bishop provided her with a permanent cell attached to the cathedral – just as holy Tuve did in Tuddal. Furthermore, she completed the physical and mental test through her stay in the deserted valley. In her cell, she even taught and helped the poor.

When Hildur was living in celibacy at the cathedral of Hólar, another woman, Gróa, daughter of Bishop Gissur Ísleifsson, decided to withdraw from society and live a celibate life at her childhood home at the cathedral of Skálholt. Gróa had been married at a young age to Ketill Þorsteinsson, later bishop of Hólar. It was after her husband's death in 1145 that she moved back to her childhood home for her vow, but she died seven years later.[46] Gróa's residency at a cathedral indicates that she was an anchoress there just like Hildur was, but as is mentioned earlier, there were no female convents in Iceland at that time where women could take vows as nuns. To live under the protection of a bishop was nonetheless a highly desirable choice. It is understandable that Gróa did not desire to remarry or be the mistress[47] or concubine[48] of another man after the death of her husband, Bishop Ketill. Various examples prove that women who belonged to the upper echelons of society were married more than once.[49] There are documents recording another anchoress, Ketilbjörg, who lived at Skálholt half a century after Gróa. She is mentioned only once in medieval written records, when her funeral was presided over by Guðmundur Arason góði (the good) (r. 1203–1237) in 1201, two years before he became bishop of Hólar. In the story, the funeral Mass was depicted as vividly memorable for all those who witnessed it, emphasizing that Ketilbjörg's holiness was established beyond all doubts.[50] By this time, one female convent had been established in Iceland, at Kirkjubæjarklaustur in the south, but Ketilbjörg chose the cathedral for her seclusion rather than a monastic house. However, she may have become an anchoress before the convent was opened in 1186.

Two other anchoresses were living in Iceland in the early thirteenth century, according to *vita*, the saga of Bishop Guðmundur góði. One of them, Úlfrún, had her residency attached to the male monastery Þingeyraklaustur, but the other, an unnamed individual, seems to have lived as a nun at Skálholt. Both Gróa and Ketilbjörg were long dead by this time, so this unnamed anchoress living at Skálholt cannot have been either of them. Nothing more is known about her. The only male anchorite living in Iceland during the Middle Ages, at the same time as Úlfrún, was Björn, who was also celibate and had a residency attached to Þingeyraklaustur but was not a monk in the monastery. Little else is known about Björn, except that he appears in a story of a miracle.[51] On the other hand, there are many stories about Úlfrún, but most of them are about otherworldly events. Apparently, she had the gift of prophecy. Úlfrún was said to live in a small hut at the monastic site and to be the mother of Simon the priest, which may indicate that she became an anchoress in her old age. The stories about Úlfrún frequently emphasize her chastity. She was said to have been so determined to keep her vow that she refused to let her own son visit her.[52] It was far from unknown elsewhere in Europe, during the eleventh and twelfth centuries, that celibate women resided in a male monastic house. Women's presence in the male monasteries appears to have most commonly taken place by the initiative of their relatives, such as through the admission of a son in the monastery, as was the case for Úlfrún.[53]

The last and most recent example of a person living in solitude in Iceland is Sister Katrín, who also was based at the male monastery, not at Þingeyraklaustur but Munkaþverárklaustur, during her initial period of celibacy. The stories about her date to the end of thirteenth century when there was still no female convent in the Hólar bishopric, to which Munkaþverárklaustur pertained. Sister Katrín's life in celibacy at Munkaþverá may have been meant to prepare her for the post as abbess in the new convent at Reynistaðarklaustur. At any rate, Katrín became the first abbess there in 1298, three years after the convent was established, but she died only one year later, in 1299.[54] To further emphasize this act, those who wished to become heads of a monastic house had to have proven their vow by spending at least three years in celibacy within an ecclesiastical institution. This probation could take place in a monastery, or an enclosure cell, as Sister Katrín's probation did, but only after completing it could the candidate be admitted to perpetual profession.[55] Katrín was not her real name, but she appears to have adopted it as a chastity name, as many of the abbesses at Kirkjubæjarklaustur had done before her.[56]

As is mentioned earlier, all the sites connected to the known hermits and anchorites in Iceland were visited and surveyed within the framework of the MMI project.[57] No excavations were undertaken, nor is it certain that the individuals residing at these sites would have left any material traces, since their residence there was usually fairly brief. However, in the late nineteenth century, a grave close to the church at Helgafell, where Guðrún Ósvífursdóttir is said to have lived in her cell, was dug up and the remains were interpreted to be hers. Some beads and human remains were found in the grave, but nothing proved conclusively that this was Guðrún's grave.[58] The grave has now been reconstructed and is legally protected. Still, on the top of Helgafell mountain (Holy Mountain) is a small hut, named the Chapel or sometimes the Shelter, which may be Guðrún's chapel, but no attempt has been made to date or investigate it.[59] In the case of Hildur, some literary research has been done with the aim of locating her cell, which is said to have been attached to the southern wall of the cathedral's choir at Hólar.[60] However, no archaeological investigations have been undertaken to prove it.

Becoming Christian

As may be read between the lines in the earlier sections, the complex process of Christianization was built not only on one-sided instructions issued by the representatives of the papacy, but predictably, it was also shaped in interaction, with all citizens of medieval Europe absorbing the politics and practices underlying Catholic ideology. Becoming Christian centered on how people synchronized their everyday lives, both religious and lay, in accordance with Christian doctrine and laws, involving an entirely new meaning of what it was to be human. In this context, one of many provoking challenges that came along with Christianity to Iceland and all other Catholic societies must have been the perception of sin and the purgatorial fire that all souls had to pass through on Judgement Day. As known, in Catholic teaching, the belief is that immediately upon death each person undergoes judgement, depending upon their behavior in life, before entering heaven, but that some can end up in the purgatorial fire and remain there eternally.[61]

To sin was introduced as an act of transgression against the will of God. The main deadly sins were defined as pride (Lat. *superbia*), envy (Lat. *invida*), wrath (Lat. *ira*), sloth (Lat. *acedia*), greed (Lat. *avaricia*), gluttony (Lat. *gula*), and lust (Lat. *luxuria*), which could appear in all human doings.[62] Still, all good work for the Church and society could reduce the pain in purgatory and, consequently, salvage the souls of the sinners. Salvation of the soul needed, however, to be accomplished through the grace of God and could only take place before death. Therefore, human life centered on the means of salvation and how souls could be released from their sins. Such penance could take place through a variety of actions, including divine offices, fasting, pilgrimage, by making the sign of the cross and washing regularly with holy water, or by giving alms. Lifelong chastity could even be applied as a penance for sins, as could the promise to feed a pauper for a certain period of time. Other monetary transactions could also serve this purpose, and these were carried out through an intermediary of an ecclesiastical institution, who in turn could promise to say Masses regularly for the sinner's soul. Moreover, it was obligatory to confess at least once a year in order to cleanse oneself from sin. Therefore, the crucial factor on Judgement Day was whether or not all of the penances practiced during one's lifetime were sufficient. Souls clean from sin would pass smoothly through the fires, but the journey was more painful for those who had not managed to be absolved of their sins before death.[63]

Praying and charity work were, however, often not enough to merit remission of sin, and in such cases the Church could also excommunicate those who had sinned. Excommunication was, as known, an institutional act meant to regulate members of the Church. Individuals subjected to such a ban were suspended from the society of God or had their membership limited. The souls of those who had been banned could only be salvaged through formal absolution granted by ecclesiastical authorities, bishops, archbishops, or – in the most serious cases – the pope himself. Excommunication was used mainly in cases involving moral transgressions, such as those involving marital matters or the birth of a child out of wedlock, but ecclesiastical authorities could provide dispensations in such circumstances.[64] Yet, excommunication was conventional practice and, certainly, applied the Middle Ages in Iceland. Still, it is worth highlighting that both canon law and medieval land laws also permitted physical punishment – whippings and even executions – for misconduct such as theft and murder. In this manner, the laws distinguished between sin and crime: slaying was a sin, for instance, while murder was a crime.[65] Physical punishment was meted out for crimes such as murder, while manslaughter and mortal sin were dealt with by churchly authorities who granted perpetrators absolution through specific penances. For example, Gissur Þorvaldsson, who was behind the slaying of the author and former lawspeaker Snorri Sturluson in 1241, was sent on a pilgrimage to Rome in order to atone for his sin. Árni beiskur, who carried out the killing with Gissur, was ordered to go along with him for the same purpose – at least, *Sturlunga saga* claims that they had their difficulties resolved by Pope Innocentius IV (r. 1243–1254) as a result of their journey.[66] Moral sins, such as those arising from consanguinity and/or childbirth out of wedlock, knowingly done, were always dealt with by excommunication, as the case of Cecilía – the founder of Skriðuklaustur – shows.

It should be emphasized at this point that in medieval Roman Catholic Christianity, the Church was the bride of Jesus Christ. All ecclesiastical houses, cathedrals, monasteries, and churches were accordingly the implements of God. Outside this framework there was no salvation (Lat. *ecclesiam nulla salus*). Nor could any human call himself an owner of a church because God was the only owner, and the clerics were his servants. This came clearly to the fore in the *Staðamál*, wherein the debate centered on the running of the *beneficia* but not the ownership of the churches. Accordingly, by fulfilling the seven sacraments, humans could be granted entrance to the Society of Jesus and the blessing of God, and perhaps most importantly, the sacraments were prerequisites for salvation. The seven sacraments were practiced by Catholic Christians as sacred ceremonies throughout their lives, from birth to death. As is mentioned earlier, matrimony and holy orders were two of them. The other five were baptism, confirmation, the Eucharist, penance through confession, and finally, the anointing of the sick. In short, baptism was necessary for entry into the Christian congregation, and confirmation reaffirmed the initiation made by the baptism. The faithful partook of the Eucharist by occasionally taking holy communion, memorializing Christ's sacrifices for humans. The sacraments of service were the aforementioned matrimony and holy orders, which underscored humans' dedication to serve the Church through marriage or religious work. The remaining sacraments were the sacraments of healing. Penance represented spiritual recovery from sin, such as provided through regular confession, but the anointing of the sick was meant to deliver the dying their last possible absolution from sin. Salvation could only begin when a person was in danger of dying from illness, injury, or old age, and the sacrament had to be administered while the person was still alive.[67]

Another highly important characteristic of the approval and general observance of the Catholic ideology was (and still is) the intercession of saints. A saint is a person who is recognized as having earned a degree of holiness closest to God. As underlined before, the so-called heavenly saints were biblical figures, while earthly saints could be kings and queens, missionaries, theologians, nuns, monks, bishops, priests, or martyrs, many of whom were members of the general public who earned sanctity because of their sacrifices for the sake of their faith. With their holiness, saints were believed to have inherited the capacity to protect people against all kinds of forces, natural or demonic. Through them, people could seek ethereal protection, any kind of help in need, or benefits from God, but obtaining such assistance required intercession through prayer, or even a pilgrimage to the shrine of a saint. The benefits or the assistance could concern any aspect of human life, but the intercession had to accord with the devotional background that each saint incorporated.[68] The connection between saints and donations was important in this respect, and it gradually became popular among people to give gifts to specially chosen saints during times of crisis, vulnerable situations in their lives, or even at their deathbed on demand of care for the souls of themselves or their relatives.[69] Saints appear frequently in Icelandic charters, votive letters, testimonies or wills, as well as in likenesses, textiles, books, and paintings, as we will see more examples on

FIGURE 4.1 A replica of the antependium from Grenjaðarstaður. Made by Helge Sigrid Vaag. It depicts the story of St. Martin. The original is on display in Musée du Louvre in Paris (Þjms_10933).

later in this book. It is important to bear in mind at this point that the concept of fine art did not exist until after the Renaissance. The images appearing in carvings, likenesses, paintings, books, or cloths were supposed to reflect the devotion of the Roman Catholic faith – personal or public – but not purposely serve as decorations. Indeed, much as the sculptures and ornaments, the architecture of ecclesiastical buildings, their interiors, objects, or the range of clerical outfit functioned similarly as the agents of Catholicism.[70]

As is discussed in the introductory chapter of this book, ninety-four saintly likenesses[71] and images were included in the preserved inventory lists from the monastic houses in Iceland, but many more were pictured on ecclesiastical fabrics and cloths or in hagiographies, often telling the stories of the lives of the saints or presenting images of them. The hagiographies were normally found in the monastic libraries (or in the homes of richer Icelanders), translated into the Old Norse/Icelandic vernacular, and even in Latin.[72] This means that the hagiographies of known saints could be read there in Icelanders' native language for the benefit of those not learned in the common language of the Church. When the stories of the saints were read from a book or a cloth, it was made it clear to the public that the earthly saints had once been human beings of flesh and blood. Also surviving is a vernacular translation of instructions, dating to 1378, on to how to make saintly likenesses in wood or alabaster, as well as painting, even in hagiographies, or embroidered cloths.[73] These guidebooks, known as model books, or *Exempla*, were used by medieval writers, textile makers, or carpenters in their work while, for example, producing books, embroidered cloths or carvings in wood, stones, and bones. It is not known how many such model books existed, but only a few have survived in Europe. One of them was made in Þingeyraklaustur.[74]

Most likely, however, the majority of saintly statues and likenesses were imported to Iceland, particularly those made of clay, alabaster, or terracotta as in the case of the likenesses of St. Barbara found in Skriðuklaustur. Some, though, were produced locally from other type of material such as wood, or perhaps from imported raw material, but neither clay nor alabaster is found naturally in Iceland. Interestingly, the iconographical instructions found in the model book made Þingeyraklaustur appear to have been followed when the ecclesiastical clothes that are preserved today were made in both Kirkjubæjarklaustur and Reynistaðarklaustur (Figure 4.1).[75] One other example is *Kirkjubæjarbók*, which was owned by the nuns in Kirkjubæjarklaustur and contains vernacularly translated stories of ten well-known female saints (see Figure 8.1). It was compiled in Iceland around 1500 and is illustrated with several colored drawings of each saint, apparently according to the standard instructions of that time.[76]

Papal Instructions and Statutes

The various events and affairs taking place in the monasteries in Iceland display episcopal interference in their operation. These interferences came either from the pope himself or from the archbishops, documented in letters. Importantly, they reminded all Icelanders to behave in the Christian manner at all times. Moreover, according to papal reforms accepted at the Fourth Lateran Council in 1215, abbots and priors were required to attend a meeting in each archdiocese every three years to review jointly the affairs of the monastic houses operating under their authority. The aim was to correct, enhance, and improve monastic life and to ensure that the chiefs of the monastic houses were equal to their job. The bishop was to be informed if they were not.[77] One clear expressions of episcopal duties in regard to the monasteries (and of course other ecclesiastical institutions) were the regular visitations made in them. These visitations were promoted by the papacy in the thirteenth century, but this meant that the local bishops were supposed to annually inspect each monastic house their bishopric.[78] Such visitations were practiced in Iceland from the early thirteenth century until the first quarter of the sixteenth century but, still, not annually (see Chapter 6).

The papal instructions issue, on the other hand, matters ranging from simple advice to formal statutes, on how to behave in accordance with canon law, such as regarding the fast, the sacraments, and the liturgical rites they required.[79] Some of them have already been cited here but not all. For instance, in 1237, Pope Gregory IX sent an interesting letter to Archbishop Sigurður in which he stressed that it was not permitted to use wine and bread made from ingredients other than grapes and wheat when celebrating the Eucharist. The letter is only preserved in a copy kept in the papal archives but has been preserved in both the *DI*, which includes commentary written in the late nineteenth century, and the *Diplomatarium Norvegicum*.[80] The general view, however, is that in this letter, the pope was rejecting a request from the archbishop for permission to use locally made wine and bread to celebrate the Eucharist, due to shortages of these items in this northernmost papal province in Niðarós. However, the letter appears to be one of the admonitions that were regularly sent out by papal authorities to the archbishops. It was directed, as was customary, at ecclesiastical institutions in the entire archdiocese of Niðarós, which included Norway, Greenland, the North Atlantic islands, and Iceland. Still, the nineteenth-century commentary on the copy of the pope's letter preserved in the *DI* speculated that it principally concerned Iceland. The supposed reason for this was that in 1203, the bishop of Garðar, Jón Árnason (r. 1189–1209), had taught Icelanders to make wine from northern crowberries during a visit to Iceland and had told them it could be used for the Eucharist celebration, as could locally baked bread.[81]

This calls to mind the persistent and well-known view of the supposed isolation of the societies of the North, which were believed to be beyond the purview of mainland Europe. However, Pope Gregory IX's concerns seem to have centered on the authenticity of the sacramental wine and bread used during the celebration of the Eucharist, rather than any supposed scarcity. The wine was to be natural, and the bread recently made, so that neither were corrupted, but both genuine and pure. It was permissible to add a certain amount of water to the wine, but only without reducing its alcohol content.[82] The ecclesiastical authorities, from the pope himself to local bishops, were obliged to ensure that canon law was followed in all possible ways. The sacramental wine – the holy blood of Jesus Christ – had to be made from vine grapes without any exceptions, and the bread – the body of Jesus Christ – from wheat only. An admonition similar to the one from 1237 had been sent to the Swedish bishops by Pope Alexander III in 1171. The pope pointed out that it was permissible, according to canon law, to add a small amount of water to the wine, but he also made it clear that he was concerned about over-dilution. Additionally, in 1220, Pope Honorius III reminded the archbishop of Uppsala how much water could be added to grape wine before it lost its purity.[83]

Thus, it may not have been the supposed shortage of the *correct* kind of materials used in the wine and bread of the Eucharist celebration that created the difficulties. The issue can rather have lain with the validity of the materials used. At any rate, no comments about the issue have been preserved from the archbishops in either Niðarós or Uppsala, only the papal admonitions. Additionally, there seems to have been no dearth of imported ingredients for the making of beer. Ceramic bottles of wine have been excavated, for instance, at Gásir, the medieval trading harbor in northern Iceland,[84] notably where the monks from Möðruvellir were accused of having gotten drunk before the great fire broke out in their monastery in 1316 (see Chapter 7). Beer appears also to have been commonly used during social gatherings, religious and non-religious, and even on fast days.[85] Although the sources, however, do not record the purchase and distribution of grape wine and communion bread in the provinces of Niðarós, both grape wine and wheat must have been imported without great difficulty from countries where both were readily available.

Analogous episcopal notifications regarding comparable matters as explained earlier are in fact preserved from local bishops in Iceland, such as in a letter from Bishop Vilchin (r. 1391–1405) in Skálholt, dated 27 June 1396. In this letter, preserved in *DI*, he emphasized that according to canon law, wine, bread, and other related items used for religious ceremonies should always be kept in a closed receptacle. Bishop Vilchin also tightened the rules regarding the celibacy of the clergy and their general performance in public. He asked priests to avoid theatrical and rakish behavior, particularly with respect to their clothes and armor. He likewise made the rules about clerical dress stricter and stressed that ecclesiastical garments should be kept clean at all times and stored in the sacristy, which had to be locked.[86] These notifications must have been done on the initiative of the papacy. Still, there is at least one case of peculiar interest in which the pope himself was involved in personal affairs taking place in a monastery in Iceland. Neither the exact details of this case nor its seriousness is known. What is known is that Abbot Jón Pálsson of Helgafellsklaustur faced difficulties during his tenure between 1458 and 1470. Two letters were sent to Jón from Pope Eugenius IV, dated 1 July 1472 and 3 July 1472, respectively; therefore, both were signed after Jón left his post as abbot. It appears that Jón was excommunicated from the Church, although he said Mass at least twice afterwards. In the letters, the pope granted Abbot Jón absolution from both of his offences, but by then, he had already lost his office.[87] The monastic houses were in this manner an inseparable part of medieval European ideology and culture, overseen by ecclesiastical officials, archbishops, bishops, and abbots, and even the general public, who equally followed the customs of Catholic Christianity.[88]

Materiality of Medieval Christendom

With the Christianization, not only did the idea of what it meant to be human change but also the material world altered interchangeably; a new world emerged, mentally and physically. For example, a new professional class appeared to people in the form of appropriately dressed priests, monks, nuns, abbots, abbesses, and bishops, which made clear the distinction between the general public and the churchly servants. As is shown with examples in the following chapters, common people could also work for the Church – in churches, monastic houses, or on bishoprics – as a means of obtaining salvation without being obliged to take religious vows. In some of the monastic institutions, there was also the possibility of receiving advanced medical treatment and nursing, whereas other institutions provided temporal shelter for pilgrims and other travelers, or even permanent shelter for the homeless and poor. Moreover, as we shall see, new opportunities were created for wealthier individuals, who could make a corrody contract with ecclesiastical institutions. Well-to-do people could also obtain an education, either theoretical or vocational, at monastic houses, or purchase textiles, manuscripts, and other products from them. All those who contributed work or gifts to these institutions of God could simultaneously cleanse themselves of sin.

The monastic houses, like all other ecclesiastical institutions in Iceland and other Catholic societies, not only offered people salvation from their sins but these were also furnished with images and paintings that continually reminded them of the upcoming Judgement Day. Furthermore, ecclesiastical buildings must have seemed otherworldly to most people to begin with, in Iceland as elsewhere, furnished as they were with symbols of the divine realm in carved likenesses, shrines containing holy relics, crosses, liturgical paxes, books, and other precious objects.[89] Even the decorated necklaces that were popular during pre-Christian times evolved into rosaries used for counting prayers, an essential practice for Catholics, in addition to charity and fasting. Rosaries were strings of beads used for devotional meditations by both the laity and the religious; for example, when asking God for a special favor or for forgiveness and salvation. They were used, either voluntarily or upon command from churchly authorities, to keep track of the prayer sequence. Each bead on the rosary represented one prayer (*Ave Maria* or *Pater Noster*), and each recitation of the rosary typically included fifty or more prayers.[90]

The church bells in ecclesiastical institutions must similarly have been ethereal but comforting, partly because their clanging could be heard from a long distance, as could the prayers or hymns. The same was true of the ceramic horns used as signaling devices, like the one excavated in Skriðuklaustur, or the hand bells used for marking the canonical hours. It was essential to be able to calculate the timing of the liturgy, and this was done with help of sun stones, hourglasses, or natural timekeepers appearing in mountains and hills.[91] In fact, a sun stone is listed in an inventory of Reynistaðarklaustur from 1408.[92] Furthermore, some place names close to the monastic sites seem to be holdovers from the calculation of canonical hours, such as Noon Hill (Icel. *hádegismóar*). Natural features of the landscape were commonly used for this purpose in all periods. Even water gained a twofold meaning with Christianization. Not only was it necessary for daily use or survival, quenching the thirst of humans and animals, but it also became sacred. Bathing acquired new meaning, as in the case of the washing of hands and feet. In the churches were liturgical basins and even *sacraria* with holy water used for various liturgical purposes, including baptism.[93] The remains of a *sacrarium* were, for example, discovered inside the monastic church at Skriðuklaustur during the excavation there.[94] Moreover, Bishop Guðmundur góði of Hólar is said to have blessed natural wells all around Iceland, and the water from them was considered healthier for body and soul than water from other wells. Such holy wells, called *Gvendarbrunnar* in Icelandic, are well known even today.[95] The water in them was believed to have curative power.[96] It should be noted here that washing – or any kind of bathing – was not only done for hygienic purposes, but was also meant to cleanse people of their sins rather than from dirt. This was done before religious services and before meals, and the water in the basins was blessed by the bishop before use. Additionally, corpses were washed before burial.[97] Nonetheless, the Church always placed great emphasis on hygiene and even ran public bathhouses outside the monastic houses for common people to bathe in, for hygiene and for good health.[98] Members of the upper classes had private baths at their homes or even hot pools such as the still-extant one Snorri Sturluson had at his residence in Reykholt.

In addition, eating habits gradually changed with the introduction of Roman Catholic Christianity, mainly due to fasting, which was one of the principal elements of official and personal penance. People could fast at any time of the year, but there were also long periods when they were obliged to do so, according to formal instructions on how and when to fast. These instructions, of course, were the same distributed all Christians through the canon law or by ecclesiastical authorities. Bishop Þorlákur, for example, gave the people in his diocese instructions on the fasting, right after he became bishop of Skálholt in 1178.[99] Besides this, clear guidelines about fasting appeared also in *Kristinréttur Árna Þorlákssonar* a century later. In them it is stated that everyone except paupers and the sick should fast after they turned fourteen years old and even that those who did eat meat during the churchly fast days faced the risk of being punished through whipping or being sent into exile.[100]

The longest fasting period each year was Lent, the forty-day period before Easter.[101] Fasting involved otherwise restricting one's intake of selected types of food during certain periods of the ecclesiastical year. During periods of fasting, one was explicitly forbidden to eat the meat of quadrupedal animals.[102] Fish and the meat of certain types of whales were permitted, as was the meat of birds without talons. The consumption of eggs, vegetables, and dairy products of all kinds was likewise permitted. Interestingly enough, consumption of the meat of narwhals, walruses, and seals was, on the other hand, prohibited on fast days[103] – at least to begin with. In a papal letter dated 6 February 1481, Pope Sixtus IV (r. 1471–1784) permits Icelanders to eat the meat of seals during the fast. The permit is provided upon a request from Bishop Magnús Eyjólfsson (r. 1479–1790) in Skálholt, and the pope underlines on this occasion that the meat of seals was already allowed while fasting in other bishoprics of the Holy See.[104]

Kristinréttur Árna Þorlákssonar includes, furthermore, codes on what was permissible to eat outside fast days and what was not. There it is stated that on non-fast days, it was permissible to eat birds that float on water and, consequently, the eggs from those birds. Bears, reindeer, and stags could also be eaten, and even walrus and seals, but not horses, cats, or dogs.[105] On a more suspicious note, it is odd to notice bears, reindeer, and stags mentioned in this vernacular version of canon law because no such animals were native to Iceland during medieval times. Only polar bears appeared there occasionally. Nevertheless, the meat of all these animals could have been imported to Iceland, but most likely these regulations were copied from European law.

Inevitably, this shift in eating habits increased demand for fish, and even meat from whales, birds, and beavers, as well as seals later on, among Roman Catholic

Christians living in Medieval Europe, from Rome to Greenland. Archaeological research and historical sources demonstrate convincingly that Icelanders, religious and lay, adopted these new dietary practices presented earlier. One interesting example of such, appearing in *Sturlunga saga,* concerns Órækja Snorrason, son of Snorri Sturluson, who wanted to obtain food for his fast. Órækja was known as one of the most vicious and violent persons in Iceland at the time of the *Sturlungaöld.* He traveled all the way to Strandir in northern Iceland to steal whale meat to eat while fasting.[106] Additionally, a recent study on dietary patterns among people buried at the Dominican priory in Västerås, Sweden, indicates that a diet rich in freshwater fish was dominant among both the laity and monks and no differences were observed between age, gender, and religious status of those buried there.[107] Notwithstanding, farms with access to the sea grew more valuable throughout the Middle Ages, gradually becoming the most valuable of all. The priors of Skriðuklaustur, for example, managed to acquire one of the largest harbors in Iceland, Borgarhöfn, in the sixteenth century, most likely to supply the inland market for whale and fish, or to export fish to mainland Europe where demand was strong. Interestingly, they paid for their share in the harbor with inland farms that were apparently of lesser value than the coastal farms.[108]

Indeed, the growing popularity of fasting and the consequent increase in the consumption of fish, eggs, and the meat of non-quadrupedal animals did, in turn, result in battle for the fish in the North Atlantic. The King of the Kalmar Union, Eric of Pomerania (r. 1396–1439), forbade any states other than the Kalmar Union to seek or trade fish in Danish territory, first for one year in 1415 but for a longer period from 1426.[109] The ban included Iceland since it was by then a part of the Union. Several examples can be used to underline how valuable the fish became, such as when one of the royal vassals in Iceland, the seneschal and knight Björn Þorleifsson, was in 1467 sent to Rif, near the west end of the Snæfellsnes peninsula, to secure that the Englishmen would not trade with fish in Iceland. During his inspection, he was brutally slain by English sailors from Lynn, but the Englishmen captured his son, Þorleifur.[110] The slaying of Björn had severe consequences and even launched the five-year-long battle, named the Anglo-Hanseatic war, lasting from 1469 to 1474. It was fought between England and the Hanseatic League about trading not only with fish but also with wool and other commodities.[111] The wife of Björn, Ólöf Loftsdóttir (1410–1479), was in Helgafellsklaustur when she heard of the slaying, but she viciously avenged it with further killings of English seafarers. According to annals, Ólöf captured three English ships in Ísafjörður, one ship in Flatey in Breiðafjörður and one in Grindavík. She also had an unspecified number of people killed there as well. Those who did not die in the conflict, when the ships were captured, were enslaved and sent to work on the construction in and around the manor at Skarð, such as to construct a new pavement to the church there. The fifty Englishmen, Ólöf is claimed to have captured, were released with a ransom but the rest were killed.[112] Eventually, she had an altarpiece made in the Netherlands in the name of her husband and her son, who she released from the Englishmen, perhaps in order to atone for her sins. In the altarpiece, which is still in the church at Skarð where the couple lived, Ólöf herself appears in a likeness of a donator handing two valuable gifts – a cloth and a walrus tusk – to Mary and Joseph.[113] This is a good example of people of the nobility buying themselves, often as donators, into ecclesiastical images and icons in the hope of God's grace.[114] At the same time, it also displays how blurry the boundaries were between the secular and sacred principles in the lives of medieval people. Ólöf's relatives even tried to compensate for the sins. In the will of Ólöf's nephew, Einar Ormsson – the first husband of Cecilía, the founder of Skriðuklaustur – it is required that a Mass for his soul be sung over the Englishmen who were killed in Grindarvík upon command of his family.[115] In addition, Ólöf's and Björn's grandson, Björn Þorleifsson 'the younger', had the so-called Reykjahólabók, containing a collection of translated stories about twenty-five saints, made around 1530–1540.[116] We will see more of Björn Þorleifsson 'the older' and his descendants later in this book because of their connection to Helgafellsklaustur.

Notes

1 Kristjánsdóttir, 'Ankorítar og hermítar á Íslandi', pp. 46–69.
2 Cormack, 'Monastic Foundations and Foundation Legends', pp. 59–82.
3 Karlsson, *Iceland's 1100 years*, p. 14; Hugason, 'Frumkristni og upphaf kirkju', pp. 66–69.
4 Harbison, 'The Early Irish Pilgrim Archaeology', pp. 90–103.
5 Foster, '*Pilgrimage Through the Pages*', pp. 1–6; Gilchrist, *Sacred Heritage*, pp. 131–132; Lane, 'The Archaeology of Christianity', pp. 148–181; Møller Jensen, 'Danmark og den hellige krig', pp. 285–328; Pelletier, 'The Pilgrim´S Badge', pp 240–253; Tarlow, 'Reformation and Transformation', p. 111.
6 Foster, '*Pilgrimage Through the Pages*', pp. 180–202; Melczer, *The Pilgrim's Guide to Santiago de Compostela*, p. 57; Stopford, 'Some Approaches to the Archaeology of Christian Pilgrimage', pp. 57–72.
7 See Guðmundsson, *Um haf innan*; Nyberg, *Monasticism in North-Western Europe*, pp. 15–16.
8 DI, pp. 170–172.
9 See, for example, Bynum, *Dissimilar Similitudes*, pp. 231–244; Arnórsson, 'Suðurgöngur Íslendinga', pp. 1–45; Møller Jensen, 'Danmark og den hellige krig', pp. 285–328.
10 *Eiríks saga rauða*; *Grænlendinga saga*, pp. 203–69.
11 Jónsdóttir, 'Hjálpi mér allir heilagir', pp. 19–29.
12 See, for example, Ó Clabaigh, 'Monasticism, Colonization, and Ethnic Tension', pp. 902–903.
13 Gilchrist, *Sacred Heritage*, pp. 31–32.
14 Egilsdóttir, 'Pílagrímur og píslarvottur', pp. 70–74; Egilsdóttir, 'Hrafn Sveinbjarnarson, Pilgrim and Martyr', pp. 29–40. His story is otherwise found in *Hrafns saga Sveinbjarnarsonar* in *Sturlunga saga* 1988, pp. 883–937.
15 DI III, p. 153; Hugason, 'Frumkristni og upphaf kirkju', pp. 349–351; Jónsson, 'Um klaustrin á Íslandi', pp. 174–265; Guðlaugsson, 'Munkaþverárklaustur', p. 231.
16 Vídalín, 'Ólafur Ormsson´s *Leiðarvísir* and its Context, pp. 212–234.
17 Aston, 'The Expansion of the Monastic and Religious Orders', pp. 9–10; Clark, *The Benedictines in the Middle Ages*, pp. 7–9; Clay, *Hermites and Anchorites of England*, pp. 1–5; Hughes-Edwards, *Reading Medieval Anchoritism*, pp. 3–4, 32–40.
18 Aston, 'The Expansion of the Monastic and Religious Orders', pp. 9–18; Clay, *Hermits and Anchorites of England*, pp. 3–6; Darwin, *The English Medieval Enclosure*, pp. 1–4; L'Hermite-Leclercq, 'Reclusion in the Middle Ages', pp. 747–764.
19 See, for example, Lawrence, *Medieval Monasticism*, pp. 26–29; Signori, 'Anchorites in German-Speaking Regions', pp. 43–44, 58.

20 Clay, *Hermits and Anchorites of England*, pp. 3–6; Gilchrist, *Gender and Material Culture*, pp. 182–186; Hughes-Edwards, *Reading Medieval Anchoritism*, pp. 41–56.
21 Jasper and Howe, 'Hermitism in the Eleventh and Twelfth Centuries', pp. 693–694.
22 Gilchrist, *Gender and Material Culture*, pp. 177–178.
23 Jasper and Howe, 'Hermitism in the Eleventh and Twelfth Centuries', pp. 685–686.
24 L'Hermite-Leclercq, 'Reclusion in the Middle Ages', pp. 758–764.
25 Karlsson, *Iceland's 1100 Years*, pp. 12–13, 66–67.
26 *DN* 5, nr. 261; Daae, *Norges Helgener*, p. 197.
27 In some sources named Unnur.
28 *Laxdæla*, pp. 5–10. See also Vanherpen, 'Remembering Unnr/Auðr djúp(a)uðga Ketilsdóttir', pp. 61–78.
29 Cormack, 'Monastic Foundations and Foundation Legends', p. 60; *Landnámabók*, pp. 3, 322–325.
30 See Jensson, 'Latin Hagiography in Medieval Iceland', pp. 892–893.
31 Jónsson, 'Um klaustrin á Íslandi', pp. 174–176; *Landnámabók*, pp. 60–65. See also Egilsdóttir, 'The Hermit and the Milkmaid', pp. 23–32.
32 *Landnámabók*, pp. 13–14.
33 *Kristni saga* is an account of the Christianization of Iceland in the tenth century, including some later church history, probably documented in the early or mid-thirteenth century.
34 Jónsson, 'Um klaustrin á Íslandi', p. 176; *Kristni saga*, p. 4; *Þorvalds þáttr víðförla I*, pp. 83–85.
35 See Jasper and Howe, 'Hermitism in the Eleventh and Twelfth Centuries', pp. 684–685.
36 *Laxdæla saga*, pp. 176–183.
37 See, for example, Gilchrist, *Gender and Material Culture*, p. 177; Hughes-Edwards, *Reading Medieval Anchoritism*, pp. 52–56; Karras, 'Marriage and the Creation of Kin in the Sagas', pp. 481–482.
38 *Laxdæla saga*, p. 186.
39 Jakosson, 'Laxdæla Dreaming', pp. 33–51.
40 Cormack, 'Monastic Foundations and Foundation Legends', pp. 70–73; *Laxdæla saga*, p. 186.
41 *Eiríks saga rauða*; *Grænlendinga saga*, pp. 203–269.
42 *Grágás*, pp. 109–110.
43 Magnani, 'Female House Ascetics', p. 230.
44 Hugason, 'Frumkristni og upphaf kirkju', p. 352; *Jóns saga ins helga*, pp. 248–252; Kristjánsdóttir, 'A Nocturnal Wake at Hólar', pp. 225–228.
45 *Jóns saga ins helga*, p. 253. See also, Egilsdóttir, 'Skjaldmær drottins', pp. 29–42.
46 *Hungrvaka*, pp. 19–21, 36.
47 'Fylgikona' (Mistress). A title of courtesy prefixed to the name of a formerly married woman of a secular leader. The fact is that men needed to divorce their wives when they took their holy orders, but they could continue nonetheless to live with them as mistresses.
48 'Frilla' (Concubine). A woman who accompanies or cohabits, as a paramour, a man without being his wife.
49 See, for example, Magnúsdóttir, 'Móðir, kona, meyja', pp. 83–92; Karras, *Unmarriages*, pp. 114–148; Skórzewska, *Constructing a Cult*, p. 82.
50 *Sturlunga saga I*, p. 196; Skórzewska, *Constructing a Cult*, p. 82.
51 *Jarteinabók II*, p. 238.
52 *Jarteinabók II*, pp. 241–242; Skórzewska, *Constructing a Cult*, pp. 82, 152–153.
53 Magnani, 'Female House Ascetics from the Fourth to Twelfth Century', p. 229.
54 *Skálholtsannáll*, pp. 198–199.
55 *Code of Canon Law*, Chapter VI, Art. 1, Can 684 §2. *Code of Canon Law*, Chapter III, Art. 2, Can 648 §3.

56 Jakobsson and Egilsdóttir, 'Abbadísin sem hvarf', pp. 7–9; Cormack, 'Monastic Foundations and Foundation Legends', pp. 74–75; Kristjánsdóttir, *Leitin að klaustrunum*, pp. 278–280.
57 See, Halldórsdóttir, 'Einsetulifnaður á Íslandi'; Kristjánsdóttir, 'Ankorítar og hermítar á Íslandi', pp. 46–69.
58 Halldórsdóttir, 'Einsetulifnaður á Íslandi', pp. 17–20.
59 Kristjánsdóttir, *Leitin að klaustrunum*, p. 232.
60 Halldórsdóttir, 'Einsetulifnaður á Íslandi', p. 26.
61 Nedkvitne, *Møte med døden i norrøn middelalder*, pp. 48–71; Pasulka, *Heaven can wait*, pp. 3–5; Roffey, 'Deconstructing a Symbolic World', pp. 341–342, 349.
62 Magnúsardóttir, 'Syndin fyrir dómstólum', p. 143.
63 Guðmundsson, 'Íslenskt samfélag og Rómarkirkja', pp. 99, 138, 279; Logan, *A History of the Church in the Middle Ages*, pp. 287–295; Nedkvitne, *Møte med døden i norrøn middelalder*, pp. 112–120; Pasulka, *Heaven Can Wait*, pp. 3–5.
64 Guðmundsson, 'Íslenskt samfélag og Rómarkirkja', pp. 32, 56–62; Magnúsardóttir, *Bannfæring*, pp. 217–296; Logan, *A History of the Church in the Middle Ages*, pp. 287–295.
65 Specifically, human slaying, or manslaughter, was when the killer declares the killing as done with purpose, but murder was a killing of another human without justification. See Júlíusson, 'Manndráp verður að morði', p. 88; *Grágás*, pp. 447–459; *Jónsbók*, pp. 101–112; Netterstrøm, 'Reformationens betydning for kriminalisering af manddrab', pp 413–418.
66 Arnórsson, 'Suðurgöngur Íslendinga', pp. 1–45; *Sturlunga saga*, p. 567.
67 Guðmundsson, 'Íslenskt samfélag og Rómarkirkja', pp. 252, 268–269, 273; Madigan, *Medieval Christianity*, pp. 85–87; Whiting, *The Blind Devotion of the People*, pp. 17, 24–41, 243–244.
68 See, for example, Cormack, *The Saints in Iceland*, pp. 49–68; Fradenberg, 'Making, Mourning and the Love of Idols', pp. 25–40; Gilchrist, *Sacred Heritage*, pp. 110–144; Hugason, 'Frumkristni og upphaf kirkju', pp. 307–311; Madigan, *Medieval Christianity*, pp. 85–94, 320–323; Simpson, 'The Rule of Medieval Imagination', pp. 4–22; Stopford, 'Some Approaches to the Archaeology of Christian Pilgrimage', pp. 57–72; Tarlow, 'Reformation and Transformation', p. 111.
69 Arnórsdóttir, 'Gender and Donation Culture', pp. 165–175; Arnórsdóttir, 'Marital Property and Change in the Donation Culture', pp. 140–156.
70 Gajewski and Seeberg, 'Art in Monastic Churches of Western Europe', pp. 999–1022; Kessler, 'On the State of Medieval Art History', pp. 179–180.
71 It is worth noting that it is not always clear which saints were depicted in the likenesses. For example, when only the name Jacobus appears on the list, it is not specified whether it was Jacobus the Great or the Greater.
72 See, for example, Wolf, *The Legends of the Saints in Old Norse-Icelandic Prose*.
73 Halldórsson, 'Líkneskjusmíð', pp. 5–15.
74 See, for example, Björnsson, *Íslenska teiknibókin í Árnasafni*; Kristjánsdóttir, *Íslenska teiknibókin*.
75 Guðjónsson, 'Skyldleiki erlendra prentmynda', pp. 71–84; Jónsdóttir, 'Gömul krossfestingarmynd,' pp. 134–141; Wandel, 'Íslenzk altarisklæði í erlendum söfnum', pp. 51–54.
76 Wolf, *A Female Legendary from Iceland*.
77 Clark, *The Benedictines in the Middle Ages*, pp. 257–258, 263–265, 288–298; *Conciliorum Oecumenicorum Decreta*, p. 241; Guðmundsson, 'Íslenskt samfélag og Rómarkirkja', p. 216; Knowles, *Religious Orders in England*, pp. 9–11; Madigan, *Medieval Christianity*, pp. 310–311, 357–358.
78 Sharp, 'Bishops, Canon Law, and the Religious, c. 1140–1350', pp. 1098–1099.
79 See, for example, DI I, pp. 235–236; DI I, pp. 237–244; and DI II, p. 52; DI IX, pp. 39–40.
80 Hereafter DN. See DI I, pp. III – XII, 513–514; DN I, no. 16.
81 DI I, pp. 513–514.

82 Madigan, *Medieval Christianity*, pp. 85–88; Schulte, 'Altar Wine'.
83 Bisgaard, 'Wine and Beer in Medieval Scandinavia', p. 70.
84 Colic, '*Medieval Icelandic Pottery*', p. 36.
85 See, for example, Bisgaard, 'Wine and Beer in Medieval Scandinavia', pp. 67–87.
86 DI III, pp. 615–616.
87 Guðmundsson, 'Tíu páfabréf frá 15. öld', pp. 64, 69–70; Jørgensen and Saletnich, *Synder og pavemakt*, p. 106.
88 See *Code of Canon Law*, Chapter II, Article 1, Can 617–630.
89 Boase, *Death in the Middle Ages*, pp. 19–45; Bynum, *Dissimilar Similitudes*, pp. 17–40; Gilchrist, *Sacred Heritage*, pp. 110–144; Fradenberg, 'Making, Mourning and the Love of Idols', pp. 25–40; Masur, 'Symbol or Presence?' pp. 4–7; Simpson, 'The Rule of Medieval Imagination', pp. 4–22.
90 Atzbach, 'Between Representation and Eternity', pp. 28–31; Gilchrist, *Medieval Life*, pp. 157–158; Masur, 'Symbol or Presence?' pp. 8–13.
91 Egilsdóttir, 'Klerkar og samfélag', pp. 364–365; Gilchrist, *Medieval Life*, pp. 13–19; McCluskey, 'Gregory of Tours, Monastic Timekeeping', pp. 19–22.
92 DI III, p. 718.
93 See, for example, Bond, 'Monastic Water Management in Great Britain', pp. 88–89; Gilchrist, *Medieval Life*, pp. 168, 186–189; Hooke, 'The Sacred Nature of Rivers, Wells, and Other Wetlands', pp. 32–57.
94 Hjartarson, 'Lífsins vatn'.
95 Hjartarson, 'Lífsins vatn'.
96 Whiting, *The Blind Devotion of the People*, p. 61.
97 Hjartarson, 'Lífsins vatn', pp. 22–24; Kerr, *Life in the Medieval Cloister*, p. 60.
98 Squatriti, *Water and Society in Early Medieval Italy*, p. 54; Thurlkill, *Sacred Scents in Early Christianity and Islam*, pp. 6–11.
99 DI I, pp. 235–236.
100 *Járnsíða og Kristinréttur Árna Þorlákssonar*, pp. 182–183.
101 See, for example, Guðmundsson, 'Íslenskt samfélag og Rómarkirkja', p. 289; Gilchrist, *Medieval Life*, pp. 14, 52; Walaker Nordeide, 'Canonical Observance in Norway in the Middle Ages'.
102 *The Rule of Saint Benedict*, Chapter XXXIX.
103 *Járnsíða og Kristinréttur Árna Þorlákssonar*, p. 185.
104 DI IX, pp. 39–40.
105 *Járnsíða og Kristinréttur Árna Þorlákssonar*, p. 184.
106 *Sturlunga saga*, pp. 365–366
107 Ahlin-Sundman, 'Masculinities and Diet', pp. 95–111.
108 Kristjánsdóttir, *Sagan af klaustrinu á Skriðu*, pp. 266–270.
109 DI XVI, pp. 126, 230.
110 The Overseas Trade of Bristol in the late Middle Ages, p. 136. There it says 18 November 1467: 'In this year Englishmen in Iceland slew the Governor, who was endeavoring to enforce the Danish king's restrictions, and the king therefore sequestered ships of Lynn and Bristol passing through the Sound'.
111 DI XVI, pp. 430–436.
112 *Vestfjarðarannáll hinn elzti*, p. 30; *Sauðlauksdalsannáll*, p. 399.
113 Júníusdóttir, *Altaristafla Ólafar ríku á Skarði*.
114 Pietraszek, *The Place and Space of Donator*.
115 DI V, p. 571.
116 Loth, *Reykjahólabók*; Kalinke, *The Book of Reykjahólar*; Wolf, 'Low German Legends of the Apostles', pp. 139–181.

5

THE MONASTIC LANDSCAPE

As was previously shown, there are a number of letters preserved from the pope himself or the local archbishops and bishops in northern Europe, emphasizing the importance of following canon law or informing ecclesiastical principals about any amendments made. Apparently, the Icelandic monasteries were not exempt from the standardized supervision provided by their orders and the ecclesiastical officials. Monasticism and Icelandic society thereby grew together in an interactive way and thus as one entity. As we will see, the monastic houses served, wherever they were run, as places not only of sanctuary, contemplation, and absolution but also of economical wealth, open to all who wished to have a share in what they offered. Accordingly, as the time went on, the bishops and chiefs of the monastic houses managed to build up a stable network around Iceland together. The monastic houses were located at more or less regular intervals along the main travel routes so as to be both accessible and clearly visible to the general public, who needed their wide-ranging services, as was customary for the Benedictine and Augustinian houses on the Continent.[1] This finely woven network also enabled them to acquire a relatively large proportion of farms in most areas of the country. However, as will be argued, the Icelandic monastic houses did not operate unchanged during the entire medieval period, although most of them adhered to the aims and objectives of their orders.

A Finely Woven Network

Although both surviving documents and archaeological remains show that the Icelandic monastic houses were situated on well-traveled routes in most areas around the country, it should be noted that no monastic institution was ever operated in the West Fjords. This is most likely because of the strong political position held by the Icelandic chieftains in the region during the early Middle Ages when the

DOI: 10.4324/9781003361077-5

number of monastic houses grew the most.[2] Otherwise, they were also, from the beginning, equally based in each bishopric so as to cover complete area around the island as possible. Notably, one female monastery was located in each bishopric, Kirkjubæjarklaustur in Skálholt bishopric and Reynistaðarklaustur in Hólar bishopric (see Figure 1.1). Soon after the establishment of the successful ones, the monasteries acquired rights to stranded valuables on their beaches. They even received donations – such as farms, physical money, books, items, or domestic animals – from people living in their closest vicinity and purchased their own farms in order to secure sufficient income. Their interests extended in this manner outwards to the coast and inwards to the remotest valleys. However, there are no indications that the monasteries competed with each other when it came to the business of selling and buying farms. Obviously, the farms were shared equally. The underlying aim may have been, as has previously been suggested, to establish a finely woven network of bishoprics and monastic institutions, providing their service to people in all four quarters of the country (Figure 5.1). At the same time, the firm political base of the Church was secured.

Predictably, all the monasteries were named after the farms on which they were established and located. This seems to have been the overall habit, because when Flateyjarklaustur was moved to Helgafell, its name was changed to Helgafellsklaustur.

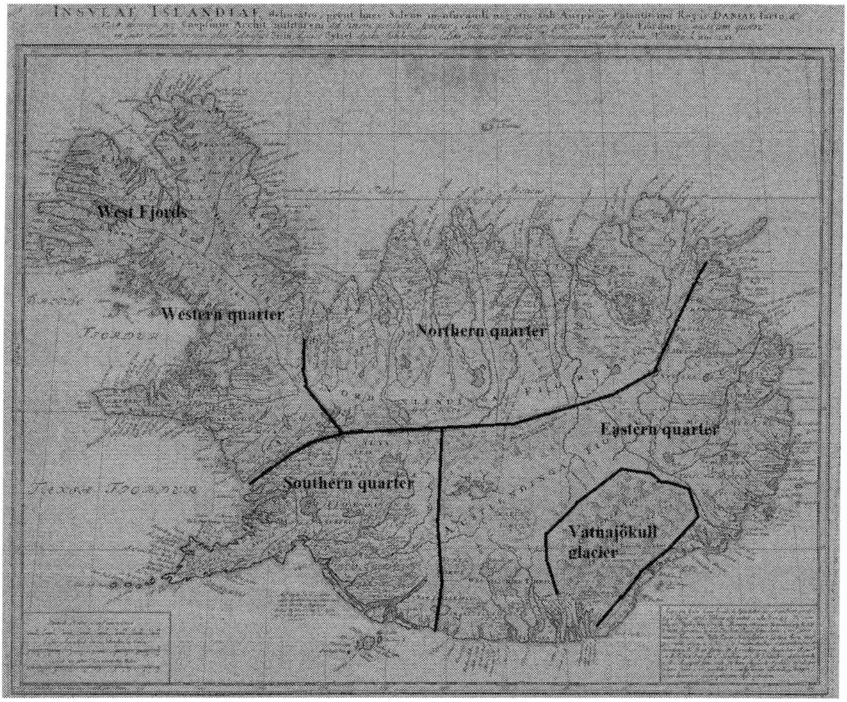

FIGURE 5.1 A map of Iceland 1734, showing the four quarters of the country.

Abbot Ögmundur, his canons, and all the monastery's possessions and equipment were moved from the island of Flatey to Helgafell in 1184. The list of goods transported is preserved in the *DI*. It is particularly interesting because it recorded equipment commonly needed for services in the monastic church, indicating that Flateyjarklaustur had begun to operate as a proper monastery and that the moving was not expected. The list included 100 books, four church bells, a shrine, and miscellaneous household equipment, in addition to twenty cows, two bulls, eight young calves, twenty horses, two boats, and seal nets. The list also named the abbot, Ögmundur Kálfsson, and three canons, Guðmundur munkur Loðmundarson, Ólafur kanúki Sigurðarson, and Eyjólfur kanúki Þorsteinsson.[3] Apparently, Flateyjarklaustur was essentially the same institution but run under a new name on a new farm at Helgafell.

The decisions made about exactly where (on which farm) the monastic institutions should be established, on the other hand, varied. Sometimes these decisions were based on otherworldly incidents, such as at Þingeyrar and Hítardalur (see Chapter 7). In other instances, the owners of the farms wanted to gain absolution from sin. This seems to have what motivated the owner of Skriða, Cecilía Þorsteinsdóttir, when donating her farm to the Church, but Skriða proved to be a convenient location for a monastic house with hospital activity, as is discussed further in the following section.[4] Moreover, it has been suggested that the locations of some of the new monastic institutions – such as at Kirkjubær, Helgafell, and Reynisnes – were based on an aura of sanctity, but they had previously been chosen as the residences of hermits or anchorites.[5] A similar example of a sanctuary associated with the establishment of a monastic house may be found at a monastic site in Norway: the Benedictine monastery established on the island of Selja in 1100, the first successful one founded in Norway. Selja's sanctuary is associated with the legend of the Irish St. Sunniva and the Seljumenn, who settled on the island while escaping the Vikings during their raids. After Sunniva's death on the island, it became an important Christian site in the north.[6] In the case of Munkaþverá and Þykkvabæjarklaustur, it appears that the owners wanted to donate their farms to the Church because they had no offspring. This was definitely true of Þykkvibær, whose owner gave his farm for the establishment of Þykkvabæjarklaustur. Munkaþverá belonged to the heir of Björn Gilsson, who gave his property to the bishopric of Hólar, where he served as bishop (r. 1147–1162) at the time (established in 1155). To reinforce his wish, on his deathbed, he donated to Munkaþverárklaustur a considerable amount of money, which he took from the episcopal see itself.[7] As a bishop overseeing all ecclesiastical houses operating in Hólar diocese, he was authorized to allocate funds in this manner.

Relatively little, however, is known about the decision to establish Bæjarklaustur at Bær in Borgarfjörður, other than that its foundation may have been a part of the endeavor, led by Archbishop Liavizos in Hamburg-Bremen, to strengthen Christianity in northern Europe. Its founder, Bishop Rudolf, came to Iceland in 1030 for the express purpose of establishing the monastery but was reportedly exhausted by the time he left two decades later, stating upon his departure that he had been among the barbarians in the north for too long. This was no wonder, given that before his time in Iceland, he had served as a prestigious Benedictine monk in Lund.[8] Ecclesiastical support in Iceland was still minimal so soon after the Conversion.

The monasteries at Keldur, Saurbær, and Viðey were, as was customary, all established on the founders' own farms, but their founding appears principally to have served to challenge the Church's most recent demands. As previously stated, in founding these monasteries, the chiefs of three prominent family clans highlighted their power and ability to operate their own ecclesiastical institutions without being dependent on instructions enforced through the archdiocese of Niðarós. Keldnaklaustur began as a monastic cell for its founder, Jón Loftsson, chief of the Oddaverjar family clan, and did not become a proper monastery until after his death in 1197. The monastery probably stood on the site of the present church and living quarters of Keldur, which was one of the Oddaverjar's main properties.[9] According to what is said in the bishops' saga of Þorlákur Þórhallsson when Jón was dying, he asked to be carried out to the door of his home in Keldur, from where he could see the church belonging to his monastery on the other side of the river.[10] Today, there are no visible houses or ruins in the area where his home is supposed to have been situated, and the present church and living quarters are located on the other side of the river. However, a geophysical survey of the field has revealed the remains of a house at least 2 m deep in the ground, making the story about the location of Keldnaklaustur even more plausible. Saurbæjarklaustur, which was established in northern Iceland by chieftain Ólafur Þorsteinsson of the Ásbirningar family clan, was closed only two years after Keldnaklaustur. By then, it had only been run for twenty-four years. No attempt was made whatsoever to locate its ruins inside the farmstead of Saurbær during the MMI project because there are almost no surviving documents that record its activities, apart from the names of the three priors who served there during its twenty-four years in operation. The monastic plant flixweed (*Descurainia sophia*) was identified in Saurbær during the study on surviving plant remains at the Icelandic monastic sites, but it is too widespread on its lands to provide a clue about where the monastic building may have been located. It was thus impossible to know exactly where to search – except beneath the present church and graveyard, which was considered infeasible from an ethical standpoint.[11]

The establishment of Viðeyjarklaustur somehow differs from the establishment of the other monastic houses in Iceland, as well as regarding how income was obtained for operating it. The course of events was that when both Keldnaklaustur and Saurbæjarklaustur had been closed down, the chieftain Þorvaldur Gissurarson, brother of Bishop Magnús Gissurarson in Skálholt, expressed concerns about the lack of a functioning monastic institution in the southern quarter of Iceland. Kirkjubæjarklaustur and Þykkvabæjarklaustur were both located in the eastern quarter of the island and Helgafellsklaustur in the western quarter. We can recall that by this time both Þykkvabæjarklaustur and Helgafellsklaustur were chaired by Hallur Gissurarson (former lawspeaker, in office 1203–1209), the brother of Bishop

Magnús and Þorvaldur. Specifically, for the establishment of Viðeyjarklaustur, Þorvaldur Gissurarson, the leader of the Haukdælir family clan, contacted another powerful chieftain, Snorri Sturluson, who was by then lawspeaker and the Sturlungar family clan leader, and asked him to take part in this enterprise. Þorvaldur had, in 1224, bought the island of Viðey for the sole purpose of locating his monastery. With the foundation of the monastery, representatives of the chieftains would be operating monasteries in all three quarters of the Skálholt bishopric, as Kirkjubæjarklaustur then operated for the time being only as a *beneficium*, not as a female convent. We can also recall that the foundation of this monastery entailed an alliance between Þorvaldur and Snorri's respective families through a marriage and concubinage, thereby securing sufficient finances for the monastery and the promise of peace between the two clans at the times of the *Sturlungaöld* conflicts. Furthermore, Þorvaldur Gissurarson convinced his brother to consecrate himself as the first prior of Viðeyjarklaustur in 1226, even though, as a secular leader, he was barred under canon law from managing a monastery.[12]

When Þorvaldur bought the island of Viðey, there were already a church and a farm there. These buildings may have been reused for the monastery, but with alterations. The charter from the monastery's establishment in 1226 has been preserved, and the details it contains seem consistent with those that were customary when an Augustinian monastic institution such as Viðeyjarklaustur was founded. At any rate, the charter is identical to that of Helgafellsklaustur, another Augustinian house.[13] This may indicate, however, that despite its political background, this ecclesiastical institution in Viðey was meant to be run in accordance with requirements. In the charter, it is noted that Viðeyjarklaustur would have three priests, two deacons, and as many canons as wanted to join the monastery. The monastery was also meant to be managed by an abbot, although under the supervision of a bishop, in this case Bishop Magnús in Skálholt.[14] Furthermore, according to the charter, the church was supposed to be equipped with two altars: one in its north aisle and another in the south aisle. The church itself was said to be dedicated to the Virgin Mary, St. John the Baptist, St. Peter, St. Paul, and St. Augustine. The altar in the north aisle was dedicated to St. Martin, St. Nicholas, St. Þorlákur the bishop, St. Agatha, and St. Lucy, while the one in the south aisle was dedicated to St. Stephen, St. Clement, St. Dionysius, St. Olaf, and St. Thomas.[15] The charter of this new monastery was presented by none other than the serving lawspeaker, Snorri Sturluson, at *Alþingi*, in 1226, where it was officially approved.[16] Thus it appears that Snorri's reward for having the charter approved by the assembly came in the form of a wealthy woman, Hallveig Ormsdóttir, provided to him by Þorvaldur Gissurarson in return for the establishment of Viðeyjarklaustur. Indeed, this was in the spirit of Snorri's well-known political interests.[17]

This was not the first time that the chieftain Þorvaldur Gissurarson had interfered with the affairs of a monastic institution in Iceland. His name appears among those who officially approved the takeover of the convent of Kirkjubæjarklaustur at the *Alþingi* in 1218. His brother, Bishop Magnús Gissurarson, also gave his blessing for this decision, as he did in regard to Viðeyjarklaustur.[18] Nevertheless, the way in which the brothers, Þorvaldur Gissurarson and Bishop Magnús Gissurarson, secured the financial future of Viðeyjarklaustur caused conflicts for a long time afterwards. The privately run *beneficium* of Viðey was certainly not sufficient to secure the monastery's financial future permanently, even with the wealth of the two founders, Þorvaldur Gissurarson and Snorri Sturluson. However, a conflict arose when the farmers in the vicinity of Viðeyjarklaustur, some of them prestigious landowners, wrote to Bishop Magnús Gissurarson to express concerns that they would be forced to donate their properties to the new monastery. They claimed that this had already happened in other parts of Iceland – which was true.[19] Their concerns were therefore justifiable, but the bishop assured the farmers that there was no need to worry, as the monastery's financial situation would be resolved by different means. However, the farmers' fear was not groundless. The solution was to impose a special cheese tax on all the farms in a wide geographical area stretching from Reykjanes peninsula in the south to the Botnsá river in the north. Under the new tax, the farmers were obliged to donate a quarter[20] of cheese or two quarters of butter to the monastery every autumn, a demand apparently made with very little concern for the farmers in question. The bishop promised that, in return, the canons of Viðeyjarklaustur would pray daily for the farmers' souls, but notably, *only for those who behaved properly*.[21] The farmers were not naïve, and they knew instantly that the tax had been imposed not by the Church but by the wealthiest and most powerful chieftains in Iceland, who had no concern for the farmers' souls. The debate about the cheese tax continued for a long time. Two men were directly involved in collecting the cheese and butter on behalf of Viðeyjarklaustur every year, and the process went slowly. Nevertheless, the area subject to taxes for the benefit of the monastery expanded gradually, and by 1280, it covered Borgarfjörður, Hvalfjarðarströnd, Akranes, Melasveit, and Leirársveit, including Andakíl. At that time, it was claimed that the episcopal seat in Skálholt had originally been entitled to collect these taxes, principally because of Bishop Magnús Gissurarson's initial involvement.[22]

When Prior Þorvaldur died in 1235, almost a decade after the founding of Viðeyjarklaustur, the post was filled by another lawspeaker and friend of Snorri, Styrmir fróði Kárason (in office 1232–1235), who held the priorship until his death in 1245. Styrmir resigned as lawspeaker, however, the year he became chief of Viðeyjarklaustur. Two years after Styrmir was appointed as prior, Bishop Magnús Gissurarson died and the Norwegian Sigvarður Þéttmarsson became his successor. It was at this point that Archbishop Sigurður Indriðason, on the command of Pope Gregory IX, refused to consecrate more representatives of the secular chiefs in Iceland as bishops. Sigvarður, the new bishop, had previously served as abbot of the Selja monastery in Norway and therefore had actual experience operating a monastery. That same year, 1238, another Norwegian monk – Bótólfur, from Helgiseter monastery in Trondheim – was officially ordained as bishop of Hólar.[23]

Location on a Well-trodden Path

As is emphasized earlier, the shift towards appointing foreign clerics for the bishoprics of Skálholt and Hólar proved to be very important for the growth of monasticism in Iceland, and it was not until after the days of Þorvaldur and Snorri that Viðeyjarklaustur became one of the wealthiest monastic institutions in Iceland, run in accordance with international standards. In 1313, Viðeyjarklaustur owned fourteen farms, and by 1395, it owned nearly fifty[24] – an impressive rate of growth. The monastery also seems at some point to have housed several poor people, as most other proper monastic institutions probably did. In fact, two years after its closure in 1539, when the Danish king took over the monastery and its properties during its dissolution, forty paupers reportedly still lived there.[25] Exactly where the monastic building stood remains a mystery, however, perhaps because they were all altered or destroyed during the Reformation. Nevertheless, the excavations carried out on the island of Viðey indicated that the monastic church was built on the same spot as the original church (and later the current church) and that the monastic building most likely stood on its western side.[26]

As in the case of Munkaþverárklaustur, the initial decision to place the monastery of Möðruvellir on this particular farm was made by the episcopal authorities in Hólar. It was little more than a century after the resolution of the *Staðamál* war in the Church's favor, that Bishop Jörundur Þorsteinsson (r. 1267–1313) began looking for a convenient farm for his canon school soon after he became bishop of Hólar. In 1293, Bishop Jörundur bought Möðruvellir in Hörgárdalur, but one year before the purchase took place, the King of Norway – who ruled Iceland at the time – had issued a letter saying that the chieftains could take over the Church's property in the country by force if needed. After this command of the king, the disputes reached their climax, even though they had often been fierce before. The chieftains subsequently took over three *beneficia* within the diocese of Skálholt, as well as taking over Möðruvellir in Hörgárdalur in Hólar diocese.[27] The seneschal Þorvarður Þórarinsson, who was in charge of the takeover on behalf of the king, finally agreed to sell Möðruvellir farm to Bishop Jörundur, perhaps because the situation had grown steadily worse for the secular authorities.[28] It was only four years later that Bishop Árni Þorláksson succeeded in his task, fulfilling Archbishop Jörundur's requirements to integrate the ecclesiastical features of canon law into the vernacular land law, with associated compromises, as has previously been noted.[29]

The only monastic institution in Iceland that seemed – at least at first – to be located totally off the beaten track, without easy access by the public, was Skriðuklaustur. Despite being the last monastery to be founded in Iceland during the Middle Ages, Skriðuklaustur managed nonetheless to secure sufficient income quickly and had about the same amount of land as other monastic houses in Iceland by the time of its dissolution in 1541. The four priors who were in charge of the monastery for around sixty years, Narfi Jónsson (r. 1496–1506), Þorvarður Helgason (r. 1506–1529), Jón Markússon (r. 1530–1534), and Brandur Hrafnsson (r. 1535–1552), clearly succeeded in raising the money for a solidly built monastic compound and an impressive church in a remarkably short span of time. Skriðuklaustur succeeded thus in satisfying the expectations of the establishers and donors, as well as the community in the surrounding region, by operating a well-equipped hospital. Food gifts, payments, and rents improved the variety of the fare that could be offered to those arriving at the monastery but how the invalids or the pilgrims made their way to Skriðuklaustur was not known until after the excavation on its ruins.

The precise location of the monastic building at the Skriða farm was revealed by geophysical survey and a test pit excavation in 2000. The monastic ruins were discovered lying hidden in the ground approximately 150 meters from the farmstead buildings. Indeed, there is a mythical story about why this field was chosen as the location for the monastery at Skriða. The story, which has strong elements from traditional folklore and demonstrates how otherworldly incidents might be used to explain important decisions, tells of a priest who intended to give the last rites to a dying parishioner in Fljótsdalur valley. Along the way, he lost his chalice and paten. When he searched for them, he found them on a tussock in this field. Moreover, the cup was full of wine and there was bread on the paten. This was considered a miracle, and a church was therefore erected in the field, with the altar placed on the tussock where the holy items had been found. When the monastery began operating shortly thereafter, it was built on that spot and dedicated to the Virgin Mary and the blood and body of Jesus Christ, symbolized by the wine and the bread.[30] Interestingly, this happened to be the location where the ruins of Skriðuklaustur were found, and it is particularly noteworthy that in the first recorded gift to the monastery in 1494, it was called the monastery of the holy blood.[31] Later, when Cecilía Þorsteinsdóttir donated Skriða farm to the Church, it was even said to be given to the holy blood of Skriðuklaustur.[32] Perhaps the name of the monastery had not yet been decided when it received its first gift in 1494 or its location was still uncertain at that time, since Cecilía also owned other farms, including in her native southern Iceland. Even though the story about the priest is certainly both mythical and otherworldly, there are factual components to it, for instance, the chalice, the wine, and the bread, and even the route that the priest followed down Fljótsdalur valley.

Nevertheless, it took a while to identify the reason the site was selected, apart from its being the only monastic house north of Vatnajökull glacier. The farm Skriða is situated near the south end of the long inland valley of Fljótsdalur, which leads to the mountain Snæfell, the Vatnajökull glacier, and the deserted highlands of eastern Iceland. The remote location of the monastery, which served as a hospital and was to be open to travelers, pilgrims, and all who needed shelter for longer or shorter periods, thus seemed peculiar at first. In fact, it was the identification of fish bones found during excavations at the site that provided an explanation. Most of the bones proved to be from large cod, ling, and haddock, which can only be caught off the southern and western coast of Iceland. The smaller fish living in the cold sea between Greenland and Iceland do not grow larger than 60–80 cm in length, but the fish bones found in Skriðuklaustur were almost all from fish that were more than a meter long.[33] This discovery pointed directly to the possibility of a forgotten route over Vatnajökull glacier to the inland areas in the east. Today it may seem improbable that people traveled and transported fish over the glacier, but this is what was done during the Middle Ages.

Furthermore, extensive research done in recent years has shown that this largest glacier in Europe (although today it is melting quickly) was much smaller at the time Skriðuklaustur was in operation than it is now and even smaller earlier on. Around 1500, Vatnajökull is known to have been divided into two smaller glaciers lying on either side of the route, which was covered in snow all year round and was supposedly about 30 km long.[34] The coastal route from the south to the eastern fjords and further into the valley in Fljótsdalur is, in fact, much longer and trickier for the transport of goods such as fish because of several deep glacial rivers that must be crossed. This is further highlighted by the business transactions of the canons, who tried to buy farms located on the southeastern coast. This was, for example, when Prior Narfi Jónsson bought a share in one of the most valuable lands in Iceland in 1504, the Borgarhöfn fishing station and harbor located in southeast Iceland. Narfi's successor, Prior Þorvarður Helgason, continued to acquire this valuable farm in the southeast and bought larger parts of it, also paying for it with two other coastal farms in the east as Narfi did. In the end, the monastery owned three-fourths of Borgarhöfn, and the bishopric of Skálholt owned the rest.[35] This was necessary because the cost of operating the monastery inevitably rose as time went by, principally due to its obligation to care for the inhabitants of the eastern half of the country. During its operation, Skriðuklaustur had, in total, forty-nine farms spread across a large area in the east and south of Iceland. Many had been donated to the monastery, while others were purchased and used to build up its financial reserves, but only until 1541, when Skriðuklaustur purchased its last farm.[36]

Further examination of written documents showed ever more clearly that people crossed Vatnajökull glacier throughout the Middle Ages, both for transporting goods and for other journeys between the south and north through Fljótsdalur valley. This implies that Skriðuklaustur may have been deliberately placed on a well-trodden path and that it was either the first or the last stopover point on the journey south or north. Likewise, several place names associated with the glacier indicate that fishermen traveled all the way from the northernmost parts of Iceland, such as Eyjafjörður, to the southern coast, most likely along the route of the Fljótsdalur valley, expressly to catch the large, valuable fish off the south coast.[37]

At times, only a few routes may have been open in the Vatnajökull glacier area, and these may occasionally have moved because of the constant changes in the glacier itself, until the route ultimately became impassable. This shift most likely took place in the mid-seventeenth century, at the peak of the Little Ice Age, when a huge icefall on the eastern part of the glacier closed the route permanently. The closure of this route had significant consequences, as it forced Icelanders to adapt both culturally and administratively to the disruption of connections between the south and the east. Initially, the eastern half was geographically the largest of the four quarters of Iceland, stretching from the Mývatn area in the north to Vík in the south and including Vatnajökull glacier. Only a century after the pathway closed, the southern part of the eastern quarter was administratively cut off, ending at the northern side of the glacier (see Figure 5.1). It has remained this way ever since.[38]

The Monastic Precincts

Since the names of the monastic houses refer in all instances to their location, it was not difficult to find the monastic sites themselves. It was more problematic, however, to identify the exact location of the monastic ruins within the farmsteads' precincts, as was done in Skriðuklaustur. The search for their ruins also showed that, in some cases, their lodgings were moved during the time of their operation, either within the same farmstead or even from one farm to another, as was the case for Flateyjarklaustur. What also hindered the search for ruins in several of the monastic sites was that churches are still in operation on them, some on the foundations of the old monastic churches, such as appears to be the case in Þingeyraklaustur, Munkaþverárklaustur, and Helgafellsklaustur, while others are parish churches established in the Middle Ages.

Apparently, operating a monastic church did not exclude an operation of a parish church within the monastic precinct. In fact, it would be not be surprising if there was parish church located on the estates of female convents because nuns were not allowed to perform parochial duties, but they could nonetheless have had their own church or chapel inside the monastic building.[39] Still, because most of the monastic institutions in Iceland were built on farms that were classified as *beneficia*,[40] it is likely that there were two serving churches, in one or two buildings, on the estates of both male and female monasteries. This can also have varied, even in time. Churches in English monasteries were often divided into two parts, one serving the monastic house and another serving as the parish church. In such cases, the parochial services took place in the western end, while monastic devotions were in the eastern end.[41] In Denmark, several monastic churches served as parish churches.[42] The question is what was practiced in Iceland. On at least three monastic estates in Iceland, there were two churches during the Middle Ages, contemporaneously operated: a monastic church and a separate parish church with full rights. Predictably, one of these sites is the female monastery, Reynistaðarklaustur, but also the male monasteries at Skriðuklaustur and Þykkvabæjarklaustur. Regarding Skriðuklaustur, only documents dating from the late sixteenth century mention two churches: a home church and a monastic church at Skriða.

Certainly, there was a church at Kirkjubæjarklaustur, but it is not fully clear from the sources if it served as a monastic church or a parish church. It may have been both as was customary in Denmark, or it could have been divided into two parts: one part serving the monastic house and another part serving as a parish church, as was done in some English monasteries. At least, according to an inventory made in Kirkjubæjarklaustur in 1218, it appears that the church was dedicated to the Virgin Mary. This may indicate that it was the nun's church. Moreover, in an inventory from 1397, the church in Kirkjubæjarklaustur is said to have twenty glass windows, indicating that the church building was relatively large (see further Chapter 6). Moreover, a judgement is preserved about an incident taking place in Kirkjubæjarklaustur in 1528, which proves the existence of a church there. This was when a priest, Jón Jónsson, attacked a carpenter, named Indriði, specifically by the church's door. Jón's family needed to pay fines not only to the nuns but also to the bishop and the cathedral in Skálholt.[43] The fact that the priest, Jón, was requested to pay fine to the nuns might show that the church belonged to their monastery.

When the female monastery of Reynistaðarklaustur was founded, Bishop Jörundur Þorsteinsson provided it with half of the estate at Reynistaður, but as is specifically mentioned in its charter, the parish church there gained control over the other half.[44] Moreover, in 1461, there were two priests and two deacons at the parish church at Reynistaður.[45] Furthermore, an unnamed man asked for burial in the narthex of the monastic church of Reynistaðarklaustur in 1431, which suggests that this particular part of the church was open to the public or was in fact the parish church to which Bishop Jörundur had given half of the Reynistaður estate over 100 years earlier.[46] In addition to this, surviving sources show that the nuns' church was quite large, as is described later (see Chapter 6).

Þykkvabæjarklaustur is one of the few monasteries that the historical sources basically state it had two separate buildings for the monastic and parish churches. In any case, Þykkvabæjarklaustur is in present days believed to have been located in the vicinity of the current church.[47] However, the space around the church does not appear to be sufficient for a monastic building on Þykkvabæjarklaustur's scale. More importantly, notes written by manuscript collector Árni Magnússon around 1700 emphasize the separation between the monastic complex and the current church site. Árni states also that it was surrounded by waterlogged ditches but does not mention the location further.[48] Therefore, the search for the ruins of Þykkvabæjarklaustur concentrated on a more plausible site about 200 m south of the present church, near the ruins of Fornufjós situated in an old fen. According to oral sources, these ruins were of a barn and cowshed. Interestingly, the geophysical survey undertaken there showed a ruin, 1800 m^2 large, rectangular in form, with several rooms beneath the ruins that were visible on the surface (Figures 5.2 and 6.4). The next step was thus to dig a trench in these remains. The identification of the tephra layers discovered in the trench (which ended up being two meters deep) and the radiocarbon dating on animal bones found in it proved that there were two building phases of a house, both dating back to the long period during which Þykkvabæjarklaustur was in operation.[49] Thus by locating the monastic complex in the field south of the church, surrounded by waterlogged ditches and fens, the residents of Þykkvabæjarklaustur were able to ensure its protection from outside attacks. A closer examination of documents preserved from Þykkvabæjarklaustur proved that it even possessed armor, which shows that it was well equipped for armed conflict, as it was in fact supposed to be.[50]

Indeed, the location of monastic buildings in fens, marshlands, and rivers appears to have been highly attractive in Catholic Europe, for example, in early medieval England, although the location of monasteries on islands was far more common.[51] Both Viðeyjarklaustur and Flateyjarklaustur provide such examples. Nevertheless,

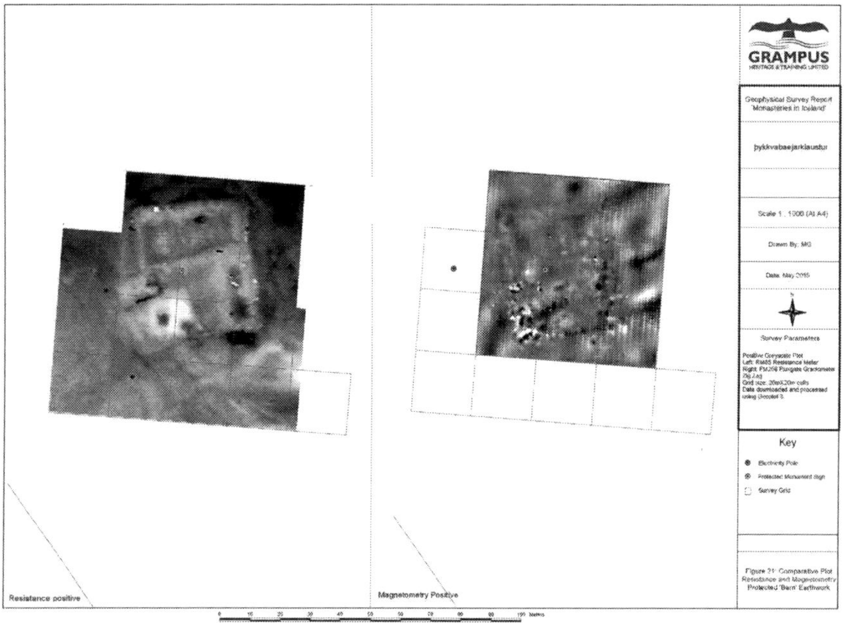

FIGURE 5.2 The geophysical survey undertaken in Þykkvabæjarklaustur showed 1800 m^2 large ruin under the surface ground. It was later confirmed that this is the ruin of the monastic house there (image in the courtesy of Grampus Heritage and Training Ltd).

Flateyjarklaustur's island remote location and inaccessibility are usually thought to be the reason for its move to Helgafell in 1184. The fact is that oceans do not necessarily isolate because they even make connections. Besides that, travel by sea was one of the most common ways to travel during the Middle Ages. The reasons for the move may rather have been economic, political, or both. It is known that shortly after the founding of the monastery in Flatey, Abbot Ögmundur was one of the candidates in the election for bishop of Skálholt, together with Þorlákur Þórhallsson, who by then was abbot of Þykkvabæjarklaustur. Although Abbot Ögmundur lost the election, he continued to operate his monastery more faithfully than ever before under the authority of the newly elected bishop. With the transfer of his monastery, Abbot Ögmundur may therefore have wanted to express his opposition to the papal authorities for whom Bishop Þorlákur worked so devotedly in Iceland. At that time, Flatey was not accepted by the Church as a *beneficium*, but Helgafell was. However, there might also have been multiple other reasons for the move. Helgafell had suffered severe damage when a fire broke out in the church in 1181. This must have had both an emotional and a financial impact on the church's owner and priest, Magnús Pálsson, who subsequently moved from Helgafell to his family estate, Reykholt in Borgarfjörður. Only three years later, Ögmundur moved his monastery to Helgafell and built the monastery there, including a new monastic church, from the ground up.[52] Sadly, Abbot Ögmundur drowned in Breiðafjörður only a few years after the move, but his successor, Þorfinnur Þorgeirsson, served at Helgafellsklaustur for the next thirty years (r. 1187–1216) and continued building up the monastery.[53]

Nevertheless, the exact location of the building of Helgafellsklaustur inside the Helgafell farm is not yet known with any certainty despite an intensive search for its ruins. The most likely spot is beneath the present church and cemetery, where it is impossible to search below the surface. In some instances, during the research for the MMI project, oral sources pointed us in an entirely wrong direction in our search for monastic ruins. Hítardalsklaustur is a case in point. Whereas documented oral sources indicated a spot, Kvíakinn, close to the eastern boundaries of the fields of the farm in Hítardalur, further survey showed that the supposed ruins were nothing more than an old volcanic crater covered in grass and heather. The most likely spot is therefore the current farmstead's quarters, where the stone with the carved face now stands above the ground (see the cover photo), much like the carved cornerstone found in front of the present church in Bær. It most likely indicates the spot where Bæjarklaustur stood. Stone sculptures of this kind are, in fact, a well-known form of churchly ornamentation during the Middle Ages. They were usually positioned near the main entrance of the church and would thus be the first thing observed before one entered the building.[54]

The approximate locations of Munkaþverárklaustur and Möðruvallaklaustur also proved difficult to determine. This is partly because they seem to have been moved within the monastic precinct during their period of operation, Munkaþverárklaustur once and Möðruvallaklaustur twice. However, the fires that these monasteries suffered greatly aided in the search for their ruins during the MMI project, especially in the case of Munkaþverárklaustur. In fact, thick layers of ash have frequently been found during groundwork at the farm of Munkaþverá, but they were all thought to have been the result of a fire that destroyed the monastery in 1429. These layers of ash were revealed, for example, when the fence around the present church was rebuilt in the early twentieth century and again in 1959 when a monument to Bishop Jón Arason was erected in front of the current living quarters.[55] Notably, when the church's fence was rebuilt, a burnt sole of a shoe was found. It was immediately thought to be from a monk's shoe, as it was found at this old monastic site at Munkaþverá. However, when the sole was examined by an expert on leather, it was determined to be from a post-medieval shoe.[56] It may be that some of the ash layers are from another house fire that broke out in November 1772, but this does not exclude the possibility that the monastic building – which was rebuilt after the fire in 1429 – may still have been standing on the same spot. The annals claimed that the fire started in the smithy and then spread to the other houses belonging to the old building where the monks once lived. It is also noted that even though the church stood nearby, it fortunately did not burn.[57] This description indicates that all the buildings stood together in a cluster. There was certainly a smithy at the monastery, as it was mentioned specifically in a corrody contract made with the couple Arnþrúður Árnadóttir and Jón Sigfússon in 1498, which states that Jón was to carry out ironwork for the abbot of Munkaþverárklaustur (see Chapter 8). The smithy from the time of the monastery may therefore still have been in use in 1772. The MMI team dug two test pits at Munkaþverá with the aim of dating the ash layers found there, and it appeared that there were two layers of ash. One was certainly from the fire in 1429, when the monastery burned down, and the other was from the fire in the smithy and nearby buildings in 1772.[58] The results also demonstrated that before the first fire broke out, the monastery stood in the southern part of the field, in front of the current living quarters of the farm of Munkaþverá, and that it was not rebuilt exactly on the same spot but closer to the present church site. Furthermore, the results showed that the monastic complex that burnt down in 1429 must have been over 900 m^2 in size, a measurement confirmed by the geophysical survey.[59]

The search for the ruins of Möðruvallaklaustur focused similarly on identifying a burnt layer from the fire of 1316. However, the history of the Möðruvellir farm is marked by fires, from its early existence to modern times. A layer of ash dating back to this early point in the monastery's operation was detected in one of the test pits dug immediately behind one of the houses belonging to the current resident priest. As before, the dating was based on tephrochronology and radiocarbon analysis. Notably, a burnt shoe sole was found, as in Munkaþverá, this one apparently in the fashion of the Middle Ages, indicating that the monastery may have stood there when the fire broke out in 1316.[60] However, a geophysical survey also revealed the outlines of a square building, approximately 35 m × 35 m in size, in an open field about 200 m south of the present church at Möðruvellir. The results of the test trench indicated that these were the foundations of a timber building. Furthermore, a tephra layer from an eruption of Mt. Hekla in 1300 proved that the building was erected after the tephra fell in this area. Therefore, this may well be the foundation of the church that blew away in 1421 and was then moved to a more sheltered spot such as the site of the present church. Thus, after three summers of archaeological work at Möðruvellir, it was concluded that the monastery had three different locations during its 250 years in operation, with the fire and later the storm precipitating moves to new sites.[61]

Places of Sanctuary and Absolution

Among the documents preserved from Iceland's medieval monastic houses are several papers that highlight the sanctity of the monastic precincts. Officially, these were places of sanctuary, as were all other ecclesiastical institutions. Church sanctuary has long been observed as one of the privileges of canon law, its purpose being to provide absolute safety for all those seeking refuge. Through the provision of sanctuary, monastic precincts offered all people physical protection, and it was utterly forbidden to carry weapons or commit any crime within them.[62] Although the Icelandic medieval land laws as presented in works such as *Grágás* or *Jónsbók* do not mention church sanctuary other than the ban on weapons, research on the phenomenon proves that it was well known in Iceland because it was highlighted in canon law.[63] The sanctuary of cemeteries is, however, highlighted in *Kristinréttur Árna Þorlákssonar*, although it was only valid for a short period of time.[64] This may be one of many examples showing that land laws were not the only regulations followed in medieval Iceland, but that canon law was observed as well.

An incident taking place in the cemetery of Helgafellsklaustur illustrates the practice of church sanctuary in Iceland and shows how serious a matter it was to disrespect it. A man who may actually have been seeking sanctuary in the monastic cemetery was killed there. This meant that the monastery had been defiled by bloodshed. The event took place in 1425. This was thus after the death of Abbot Vermundur Örnólfsson in 1416; however, it is uncertain when his successor took over, and there may have been no abbot at all in charge of Helgafellsklaustur at the time. The annals all agree about the severity of the matter, but the serving monks unsuccessfully tried to defend the monastery from being defiled. The desacralization was so severe that no Mass was sung there for a full four years, when the church could be re-consecrated by the bishop, but unfortunately, the perpetrators managed to escape all the way to England without being caught.[65] It was not until 1429 that Jón Vilhjálmsson Craxton,[66] who by then was serving as bishop of Hólar, took on the task of re-consecrating the monastery. Actually, Helgafellsklaustur lay in the bishopric of Skálholt, but Bishop Árni Ólafsson had not returned from a trip abroad and his successor, Jón Gerreksson, did not move to Iceland until 1430. The matter could not wait; otherwise, the damage would have been permanent and Helgafellsklaustur would have collapsed. Therefore, Bishop Jón Craxton cleansed the monastery, the church, and the cemetery so that it could function properly again. The bishop also chose Njáll Bárðarson to be the new abbot and tasked him with restoring the reputation of the institution.[67]

The calamity of 1425 was not the first time Helgafellsklaustur was disturbed by bloodshed or involved in a case of manslaughter. When Ólafur Hjörleifsson served as abbot there during the period 1258–1302, he had a steward named Marteinn Másson whose task was to take care of the monastic building there and perform other domestic labor on its farm. At one point, a man named Guðlaugur Tannason tried to slay the steward, although not on the monastic precinct at Helgafell. His actions were not unprovoked, though, as Marteinn was a murderer himself, having killed Guðlaugur's father when still a child. In fact, this was not the first time someone tried to avenge Guðlaugur's father's death, but in an earlier attempt, Marteinn's brother was killed.[68] What is particularly noteworthy in this case is that a man like Marteinn, with a criminal record, held a position as steward in a monastic institution. Indeed, it appears that his work at the monastery was part of his penance. Absolution was supposed to be for the benefit of society as a whole, and the steward's work at Helgafellsklaustur can certainly be classified as such. In addition to his work, Marteinn had donated the farm Höskuldsey in Breiðafjörður to the monastery in 1281, most likely in atonement for his sins.[69] This was customary, in fact, because bishops could request that an economic transaction would be a part of absolution, as was the case here.

Indeed, there are other known examples where sinners were provided the opportunity to fulfill their penance there. In one instance, two thieves were granted remission of their sins by working for Skriðuklaustur. According to the verdict, written by Bishop Ögmundur Pálsson at Skálholt on 1 October 1524, they had stolen brushwood from the monastery's land, and their absolution was subject to the condition that they work on the enlargement of the monastic cemetery.[70] They seem to have fulfilled this condition because an extension of the cemetery and subsequent reconstruction of its wall was identified during the excavations at Skriðuklaustur in 2002–2012.[71] Oddly enough, this is not the only case of this kind from Skriðuklaustur. That same year, 1524, Brother Jón Jónsson was granted absolution in return for undertaking useful work for the monastery at which he served. What may also be detected in this case is the holiness not only of the monastic precincts but also of the relics belonging to them. Brother Jón had been tasked with watching over the schoolchildren studying there, a boy and a girl named Jón and Guðrún, respectively, but he had allowed them to wander freely around inside the monastic building: even enter the most sacred areas inside the church. Unfortunately, the children had touched some unspecified relics, which then had to be re-consecrated.[72] Þorvarður Helgason, the prior in charge at Skriðuklaustur, was obliged to report the incident to Bishop Ögmundur Pálsson in Skálholt, who in turn needed to grant absolution to Brother Jón, which he did. Brother Jón was therefore absolved of his sin, but the credibility of Skriðuklaustur could have been at stake if word had spread that a sacred member of the monastic house had broken the rules of the order and, consequently, of divine law. Both the bishop and the head of the monastic institution, as in the case of Skriðuklaustur, were obliged to ensure that everything operated as expected, not at least for the sake of its benefactors but also for the surrounding community. Examples exist from monastic houses in Europe in which benefactors expressed concerns about how their donations were spent.[73] It is, therefore, likely that this was the case in the Icelandic monasteries as well.

Predictably, Brother Jón was granted absolution in accordance with canon law. He had to confess, but what is more surprising is that he was also appointed sacristan of the monastery. According to the document preserved about the case, the argument for his absolution was that he was, after all, a useful servant of God and could therefore atone for his sins by doing good work within his monastery. A detailed description is given of his duties as sacristan: to guard the cloister gate, to call the other canons to services day and night, and to supervise the singing of masses held when the prior was not at home.[74] Usually, the sacristan's duties were to ensure that there were sufficient candles and oil in the monastic building in which he was serving, besides preparing the masses and organizing the events when the novices made their profession of faith.[75] This may have been Brother Jón's task as well, although this is not specifically mentioned in the document. The content of the penance in question seems to have been rather weighty, but its severity may be explained by the fact that this was not the only sin from which Jón needed forgiveness. In the 1 October 1524 document describing the case of the schoolchildren, the bishop announced that Brother Jón would concurrently be absolved of the sin of having had a child with his cousin, Oddný Hallvarðsdóttir.[76] The substance of this sin was twofold: first, breaking the vow of celibacy and, second, having a child with a close relative. The document indicates, however, that losing track of the schoolchildren in his care was much more serious than breaking his vow of celibacy because of the sanctity of the churchly objects involved.

Furthermore, the record of Brother Jón's misconduct demonstrates how disobedience was handled at the highest possible churchly level in Iceland. In some cases, the bishops had to intervene in matters that may not have seemed all that serious but could not be resolved by those involved. Vermundur Örnólfsson, formerly a priest in Selárdalur in Arnarfjörður, had only served as the abbot of Helgafellsklaustur for one year in 1404 when his first misfortune occurred. His horse was stolen, including his saddle and bridle, while he was visiting the church site and cemetery in Snóksdalur. Vermundur took this very seriously and considered it an unforgivable sin, perhaps because of the formal and legal sanctity of the church and the cemetery in question. Besides this, stealing the horse of an ecclesiastical man, and on holy precinct, was completely different from stealing a horse from a farmer or from an ordinary farm. In an official letter, Bishop Vilchin urged the abbot to contain his anger and appointed a negotiator to mediate in the dispute between the abbot and the thief. Moreover, the bishop pleaded with Vermundur to set aside his recommended verdict on the guilty man, Guðmundur Einarsson of Hrafnabjörg, and promised the abbot that the loss would be fully compensated.[77] This arrangement permitted both parties to maintain their dignity and honor. It is unclear from the sources precisely how the matter was resolved, but certainly it was the duty of Church officials to show sinners understanding concerning their transgressions and to provide them with an opportunity for introspection, as Bishop Vilchin clearly did.

The sanctuary of monastic churches and cemeteries may also have reached beyond the living in other ways by protecting sinful souls. This is especially evident from examples of men who died in battle or by other violence and were rushed to the monasteries and buried there rather than at the nearest churches. For example, the bodies of those killed at the Battle at Örlygsstaðir in 1238 were transported from Skagafjörður to Munkaþverárklaustur and buried in its cemetery.[78] Even after the battle at Þverá in Eyjafjörður in 1255, the dead and wounded members of both warring families were brought to Munkaþverárklaustur.[79] When the chieftain Þorgils skarði was slain in Hrafnagil in January 1258, Abbot Eyjólfur Brandsson in Munkaþverárklaustur was informed immediately. Þorgils' disfigured body was first transported to the church of Grund in Eyjafjörður, but Abbot Eyjólfur had him brought to his monastery and buried there.[80] A similar story can be told of the case when seneschal and knight Björn Þorleifsson was slain by English sailors in 1467. The Englishmen chopped him into pieces, but his badly mutilated remains were brought for burial to Helgafellsklaustur, where his soul would surely be saved, rather than to the church at Skarð in Skarðsströnd, where Björn lived.[81] Nevertheless, such cases did not have to be connected to death due to manslaughter or murder as the aforementioned examples indicate but could also be found for accidental deaths. In 1307, a woman named Sólveig Loftsdóttir drowned in Hörgá river in Eyjafjörður on her way to Mass along with another woman. Her body was found and brought to Munkaþverárklaustur for burial. Her husband, Þorvaldur Geirsson, donated valuables to the monastery in the name of the poor and for his own eternal welfare. To the church at Bægisá, where Sólveig should have been buried, he donated much less.[82] Interestingly, this case is documented because of disputes that arose about Sólveig's body and the fee that was donated to Munkaþverárklaustur in connection with her burial.

There are other noteworthy examples preserved about relatives trying to compensate simultaneously for their own sins and those of a deceased family member. These examples may in turn highlight the status of monastic houses as sacred places open to all those who wished to withdraw from the outer world – including sinners. For example, Margrét Bjarnadóttir, who became a nun at Reynistaðarklaustur in 1432, donated to the convent sixty *hundruð*[83] in money and one farm, Hólar in Láxárdalur, to the Hólar bishopric.[84] Two years later she donated Reynistaðarklaustur another valuable farm, Skefilsstaðir on Skagi.[85] An examination of Margrét's background is revealing. She was married to the lawman Hrafn Guðmundsson, who in 1431 was a judge in a case about the rights over a shipwreck. One of the parties involved was Jón Craxton, bishop of Hólar. Hrafn Guðmundsson ruled against the bishop, who refused to accept the verdict and consequently excommunicated the lawman.[86] Hrafn Guðmundsson died that year without having had a chance to compensate for his 'crime'. It was thus the widow's task to try to quench the fires her deceased husband faced in his journey through purgatory. Not only did she become a nun and give two farms and money to the Church, but also, through her donation to Hólar, she was promised thirty masses for her soul[87] in the cathedral and many more in other churches in the bishopric to spare her from purgatorial fire.[88] Margrét could have chosen to make a corrody contract with Reynistaðarklaustur, as women of her status commonly did, but the fact that she joined the convent suggests that she preferred a life of religious celibacy.

Churchly sanctuary was abolished in Iceland with the Reformation in Skálholt in 1541 and in Hólar in 1550.[89] Written documents show that its abolition was indeed quickly implemented. For example, the last Catholic bishop in Hólar, Jón Arason, tried to seek sanctuary in the cemetery of Sauðafell in Dalir along with two of his sons in September 1550, where they were nonetheless captured and brought for execution at Skálholt.[90] The cemetery had no meaning any more as a place of sanctuary, and these executions were the first to take place in Iceland under the new Lutheran customs and civil laws.

Divine Manifestation

Divine manifestation applies to certain tasks carried out in the meaning of doing something of compassion, gratitude, and awareness, such as when offering aid to those in need. Such manifestation appears clearly in how devotedly Icelanders followed Catholic teachings, not least through the assistance and service provided by the monastic houses. The fact that an advanced hospital was run in Skriðuklaustur monastery underlines, in this manner, its meaning as a place of safety and, at the same time, a place for cleansing and purification from sin appearing in the diverse form of ailments. The excavation showed that the canons there served people of both sexes, all ages, and all social classes, and the bones of fetuses, neonates, young children, adolescents, and adults were discovered in the graves. More than half of the skeletons dug up from its cemetery showed identifiable signs of various chronic diseases, illnesses, or traumas, including syphilis, tuberculosis, hydatid disease, lung infection, cleft palates, various kinds of gum diseases, tumors, broken bones, and scurvy, in addition to some unidentified infections and severe handicaps.[91] In fact, monastic institutions were generally obliged to bury all those who died in their charge, not only the serving canons, so these were most likely their clients. It was also important for them to ensure that the benefactors of the monastic house in question were buried within the monastic complex in order to guarantee an eternal link between them and the monastic institution.[92] These burials all took place at Skriðuklaustur, but the inhabitants of the nearby valley must have been buried at their parish church, situated only two kilometers away at Valþjófsstaður.

Interestingly enough, several pieces of evidence shed light on Kirkjubæjarklaustur's focus on the general protection of women, a focus probably shared by Reynistaðarklaustur. Indeed, one official letter demonstrates that Kirkjubæjarklaustur served as a shelter or sanctuary for women who had been subjected to violence by their husbands. The letter was written by Gissur Einarsson, bishop of Skálholt, in 1543. This was two years after the adoption of Lutheranism in 1541, but it may nevertheless highlight a common custom practiced in the convent while it was still operating. The bishop apparently still respected the abbesses' independence, even though their convent was about to be closed permanently. In the letter, the bishop kindly asked the last abbess of Kirkjubæjarklaustur, Halldóra Sigvaldadóttir, to allow an unnamed woman to return to her husband. According to the letter, the woman had escaped to the convent because of his violent behavior. The bishop, Gissur, underlined that wife-beating, which in this case had taken place, was not a legally accepted reason for divorce.[93] The husband is mentioned by name in the bishop's letter, so he was easy to trace, and further research showed that he, Bergur Ingimundarson, was a lawman working and living in western Iceland. This meant that his wife had to travel a long distance over mountains and rivers to get the shelter she needed – most likely a permanent refuge in the female convent in Kirkjubær, as Kirkjubæjarklaustur was located far away in the southeast. According to this, she did not run to a nearby farm or to the bishopric of Skálholt for help; she chose to flee to a shelter that was officially open for all women in need, thus all the way Kirkjubæjarklaustur.

Undoubtedly, medieval Icelandic women were quite familiar with the advantages of establishing their own monastery in Iceland, not least as a place of sanctuary, exclusively for their own needs. Women were no less well read than men, as was discussed, for example, in the context of the pilgrimages they took or when they made their choice to live as anchorites, long before the founding of the convent in Kirkjubær. Monasticism had already gained a firm foothold in Iceland, and the addition of a female convent to the male convents enabled Icelandic women to follow the trends and policies prevailing elsewhere in medieval Christian Europe. By the time Bishop Þorlákur established Kirkjubæjarklaustur in 1186, female monasteries had been founded in most societies in northern Europe, and on that occasion, he announced officially that it was to be operated under the full control of an abbess. This may certainly have helped Icelandic women to strengthen their position and protect their lay sisters as much as their religiously consecrated sisters.

It must thus have been a serious setback, not only for the nuns in Kirkjubæjarklaustur, but for Icelandic women in general, when Bishop Magnús Gissurarson appointed the chieftain Digur-Helgi Þorsteinsson to supervise Kirkjubær as a *beneficium* in 1218 and closed down the convent at the same time. On this interesting case of Kirkjubæjarklaustur's closure, historians Björn Þorsteinsson and Jón Jóhannesson both noted in their publications from around the middle of the twentieth century that the abbesses appeared to be unable to run their convent in Kirkjubær, as they were supposed to do, so the bishop needed to hand it to the chieftains. Jón claimed that the problems the abbesses encountered were mainly financial but did not explain that further.[94] Fortunately, Bishop Magnús ordered that the properties and operation of the convent should be inspected in 1218, and the inventory taken at that occasion proved that it had been splendidly run. This inventory does not indicate any justifiable reason not to trust the nuns to continue operating their monastic house, other than the chieftains' wish to acquire control over all ecclesiastical properties in Iceland during the times of the *Staðamál* conflicts. According to the inventory, which was made only twenty years after the convent's establishment, Kirkjubæjarklaustur owned all or part of nine farms, in addition to receiving rents from another nine farms owned by others.[95] Such a substantial support from their benefactors must have been very important to the nuns, but it also shows that the convent was an institution that people trusted.

Although historical sources do not mention Kirkjubæjarklaustur again as a female convent until the end of the thirteenth century, it appears to have reclaimed its previous status as a religious house for women and was supported by the local community after its reopening. This can be inferred from the aforementioned example about the woman who sought shelter there. The Kirkjubæjarklaustur nuns' emphasis on women's work and women in general may even be witnessed in their library, further highlighting the gendered difference between male and female monasteries. The so-called *Kirkjubæjarbók*, which was found in Kirkjubæjarklaustur after the final closure of the convent during the Reformation, is one of the best examples of this emphasis. As has been mentioned previously – and will be discussed again – this book contains a collection of stories about ten female saints, all of whom were invoked as the protectors of women, their work, and their duties in life, such as childbirth or breastfeeding. This protection also extended to cases of sexual abuse.[96]

Boundaries

The monks and nuns seem to have needed to show in practice that they were honest and could be committed to guard the property and the souls of members of the community. The monastic buildings likewise needed to be correctly furnished and arranged in accordance with their aims and objectives, and it is apparent that resources available locally did not prevent them from fulfilling these requirements. Skriðuklaustur is a good example on that. The fact that nearly 300 individuals – canons, patients, lay people, and even pupils studying at the monastery – found a final resting place there, despite its brief period of operation, demonstrates that it was an influential, well-run institution that people trusted.

Since the monastic houses were meant to provide service to the general public, this demanded that their buildings would be constructed with certain spaces for non-consecrated residents. Such divisions are well known from both Augustinian and Benedictine houses on the Continent. The laity, students, and guests were usually not allowed to enter areas other than those specifically designated for them, such as inside the cloister garth, the guest house, the infirmary, and the domestic buildings.[97] The Cistercians, who were more restrictive than the Benedictines in this regard, allowed lay people or guests only to enter specific areas in their houses. In female convents, gender-based segregation was also necessary, mainly because of the nuns' abstinence from ecclesiastical and husbandry tasks. Both female and male monastic houses' social ties with the laity and the local communities – ties that grew steadily stronger throughout the Middle Ages – were vital for their existence. These relationships were based on different approaches in the case of each individual monastic house. Still, it may occasionally have been difficult for the nuns and monks to keep sacred and secular work separated when a considerable part of it took place in the local community – and thus outside the monastic buildings.

A good example of the emphasis on trust, as well as the importance of sacred and lay boundaries, may be deduced from the incident in Skriðuklaustur in 1524, when Brother Jón lost track of the schoolchildren studying there. This demonstrates, among many other things, that certain areas of Skriðuklaustur were not open to non-ecclesiastics. Apparently, access to the monastic building was to some extent available to lay people, since Brother Jón was thought to have guarded the cloister gate there. He was told to make sure that those who came to the monastery would only enter the areas that were open to them, such as the infirmary.[98] Thus, access within the house had to be firmly regulated by those in charge. In fact, the division between sacred and lay areas was clearly visible in the ruins of Skriðuklaustur, although it is not certain which rooms or areas the schoolchildren entered or which relics they touched when they committed their transgressions. Found in the center of the ruins of the monastic building was a set of steps that apparently divided the building into sacred and lay areas.[99]

The entire arrangement of the building there must have been planned in advance, although not all parts of it were completed at the same time. The results from the excavation indicated that the guesthouse may have been the first room built in the monastic complex, most likely in 1493 – or even earlier, as it could have served travelers heading across Vatnajökull glacier. Thereafter, the boundaries of the cemetery were marked out and consecrated in 1496, as was documented in a letter from Bishop Stefán Jónsson.[100] The rest of the rooms were gradually built on the western, northern, and eastern sides, and the church was finally finished in 1512, nearly twenty years after the establishing of Skriðuklaustur.[101] According to official documents, the work of the priors, Narfi Jónsson and his successor Þorvarður Helgason, had been characterized until then by attempts to finance the church building, not only through the exchange of properties but also through the purchase of the timber.[102] In addition to the priors' efforts to raise funds to finish building the church, the monastery must have benefited from the financially based contributions from its benefactors and the general public.

Notably, the monastic church at Skriðuklaustur stood on the south side of the monastic building instead of on the north side, as was more typical of the standard monastic plan. However, such placement of monastic churches is certainly not unknown, especially in northern Europe, that is, Norway, Denmark, and England. In England, one-third of monastic buildings were designed with the church on the southern side.[103] Nevertheless, this arrangement implies that the rooms designated for the clergy stood in the western wing of the building at Skriðuklaustur. Due to this spatial arrangement, it was impossible for lay people to enter this wing, even long-term guests of the school or the hospital. The western wing was connected to the church by the night stairs – a narrow corridor – so that the canons would be able to attend services in the church day and night. The monks always needed to be ready upon signal to go quickly and work for God – they even slept in their clothes so they could rise without delay.[104] From this corridor, it was possible to enter the dormitory and the prior's lodgings. The lodgings may also have served as a warming room, since they were furnished with both a stove and a shelf. These rooms were located closest to the church and were some of the finest in the entire monastic complex, since both the floors and the walls were lined with timber. In the northern end of the corridor was the chapterhouse, possibly used as a chapel until the monastic church was completed and consecrated in 1512. Next to the chapterhouse in the northern wing was the refectory. A small door made it possible to enter it from the chapterhouse. In the north-western corner was a brewery with an entrance from the outside. One of the main entrances was located further east on the northern side. Most likely, this entrance was also open to the public and would have been where people came to get food from the kitchen, which was placed east of the entrance. By the end of this public entrance were the stairs that separated the sacred area from the laity in the eastern wing.[105] The eastern wing consisted of an outer kitchen, and storage facilities and even a second-floor infirmary situated above the guesthouse. Another staircase was found, which led to the second-floor infirmary.[106] The gates to the monastic garden and the infirmary were located in this area too (see Figure 1.2).[107]

The following chapter provides detailed descriptions of most of the other monastic houses run in Iceland during the Middle Ages, but it draws primarily on information from the official visitations, unlike what was made possible through the excavation at Skriðuklaustur. At this point, it is even appropriate to stress once again that Iceland's medieval monastic institutions followed either the Benedictine or Augustinian order – as Skriðuklaustur monastery did – or a subordinate order of the Augustinians, the order of St. Victor. No other religious orders are known to have been active in Iceland during the medieval period. Even Rudolf, the abbot of earliest monastic house in Iceland, Bæjarklaustur, was a Benedictine monk. Although the order followed at Hítardalsklaustur has not been confirmed, it was very likely run in accordance with the Benedictine Order too, which was spreading quickly across northern Europe at the time the monastery was established. Moreover, one of its first abbots, Hreinn Styrmisson, came from the Benedictine monastery at Þingeyrar. It seems, however, that the operational differences between Benedictine and Augustinian houses in Iceland were minimal, at least during the last two or three centuries of monasticism in Iceland. One incident – when Bishop Jón Sigurðsson (r. 1343–1348) changed the allegiance of Viðeyjarklaustur from the Augustinians to the Benedictines and his successor changed it back – underlines the lack of any material difference between them. Still, for unknown reasons, the Benedictines seem to have been stronger in Hólar diocese, with the three main monastic institutions belonging to that order, as opposed to one following the Rule of St. Augustine. Conversely, the Augustinians were stronger in Skálholt diocese, with four monastic institutions affiliated with that order and only one – the female convent of Kirkjubæjarklaustur – following the Benedictine Order as the other female convent, Reynistaðarklaustur, did too.[108]

Notes

1 See, for example, Berman, 'Later Monastic Economies', pp. 836–837; Bond, *Monastic Landscapes*; Röckelein, 'Monastic Landscapes', pp. 821–822.
2 Kristjánsdóttir, *Leitin að klaustrunum*, pp. 59–60. Perhaps this was even the reason why no monastic house was ever established on the Faeroe Islands.
3 DI I, pp. 281–282.
4 Examples of such motivations behind establishing a new monastic house are well known from other societies in Europe, see Lyon, 'Nobility and Monastic Patronage', pp. 852–857.
5 Cormack, 'Monastic Foundations and Foundation Legends', pp. 61–82.
6 Hommedal, 'St Sunniva, the Seljumenn, and St Alban', pp. 45–60.
7 Kristjánsdóttir, *Leitin að klaustrunum*, pp. 131–132, 190–191.
8 Þorsteinsson, *Íslensk miðaldasaga*, pp. 74–75, 125–126; Kristjánsdóttir, *Leitin að klaustrunum*, pp. 67–78.
9 Kristjánsdóttir, *Leitin að klaustrunum*, pp. 300–312.
10 *Þorláks saga B*, pp. 180–181.
11 Kristjánsdóttir, *Leitin að klaustrunum*, pp. 313–324.
12 See DI I, p. 291; Kristjánsdóttir, *Leitin að klaustrunum*, p. 330.
13 See DI I, p. 282; DI II, pp. 115–116.
14 DI I, pp. 498–499.

15 DI I, p. 498.
16 DI I, p. 496.
17 Arnórsdóttir, *Konur og vígamenn*, pp. 92–93; Magnúsdóttir, *Frillor og fruar*, pp. 66–70; Jakobsson, *Auðnaróðal*, p. 160.
18 DI I, pp. 392, 394–395. See also DI I, p. 485 and *Sturlunga saga*, pp. 49, 388.
19 DI I, pp. 491–492.
20 One quarter equals 4.3 kg.
21 DI I, pp. 493–496.
22 DI I, p. 496; DI II, pp. 194–195. See also Jóhannesson, *Íslendinga saga I*, pp. 233–234.
23 DI I, pp. 485–486; Þór, 'Hólabiskupa ævir', pp. 407–408.
24 DI II, p. 377; DI III, pp. 597–598.
25 DI X, pp. 502–505. See also Ísleifsdóttir, 'Öreigar og umrenningar', pp. 91–126.
26 Kristjánsdóttir, *Leitin að klaustrunum*, pp. 325–355. See also Hallgrímsdóttir, 'Fornleifarannsókn í Viðey 1987'; Kristjánsdóttir 'Klaustureyjan á Sundum', pp. 29–52.
27 *Árna saga*, pp. 207–209; Kristjánsdóttir, *Leitin að klaustrunum*, pp. 391–392.
28 DI II, pp. 323–325.
29 DI II, pp. 282–298; *Árna saga*, pp. 208–209; Guðmundsson, 'Íslenskt samfélag og Rómarkirkja', pp. 84–93; Stefánsson, 'Um staði og staðamál', pp. 139–166.
30 Magnússon, 'Um klaustrin', p. 34; Sigurðsson, 'Um Skriðuklaustur', p. 238.
31 See DI VII, p. 233. There it says: 'In primis gefur ec austur til helga blod þess(ar) iij jarðir'.
32 DI VII, p. 525.
33 Hamilton-Dyer, 'Skriðuklaustur Monastery – Animal bones 2003–2007', pp. 33–37; Kristjánsdóttir, 'Lost Paths', pp. 1–8.
34 Björnsson, *Jöklar á Íslandi*, p. 243.
35 Steinsson, 'Saga munklífis á Skriðu', p. 108.
36 Steinsson, *Munklífi á Skriðu*; Steinsson, 'Jarðir Skriðuklausturs og efnahagur', pp. 74–103; Kristjánsdóttir, *Sagan af klaustrinu á Skriðu*, pp. 267–274.
37 Magnússon, *Chorographica Islandica*, pp. 82–83, 228; Guttormsson, *Við rætur Vatnajökuls*, pp. 145–147.
38 Kristjánsdóttir, 'Lost Paths', pp. 6–7.
39 Gajewski and Seeberg, 'Art in Monastic Churches of Western Europe', pp. 1014–1015.
40 Meaning that the Church had proprietorship of more than a half of the monastery's land, but in most cases, it had full proprietorship and rights of it.
41 Gilchrist, *Gender and Material Culture*, pp. 101–103; Scott, 'Romsey Abbey', pp. 159–160. See also discussion on gendered appearances of monastic liturgy in Muschiol, 'Gender and Monastic Liturgy in the Latin West', pp. 806–809.
42 Seesko, 'Between King and Congregation', p. 274.
43 DI I, p. 394; DI IV, p. 238; DI IX, pp. 480–482.
44 DI II, p. 300.
45 DI V, p. 361.
46 Kristjánsdóttir, *Leitin að klaustrunum*, pp. 337–339.
47 Kristjánsdóttir, *Leitin að klaustrunum*, pp. 190–191.
48 Magnússon, 'Um klaustrin', p. 34.
49 Kristjánsdóttir, *Leitin að klaustrunum*, pp. 210–217.
50 DI IX, p. 192; Kristjánsdóttir, *Leitin að klaustrunum*, pp. 201–203.
51 Hooke, 'The Sacred Nature of Rivers, Wells, and Other Wetlands', pp. 36–46.
52 Kristjánsdóttir, *Leitin að klaustrunum*, pp. 223, 234.
53 Kristjánsdóttir, *Leitin að klaustrunum*, p. 548.
54 Ó Clabaigh, *The Friars in Ireland*, pp. 249–253; Kristjánsdóttir, *Leitin að klaustrunum*, pp. 178–182.
55 Kristjánsdóttir, *Leitin að klaustrunum*, p. 141.
56 Kristjánsdóttir, *Leitin að klaustrunum*, pp. 140–141.
57 *Ketilsstaðaannáll*, p. 423; *Húnvetnskur annáll*, p. 625.

58 Kristjánsdóttir og Gunnarsdóttir, *Kortlagning klaustra á Íslandi*, pp. 7–10.
59 Kristjánsdóttir, *Leitin að klaustrunum*, pp. 140–145.
60 Kristjánsdóttir, *Leitin að klaustrunum*, p. 415.
61 Kristjánsdóttir, *Leitin að klaustrunum*, pp. 412–417.
62 Shoemaker, *Sanctuary and Crime in the Middle Ages*; Walgenbach, 'Church Sanctuary in the Contemporary Sagas', pp. 103–105.
63 Walgenbach, 'Church Sanctuary in the Contemporary Sagas', pp. 106–107.
64 *Járnsíða og Kristinréttur Árna Þorlákssonar*, pp. 151–154.
65 *Lögmannsannáll*, p. 294; *Nýi annáll*, p. 24; *Skarðsárannáll*, p. 24.
66 Referred to hereinafter as Jón Craxton.
67 Grímsdóttir, 'Biskupsstóll í Skálholti', p. 42; Þór, 'Hólabiskupa ævir', p. 415.
68 DI VI, p. 6; Pálsson, *Helgafell*, pp. 67–68.
69 DI II, pp. 331–332.
70 DI IX, pp. 244–246.
71 Kristjánsdóttir, *Sagan af klaustrinu á Skriðu*, p. 40.
72 DI IX, p. 245.
73 Jamroziak, 'Spaces of Lay-Religious Interaction', pp. 37–58; Lyon, 'Nobility and Monastic Patronage', pp. 857–862.
74 DI IX, pp. 244–246.
75 Gajewski and Seeberg, 'Art in Monastic Churches of Western Europe', p. 1008; Kerr, *Life in the Medieval Cloister*, p. 207.
76 DI IX, p. 245.
77 DI III, pp. 697–698.
78 *Sturlunga saga*, p. 424.
79 *Sturlunga saga*, pp. 696–702; 704–706.
80 *Sturlunga saga*, pp. 736–737.
81 Sigurjónsson, *Vestfirðingasaga 1390–1540*, pp. 192–198; DI XII, pp. 47, 50.
82 *Lárentíus saga*, pp. 277–280.
83 *Hundrað (pl. hundruð)* was a unit of measurement. One *hundrað* was equivalent in value to six cows. A farm, for example, could be valued at twelve, sixty, or 100 *hundruð*.
84 DI IV, pp. 520–521; 521–523.
85 DI IV, pp. 551–552.
86 See DI IV, pp. 487–488.
87 In Icelandic, *sálumessa*; that is, a mass for the soul.
88 DI IV, pp. 521–522.
89 DI XII, pp. 687–688. See also Walgenbach, 'Church Sanctuary in the Contemporary Sagas'.
90 DI XII, pp. 687–688; Schwarz Lausten, *Luther og Danmark i 500 år*, pp. 69–70; Ísleifsdóttir, *Byltingin að ofan*, p. 256.
91 Ahlin Sundman, 'Osteological Analysis of the Human Remains'; Collins, 'An Osteological Analysis of the Human Remains from the 2009 Excavation Season'; Collins, 'An Osteological Analysis of the Human Remains from the 2010 Excavation Season'; Zoëga, 'Fornmeinafræðileg rannsókn á fimm beinagrindum úr klausturgarðinum á Skriðu'; Pacciani, 'Anthropological description of skeletons from graves no. 4, 62, 63, 65, 66, 67 and 68'; Pacciani, 'Anthropological description of skeletons from graves no. 5, 17, 27, 34, 54, 74, 75 and 80'; Pacciani, 'Anthropological description of skeletons from graves no. 83, 84, 85, 87, 88, 95, 96, 97 and 99'; Pacciani, 'Anthropological description of skeletons from graves no. 123, 124, 125, 126, 127, 128, 129, 130, 131, 132, 133, 134, 135, 136, 141, 142, 143, 145 and 146'; Kristjánsdóttir and Collins, 'Cases of Hydatid Disease', pp. 479–486.
92 Gilchrist and Sloane, *Requiem*, p. 63; Ó Clabaigh, *The Friars in Ireland, 1224–1540*, pp. 107–110; Stöber, 'Bequests and Burials', pp. 131–146.
93 DI XI, p. 271. See also Arnórsdóttir, *Property and Virginity*, p. 143.
94 Þorsteinsson, *Íslenska þjóðveldið*, p. 223; Jóhannesson, *Íslendinga saga*, p. 234.

95 DI I, p. 394, also pp. 395–396.
96 See, for example, Wolf, *The Legends of the Saints in Old Norse-Icelandic Prose.*
97 Gajewski and Seeberg, 'Art in Monastic Churches of Western Europe', pp. 1015–1016; Lauwers, 'Constructing Monastic Space', p. 331–333.
98 DI IX, pp. 244–246.
99 Kristjánsdóttir, *Sagan af klaustrinu á Skriðu*, pp. 119–121.
100 DI VII, p. 309.
101 DI VIII, pp. 403–404.
102 DI VIII, pp. 401–404; Kristjánsdóttir, *Sagan af klaustrinu á Skriðu*, pp. 44–46.
103 Gilchrist, *Gender and Material Culture*, pp. 128–133; Gunnes, 'Klosteranlegg i Norge', p. 90; Møller-Christensen, *Æbelholt kloster*, p. 26.
104 See Chapter XXII of the Benedictine rules, which appear to have been like the Augustinian ones, at least as they were practiced during the last phases of monasticism in Iceland.
105 Kristjánsdóttir, *Sagan af klaustrinu á Skriðu*, pp. 103–114.
106 Kristjánsdóttir, *Sagan af klaustrinu á Skriðu*, pp. 59–140.
107 Kristjánsdóttir, *Sagan af klaustrinu á Skriðu*, pp. 115–130.
108 As was customary for the female convents in northern Europe, both Kirkjubæjarklaustur and Reynistaðarklaustur followed the Benedictine Order (with exemptions though). *The Regula Benedictit* was originally written by Benedict of Nursia in 540 CE as guidelines for male monasteries in Italy. When the female convents following the Benedictine Order grew in number, mainly in the eleventh and twelfth centuries, the request was raised by several religious women in Central Europe, such as Heloise of Paraclete and Hildegard of Bingen, to modify the rules. As a result of this request, the Benedictine's rules were recontextualized for the female convents, although neither women, abbesses, nuns, nor sisters have ever appeared directly in them. See, for example, Madigan, *Medieval Christianity*, p. 158; Lichtenberg, *Gender Issues in the Benedictine Rule*, pp. 1–6.

6

VISITING THE MONASTIC HOUSES

The excavation of Skriðuklaustur offered an important view of the lodgings and furnishings of a monastic building dating from the last decades of monasticism in Iceland. The case of Brother Jón, described in the previous chapter, certainly adds to the picture but it also demonstrates that ecclesiastical authorities strived to run their institutions in accordance with requirements. However, the inventories provide us perhaps with the most detailed description of eight of the other monastic settlements operating longest in Iceland. These are assessed in the following sections, with the aim of shedding light on the monasteries' overall lodgings and furnishings, but in combination with muniments, contracts, and letters describing various incidents. Still, before proceeding, it is necessary to bear in mind that the inventories were recorded on the behalf of ecclesiastical authorities and, thus, offer the more official view of the monastic houses compared to that offered by many other documents or remains. The oldest inventory from a monastic house in Iceland is the one made in Kirkjubæjarklaustur in 1218, if the list of goods transported when Flateyjarklaustur was moved to Helgafell in 1184 is not considered a formal inventory. Particularly detailed inventories – listing their buildings, interiors, furniture, and possessions – were those made in the four monastic houses in Hólar diocese in 1525. These inventories were carried out on behalf of Bishop Jón Arason the year after he was elected to office. Most of the inventories from the monastic institutions in Skálholt diocese were, on the other hand, made during different periods.

The Benedictines at Munkaþverárklaustur

The Benedictine monastery at Munkaþverá produced the most detailed inventory of any monastic institution operating in Hólar bishopric in 1525. Indeed, it is so detailed that it is possible to follow the bishop's agent through the building

DOI: 10.4324/9781003361077-6

and draw an artist's impression of what the monastery would have looked like (Figure 6.1). The inventory lists the name of each room, along with the items kept in each, thereby providing further insight into how the rooms were used. It appears that the eastern wing of the complex included the abbot's lodgings, a sacristy, a chapterhouse, a schoolroom, and day and night staircases leading to the chapel. Outside the eastern long wall was a brewery that could only be entered from the outside. In the southern wing were a dormitory and a refectory. The refectory stood on the eastern side of an entrance to the cloister garth, and on the western side of this entrance were two pantries of different sizes. In the western wing there were a kitchen, a smithy, and a storage room. Outside the western wing were the houses meant for the laity – corrodians, occasional guests, and paupers. According to the inventory, in addition to the monastic church, which encompassed the whole of the northern wing, there was a chapel and a freestanding bell tower – a steeple – right outside the western entrance of the church. In the center was the cloister garth.[1]

The bell tower or steeple of Munkaþverárklaustur seems to have been of the same type as those in the monasteries at Þingeyrar, Þykkvibær, Kirkjubær, and Reynistaður. The steeples at Þingeyraklaustur and Reynistaðarklaustur will be mentioned later in the context of payments for burials inside them, but in a documented incident taking place at Þykkvabæjarklaustur, the steeple collapsed in a storm with the Augustini church bell.[2] The steeple in Kirkjubæjarklaustur is only

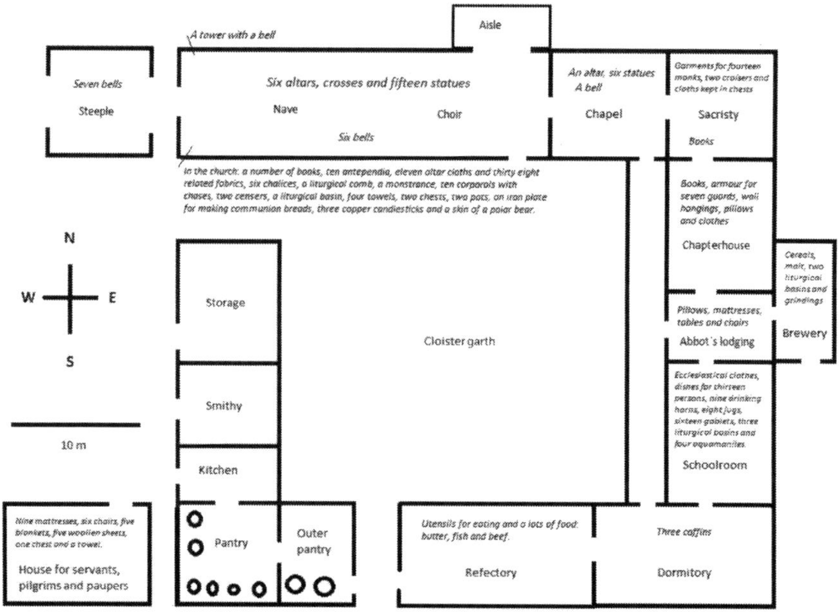

FIGURE 6.1 A plan of the building of Munkaþverárklaustur, based on the inventory of 1525. Some of the main possessions are listed.

mentioned during the period when the convent had been taken over by chieftains in the early thirteenth century. The steeple had a door, so it must have been possible to enter it, although neither its size nor any other details are known.[3] Moreover, the foundations of a steeple, circular in form, were found during the excavation of the ruins of Skriðuklaustur. It was located in the garth, close to the well and thus in the vicinity of the cloister gate in the west of the monastic complex.[4] Otherwise, the church in Skriðuklaustur was long and narrow, with one aisle on its northern long wall. Internally, it was 15×5.7 m in size, with the aisle only measuring 2.5×3 m.[5] On the other hand, the monastic church of Munkaþverárklaustur seems to have been much larger, up to 30 m in length, based on an estimate from the inventory compiled in 1525.

Moreover, according to the inventory of 1525, the monastic church of Munkaþverárklaustur was divided into a nave, a choir, and a chapel, as was customary. There were a total of six altars in the nave and choir and a seventh one in the chapel. From the chapel, it was possible to enter the sacristy, which could also be accessed via the chapterhouse, as it was located in the north-east corner of the monastic complex. In addition, an aisle was attached to the north wall of the church, with an opening from the chancel. The main altar in the choir was dedicated to the Virgin Mary, as were two other altars in the church, including the one in the chapel. The other altars in the church were dedicated to Bishop Jón Ögmundsson, St. John the Baptist, St. Anne, St. Michael, and St. Benedict. All were fitted with elaborate likenesses of the saints to which they were dedicated. In all, there were fifteen such likenesses in the church itself, commemorating fourteen saints. These were Saints Andrew, Anne, Anthony, Bonaventure, Hallvard, John the Baptist, Magnus, Martin, Michael, Olaf, King of Norway, and Zita, as well as the Holy Trinity, two of Bishop Jón, and finally, four of the Virgin Mary, one of which is said to have been large and gilded.[6]

The inventory from 1525 is not the only one that can be used to shed light on the furnishings of Munkaþverárklaustur because Bishop Jón Craxton also made one in 1429, soon after the great fire. It should be emphasized here that the 1429 inventory was completed while the monastery was still under reconstruction. At that point, the church owned fourteen chasubles, eighteen gowns, five antependia, four vestments (see Table 8.1), eight tablecloths, two unspecified likenesses, and one statue of the Virgin Mary in an open retable.[7] Nonetheless, the inventory of 1525 certainly highlights the growth of Munkaþverárklaustur during the century that had passed since the reconstruction after 1429. On the roof at the west end of the church was a tower with a bell. Another church bell was in the chapel, seven others in the so-called house of bells (which could have been the steeple), and six (four of them small) inside the church. This was certainly not all. The church possessed at least ten antependia, eleven vestments, and many other related fabrics for church custodians embroidered with saintly figures and other ecclesiastical ornaments. Inside the church building, the main items listed were six chalices, a liturgical comb, a monstrance, ten corporals with seven corporal cases, two censers, a liturgical basin for washing hands, four towels, two chests, three more church bells, two pots, a wafer host for making communion bread, three copper candlesticks, and thirty-eight cloths of different kinds (some made of silk) for ecclesiastical services.[8]

Interestingly, a polar bear skin was among the items listed in the church in 1525. Such skins were very valuable and were commonly owned by the best-equipped ecclesiastical institutions in Iceland during the Middle Ages.[9] The library, which contained eighty books, seems to have been housed mainly in the church, but books were also listed among the items in two other rooms, the sacristy and the chapterhouse. These books ranged from religious psalms written in Latin to more historical texts written in Old Norse/Icelandic. Those in the sacristy included books containing stories about unspecified persons and books used for religious services. One of the most interesting among them was a missal with a sealskin cover. The chapterhouse contained various books, including an 'old' Altar book, hagiographies of the Virgin Mary, St. Barlanus, and St. Peter, unnamed stories of two female saints, and the bishops' sagas of Guðmundur góði and Jón Ögmundsson, to mention a few.[10] In addition to these was an office book, which had also been recorded when Bishop Jón Craxton had his inventory compiled nearly 100 years earlier, as well as some other unnamed books. However, the library had clearly expanded considerably between 1429 and 1525.[11] In the sacristy, there were also garments of various kinds sufficient for at least eighteen or nineteen monks and a deacon – a similar number was also listed in the inventory of 1429 – besides two crosiers, two chests, and one smaller casket.[12]

The sacristy is mentioned three times in documents after 1429, in addition to the inventory of 1525. Twice in 1467, Abbot Einar Ísleifsson used the room for financial purposes. On the first occasion, he used it to sign a contract with a female corrodian, Þuríður Halldórsdóttir, in return for her donation of Uppsalir farm in Eyjafjörður to the monastery. The second time the sacristy was used that year was when the accounts of the church at Einarsstaðir in Reykjadalur were delivered to the bishop, Ólafur Rögnvaldsson, who was there for the occasion.[13] Why the accounts of this particular church were kept in Munkaþverárklaustur is not clear. The third time the sacristy appears in documents is in 1478, when the Reverend Magnús Ásgrímsson handed his farm Eiðar on Langanes over to Hólar cathedral as penance for a crime he had committed. The crime is not specified, but both Bishop Ólafur and Abbot Einar were present when the fine was paid, as were some other priests.[14] Abbot Einar Ísleifsson was the longest serving abbot in Iceland. He served Munkaþverárklaustur for more than a half century, from 1435 to 1487. It was in this period that the monastery there acquired most of its farms.[15]

The next room in Munkaþverárklaustur visited by the bishop's agent in 1525 was the chapterhouse. It contained a wide variety of objects, including three chests, a bowl, five pots, a cauldron, ecclesiastical cloths, and pillows, as well as the books listed earlier, which were kept in the chests. The walls were even covered with wall hangings. Furthermore, for some odd reason, the chapterhouse also contained grinders for both pepper and mustard, along with some assorted tools for the preparation of funerals, such as a spade for digging graves. In addition, there were plates of armor for at least seven guards – or men-at-arms (Icel. *sveinar*).[16] The chapterhouse thus seems to have been rather comfortably equipped, but in fact, it was one of the rooms listed in the monastic complex at Munkaþverá after the great fire of 1429.[17] The question is, however, whether it was common to store such equipment in chapterhouses, which were otherwise intended for the daily meetings of the religious community. It is plausible that the organization of the cemetery was a matter that needed to be discussed with the burial tools at hand. The same could be said of the defense of the monastery. It is even conceivable that some of these items were actually kept in the brewery, whose tools were listed immediately after those in the chapterhouse or that certain items may simply have had no fixed storage place. In the brewery, there was equipment for making beer, in addition to barrels of meal and other cereals, and two liturgical basins. What was even more noteworthy is that the brewery was locked from the outside, so it could only be entered from the abbot's lodgings, which came next on the list. Relatively few items were stored there: just three tables (one with chairs), wall hangings, nine upholstered seats, and a few different mattresses.[18]

The abbot's lodgings are actually mentioned twice among the rooms of Munkaþverárklaustur before the great fire in 1429. The first reference appeared in the story of the chieftain Þorgils skarði in 1255.[19] The second one was in papers from 1415, when a couple, Benedikt Brynjólfsson and Margrét Eiríksdóttir, handed all that they had inherited from the Reverend Steinmóður Þorsteinsson over to the bishop of Hólar, Árni Ólafsson.[20] It seems thus to have been an old tradition to sign the papers of Hólar cathedral in the abbot's lodgings at Munkaþverárklaustur, although the sacristy was later used for such purposes as well. The abbot's lodgings appear to have been rebuilt after the fire, indicating that they were among the most important rooms in the entire monastery. They are mentioned not only in the inventory of 1525 but also in the one from 1478, when a contract was signed concerning the donation of Ljósavatn farm in Bárðardalur to Hólar cathedral.[21]

The next room mentioned in the inventory was the schoolroom, and this is the only time it appears in documents from Munkaþverárklaustur. The room contained various items useful for the students, and in addition to different kinds of ecclesiastical clothing, there were dishes for thirteen persons, nine drinking horns, eight jugs, sixteen goblets (five of them from the Netherlands), and other tableware. Furthermore, three large liturgical basins and four aquamaniles were also on the list of items in the schoolroom. There was thus a total of six basins in the monastery.[22] After the schoolroom, the bishop's agent listed the items in the southern wing, starting with the canons' dormitory located on the corner of the monastic complex. The dormitory contained little apart from three coffins, one without a lid. Next was the refectory, which could be entered from the dormitory. In it, there were both utensils for eating and a large amount of food: butter, fish, and beef, to mention a few items. In the two storage rooms west of the refectory, even more food was kept in barrels and containers. Also kept in the storage rooms were some tableware, tools such as churns, tubs, buckets, and twenty bowls.[23]

It is not clear why the storage rooms had two different names – storage room and anterior storage – as there appears to be very little difference between them as regards supplies. In the kitchen, which was located next to the storage rooms but in the western wing, there were three old boilers and one new one, among other utensils. In the smithy, which came next, were all the items that might be expected in such a room, but also equipment for the transport of goods by horses, such as twenty packsaddles. There were also nine ropes for horses, as well as a quantity of *vaðmál*[24] and a loom.[25] Apparently, it was here that the couple Arnþrúður Árnadóttir and Jón Sigfússon carried out their work for the abbot of Munkaþverárklaustur in 1498: she did the weaving and he, the ironwork.[26] Finally, in the last building listed, which was meant for lay people and was located immediately outside the monastic complex, there were nine mattresses, six comfortable chairs, five blankets, five woolen sheets, one chest, and a towel specifically meant for drying the hands after washing them in the liturgical basins. One room seems to have disappeared with the fire in 1429: *munkastofa* (the monks' room), which is only mentioned in 1313, when Lárentíus, who later became bishop of Hólar, was a monk in Munkaþverárklaustur and heard of the death of Bishop Jörundur in Hólar, whereupon the monks were immediately called for service in the church and all the church bells were rung at the same time.[27]

There are, moreover, two seals preserved from Munkaþverárklaustur, but they may hint about its housings. One is attached to a contract dated 19 May 1375, when Munkaþverárklaustur had to sell one of its farms due to a temporary financial crisis it was experiencing. The image on the seal is especially interesting because it is a three-dimensional picture of a church. It has been suggested that the seal may show what the monastic church at Munkaþverárklaustur actually looked like. The reason for this interpretation is that when Munkaþverárklaustur was rebuilt after the fire in 1429, it obtained a new seal with an image of an architecturally different church.[28] However, the seals can also depict a conventional image of a Continental monastic church because they are very similar to many other seals from other Benedictine monasteries outside Iceland. The later seal from Munkaþverá, for example, is almost identical to a seal of the Benedictine Abbey at Hronský Beňadik in Budapest, dating back to 1232.[29] The two seals from Munkaþverárklaustur may thus have been based on conventional ideals for a Benedictine monastery and been purchased from abroad, as in fact most of the other items used in the Icelandic monastic houses were. This example could therefore rather be an indication that the Icelandic monastic houses were designed in accordance with a traditional form of monastic architecture that was used regardless of geographical location.

The Other Three Benedictine Houses in Iceland

The 1525 inventories of the other Benedictine houses of Hólar, Þingeyraklaustur and Reynistaðarklaustur, represent similarly well-equipped buildings. Still, the inventories from these two monastic houses are patchier than the one from Munkaþverárklaustur and thus more difficult to follow as regards specific rooms. In the case of Þingeyraklaustur, only one room is mentioned by name in the inventory of 1525: the smithy. Otherwise, the description merely covers the church and the monastic building as a single complex.[30] Some specific rooms, however, are mentioned explicitly in preserved contracts from Þingeyraklaustur, such as a hall and corrodians' house, as well as the church and the aforementioned steeple.[31] For example, in the bishops' saga of Lárentíus, a church and a convent at Þingeyraklaustur are mentioned together.[32] Actually, in some cases it is not completely certain whether or not 'convent' refers to the monastery itself, because sometimes specific rooms appear to be named as such. This can also be seen in the inventories from the Augustinian monasteries at Helgafellsklaustur and Viðeyjarklaustur, discussed in the next section. The historical documents are otherwise silent about the names of any rooms that must nevertheless have been there, such as a refectory wherein a meal must have been served to farmers from Vatnsdalur but not to Bishop Lárentíus during his visit there in 1328. This was when disputes arose because of the financial support the monastery received from Hólar when it was established by Bishop Jón Ögmundsson more than two centuries earlier.[33]

In 1525, the church and monastic building at Þingeyraklaustur contained nine vestments, fifteen chasubles, five robes, nine gowns, four dalmatics, three crosiers, one meter, an altarpiece with nineteen gilded plaquettes (one made of alabaster), three altar cloths, four altar stones, and four fully equipped altars, one of them dedicated to St. Benedict. There were also three corporals, four corporal cases, three silver gilt shields, nine other silver gilt shields, six chalices with patens (four of them gilded), one cloth for a paten, four towels, three paxes, three aquamaniles, a badge, an old silver gilt shrine, a *propitiatorium* with silver, ten copper candlesticks (although some were broken), and three copper crosses over the high altar. The church possessed three images of the Holy Trinity and likenesses of Saints Andrew, Benedict, Catherine, Clare, Jesus, Jacobus, King Olaf, Peter, Paul, and Zita, as well as two likenesses of Bishop Jón, two of John the Baptist, and four of the Virgin Mary. Embroidered cloths covered them, and the one covering the Virgin Mary was made of silk. There were also eight good church bells, three small bells, six chests, a scale with weights, a wafer host for making communion bread, two liturgical basins, two chairs, an iron helmet, and a large iron bar. There were numerous reading books, such as homilies, hymns, psalters, a periodical book, a rule book, two choral books, and many other unnamed books in Old Norse/Icelandic and Latin. In addition to these were hagiographies of the Virgin Mary and St. Barlanus, Peter and John the Baptist, *vita patrum*, as well as the bishops' sagas of Jón Ögmundsson, Guðmundur góði and St. Þorlákur Þórhallsson. Finally, there was also the story of Pope Gregory.[34] The equipment related to the household included eleven troughs, eleven tin troughs, and five wooden troughs, twenty-six table plates, thirty-five kettles (five of them in poor condition), one large kettle, a table towel, two woolen cloths, and three pepper grinders. There was also one skin, eleven ropes, numerous tools for cutting turf, two axes, nine different kinds of barrels, sixteen smaller barrels, seven buckets, one drinking pot, ten bowls, two cereal boxes, five pots, four churns, two chests, one copper pot, two large tin jugs and three old ones, ten goblets, three wooden bowls, nine mattresses, nine chairs, one saloon cloth, a basin, a towel, three boats, and a quantity of butter (285 kg in all).[35]

The 1525 inventory of Reynistaðarklaustur only mentions the church and chapterhouse. However, other documents mention rooms such as the hall, steeple, narthex, sacristy, and living room, in addition to the domestic ones, such as storage cupboards, pantry, and dungeon. In 1525, the church at Reynistaðarklaustur contained three likenesses of the Virgin Mary in tabernacles with doors, one of which was silver gilt, and one likeness each of saints Þorlákur, Catherine, John the Baptist, Thomas, Bishop Jón, and Olaf the King. There were also nine chests, eight altar stones, two candlesticks, two altarpieces, two censers, five chalices with patens, a *propitiatorium* with silver, ten large church bells and two small ones, two shrines, and a number of other smaller ecclesiastical items. In addition to these, there were thirty-seven books, ranging from Bibles and psalms to stories about saints.[36] It is, however, noteworthy how few vestments the convent possessed in 1525, but they were only seven by then. On the other hand, according to the inventory compiled due to changes in stewardship at Reynistaðarklaustur in 1408, there were at that point twelve chasubles, six gowns, ten dalmatics, ten vestments, and thirteen antependia (see Table 8.1). Perhaps fewer priests served the convent by then, in contrast to earlier times. Alternatively, if the liveries were a part of the convent's manufacturing output and not intended for use in the chapel, they may have been sold. Nevertheless, it is plausible that the political upheavals of the Reformation, which by then had begun within the Danish kingdom, caused a decline at Reynistaðarklaustur or that there was a shift in emphasis regarding ecclesiastical services provided by the convent. Importantly, the inventories from 1408 to 1525 do not otherwise indicate a reduction in the convent's wealth as the Reformation approached.

Furthermore, the inventory of 1408 is much more detailed than that from 1525, although it may seem odd that no saintly likenesses were listed in the 1408 inventory, whereas seven were recorded in 1525. There must have been some, as in all other ecclesiastical houses of that time. Still, among the other items in Reynistaðarklaustur in 1408 were nine corporals, four chalices, a fifth broken one, two iron plates for making the host, six large church bells (which increased to ten in 1525), two small bells, three copper censers (but only two in 1525), seven golden rings and one ring of silver, two bowls of silver and two others unspecified, two beakers, two silver gilt crosses, a vessel with a silver gilt rack, and an ivory crosier inlaid with silver. There were also scales and weights, one mirror, a broken aquamanile, five liturgical basins (three of them damaged), thirteen chests (three of them locked), six different kinds of tapestries (including one of wool), and some other textiles and church objects, as well as the sun stone already mentioned in this book. The list also includes some household items, such as forty troughs, thirty-nine pots (fourteen of which leaked), thirty-five dishes, five small boxes, twenty cups, fifteen spoons (three of them silver gilt), six bottles, four tinned discs, three broken cans, three boilers, a hammer, a shovel, a turf cutter, two axes, a sharpener, a stave, and some raw iron. Some food is listed as well, including fish, butter, flour, and oil. Bedding was also registered on the same occasion, for example, ten mattresses, twenty-two blankets, and eight quilts.[37]

Interestingly, there is one surviving official document that provides hints about what the nuns owned personally. This is the will in which an unnamed man donated various items to the sisters in Reynistaðarklaustur in payment for his burial in the narthex of the convent's church at the time of the smallpox outbreak in 1431. According to his testimony, the nuns Helga Bjarnadóttir and Agnes Jónsdóttir received one chest each. Both were among the eight nuns who took holy orders in 1431. The chests were not empty. The one that Helga received contained blankets, and in the one that Agnes received, there were both blankets and scissors for making clothing. Additionally, the prioress, Þórunn, was given a brown horse, Þuríður a white cloth and seven candlesticks, and Sigríður a cow, which was then located at Bessastaðir. Þóra Finnsdóttir, later abbess, was supposed to inherit a piece of blue linen. The rest of the nuns, who are not named individually, received investments in the form of *kúgildi*.[38] Finally, the steward, Illugi Björgólfsson, was supposed to inherit the man's sword and gloves. Many more relatives and friends across the country also received promises of inheritance, ranging from horses to dresses. According to the unnamed testator's will, a man named Þorsteinn Jónsson, of whom no further details are known in the context of Reynistaðarklaustur, received a saddle and a bridle for a horse – notably, on the condition that Þorsteinn himself survived the smallpox.[39]

How the rooms in Reynistaðarklaustur were arranged is difficult to determine from the surviving documents, but the seal of the convent clearly displays an image of a timber church, identical to the Norwegian stave churches, with dragon heads on the roof and the bell tower (Figure 6.2). The question is whether the seal actually shows the nuns' church or chapel at Reynistaður, as has been suggested by some scholars,[40] or simply depicts a standard image of a Scandinavian medieval church, as seems to have been the case for the seal of Munkaþverárklaustur. This may certainly be the case if the seals were generally produced abroad, purchased, and then imported to Iceland. However, it is equally possible that many of the monastic churches in Europe had a number of similarities in terms of architecture and layout. The furniture and rooms of the monasteries in these societies followed the same fashions. Common imported artifacts could have a major impact on local

FIGURE 6.2 The seal from Reynistaðarklaustur.

production because the tendency to follow the latest fashion appears to have been strong at the time, as it is today. After all, it is therefore possible that the seal in question depicts the church of Reynistaðarklaustur, which resembled other monastic churches built of timber, such as the church at the archbishopric of Niðarós. Interestingly, further information is preserved on the church of Reynistaðarklaustur. This information dates from the time after the Reformation, when the church was torn down on the orders of the Danish king, but the church is said to have been built of timber rather than the turf and stone more commonly used in Iceland. Moreover, in this document, the convent's church at Reynistaðarklaustur is said to have been so large that the *sanctum sanctorum* (the chapel, or possibly only the choir) of it was big enough to serve as a Lutheran chapel for Reynistaður.[41]

The seal and in fact several other documents indicate that the convent's church was architecturally similar to the Norwegian stave churches – and that there was a proper church, not merely a chapel. The church at the school in Möðruvellir may also have been of timber, rather than turf and stone, since it broke into pieces in the storm of 1421. Both these ecclesiastical institutions, although differently run, belonged to Hólar diocese and were established almost in the same year: at the end of the thirteenth century, in 1295 and 1296. According to both the inventory from 1525 and other documents, the church of the convent in Reynistaður appears otherwise to have consisted of a nave, a chancel, and a narthex, as well as a steeple and a chapel (if *sanctum sanctorum* refers to a chapel). The narthex may thus have served as the parish church if not situated in a separate building.

The specific rooms of the third Benedictine monastic house described here, the female convent of Kirkjubæjarklaustur, located in Skálholt diocese, are barely mentioned by name in surviving documents, apart from the church, the church's door, the choir, the steeple and its door, a hall, and an outer kitchen. Nevertheless, three important inventories survive from Kirkjubæjarklaustur, in addition to a specific one listing the nuns' silver possessions, which was made by Bishop Stefán Jónsson in 1494.[42] The first inventory is the one carried out when the chieftains took over the convent in 1218. Unfortunately, the list of possessions is not very detailed, as the compiler seems to have been interested mainly in the finances of the convent. The agent lists only the value of the possessions, without any further description. It is in this inventory that it is stated, however, that the church at Kirkjubær was dedicated to the Virgin Mary and that it possessed ecclesiastical cloths, church bells, and books worth 220 *hundruð* in all. The value of the convent's nine farms is also listed.[43] Although the items are not listed in detail, the inventory nevertheless shows, as has been previously highlighted, that the convent was relatively wealthy at the time of the takeover, most likely thanks to the nuns and the two abbesses who had been in charge since its establishment in 1186.

Bishop Jón Sigurðsson had the second inventory of Kirkjubæjarklaustur compiled in 1343. The inventory confirms a rate of growth similar to that seen in the other monastic institutions at that time, since those that had survived the Staðamál conflicts became very wealthy. In 1343, for example, Kirkjubæjarklaustur owned nine chalices, eight church bells, nine missals, seven rosaries, four censers, a shrine, an altar piece, a baptismal font, six crosses, seven candlesticks for the high altar, and two large painted statues of the Virgin Mary and St. Catherine. Most outstanding, however, were the textiles. The inventory listed not only the wall hangings around the church but also fourteen antependia, twelve cloths for the lectern, twenty-two chasubles (including twelve made of elaborate silk), twenty gowns, six dalmatics, and eight robes. Oddly enough, the most elaborate chasuble, which was blue, is listed separately.[44] It may have been meant for someone special, perhaps even for the bishop himself, or it may have been intended for sale as part of their textile manufacturing output (see Table 8.1). When Kirkjubæjarklaustur was inspected for the third time, notably by Bishop Vilchin in 1397, there were twenty-four chasubles, thirteen gowns, five dalmatics, four robes, and eight vestments, in addition to fourteen antependia and numerous other ecclesiastical garments. The chasubles were said to be ready for use because they had already been consecrated.[45] Furthermore, there were six corporals, two crosiers, two lecterns, four altarpieces, four censers, three posts to hold up the tapestries, the shrine (now said to contain holy relics), six crosses instead of five, nine candlesticks instead of eight, a basin, an aquamanile, two pax boards, a box for the altar bread, and some other liturgical items. Moreover, in 1397, it possessed seven likenesses, for example, as opposed to two at the time of the previous inventory in 1343. There was also a library by then, containing fifty-one books in Latin and Icelandic/Old Norse, as well as an unspecified number of reading books (Icel. *lesbækur*). In 1343, on the other hand, there were only nine books.[46] Furthermore, as has been said before, in 1397, the church at Kirkjubæjarklaustur had twenty glass windows – most likely stained-glass windows because pieces of them were found during the recent excavation there.[47]

Windows with stained glass are thought to have been very rare in Iceland during the Middle Ages and were not owned by ordinary people. On the Continent, however, stained glass was common in the windows of ecclesiastical buildings such as cathedrals and monasteries, and the light that shone through them was seen as the manifestation of the heavenly light.[48] The windows in the church of Kirkjubæjarklaustur must thus have been eye-catching and must have highlighted the heavenly purpose of the convent. This must also have increased trust and belief in it as a proper ecclesiastical institution. Kirkjubæjarklaustur was not the only monastic institution in Iceland with stained-glass windows; eight windows were also listed in an inventory from Helgafellsklaustur in 1397.[49] Moreover, the excavations at Skriðuklaustur found pieces of stained glass; these were coated with ecclesiastical images and texts.[50] The glass in the windows in these three monastic institutions – Kirkjubæjarklaustur, Helgafellsklaustur, and Skriðuklaustur – suggests that stained glass may have been common in ecclesiastical buildings in Iceland. The window glass must have been imported, like many other precious items the monastic houses owned, since no glass production took place in Iceland during the Middle Ages.

The inventory from 1397 was not the last one made at Kirkjubæjarklaustur. For some unknown reason, Bishop Stefán Jónsson recorded the nuns' silver and gold possessions in 1494. The silver items they then owned included one larger bowl, four smaller bowls, one cup with a lid, one without a lid, one larger beaker with a lid, one censer, two chalices, one silver gilt horn, and a crucifix. Finally, on the list were four golden rings and a fifth broken one. The bishop took the broken one with him but gave Abbess Halldóra a new one instead.[51] The rings emphasize the nuns' special relationship with their convent; in taking their vows, they became the brides of Christ. The number of rings may also give an idea of how many nuns there were at Kirkjubæjarklaustur at this point, although it is not known whether they all wore a ring. As is mentioned earlier, in 1408, Reynistaðarklaustur had seven golden rings and one silver ring.[52] Golden rings are not often listed in the inventories of the monasteries, but the abbots and the monks needed to own rings, too. The prior of Skriðuklaustur certainly had one: the ring that was found in his grave. However, another one is in fact listed in a gift from Einar Ormsson's family to the monastery in 1494.[53] Thus, the continued growth of Kirkjubæjarklaustur throughout the fourteenth century can be observed from the inventories, but the same can also be said about Reynistaðarklaustur during the fifteenth century, particularly when it came to livestock and textile making, as will be discussed further in Chapter 8.

As has been highlighted, the four Benedictine houses described here – Munkaþverárklaustur, Þingeyraklaustur, Reynistaðarklaustur, and Kirkjubæjarklaustur – were located in both Icelandic dioceses, Hólar and Skálholt. When we compare the inventories of the Benedictine houses with those of the Augustinian monastic houses from both dioceses, the difference between the two orders appears to have been minimal as regards lodgings and furnishings. However, as in the case of the Benedictine houses, the Augustinian inventories vary in terms of what is recorded and what is not. In some cases, only the furnishings of the church are listed, while others included lists of day-to-day items and even livestock at the monastic farms (see Chapter 8). Most importantly, the different inventories from the Icelandic monastic houses demonstrate clearly that they were well-furnished and equipped and, on the whole, operated according to the highest standards of monasticism until the last decades prior to the Reformation.

The Augustinian Houses, Furniture, and Items

The five Augustinian monasteries in Iceland: Möðruvallaklaustur, Þykkvabæjarklaustur, Helgafellsklaustur, Viðeyjarklaustur, and Skriðuklaustur will now be visited. Unfortunately, the inventory compiled in 1525 of the assets of the Augustinian school at Möðruvallaklaustur is as sparse as those made for the monasteries at Þingeyrar and at Reynistaður. The names of the rooms of Möðruvallaklaustur are recorded in other historical documents; however, only a church and a sacristy are mentioned in the context of the great fire in Möðruvallaklaustur in 1316. Until the second rebuilding, which took place after the monastic church collapsed in a storm in 1421, only three rooms are mentioned by name, in addition to the church. The first one is the *miklastofa*, where the bishop's meal was served during his memorable visit to the monastery around Easter of 1328, as is described in Chapter 7. The chapterhouse is also named two days later in the account of the same visit. In addition to this, a living room is mentioned in the only corrody contract made in Möðruvallaklaustur, but this happened nearly a century later, in 1431.[54] While the inventory from 1461 is extremely useful for shedding light on the library of Möðruvallaklaustur, almost nothing else is listed there. By then, the library contained 114 books and, importantly, all are specifically named.[55] Only Helgafellsklaustur appears to have had a larger library, which comprised nearly 200 unspecified books in 1397. Viðeyjarklaustur had sixty books in 1397, and the other Augustinian monasteries had fewer.[56]

The inventory from 1525 offers, on the other hand, quite detailed information on the furniture and items owned by the monastery at Möðruvellir. At this point, the church had two crosses above the altar, one large statue of the Virgin Mary, and another smaller one. There were also other nine likenesses of Saints Augustine, Bartholomew, Nicholas, Anne, John the Baptist, Peter, Magnus, Jesus, and Olaf, King of Norway. The church also held a shrine, a *propitiatorium* with silver, a large cross above the altar, two church bells inside the church and six outside, four altar stones, six chalices (two of them gilded), and some other liturgical items. Furthermore, ten vestments are listed, including two chasubles, twelve gowns, seven robes, three dalmatics, a number of other garments, and towels. In addition, there were two basins, two iron plates for making the host, an aquamanile, a baptismal font, tools used for burials, and eight chests. Next, seventy-six books are listed – far fewer than in 1461 – and finally, the skin of a polar bear, like the one owned by the neighboring monastery at Munkaþverárklaustur.[57] Furthermore, in the monastic building, there were a number of tapestries and other fabrics, including thirteen mattresses and quilts, thirteen blankets, seven chests (one of them locked), and armor for six men-at-arms (Icel. *sveinar*). There were also thirteen jugs, thirteen goblets, two tin goblets, ten tin plates, nine drinking horns, thirty-seven platters (some with unspecified images), twenty dishes (ten of them new), twenty wooden trays, sixty troughs, thirteen tubes, thirty bowls, three wooden bowls, twenty churners, twenty-four spoons, five small pots, one large pot, nine kettles, one linen cloth, twenty woolen cloths, and four towels. In addition to this, there were three grinders: one for mustard, another for pepper, and the third for malt. Finally, there was about 20 kg of wax.[58] Again, all these items highlight the wealth of Möðruvallaklaustur, particularly after its long period of disruption. Furthermore, although it was operated mainly as a monastic school, it does not appear to have been less well-equipped than the other monasteries in Iceland.

For Iceland's four other Augustinian monasteries, all of which were located in Skálholt diocese, a number of inventories were compiled: for Helgafellsklaustur *c.* 1274, *c.* 1377–1378, and 1397; for Þykkvabæjarklaustur, in 1340 and 1523; and for Viðeyjarklaustur, in 1234, 1313, and 1367, but as has been noted previously, no inventory exists for Skriðuklaustur. The 1184 list of possession, made when Helgafellsklaustur was moved from Flatey island to the mainland, shows that there were already one hundred books, in addition to four church bells, a shrine, a variety of household equipment, livestock totaling sixty animals, two boats, and seal nets.[59]

The first formal inventory was, on the other hand, compiled on behalf of Bishop Árni Þorláksson in the late thirteenth century, but unfortunately, it covers only the possessions of the monastic church and nothing else. It thus appears as though there were very few buildings at Helgafell so early on or that they simply did not matter for the bishop's accounting. However, the church of Helgafellsklaustur was already well equipped around 1274. By then, it owned one chalice of gold and five silver chalices, of which two were gilded but three were not. There were six church bells and one altar stone, in addition to two shrines – instead of one in 1184. Furthermore, the church owned garments for twelve monks, as well as nine gowns.[60] This demonstrates impressive growth during a difficult period. At the time, Hallur Gissurarson – brother of the bishop of Skálholt, Magnús Gissurarson – was abbot there (r. 1221–1225) while simultaneously serving as abbot of Þykkvabæjarklaustur (r. 1224–1230).

It was not until the *Staðamál* were settled around 1300 that a shift in the operation of Helgafellsklaustur became particularly noticeable. Around this time, in 1308, the church was enlarged, and several new contracts were made with corrodians. Luckily, the second and third inventories were made after that time, namely, in 1377–1378 and 1397. The exact date of the 1377–1378 inventory is not known with any certainty. It is thought to have been made initially by Bishop Gyrðir Ívarsson (r. 1350–1360) but subsequently amended to include some later additions because the list of properties owned by Helgafellsklaustur included farms acquired around 1377–1378.[61] The inventory from 1397, on the other hand, was compiled after the well-recorded visitation of Bishop Vilchin around his diocese of Skálholt. Judging by the 1377–1378 inventory, the number of furnishings and possessions owned by Helgafellsklaustur appears to have grown enormously during the single century that had passed since the previous inventory had been compiled in 1274 (Figure 6.3). Nonetheless, as before, the inventory from 1377 to 1378 covers only the furniture and possessions of the church. By then, there were vestments for fifteen clerics, twenty chasubles, fourteen gowns, twelve robes, four dalmatics, and a variety of other ecclesiastical cloths for the altars (Table 8.1). There were three likenesses: one each of St. Augustine, Bishop Jón, and St. Olaf, King of Norway. There were also two crosses (one of them a large one), seven chalices (one of them gilded), one pax, one censer, one shrine, four antependia, an unspecified number of books, and tableware.[62]

By the time Bishop Vilchin compiled his inventory a few years later, the possessions of Helgafellsklaustur had continued to increase, but it should be borne in mind that his inventory is much more detailed than its predecessors. In 1397, Helgafellsklaustur owned garments for thirty monks, as compared with twelve in 1275 and fifteen in 1378. These garments were kept in the church. Otherwise, the inventory from 1397 lists nearly the same number of other ecclesiastical clothes as in 1378 (see Table 8.1). However, this was certainly not all. In the church were three antependia, which were embroidered with images of the Apostles, as well as two other larger antependia and six smaller ones.[63] Other valuable items included in Bishop Vilchin's inventory were ecclesiastical cloths of various kinds for covering

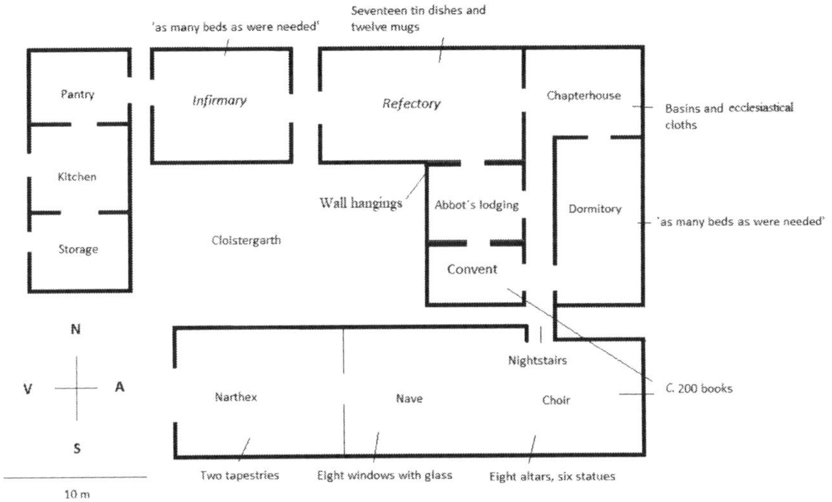

FIGURE 6.3 A plan of the building of Helgafellsklaustur, based on the inventory of 1397.

the altar and other similar purposes, an altarpiece, eight chalices, two pax boards, one liturgical basin for handwashing, and four crosses with and without figures of saints. Furthermore, there were three statues of the Virgin Mary and one each of St. Augustine, Bishop Jón, and St. Olaf King of Norway, iron candlesticks standing around the statues, twelve church bells (five of them small), four altar stones, two crosiers, five iron plates for making the communion bread, and one baptismal font.[64] The library's books had doubled in number from the time of its move: according to Vilchin's inventory, it held nearly 200 books, including twenty-five missals, thirty-five books in Old Norse and 100 in Latin, and a number of unspecified ecclesiastical books. Eight glass windows were also listed in the church. Interestingly, listed among Helgafellsklaustur's possessions in 1397 were two boats, just as it had at the time of the moving from Flatey in 1184.[65]

The inventory of 1397 also reveals that the monastic church at Helgafellsklaustur was divided into three parts – a choir, a nave, and a narthex – as monastic churches were traditionally divided. Interestingly, these details are not mentioned in earlier documents and therefore do not appear until almost a century after the church was enlarged. It is not certain what the extension entailed, but it is possible that the narthex was added at that point since it was not mentioned until 1397. In any case, the extension was significant enough to require re-consecration of the church.[66] In 1397, there were six altars in the church, and two of the narthex walls were covered with 'good' tapestries – as is specifically noted in the inventory. This was certainly not all; attention should be drawn to how many precious fabrics, both wall hangings and cloths, Helgafellsklaustur owned. The abbot's lodgings, the sacristy, the 'convent' [*sic*] and a room named *miklastofa* were all furnished with fabric wall hangings. These were the rooms the bishop's agent entered after he had registered the valuables in the church.[67]

According to this, it seems that the church took up the southern wing of the monastic complex, as was the case at Skriðuklaustur. In the eastern wing were the abbot's lodgings, and next to them was the 'convent'. In the northern wing were the chapterhouse and the *miklastofa*. More rooms are listed, such as the dormitory, which must also have been located in the eastern wing next to the abbot's lodgings and the 'convent'. Between these rooms and the dormitory were the night stairs leading to the church. In the abbot's lodgings and the 'convent' were pillows, bolsters, blankets, and even a considerable part of the library. In the chapterhouse were basins and some cloths, and in the dormitory were as many beds 'as were needed', according to the inventory. The *miklastofa* seems to have been the refectory of the monastery because seventeen tin dishes and twelve mugs were stored there.[68]

The name *miklastofa* appears not only at Helgafellsklaustur and Möðruvallaklaustur but also at Þykkvabæjarklaustur. However, at Þykkvabæjarklaustur, both a *miklastofa* and a refectory are mentioned in the inventory made by Bishop Jón Indriðason in 1340. It is thus difficult to identify the exact purpose of the two rooms in Þykkvabæjarklaustur because the inventory does not list the specific items stored in them. In Bishop Vilchin's inventory of Helgafellsklaustur from 1397, *mikliskáli* is mentioned but there it seems to have been some sort of infirmary or guesthouse, or the room where the laity lived. In it, were as many beds 'as was required'.[69] The difference between *mikliskáli* and *miklastofa* is otherwise not clear. In the case of Helgafellsklaustur, houses for corrodians were first mentioned in 1390, and then again in 1493, 1497, 1508, and 1513. The more household rooms, such as storage chambers and the kitchen, are not mentioned at all, but they must have been there as well.

As was done in the inventories of a few other monastic institutions, the silver owned by Helgafellsklaustur is listed last as a separate entry in Bishop Vilchin's inventory from 1397, not in the context of any of the rooms mentioned earlier. The list includes a silver cup, three silver gilt drinking horns, seven silver vessels, two beakers, two bowls, and seven silver spoons. On the same list is a *propitiatorium* with silver, a censer, a silver gilt wooden cup, one cup of gold, a crucifix with silver fasteners, a likeness of St. John the Baptist with alabaster, and finally, four candlesticks with copper.[70] It is not surprising that there was a precious likeness of St. John the Baptist in Helgafellsklaustur and that it was included on the list of silver the monastery owned, because the church itself was dedicated to him.

The two inventories preserved from Þykkvabæjarklaustur are also very informative, displaying the furnishings of the monastic building in greater detail than in many other monasteries – again, they highlight the different approaches and interests of the bishops' agents. The inventories from Þykkvabæjarklaustur are also particularly interesting in light of the results of the aforementioned geophysical survey of its ruins at Fornufjós, undertaken by the MMI project (see Figure 5.2). Moreover, as in Helgafellsklaustur, the tapestries and wall hangings are very important entries in the inventories from Þykkvabæjarklaustur. Once again, it may be inferred that they were produced by the nuns in Kirkjubæjarklaustur, although the possibility cannot be excluded that some of the fabric may have been imported. At least some of the material used in the production, such as the silk, linen, and ingredients for some of the dyes, must have been imported – as was necessary for the book production that also took place in some of the Icelandic monasteries. On the other hand, wool was plentiful, for example, at Kirkjubæjarklaustur (see Chapter 8).

In the church of Þykkvabæjarklaustur, for example, there were thirty chasubles, twenty-nine gowns, thirty antependia, eleven robes, and nineteen dalmatics in 1340 (see Table 8.1). Additionally, in the monastic building, there were thirty beds and various kinds of blankets. Four of the beds were surrounded by wall hangings, as were the hall, the abbot's lodgings, the *miklastofa*, and the refectory (Figure 6.4). Apparently, there were clothes and spaces for thirty clerics, although some of them may have been deacons or novices. In addition to this, Þykkvabæjarklaustur owned seven chalices (five of them gilded), one corporal, one shrine, three crosses, three crosiers, ten church bells, and five likenesses: three of the Virgin Mary, one of St. John the Baptist, and one of St. Þorlákur. Furthermore, there were three crosses with the images of unnamed saints. The food was also listed. There were 105 kg of flour, 35 kg of butter, 3½ barrows of the dairy product *skyr*, nine carcasses of bulls and sheep, and the suet of seventy-five animals.[71]

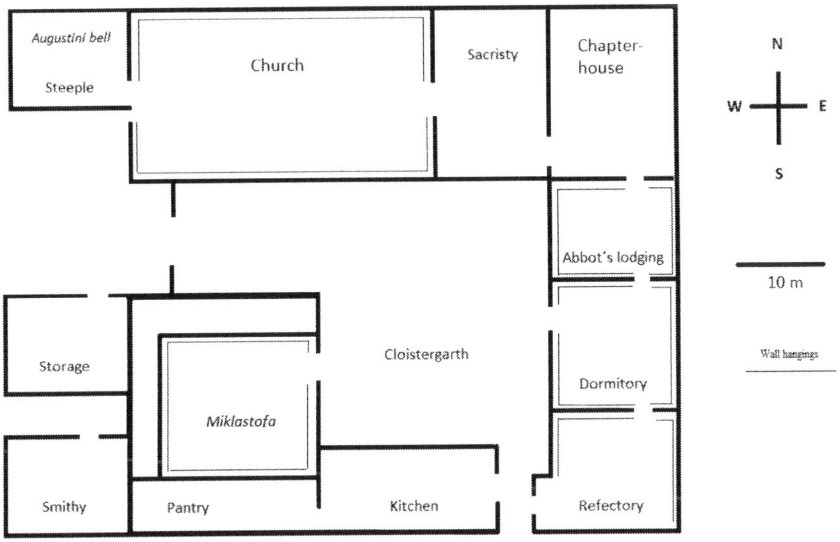

FIGURE 6.4 An illustration of the monastic building of Þykkvabæjarklaustur, based on the inventories of 1340 and 1523, and the results from the geophysical survey.

The latter inventory in Þykkvabæjarklaustur was made by Bishop Ögmundur Pálsson (r. 1521–1540) during his first visitation of his diocese of Skálholt in 1523. Apparently, as in the case of the other monastic houses, much had changed since the previous inventory, undertaken by Bishop Jón Indriðason (r. 1339–1341) in 1340. In 1523, there were twenty vestments rather than thirty, three robes instead of eleven, thirteen gowns instead of twenty-nine, and four priests' surplices that had not been on the list two centuries earlier. The nineteen dalmatics were gone. Nonetheless, there were twelve 'good' chasubles and three worse ones, two stoles, one miter, and one pair of gloves. Among other items were ten corporals, one *propitiatorium*, one cloth of silk, five piscina towels, six chalices, four censers, one shrine with two silver crosses, two alabaster altarpieces, three Irish crosses (one of them gilded), three altar stones, one baptismal font, four candlesticks, and two pax boards. In contrast to 1340, by 1523 there were only two statues of the Virgin Mary, although the monastery still possessed the likenesses of St. John the Baptist and St. Þorlákur, which were said to be old and made of wood. In 1523, however, there appear to have been nine new likenesses of both old and new saints. These were of Saints Augustine, Olaf, Andrew, Anne, Catherine, Veronica, and Roch. There were two likenesses of St. Augustine, one of which was large, polychromed and gilded, and there was even one new one of St. John the Baptist. There were also images of the Holy Trinity in the church.[72]

Apparently, the growth of Þykkvabæjarklaustur had reversed. There were only ten beds instead of the thirty listed in 1340 and relatively few chairs and blankets. However, while the religious members of the monastery were reduced in number, the tableware listed in the inventory of 1523 indicates that a large number of lay people may have resided there. In this inventory made by Bishop Ögmundur, fifteen table plates were listed, as well as thirteen small ones, and forty large wooden plates. In addition, sixteen drinking horns were recorded, along with six cups and twelve pitchers.[73] Drinking horns were extremely valuable at that time, particularly if they were carved and/or silver gilt. The carving on them was usually considered a great work of art.[74] In the smithy, numerous farming implements were listed, in addition to 1½ barrels of tar that must have been used to maintain the timber walls of the monastic building. Interestingly, full armor and equipment for up to ten men-at-arms appeared in Þykkvabæjarklaustur's inventory for the first time in 1523.[75] By then, Protestant-related unrest had begun to flare up on the Continent, which may have caused a decline in the activities at Þykkvabæjarklaustur, as at Reynistaðarklaustur. At any rate, it appears that the monks were better prepared for battle in 1523 than they had been previously.

The last Augustinian monastery included here is Viðeyjarklaustur. Its most detailed inventory was the last one, compiled in 1367 by Bishop Oddgeir Þorsteinsson (r. 1339–1341). Its properties had previously been counted at least twice, in 1234 and 1313. No interiors or furnishings were recorded on these two occasions, only farms and livestock.[76] However, as has previously been noted, Viðeyjarklaustur's founding charter from 1226 specified how the church was to be furnished, although it is not known whether the instructions were ever followed. According to the charter, the monastery should have possessed likenesses of Saints John the Baptist, Peter, Paul, Augustine, Martin, Nicholas, Þorlákur the Bishop, Agatha, Lucy, Stephen, Clement, Dionysius, Olaf, King of Norway, and Thomas.[77] In 1367, however, only two likenesses of saints were among its possessions, both of the Virgin Mary.[78] This is not surprising since the church at Viðeyjarklaustur was dedicated to her, but it may suggest that the church was never furnished as had been planned in 1226. The discovery of the figurine of St. Dorothy in the ruins of Viðeyjarklaustur indicates, however, that the inventories of the monastic institutions do not tell the whole story, although this particular likeness could certainly have been brought to the monastery after the fire in the church in *c.* 1495.

Although this inventory from 1367 generally does not record the names of specific rooms at Viðeyjarklaustur other than the church and the chapterhouse, in some cases the agreements, contracts, documented activities, and events recorded do mention a few, such as the abbot's lodgings, dormitory, hall, and a corrodian's house, in addition to the 'convent'. Some of these rooms are named, either for the first time or in a subsequent mention, in the context of the monastery's dissolution in 1539, when the monastic building were demolished by the Danish king's men (see Chapter 9).[79] Nothing in the 1367 inventory from Viðeyjarklaustur is otherwise unexpected in comparison with the inventories from Iceland's other monasteries. At that point, there were thirteen good chasubles and twelve in worse condition (see Table 8.1). In addition, there were sixteen vestments, seven dalmatics, twenty-one gowns, eleven robes, twelve antependia at the high altar with thirteen other embroidered cloths, four chalices, one large bowl of gold, three unnamed likenesses of silver, thirteen corporals, one red silk cloth, one crosier made of walrus tusk, nine candlesticks, six piscina towels, one pillow of silk, six liturgical books, an iron plate for making hosts, two censers, two cists in the church, twelve bells of two different sizes, an altarpiece over the altar, the two statues of the Virgin Mary, one cross over the high altar and another with saintly likenesses, three other crosses (one of them of gold), a crucifix in the chapterhouse, one baptismal font, one liturgical basin for handwashing, one shrine with relics, and some other smaller items. Finally, as in Helgafellsklaustur, the silver was listed separately – or at least some of it was, because silver items also appear on the other list. The main items on this list from Viðeyjarklaustur included five silver gilt drinking horns, eleven spoons, four bowls, another bowl with a silver lid, nine roses,[80] and two candlesticks.[81]

Notes

1 DI IX, pp. 305–307.
2 Kristjánsdóttir, *Leitin að klaustrunum*, pp. 198–199.
3 *Sturlunga saga*, pp. 554–555.
4 Kristjánsdóttir, *Leitin að klaustrunum*, p. 444.
5 Kristjánsdóttir, *Sagan af klaustrinu á Skriðu*, p. 80.
6 DI IX, p. 305.
7 DI IV, p. 374.
8 DI IX, pp. 305–307.
9 Teitsson, 'Bjarnarfeldir í máldögum', pp. 23–47.

10 DI IX, pp. 306–307, 317–318; Olmer, *Boksamlingar i Island 1149–1490*, pp. 71–76.
11 Jensson, 'Þingeyrar Abbey in Northern Iceland', pp. 152–160.
12 DI IV, p. 374.
13 DI V, pp. 471–472.
14 DI VI, p. 158.
15 Kristjánsdóttir, *Leitin að klaustrunum*, p. 546.
16 DI IX, p. 307.
17 Kristjánsdóttir, *Leitin að klaustrunum*, p. 164.
18 DI IX, pp. 307–308.
19 *Sturlunga saga*, p. 713.
20 DI III, pp. 761–762.
21 DI VI, p. 162.
22 DI IX, pp. 306–308.
23 DI IX, p. 308.
24 Wadmal.
25 DI IX, p. 308.
26 DI VI, pp. 684–685.
27 *Lárentíus saga*, p. 314.
28 Harðardóttir, 'Myndefni íslenskra klausturinnsigla', p. 220; Kristjánsdóttir, *Leitin að klaustrunum*, pp. 135, 155.
29 Oulíková, 'Sphragistic Artefacts of the Benedictines', pp. 378–379.
30 DI IX, pp. 313–316.
31 Kristjánsdóttir, *Leitin að klaustrunum*, p. 98.
32 *Lárentíus saga*, p. 332.
33 See DI II, pp. 304–314.
34 DI IX, pp. 312–314.
35 DI IX, p. 316.
36 DI IX, pp. 320–322.
37 DI III, pp. 717–718.
38 *Kúgildi* was a unit price used in trade. It is the value of one cow, or six ewes with wool and lambs.
39 DI IV, pp. 483–484.
40 See, for example, Harðardóttir, 'Myndefni íslenskra klausturinnsigla', p. 218.
41 Kristjánsdóttir, *Leitin að klaustrunum*, pp. 377–379.
42 DI VII, p. 232.
43 DI I, pp. 394–395.
44 DI II, p. 781; DI VIII, p. 5.
45 DI IV, p. 238.
46 DI IV, p. 238.
47 DI IV, p. 238; Mímisson and Einarsson, '"*Ora et labora*"', pp. 53–54.
48 Gilchrist, *Medieval Life. Archaeology and The Life Course*, pp. 96, 139, 172–174; Guest, 'Stained Glass and Liturgy', pp. 271–285; Kurmann-Schwarz, 'Gothic Stained Glass', p. 469; Ó Clabaigh, *The Friars in Ireland*, pp. 245–248.
49 DI IV, pp. 170–171.
50 Kristjánsdóttir, *Sagan af klaustrinu á Skriðu*, p. 88.
51 DI VII, p. 232.
52 DI III, p. 717.
53 DI VII, pp. 232–234.
54 DI IV, p. 471.
55 DI V, pp. 286–291; Olmer, *Boksamlingar i Island 1149–1490*, pp. 71–75.
56 Olmer, *Boksamlingar i Island 1149–1490*, pp. 67–68.
57 DI IX, pp. 316–318.
58 DI IX, p. 319.
59 DI I, pp. 281–282.

60 DI II, pp. 115–116.
61 See forewords written by Árni Magnússon in DI III, pp. 325–326.
62 DI III, pp. 328–329.
63 DI IV, pp. 169–170.
64 DI IV, p. 170.
65 DI IV, pp. 170–171.
66 See *Gottskálksannáll*, p. 341; *Flateyjarannáll* p. 391.
67 DI IV, p. 171.
68 DI IV, p. 171.
69 DI IV, p. 171.
70 DI IV, pp. 171–172.
71 DI II, pp. 738–739.
72 DI IX, pp. 190–191.
73 DI IX, pp. 191–192.
74 Magerøy, 'Islandsk hornskurd', pp. 34–36.
75 DI IX, p. 192.
76 DI I, p. 506; DI II, p. 337.
77 DI I, p. 498.
78 DI III, p. 214.
79 Kristjánsdóttir, *Leitin að klaustrunum*, pp. 338–342.
80 The privileged symbol of Virgin Mary.
81 DI III, pp. 213–215.

7

DISRUPTIVE EVENTS

The Icelandic monastic houses were far from immune to disruptive events, making their stories so varied. The residents of the monasteries were involved in a wide range of activities, both virtuous and sinful, while nonetheless striving to follow medieval Christian doctrine and the monastic agenda. In this context, it is particularly interesting to observe how religious servants, as well as the laity, dealt with various calamitous setbacks caused by events beyond their control. One of the worst catastrophes the monastic institutions in Iceland were forced to face was the Black Death, referred to here as the plague. This deadly pandemic struck Iceland twice during the Middle Ages. The first wave struck soon after 1400, some decades after it had swept through most of Europe, and the second came towards the end of the fifteenth century. The monasteries also endured scandals, were hit by destructive fires or storms, and suffered internal conflicts over their general operations. For example, the convent of Reynistaðarklaustur in northern Iceland was twice beset by pregnancies, and sensational disputes arose between the Hólar bishops and the priors at Möðruvallaklaustur after they lost their building and all its contents in a fire in 1316. We call to mind that Munkaþverárklaustur was also destroyed by a deadly fire in 1429, and two churches on monastic sites burned down – the first at Þingeyraklaustur in 1157 and the second at Viðeyjarklaustur around 1495 – although the other buildings of those monasteries escaped the flames. The vicious storm that blew Möðruvallaklaustur church to pieces in 1421 should be listed here as well. Several other sudden events occurred, causing varying degrees of devastation. Yet despite various tragedies, the monasteries did not lose their public trust or their assets until the Reformation.

Catastrophic Fire in Hítardalur 1148

The fires at Þingeyraklaustur, Möðruvallaklaustur, Munkaþverárklaustur, and Viðeyjarklaustur have already been mentioned several times before in this book.

DOI: 10.4324/9781003361077-7

One fire, however, has not yet been cited as a monastic site because it took place not in a monastic building but rather at the farm of Hítardalur, where Hítardalsklaustur was established shortly thereafter. The fire can tell us quite a bit about the ideas held in medieval Iceland about human sin and how it might be mitigated by good works in the name of God. It broke out late in the evening on Michaelmas, 30 September 1148. The annals claimed it started because a bolt of lightning hit the farmstead's living quarters,[1] a large hall or a longhouse that most likely was built of turf, driftwood, and stones, as was the custom. There, chieftain Þorleifur beiskaldi Þorláksson held feasts for those traveling between the south and the west of Iceland. Hítardalur was his residence, but for long periods before and after the fire, it was also a well-known stopover on the main route between the cathedral of Skálholt and the West Fjords.

It is, in fact, not surprising that written documents of the time claim that a tragedy on such a scale had never happened before in Iceland. Over seventy men perished in the fire, eight of them priests from churches within the diocese of Skálholt.[2] Among the dead was Bishop Magnús Einarsson (r. 1134–1148) himself, who was in Hítardalur that fateful evening. He, his priests from Skálholt diocese, and their entourage were staying together there, as they commonly did.[3] There were a few survivors, including the host himself, Þorleifur beiskaldi, who managed to escape the burning house along with several guests by slipping through a gap that was made in the roof of the longhouse. Bishop Magnús refused to leave the hall, however, claiming that this was God's will, and consequently died in the fire.[4]

The actual size of the longhouse in Hítardalur is not known, so it is difficult to speculate how many people could gather there. The ruins of the burnt hall were not found during the MMI project despite an intensive search; however, the remains of a longhouse built immediately after the fire, still visible in 1891, were 30 m in length.[5] It is thus possible that the longhouse lost in the 1148 fire was of a similar size. A longhouse of the same length has been excavated at Hofstaðir in the Mývatn area in northern Iceland. It was used until the late twelfth century to hold large feasts, much like the longhouse in Hítardalur, so the two may have been comparable in size.[6] In any event, it is likely that the deaths in the Hítardalur fire in 1148 were due to toxic fumes produced by the burning turf rather than to the fire itself. It is not known where the bodies of those who died in the fire were buried, so the cause of death has not been examined scientifically.

There is no reason to doubt the death toll because the side effects of this accident were long-lasting and highly significant, lending credence to the descriptions of the incident. The fire in Hítardalur may have been one of the most disastrous in the history of Iceland. It appears to have had a profound impact on the Icelandic Church, the development of monasticism in Iceland, and Icelandic society in general long afterwards. One of the decisions made by the surviving episcopal authorities was to establish a monastery, the first one in Skálholt diocese, at the farm in Hítardalur in order to propitiate for the deadly fire, which was immediately interpreted as God's punishment for the sins of humankind. Bishop Magnús Einarsson was believed to have had plans to establish the first monastic house in the southern diocese (there were already two in the northern bishopric) in the Westman Islands, but obviously, his untimely death put an end to these plans. It therefore seems likely that Þorleifur beiskaldi decided to donate his farm, where Bishop Magnús died according to God's will, to the Church in order to establish the monastery there rather than in the Westman Islands.[7] It was the bishop's successor in Skálholt, Klængur Þorsteinsson (r. 1152–1176), who fulfilled these wishes and established this third monastery in Iceland at Hítardalur in 1166, twenty years after the fire.

There were other even more momentous side effects of the fire. The loss of so many serving clergymen caused a general dearth of priests in Skálholt diocese. In fact, the shortage was so dire that it was decided to allow all those who wished to serve as priests or deacons be consecrated even if they were not old enough.[8] There was no bishop at Skálholt for four years after the fire, until Bishop Klængur was consecrated by Archbishop Eskil in Niðarós in 1152. In the meantime, the bishop of Hólar, Björn Gilsson (r. 1147–1162), carried out the tasks of the bishop of Skálholt. These included consecrating all the new priests and deacons, which was accomplished in a single ceremony in 1151.[9] One of the young men chosen to become a priest on this occasion was, in fact, Þorlákur Þórhallsson, who later became bishop of Skálholt and, as is described in Chapter 3, profoundly influenced the development of the Church in Iceland during his term, which lasted from 1178 to 1193.

Þorlákur was only nineteen years old when he was consecrated as a priest. At that time, he was studying for the priesthood at Oddi in Rangárvellir, but afterwards, he moved abroad for further studies (most likely between 1155 and 1160). In his bishops' saga, *Þorláks saga helga*, it is emphasized that Þorlákur had met high-level ecclesiastical officials during his six-year stay in Paris, then main center of clerical education in Europe. This shaped both him as an individual and his views on the operation of the Church.[10] As has been described previously, when Þorlákur finally took office as a bishop in Skálholt bishopric, he immediately began to reform the Church there in accordance with the knowledge he had gained during his studies abroad. Consequently, the monasteries were strongly affected by his ecclesiastical reforms. We should recall here that Snorri Sturluson was also educated at Oddi, three decades after Þorlákur obtained his education there. Both became prestigious leaders in Iceland: Þorlákur of the Church and Snorri as a lawspeaker and a chieftain.[11]

The well-known success of Þingeyraklaustur may have led people to hope they could avoid supernatural events such as the one occurring at Hítardalur in September 1148. Medieval Christians believed strongly that all kinds of setbacks could be mitigated by good deeds done in the name of God.[12] When Þingeyraklaustur was established in 1112, it was claimed to have been founded specifically for the spiritual purpose of improving living conditions in Iceland, although political and economic factors must also have been pivotal in decisions as significant as the founding of a monastic institution.[13] Environmental factors had, in fact, been unfavorable for Icelanders for some time. For example, the eruption of Mt Hekla in 1104 had caused serious harm to the vegetation in large areas of the island. Furthermore, inclement weather had caused harvest failures and other difficulties in the agricultural sector on which Icelanders relied so strongly. Fishing became more difficult for the same reason.[14]

Otherwise, very little is known about the activities of Hítardalsklaustur during its short period of operation from 1166 to –1201, perhaps because of the shortage of written documents from this early period. It does not seem to have been operated as a proper monastery after 1201, when there were no longer any resident abbots. Instead, there were only sub-abbots, the last of whom was the chieftain Runólfur Sighvatsson, who is mentioned in written sources as late as 1237.[15] Nor are there any other documents recording the monastery's supposed activities, such as investments in farms or religious donations, unlike what is preserved from other monastic institutions from the same period. As has previously been suggested, the *Staðamál* disputes appear to have eroded general support for the operation of Hítardalsklaustur.

However, even after the deadly fire, Hítardalur remained a regularly used stopover place for those traveling between the south and west in Iceland. It was located on one of the main routes across the island, and the fire did not change that. For instance, Bishop Páll Jónsson rested for four weeks in Hítardalur when he suddenly became ill while returning home to Skálholt from a visitation to the West Fjords in 1211. Bishop Páll managed to reach Skálholt shortly before his death, but no monastery is mentioned in context of his final stay in Hítardalur, only the farmstead, which apparently had gained the status of *beneficium*.[16] More than four decades had passed since the monastery there had been founded, but it seems at least to have stopped functioning as a proper monastic institution some time before the ill bishop lay there. Nevertheless, the cornerstone with the carved face preserved at Hítardalur indicates probably the spot where the building of Hítardalsklaustur stood, thereby providing some confirmation of the monastery's existence and perhaps the location of the longhouse destroyed in the fire.

Monasteries on Fire

Other fires deserve to be discussed in detail here, particularly those at Möðruvallaklaustur and Munkaþverárklaustur, because they also had consequences for monastic Iceland, albeit to a different degree and in another manner than the fire in Hítardalur. Virtually nothing is known about the fires in Þingeyraklaustur in 1157 and Viðeyjarklaustur in 1495, but the damage they caused may have been minimal. In the case of Þingeyraklaustur, Bishop Finnur Jónsson's ecclesiastical history of Iceland records only the year of the fire, nothing else.[17] Similarly, the fire in Viðeyjarklaustur's church is recorded only through a single letter, which confirmed the ownership of driftwood to be used for its reconstruction.[18] The 1316 fire in Möðruvallaklaustur, on the other hand, caused a bitter and long-lasting struggle between the bishop of Hólar and the canons. As we will see, the archbishop of Niðarós had to intervene frequently in the dispute, and the monastery stopped functioning for an entire decade as a result of the fire. Still, none of these three fires was fatal, unlike those at Munkaþverárklaustur and Hítardalur.

The protracted struggle caused by the fire in Möðruvallaklaustur gives an indication of how heavily the monastery there relied on the support and interests of the serving bishops in Hólar. It is important recalling the situation in Munkaþverárklaustur, where Bishop Brandur Sæmundarson of Hólar allowed its building to collapse and neglected to appoint a new abbot when the incumbent died in 1196. The reasons for the lack of interest in operating Munkaþverárklaustur and Möðruvallaklaustur differed, though.[19] Möðruvallaklaustur was founded on the initiative of the bishop of Hólar, Jörundur Þorsteinsson (r. 1267–1313), whose apparent intention from the outset was to open a school in Möðruvellir – a *scola claustrum* – for the purpose of educating priests to serve in his diocese. Demand for educated clerics was increasing quickly at that time, in line with the growth of the Church in the wake of the *Staðamál*.[20]

While it was common on the Continent to operate monastic schools in the cathedrals themselves, they were often found in both Augustinian and Benedictine monasteries as well. But operating a proper school required good libraries.[21] The Augustinian monastery at Möðruvellir definitely had one – at least it did later on. When the titles were recorded in 1461, it contained 114 books, which made it the second-largest monastic library in Iceland; the largest one was always based at Helgafellsklaustur. Helgafellsklaustur was, moreover, the only monastery in Iceland that can with certainty be linked to the Order of St. Victor, which was known for its emphasis on clerical education.[22] In any case, according to written documents, Bishop Jörundur appears early on to have been enthusiastic about operating such a school for his future canons, who would serve the episcopal area within Hólar diocese. He had planned to open a school of this kind for the cathedral clergy in Hólar as early as 1267, and he even obtained the archbishop's permission for it, as canon law stipulated. However, the establishment of a cathedral school under his protection at his episcopal see did not take place at that time, most likely because of the disagreement between the Icelandic authorities and Archbishop Jón II rauði (the red) (r. 1267–1282).[23]

Nevertheless, Bishop Jörundur's plans came to fruition before the end of the thirteenth century with the establishment of the canon school at Möðruvellir in Hörgárdalur valley, which was called Möðruvallaklaustur from then on. This was in 1296, when Archbishop Jón II rauði had been replaced by Archbishop Jörundur (r. 1287–1309), the namesake of Bishop Jörundur in Hólar. The bishop himself became abbot of the canon school, and priors oversaw the monastery itself. According to a charter written in the context of Möðruvallaklaustur's founding in 1296, when the profits from the home farm at Möðruvellir were deemed insufficient start-up capital for the school's operation, Bishop Jörundur provided additional resources that he took from the episcopal see itself.[24] A year later, in 1297, Bishop Jörundur hired the first prior, Teitur, to take charge of the canon school in Möðruvellir. The bishop also arranged for the construction of a church, together with all that was needed for the new institution. The church was first used for a service in the monastery in 1302.[25]

The plan to found and operate a canon school at Möðruvellir seems to have been well received and generally accepted initially, but later it turned out to be the opposite. Bishop Jörundur died in 1313 at the age of eighty-three and was succeeded by Auðun rauði (r. 1313–1322), who had previously served as a canon at the cathedral of Niðarós and was thus one of the foreign bishops appointed to office in Iceland after 1238. In contrast to Bishop Jörundur's preferences, Bishop Auðun rauði wanted to have the school located at the bishop's seat in Hólar rather than in Möðruvellir. However, there were times when Auðun seemed to be opposed to the school's operation altogether. For example, he accused Prior Teitur and his canons, who oversaw the operation of Möðruvallaklaustur, of having been inattentive to their tasks following the death of Bishop Jörundur. Rumors were circulating about inadequate management at the school, which must have encouraged the bishop to actively think about moving it to Hólar, and he frequently expressed his concerns about the high cost of operating the school at Möðruvellir. This gave rise to serious disputes between the bishop and Prior Teitur. Among the bones of contention was not only Möðruvallaklaustur's location but also the properties Bishop Jörundur had taken from the episcopal see itself in Hólar and given to the school in 1296. Included in the grants were the associated rights to the driftwood and whales found on their beaches. The bishop wanted all these earnings to revert to his episcopal institution in Hólar.[26] It is worth drawing the attention to it here that when the trouble began at Möðruvallaklaustur, Bishop Auðun was already embroiled in a dispute with the abbot and monks of Þingeyraklaustur, in a bid to reclaim the capital given to that monastery by Bishop Jón Ögmundsson nearly 200 years earlier.[27]

It was around this time that Möðruvallaklaustur burnt down. The building were destroyed, including the church with all the relics, ornaments, and interior furnishings Bishop Jörundur had provided. Soon after this disastrous event, which occurred on 16 September 1316, Bishop Auðun rauði blamed the canons themselves for having burnt down their own monastery after getting drunk during a visit to the trading harbor at Gásir, on the coast of Eyjafjörður. Later, when the incident was still under investigation by the clerical authorities in both Iceland and Norway, the turn of events was described in detail by Auðun rauði's successor, Bishop Lárentíus Kálfsson (r. 1324–1331). In fact, Lárentíus stressed that his account was based on what Auðun rauði told him before his death in 1322. In that account, Bishop Lárentíus said that on the night in question, the canons had handled lit candles carelessly after their return from Gásir. A fire broke out and spread quickly to the tapestry in the choir, and from there into the sacristy, whereupon it became utterly uncontrollable.[28]

To this day, no one knows exactly what happened. Bishop Auðun rauði knew well that if Möðruvallaklaustur were to continue operating, considerable money would have to be spent on its reconstruction. Ornaments and church furnishings would also have to be provided again by the bishopric of Hólar. However, while this certainly could have been arranged, the damage caused by the fire was more than merely financial. The reputation of the monastery – and the bishopric as well – had suffered a serious setback. It was always possible to build new houses, but respect and reputation were more difficult to regain. Sadly, less than two decades after Möðruvallaklaustur was founded, there was neither a monastic building nor any canons left. Two of the canons, Þorgeir and Þórður, took office in nearby churches. Two others, Þorbjörn and Brandur, went home to Hólar but died shortly thereafter. The fifth, Ingimundur Skútuson, left the country and became a monk in the monastery at Helgisetur in Trondheim, Norway.[29] Prior Teitur seems to have died the same year the fire broke out, as he disappears from the record after 1316.[30]

The consequences of the Möðruvallaklaustur fire soon became a kind of never-ending story because the canons refused to accept the accusations levelled against them by the bishop. In 1324, when Lárentíus was in Niðarós for his own consecration as bishop, Ingimundur Skútuson, the canon who had fled to Helgisetur monastery after being expelled by Auðun rauði from Möðruvallaklaustur, popped up once again. Ingimundur was lodging a complaint with the archbishop, Eilífur korti Árnason (r. 1311–1332), stating that the school at Möðruvellir had been closed down without the archbishop's approval. Moreover, Ingimundur contended that Bishop Auðun had stolen all the earnings from Möðruvallaklaustur's properties after the fire in 1316. In the defense against these accusations, the incoming candidate for the episcopal see in Hólar, Lárentíus, claimed that he was completely innocent of the charges because the decision had been solely in the hands of Bishop Auðun. However, Archbishop Eilífur took the matter into his own hands and appointed the bishop of Skálholt, Jón Halldórsson, and the abbot of Þykkvabæjarklaustur, Þorlákur Loftsson, to be the negotiators and judges – *judices delegati* – in this complex matter. Obviously, the new bishop of Hólar, Lárentíus, was not permitted to participate in the investigation. The archbishop demanded, moreover, that Bishop Lárentíus would reconstruct the monastery at Möðruvellir and immediately return its property, providing it with new cloths and relics. The bishop eventually did as he was ordered to do, and Möðruvallaklaustur was at last reopened in a new building in 1326, ten years after the fire. Even Ingimundur Skútuson and two of the canons, Þorgeir and Þórður, returned to it. The archbishop had claimed that if they were guilty of the fire, they were best kept in a monastic institution anyway. In fact, Þorgeir was appointed as prior.[31]

The repercussions of the Möðruvallaklaustur fire were far from over at this point. Indeed, the bishop's interference in the monastery's operation continued as never before, which was perhaps to be expected, but the bishop's concerns seem to have extended well beyond regular administrative work. Although Bishop Lárentíus had reopened the monastery in 1326, in accordance with Archbishop Eilífur korti Árnason's orders, he apparently did not trust the canons to operate it properly. He therefore decided, since he was forced to pay for the operation of Möðruvallaklaustur anyway, to move the school from there to Hólar. He sent the two negotiators, Jón and Þorlákur, to Möðruvellir on 29 July 1327 with a formal contract (*pactum*) providing for the transfer of Möðruvallaklaustur to the bishop's seat at Hólar. Once again, the move was opposed by the prior, Þorgeir, and the other canons.

Subsequently, it was decided to send two new negotiators, the priests Egill Eyjólfsson and Arngrímur, to the archbishop in Niðarós in order to settle the case.[32]

Meanwhile, Prior Þorgeir and Bishop Lárentíus continued their quarrel, obviously disagreeing about the division of power between them. Bishop Lárentíus stated officially that the canons had full authority over the ecclesiastical affairs of their monastery, but notably not over affairs such as its financial management. He referred to both Bishop Jón Ögmundsson and the Order of St. Augustine in support of his case.[33] Furthermore, the bishop underlined that if the canons lacked necessary items such as furniture, clothing, or food, they should simply request them from Hólar. Prior Þorgeir claimed that the bishop had never returned all the money the monastery initially received, as he had promised the archbishop he would, and that Möðruvallaklaustur was suffering financially as a result. He had already appealed to Bishop Jón Halldórsson of Skálholt, whom the archbishop had previously appointed as one of two negotiators to solve the initial dispute between the bishop and the prior. Bishop Jón was quick to respond and gave Möðruvallaklaustur a gilded chalice and two chasubles as compensation for the losses inflicted on the canons by Bishop Lárentíus.

While the case was being discussed once again at the seat of the archbishopric of Niðarós, Bishop Lárentíus decided around Easter 1328 to ride to Möðruvallaklaustur to see if all was well there. He claimed that he had heard rumors about a shortage of hay and food at the monastery and wanted to investigate the cause – in particular, to determine whether the shortage was due to continuing carelessness on the part of the canons, such as that which had caused the fire in 1316. However, this action by the bishop and the suggestion that the reported lack of hay and food was the canons' own fault can hardly be regarded as anything but mistrust of them, after all that had happened in the past. The canons at Möðruvallaklaustur knew that the bishop was coming for a visit and immediately prepared their protest against him. By the time he arrived, a large group of farmers from both Hörgárdalur and Eyjafjörður, as many as forty people, had joined them and were guarding the monastery. There was no welcoming procession staged to mark Bishop Lárentíus' arrival at Möðruvallaklaustur, as there should have been. And this was not all; the canons protested further. They did not greet the bishop when he entered the church, and when he sat down for a meal in the *miklastofa*, the canons served far better food to the farmers than to the bishop himself.[34] Such support from the local community is well known from monastic houses in Denmark and England.[35] In fact, this protest is also reminiscent of the Þingeyraklaustur canons' response ten years earlier, when Bishop Auðun visited their monastery in 1318, intending to discuss the initial financial support the monastery had received from Bishop Jón Ögmundsson of Hólar. On that occasion, just as during the visit to Möðruvallaklaustur in 1328, the bishop was met by neighboring farmers – these from Vatnsdalur, the valley nearest Þingeyraklaustur – who had gathered to guard the monastery. Bishop Auðun was not received with a procession upon his arrival at Þingeyraklaustur, as he should have been, nor was he served a meal like the one the farmers received from the canons.[36]

The incident in Þingeyraklaustur in 1318 was resolved with assistance from the archbishop of Niðarós and settled in favor of the monastery, but the story of the Möðruvallaklaustur incident did not end well for Prior Þorgeir and his canons. After being deeply insulted at Möðruvallaklaustur, Bishop Lárentíus had had enough, and he fled to Abbot Bergur Sokkason at Munkaþverárklaustur, located nearby in Eyjafjörður. He stayed there for two nights rather than staying at Möðruvallaklaustur, as he had planned. He then returned to the monastery in Möðruvellir, by which time the farmers had all left. Bishop Lárentíus insisted on a meeting with Prior Þorgeir and his canons in the chapterhouse and demanded to examine their hay and food supplies. They refused. Bishop Lárentíus then fired Prior Þorgeir and immediately appointed another man, Steindór Sokkason, to replace him.[37]

What makes this act rather suspicious is that Steindór Sokkason was the brother of Bergur Sokkason, abbot of Munkaþverárklaustur, where Bishop Lárentíus had stayed the night before. However, in the autumn of 1329, the two negotiators, Egill and Arngrímur, returned to Iceland from the archbishop of Niðarós with the news that the monastery would not be moved to Hólar. This was the end of that story. Egill even received a silver bowl and a book on canon law from the archbishop for his splendid and successful work.[38] Egill later succeeded Lárentíus as bishop of Hólar. Prior Steindór, however, retained his post from 1328 to 1352. In the end, he was forced to resign when a new bishop of Hólar, Ormur Ásláksson, once again planned to move Möðruvallaklaustur to the bishop's seat. This was in 1349, the year the plague ravaged Norway.[39] The move never took place, perhaps because of the chaotic situation at the archbishopric's seat in Niðarós in the wake of the epidemic. Thus, the school at Möðruvallaklaustur was always based in Hörgárdalur, until it was permanently closed shortly after the Reformation.

The circumstances surrounding the destruction of Munkaþverárklaustur in a fire in 1429 were totally different from those at Möðruvallaklaustur. The Munkaþverárklaustur fire did not have any negative or long-term consequences beyond the terrible loss of life. The Benedictine monks in Munkaþverárklaustur were much more independent than the Augustinians in the canon school of Möðruvallaklaustur because the Benedictines were commonly not subject to episcopal authority. The fire of Munkaþverárklaustur broke out in its building on a February evening in 1429. Just as in Möðruvallaklaustur, the blaze devoured everything. Worse, two monks perished. One of the surviving monks was Þorgils, who had served as a prior in the monastery, but he was so badly injured that for a while he was not expected to survive. He did survive, however, and, shortly after the fire he was appointed as abbot there, but he never recovered physically from the fire and died after serving in office for only four years. Still, this was an important period of recovery for the monastery, as we will see.[40]

This second time Munkaþverárklaustur was in danger of closing, the monks managed to rebuild their institution with steadfast assistance from the bishop of Hólar, Jón Craxton. Craxton and Abbot Þorgils were obviously looking to the future. It was at this point that a brand new altarpiece, produced in Nottingham, was purchased for the new monastic church. It is one of the three English alabaster altarpieces that have survived in Iceland. Bishop Jón Craxton also registered the possessions of Munkaþverárklaustur late in 1429, the same year the fire broke out. The inventory lists nineteen chasubles, eighteen gowns, three robes, five vestments, eight cloths for the altar, one candlestick, and two unspecified likenesses, including one retable with a sculpted likeness of the Virgin.[41] The alabaster altarpiece is not on the list, however, and was clearly not acquired by the monastery until shortly afterwards. Hence, as we saw from the inventories listed in Chapter 6, Munkaþverárklaustur did recover successfully, but it took a while.

The Plague

It was rare for a Benedictine monastery of Munkaþverárklaustur's scale to be overseen not by an abbot but by a prior, as was the case when the fire broke out in 1429. A prior is usually the head of a priory, and Munkaþverárklaustur was never a priory. Still, the prior was always the second in command in proper monasteries, and his task was to assist the abbot and act as his deputy, just a prioress was second in command in a female convent. The reason for the arrangement in Munkaþverárklaustur may have been that the last serving abbot, Hallur, had died during the outbreak of plague in northern Iceland in 1402. The monk Þorgils was appointed as prior to temporarily take care of financial matters and the daily operation of the monastery; thus, Munkaþverárklaustur had no abbot for twenty-seven years, until Prior Þorgils was made abbot after the fire in 1429.[42]

This situation shows how long it took Munkaþverárklaustur to recover from the plague, but in fact, it took a while for most of the other monastic houses in Iceland to recover as well, not least due to the loss of both lay and religious personnel. It appears, however, that even though the monasteries lost many of their own people, they reaped enormous financial benefits from the epidemic at the same time, as people believed that donations to ecclesiastical institutions would put an end to the plague, which was generally viewed as divine punishment for the sins of humans. It is appropriate noting, though, that the plague was not the only catastrophic event that encouraged the giving of gifts to ecclesiastical institutions. Other epidemics had the same effect. The unnamed man who requested burial in the narthex of the church of Reynistaðarklaustur in 1431 offers a good example. The wording of his will suggests that he was either ill with smallpox or simply afraid of catching it, as Iceland was in the throes of a widespread smallpox outbreak at the time.[43]

How and where the plague eventually reached Iceland is yet an unsolved mystery. Caused by the bacterium *Yersinia pestis*, it is known to appear in at least three distinct contagious forms that spread in different ways: from rats, from fleas carried by the rats, through the air, or through contact with human body fluids.[44] There were no rats in Iceland during the Middle Ages – at least, no rat bones have yet been discovered in archaeological excavations in the country. Although the progression of the disease is considered to have been short, only a few days, people could nonetheless have been infected while aboard a ship sailing to Iceland and have arrived alive but contagious. It is even plausible that the rats' fleas were still alive in clothes or goods transported with the ships. This is all based on speculation. Nevertheless, scholars have concluded that the plague first arrived in 1402 with a ship sailing to Maríuhöfn, a harbor in Hvalfjörður used by the bishops of Skálholt. It is then thought to have spread to the north, but by then many people in the south of Iceland had already died of it.[45] However, this may not be true because, as we will see, it appears that the abbots and abbess in Hólar diocese were already dying of plague in 1402, whereas the abbots and abbess in the diocese of Skálholt did not die until in 1403. This indicates that the plague may have spread around Iceland in the opposite direction, but where it arrived first is one of many unanswered questions about it.

In any case, the story goes that the plague initially came to Iceland with a blue cloth on a ship that had sailed from England. After that, it is claimed that the disease turned into a bird.[46] Obviously, this story is mythical, and the disease may well have come from other areas of Europe. Sailings from Norway, for example, had resumed after the plague had subsided there in 1350. Ships also sailed frequently from Germany to Iceland at the beginning of the fifteenth century, owing to the fishing opportunities. The truth is that although the plague had swept across most, though not all, regions on the Continent between 1347 and 1352, it flared up again and again, causing local outbreaks in Europe at least until the seventeenth century. There was no known outbreak in England between 1374 and 1437, for instance, whereas Italy experienced further outbreaks in 1400 and 1405.[47] Thus the plague could have arrived in Iceland from any area with which Icelanders were in contact at the beginning of the fifteenth century.

The epidemic's late arrival to Iceland has made scholars doubt whether the disease was actually the plague;[48] however, the staggering death rate in Iceland suggests that it can hardly have been anything else. When the epidemic first hit Iceland in 1402–1404, the death rate is thought to have been as high as 40–60%, which is comparable to the rates seen in neighboring countries.[49] During Iceland's second wave, in 1494–1495, the death rate was considerably lower.[50] However, due to the absence of material evidence to match written sources, the scale of the mortality in Iceland during the two waves of plague is debated, as is the origin of the disease.

So far, no systematic research has been done on the burial sites in Iceland that were in use during the first phase of the plague. Such research, based on a contextual ancient DNA analysis, might shed further light on the origins and development of the disease. Only one cemetery dating back to the period of the plague has been excavated in Iceland – the cemetery belonging to a parish church at Hafljarðarey. When it was dug up, first in 1905 and again in 1947, no mass grave was found that might have indicated a large number of deaths resulting from a disaster such as the plague.[51] The cemetery at Kirkjubæjarklaustur was not included in the excavation carried out there from 2002 to 2006, and the excavation at Viðey, where Viðeyjarklaustur was located, revealed primarily post-monastic graves. The monastic cemetery at Skriðuklaustur may be mentioned here as a potential burial place for second-wave plague. Although was not consecrated until 1496, as is borne out by a letter written by Bishop Stefán Jónsson in Skálholt on 23 August of that year, this was right after the second outbreak of plague in Iceland.[52]

Notwithstanding the debate described earlier, the plague should be regarded as the deadliest crisis that Icelanders encountered during the Middle Ages, at least according to the descriptions in written sources. Furthermore, the annals and official documents indicate that the highest death rate in Iceland was among the clergy. For example, the annals specifically state that all priests in the province of the Hólar bishopric died of plague in 1402.[53] Moreover, according to the annals, the winter of 1403–1404 was particularly deadly in the Skálholt episcopal see, with both lay and religious residents decimated by the plague.[54] In an entry, it is stated that the year before eight of the fourteen nuns in Kirkjubæjarklaustur died, including Abbess Halldóra Runólfsdóttir.[55] Additionally, according to other sources such as the historical records of the bishop, only one monk survived the first wave of plague in Þingeyraklaustur in 1402. The abbot there, Sveinbjörn Sveinsson, was among those who died.[56] In Þykkvabæjarklaustur, six of the twelve monks died in 1403, including the abbot, Runólfur Magnússon.[57] Other ecclesiastical houses smaller than the monasteries, such as parish churches, were also hit hard by the epidemic. Recent research has shown that after the early fifteenth-century outbreak, only thirty-five of the seventy-two parishes in northern Iceland still had priests. In the south, only fifty-three out of 105 parishes had surviving priests.[58] Further research on the numbers of plague victims, based on the annals, estimated the death rate among the clergy at between 80% and 95%.[59] In this regard, the situation was in fact no different in Iceland than elsewhere in Europe, where the death rate among the clergy was generally higher than among ordinary people.[60]

It is certainly noticeable that except in Möðruvallaklaustur, all of Iceland's abbots and both abbesses died during the first outbreak of plague. In the second wave, on the other hand, only three abbots died, while five abbots and both abbesses survived. The annals report not only on the deaths of the nuns at Kirkjubæjarklaustur; they also report that on three occasions in 1402 or 1403, there were no lay people left in the convent because of the plague. The same annals even state that at one point, 775 people were buried there, all of them plague victims.[61] Moreover, other annals describe the situation as such that on average, when fifteen people accompanied corpses to be buried, only four returned.[62]

By being on the front lines of the epidemic, the residents of the ecclesiastical houses, both religious and lay, were automatically at much greater risk of infection than anyone else. The role of Iceland's monasteries in providing relief to the general public during hard times appears at least to have been more vital during the plague than often before. In the *DI*, for instance, there are two votive letters encouraging people to go on pilgrimages to the monasteries in Hólar diocese in order to stop the spread of the disease. The first letter was written in Grenjaðarstaður church in the north on Christmas Day 1402, and the second one was written in Munkaþverárklaustur itself on 14 January 1403.[63] Ironically, all of this must have helped the plague to spread even faster and over larger geographical areas than would otherwise have been possible.

In the Grenjaðarstaður letter, people were encouraged to go on pilgrimage 'til sáluhjálpar og syndalausnar og sérlega mót þeirri ógurlegu drepsótt sem þá fór vestan eftir landinu og felldi bæði ríka og fátæka, leika sem lærða' (for the salvation and absolution of people due to the terrible plague, which had by then gone west across the country and killed both rich and poor, clerics and lay people).[64] These acts of pilgrimage were supposed to be undertaken in the name of the Virgin. The letter claims that both Húnavatnssýsla county and Skagafjörður were already nearly bereft of religious and common people alike. It also expressed fears that this great pestilence would spread to the west and south, where many people resided. Furthermore, the letter from Munkaþverárklaustur indicates that direct gifts of money to the Church were meant to alleviate the ongoing crises caused by the plague.[65] Moreover, on the way to their destinations, the pilgrims were told to kneel 150 times while saying the prayer *Ave Maria* aloud.[66] This was not all. All those who were healthy were supposed to fast on water before each St. Mary's Mass – if it took place on a Monday; furthermore, on each night of fasting, they were to recite the *Paternoster* and the *Ave Maria* fifty times each, while bowing at the same time. People were also urged to give alms, and the monastic houses were among the institutions responsible for distributing the offerings made.[67] What is more, the votive letter written in Munkaþverárklaustur in January 1403 was not only addressed to the Virgin, as the one written at Grenjaðarstaður was, but it also appealed to Jesus Christ and the deceased Bishop Guðmundur góði for help in alleviating the plague. Of great importance here was the invocation of saints such as St. Barbara, St. Roch, and the Virgin Mary, whose assistance one could seek through intercessory prayer while requesting assistance from Almighty God. All the priests serving at that time were supposed to sing for the Virgin (*virgo mater Christi*) after all masses except requiems. In the name of the bishop, Guðmundur góði, all people should give the pope an *alin*[68] from each *hundruð* in suitable money.[69]

Interestingly, the letters from Grenjaðarstaður and Munkaþverárklaustur explicitly mention both Munkaþverárklaustur and Þingeyraklaustur, in addition to Hólar cathedral, as the destinations for pilgrimages – but not Möðruvallaklaustur or Reynistaðarklaustur. Thus, the people from the area between Reykjahlíð and Vaðlaheiði were supposed to walk to Munkaþverárklaustur, while those living in Húnavatnssýsla county and in Skagafjörður were asked to go on pilgrimage to Þingeyraklaustur and Hólar. The letters therefore indicate that a large number of people – possibly sick people – were walking specifically to the monasteries at Þingeyrar and Munkaþverá, and to Hólar, when the plague was at its peak. In this context, it is noteworthy that Möðruvallaklaustur was the only monastic institution in Iceland to lose none of its inhabitants in either wave of the plague. The reason for this may be that the monastery served as a canon school and was thus not open to ordinary people. The other monastic houses, like most ecclesiastical institutions in Iceland, were supposed to bring comfort to the dying through prayer or the provision of medical care. They were even responsible for organizing the burials of plague victims and providing support to mourners. That being the case, it should not be surprising that they were profoundly affected by the plague.

The historical sources show, moreover, that in the wake of the first wave of plague, there was a distinct shift in the operation of Iceland's monastic houses, which enjoyed a general economic recovery while simultaneously struggling with the decimation of their lay and religious population. This also seems to have happened elsewhere in medieval Christian Europe: donations to ecclesiastical institutions soared between 1300 and 1500, the period when the plague struck the Continent.[70] Apparently, the economic recovery from the plague started as soon as the disease had passed.

Post-Plague Recovery

Although the post-plague recovery of monastic institutions has been investigated in certain areas of Europe, such as England, Germany, and some regions of Italy, the basis and consequences of the recovery remain to be examined in greater depth. The studies that have been undertaken suggest that although the monastic economies were particularly resilient in the face of the short-term consequences of the plague, the gains they made were part of a longer process.[71] The post-plague recovery seems to have been similar in Iceland, although it is difficult to identify because the plague's side effects on the monasteries have only been partly examined. Official letters preserved from Iceland demonstrate clearly that individual donations to ecclesiastical institutions were popular during both outbreaks of plague, when people were trying to protect themselves from the disease. Often these gifts included both precious items and valuable farms. One such gift was Ytri-Ey on Skagaströnd in the north, which was donated to Þingeyraklaustur by a woman named Valdís Helgadóttir in 1403, together with all the resources pertaining to it, as was usually specified. At any rate, in the letter of donation, Valdís promised to give the farm to the monastery, but only if she should die of plague.[72] Valdís' fate is not known for certain, but the monastery apparently received the farm Ytri-Ey because twenty years later, Abbot Ásbjörn Vigfússon sold it to Einar Bessason at a substantial profit.[73]

One similarly interesting gift, which has been mentioned previously, is the donation made to Skriðuklaustur in 1494 by Einar Ormsson's aunt, Ingibjörg Þorvarðardóttir, signed by her husband, Páll Brandsson.[74] This was just around the time the monastery there was established. When Páll wrote his will, Ingibjörg was already dead, as was the couple's son, and he himself was seriously ill with the plague. Páll died soon afterwards, and in the will, he expressed his desire to be buried at his home church at Möðruvellir in Eyjafjörður, next to his late wife. As has been described previously, the gift to Skriðuklaustur consisted of three valuable farms, as well as cattle, cash, and various items for the operation of the monastery that was about to be established.[75] In the will, Páll Brandsson praised the Virgin, St. Peter the Apostle, St. Nicolaus, the Archbishop of Niðarós, Bishop Guðmundur góði, and even St. Barbara.[76] He also bequeathed a share of his properties to family members, friends, and other churches, although Skriðuklaustur received the largest share. Ingibjörg Þorvarðardóttir and Páll Brandsson may well have intended these donations as a means of securing salvation for the souls of Einar Ormsson and Cecilía Þorsteinsdóttir, as well as their own. The votive letters described in the previous section and the wills mentioned earlier are good examples of wishes that are directed to specially chosen saints during times of vulnerable situations or crisis.[77]

The list of farms owned by the Icelandic monasteries indicates that their holdings increased significantly in number soon after the first outbreak of the plague. In the case of Helgafellsklaustur, seven farms were donated to it in the first twenty years after the plague hit Iceland. More specifically, Helgafellsklaustur owned fifty-three farms in 1397 but, according to preserved documents, purchased additional farms in 1407, 1417, 1431, 1440, and 1448.[78] It also received as gifts (or bought by selling others) a total of thirteen farms during the period 1490–1494, when the plague struck again.[79] Another example may be taken from Munkaþverárklaustur, which owned twenty-three farms in 1318. By 1446, however it had forty-two, double the number it had held some 130 years earlier. Even so, six of the monastery's farms were deserted in 1446,[80] indicating that the economic value of many farms may have been reduced because of the plague.

We should draw attention to it here that during long periods in the fourteenth and the fifteenth centuries, conditions were generally difficult in Iceland. There were not only various diseases, smallpox among them, but also natural disasters such as earthquakes, volcanic eruptions, and severe winters followed by crop failures.[81] Official documents mention specifically, for example, that in 1355, many of cattle at Munkaþverárklaustur died as a result of these harsh conditions.[82] This was acknowledged as a financial loss for the monastery. Natural disasters were not the only source of difficulty, however. For some years after the plague struck Norway in 1349, very few ships, if any, sailed from there with goods to Iceland. The same was true of ships from other countries, such as Germany and England.[83] In fact, the economic situation in Munkaþverárklaustur became so dire in 1375 that the abbot, Árni Jónsson, sold a part of Skriðuland in Öxnadalur to a neighboring farmer, Guðmundur Sigurðsson, 'fyrir þröngvandi nauðsyn staðarins' (for the urgent financial necessity of the monastery), as is stated in letters written on 25 March and 19 May of that year.[84] It is noteworthy that the land in question was initially a gift from a woman named Gróa Oddsdóttir, who donated it to the monastery in connection with a corrody agreement.[85] The letters demonstrate how precarious the finances of the monastery were by the end of the fourteenth century. They may even indicate that the monastery's finances were in a serious disarray. On the other hand, in 1429, the monastery could afford to rebuild some of the monastic building, including the church, and even purchased some new items for it over a period of a few years.

By 1525, when the inventory of the monastic institutions in Hólar diocese was compiled, it appears that Munkaþverárklaustur was very well equipped and furnished. In its monastic building and church, for example, were the twenty-one saintly likenesses, six chalices, eighteen bells, and many other precious items described in detail in Chapter 6. Improved economic circumstances after the first outbreak of the plague can also be observed from the monasteries at

Viðeyjarklaustur, Reynistaðarklaustur, Kirkjubæjarklaustur, Þykkvabæjarklaustur, and Möðruvallaklaustur. Even so, the constant fear of a worsening situation may have given rise to the idea of opening a monastery that could provide health care to the people in eastern Iceland, where there were no other monastic institutions. This idea is supported by the archaeological excavations at Skriðuklaustur, which indicated that the monastery's main function was to serve as a hospital, and the timing of its establishment, as the planning and construction of the monastic complex took place during the second outbreak of plague in Iceland.

While the post-plague economic growth experienced by the monastic houses is noteworthy, the devastation by the loss of both lay and religious servants is also worth mentioning. For example, Bishop Vilchin Hendriksson of Skálholt (r. 1391–1405) had only recently praised all the noteworthy and precious fabrics produced by the nuns in Kirkjubæjarklaustur when more than half of them died of plague, together with their highly respected abbess, Halldóra Runólfsdóttir. The nuns in Kirkjubæjarklaustur are also said to have faced significant difficulty with the loss of the lay people responsible for the non-ecclesiastical work in their convent. The situation was so dire at one point that the surviving nuns themselves had to do farm chores such as milking the cows, for which they had neither the skill nor the knowledge, according to the annals.[86]

When Abbess Halldóra Runólfsdóttir died of plague in 1403, a new abbess, Guðrún Halldórsdóttir, replaced her immediately,[87] but this was certainly not the case in all the monastic houses in operation in Iceland at that time. It took over three decades to fill some of the posts of the abbots and abbesses, including in the case of Munkaþverárklaustur. The female convent in the northern bishopric, Reynistaðarklaustur, was without an abbess for thirty-five years after Ingibjörg Örnólfsdóttir died of plague in 1402. Ingibjörg's father had paid one hundred *hundruð* in livestock with her when she became a nun there. She then rose to prominence and took post as abbess in 1390. After her death, Reynistaðarklaustur was ruled by a prioress, and by the stewards and assistants. Thus, it was during the period from 1408 to 1435 that the prioress, Þórunn Ormsdóttir, ruled Reynistaðarklaustur along with an assistant for one year, the nun Þuríður Halldórsdóttir. Another member of the ruling team was a steward, Björgólfur Illugason, who also served as the convent's priest and confessor for a while. However, in 1408, a new steward and priest, Logi Stígsson, was hired for the convent.[88] At least, it seems that everything was done to keep it going, albeit without an abbess, until 1437. The new abbess, in fact, was one of the nuns, Þóra Finnsdóttir, who had joined the convent in 1431. Interestingly, when she became abbess, she changed her name to Barbara – the name of the saint who was supposed to protect against fever such as that caused by the plague.[89]

In Þingeyraklaustur as well, there was no abbot for twenty-two years after Abbot Sveinbjörn Sveinsson died of plague in 1402. When the plague struck the monastery for the second time in 1495, the abbot, Ásgrímur Jónsson, also died, but he was replaced that same year by Jón Þorláksson.[90] As is discussed earlier, there was likewise no abbot in Munkaþverárklaustur for twenty-seven years after Hallur

FIGURE 7.1 The antependium from Skarð. The name of Sólveig Hrafnsdóttir, the last abbess to serve Reynistaðarklaustur, is embroidered in it. It even depicts embroidered images of St. Benedict; St. Egidius; St. Hallvard; St. Magnus, Earl of Orkney; St. Olaf, King of Norway; and St. Þorlákur, bishop of Skálholt (Þjms_2028).

died, but this changed when Þorgils, who had been severely injured in the 1429 fire, took over the post.[91] The abbot in charge of Munkaþverárklaustur during the second wave of the plague, Jón, died in 1494 but was replaced the same year by Einar Benediktsson, who had previously served as a priest at both Grenjaðarstaður and Hólar cathedral.[92] The situation was similar in most of the monastic houses. Abbot Runólfur Magnússon, who had been in office at Þykkvabæjarklaustur for forty-two years, died of plague in 1403. Unfortunately, his successor, Jón Hallfreðarson, drowned accidentally in Kollafjörður bay, only six years after his consecration in 1416. As is noted earlier, both Viðeyjarklaustur and Þingeyraklaustur lost their abbots in both waves of the plague. However, it took a much shorter time for Viðeyjarklaustur to fill the void than for Þingeyraklaustur. Abbot Páll kjarni Magnússon was replaced by Bjarni Andrésson only two years after the plague first hit Viðeyjarklaustur. During the second wave, when Abbot Jón Árnason died in 1494, he was succeeded by Árni Snæbjörnsson that same year.[93] Similarly, at Helgafellsklaustur, the abbot, Þorsteinn Snorrason, died in 1403 and the new abbot, Vermundur Örnólfsson, was selected for the post the following year.[94]

Preserved documents indicate, moreover, a sudden and intriguing shift in farming practices in the monastic houses around this time, perhaps caused by the plague. Still, because so few existing inventories list both pre-plague and post-plague possessions for the same monastic institution, it is difficult to gain a clear overview of the matter. The ones that do survive indicate that the monastic houses engaged in more mixed farming practices after the plague, raising both cattle and sheep, as will be discussed further in Chapter 8. For example, the inventories made in Reynistaðarklaustur in 1408 and 1446, respectively, show that the stock expanded enormously in the interim, especially regarding sheep.[95] This may suggest that the convent had recovered well from the epidemic. The monastery of Helgafellsklaustur provides another similar example. Anyhow, the monasteries at Reynistaður and at Helgafell, at least, were wealthy despite the troubles they weathered during the epidemic. An analysis of animal bones from the monastic sites could shed further light on the matter, but no such analysis has been carried out to date, except from those excavated at the site of Skriðuklaustur that was not operated until late fifteenth and mid-sixteenth centuries, so this question on how the general operation of the monastic institutions changed may remain unanswered for a while to come. However, a pilot study undertaken under the auspices of the MMI project examined evidence of a possible change in vegetation, which may have occurred as a result of the plague and the dissolution of the monastery of Þingeyraklaustur. The results showed clear evidence of a change in land use. Interestingly, the study suggests that the reduced population may have shifted the monastery's emphasis from cattle farming to sheep herding, most likely because it was less labor intensive.[96] Similar studies in Sweden have shown comparable results, even indicating that the plague caused wide-ranging alterations in people's way of living.[97]

The shift in farming due to the plague may, in turn, have affected both textile production and manuscript making in the monastic houses. This would then have affected land management in general, as well as many other aspects of life. The plague certainly hit the monastic houses hard, but personal scandals also had a detrimental impact, albeit an entirely different one, as the following examples demonstrate.

Scandals

Religious celibacy was supposed to place the clerical male above the male layman.[98] However, a number of examples presented in the previous chapters show that many of the complications that arose in Iceland's monasteries stemmed from a failure to honor their vow of celibacy. It appears that most of those who violated this oath were religious men, and that religious women – that is, abbesses and nuns – rarely broke their vows. The examples show, in fact, that most of the bishops, abbots, monks, and priests serving the Church in Iceland throughout the Middle Ages had mistresses or/and concubines, and even children. Only three bishops – St. Þorlákur Þórhallsson, Guðmundur góði, and Stefán Jónsson – are known by certainty to have devotedly kept their vow of celibacy and emphasized its value in their work. However, the two sole examples of nuns having children are from the same convent, Reynistaðarklaustur, and both instances date from the same year, 1431. One of these cases involved a butler from Hólar and the other, the convent's priest. The nuns who gave birth were Þóra Illugadóttir, daughter of the acting steward, Illugi Björgólfsson (himself the son of the former steward, Björgólfur Illugason), and Þuríður Halldórsdóttir, the former assistant prioress of Reynistaðarklaustur.

Þuríður Halldórsdóttir immediately claimed that the child's father was the butler at Hólar cathedral, Þorlákur Sigurðsson. Although he did not belong to the clergy there, the case must nonetheless have been considered a serious one. However, it was quite easily resolved through absolution granted by the bishop of Hólar, Jón Craxton, in return for the butler's promise of obedience and penance thereafter.[99] No other documents on the couple's absolution are preserved, but they may be lost. The butler clearly remained in his post at Hólar, because he is named in later documents and referred to there as the butler.[100] But this only tells half of the story. Apparently, the prioress, Þórunn Ormsdóttir, was deeply concerned about defending the honor of her convent during the difficult decades, especially after the plague. Þóra Illugadóttir admitted that the father of her baby was in fact the serving priest of the convent, Þórður Hróbjartsson, who was therefore the father confessor of the nuns there as well. Þóra must have been already pregnant when she took her vow in 1431 because the baby was born only four months after she entered the convent.[101]

The consequences for the priest, Þórður, appear to have been more severe than for the butler, Þorlákur. This was perhaps because, as a priest, he had promised before God to live his life in celibacy. For his wrongdoing, Þórður lost his post as the convent's priest and confessor. As part of his penance, he was required to spend his life in celibacy in a monastery, although he was permitted to choose which one. Moreover, he was ordered to leave the convent at Reynistaður immediately. This was not all. Þórður had to fast regularly for the next seven years, and during that period he was required to go on a barefoot pilgrimage throughout Hólar diocese every Saturday and read the psalter in all the main churches there.[102] There is no record of how Þóra was absolved of her sin, despite of her obvious role in the affair. Interestingly, it seems that the absolution Þórður was granted was honestly not meant to break up the relationship between him and Þóra. Even if that was the intention, the attempt was clearly unsuccessful, because the couple had two more sons: Illugi, born in 1440, and Þórður, born in 1445.[103] Their firstborn child may have been left behind in the convent, or perhaps it died in the smallpox epidemic that hit Iceland in 1431, the year of its birth. At all events, the child is not listed in the online database with its two brothers.

Apparently, Þóra and Þórður left Reynistaðarklaustur soon after their first child was born. Þórður appears not to have moved to another monastic house as a monk or a priest, as he was supposed to do. He may instead have gone to live somewhere else with Þóra. Perhaps they lived as corrodians under the protection of a bishop or a monastic house, although there are no documents to support this theory. According to canon law, this was indeed an option. When a woman had finished her novitiate, ranging up to two years, she had the right to decide to leave the convent, though she needed the permission of her superior, the abbess or the bishop. Still, she was even allowed to marry and live a normal life in the world after leaving it.[104] A priest, on the other hand, could never marry because his vows were supposed to last forever. He could be permitted to leave the priesthood, but he was thereby formally excommunicated. In such a case, he was no longer allowed to say Mass or be called Father, but he never ceased to be a priest.[105] If it is true that Þóra left her convent immediately after her novitiate, it is tempting to speculate that she initially came to Reynistaðarklaustur not of her own free will, but rather at the behest of her father, Illugi Björgólfsson, because of her pregnancy and her relationship with the convent's priest, Þórður. Most likely, Illugi was living in the convent with his family anyway while working as a steward there.

Indeed, the aftermath of the relationship of Þóra Illugadóttir and Þórður Hróbjartsson stands out due to the severity of the punishment imposed on Þórður. In contrast, as has been noted previously, many priests, abbots, and even bishops were known to have had children out of wedlock throughout the Middle Ages without being punished. Many of the numerous examples of the clergy's mistresses and concubines are listed in Chapter 3. This brings us back to the case of the abbot of Þingeyraklaustur, Helgi Höskuldsson, who was sent on pilgrimage to Rome three times by Bishop Jón Arason to atone for having children while in office.[106] In Helgi's case, it is difficult to understand why he should need to seek absolution, as the bishop was himself the father of nine children. There are other peculiar cases as well, such as when the priest Eiríkur Eiríksson was sent to Jón Þorvaldsson, abbot of Munkaþverárklaustur, as a novice for twelve months in 1487. Unfortunately, Eiríkur had a child during his novitiate. He immediately promised to live a life of obedience and penance forever thereafter, but this appears not to have been enough. At least, the bishop of Hólar, Ólafur Rögnvaldsson, made it clear that fatherhood and respectable service in holy orders were utterly incompatible.[107] Eiríkur was therefore denied the opportunity to become abbot.

To give in to sexual temptation should have been observed as one of the mortal sins. The consequences of such behavior were made apparent not only by the number of illegitimate children but also by the sexually transmitted disease syphilis, which, from the end of the fifteenth century onwards, spread among the clergy just as quickly as among the common people in Europe. The research at Skriðuklaustur showed that the disease had reached Iceland by this time, as at least eighteen people who died of syphilis were buried in the monastic cemetery there.[108]

Syphilis

No cases of death due to syphilis had been known in Iceland, until the disease was found in both its venereal and congenital forms during the excavation of the monastic cemetery at Skriðuklaustur. Notably, the syphilis cases found there are also the earliest yet discovered in Iceland.[109] The venereal form of syphilis is explicitly transmitted through sexual intercourse between individuals, and the congenital type is transmitted when a fetus is infected through its mother, either *in utero* or during birth. In some instances, when the infection is transmitted from the diseased mother to her unborn child, it can cause stillbirth. If they survive the birth, however, individuals with congenital syphilis can reach early adulthood, as some of the cases from Skriðuklaustur demonstrate.[110]

Both the venereal and congenital forms of syphilis develop in three stages – primary, secondary, and tertiary – a process that can take up to thirty years, although the secondary stage begins some days or weeks after the primary infection. The symptoms of the disease vary from one stage to another. As a long-term illness, it rarely causes bone deformation during the initial stages, although this is nonetheless known to appear in some cases. During the two later stages of the disease, particularly the tertiary stage, significant changes occur in the bones and skin, and the central nervous and cardiac systems can be severely damaged. This is often accompanied by outer lesions and pimples on most parts of the body. The tertiary lesions occur progressively, between two and ten years after the initial infection.[111] In fact, all three stages were identified in the eighteen skeletons with syphilis found in Skriðuklaustur's burial grounds. The skeletons belong to both male and female individuals who range in age from adolescents to adults. Yet it seems that the syphilis cases identified at Skriðuklaustur were more common among females than males. Of the eighteen syphilis patients, ten were females, five were males, and three were adolescents who had not matured sexually. The youngest individual to die there of syphilis was little more than fourteen years old.[112]

Taking care of the patients seeking help in the monastery must therefore have been extremely demanding for all of those involved in healing or nursing. This would particularly been the case for the patients with syphilis, given that during the tertiary stage, the bacterium that causes the disease even affects the central nervous system, causing serious mental illnesses. In addition to the mental impact of the disease, the lesions, and wounds that syphilis causes on both skin and bones make the individual virtually unable to function normally. Interestingly, nearly all the syphilis cases from Skriðuklaustur were found in graves located in the cloister garden and east of the choir. These were the areas of the cemetery that were designated for patients, indicating that the canons there were free from the disease.[113]

Before the identification of syphilis in skeletons found in Skriðuklaustur's monastic cemetery, the disease was generally not believed to have been present in Iceland until the modern era, principally because there had been no evidence of its presence. However, written sources inform us about a barber-surgeon (Icel. *bartskeri*) who came to Iceland in the early sixteenth century to heal Icelanders of this particular disease. Barber-surgeons were particularly adept at treating syphilis. They are even thought to have been capable of performing some exterior operations on their patients, but most commonly they used mercury or other liquids in their treatment regimens. Mercury was, in fact, the earliest known remedy for diseases such as syphilis and leprosy during the Middle Ages. Its use has been identified at the medieval hospital at the Øm monastery in Denmark, as well as at Skriðuklaustur.[114]

The first barber-surgeon who came to Iceland was Lazarus Mattheusson. He was originally from Germany but came to Iceland in 1525 at the request of Bishop Ögmundur Pálsson, who must have recognized the harm the disease was already causing. Ögmundur was the last Catholic bishop of Skálholt. Before his elevation to the episcopate, he was abbot of Viðeyjarklaustur from 1515 to 1520, and a year later, in 1521, he was consecrated in Niðarós as bishop of Skálholt. He had been well-educated in schools in England and the Netherlands, where he must have acquired knowledge of the barber-surgeons working on the Continent.[115] According to the contract made with Lazarus, he was supposed to be rewarded with the farm of Skáney in Borgarfjörður, where he had initially stayed, in return for healing 100 Icelanders. Furthermore, according to the contracts made between Lazarus and the bishop, all equipment and ointments were to be provided by Lazarus. It is particularly interesting to reflect on the name of this barber-surgeon: Lazarus. We might speculate that when he became a healer, he chose to adopt the name of St. Lazarus, who was believed to protect against epidemics.[116] At the very least, such a name may have given his patients hope that they might be cured.

Eventually, Skáneyjar-Lassi, as Lazarus was commonly called, received the promised farm at Skáney in return for his work, although it is not likely that he managed to heal all those he was supposed to heal. Still, while Icelandic scholars have certainly not rejected the existence of Skáneyjar-Lassi – he had a wife and children in Iceland – they have argued that the cases of syphilis he was supposed to treat were most likely leprosy, tuberculosis (or scrofula), scurvy, or a combination of these.[117] For example, it has long been claimed that when the first Lutheran bishop of Skálholt, Gissur Einarsson, suffered from the disease himself, it was not really venereal syphilis but a combination of leprosy and scurvy.[118] Because syphilis was usually associated with promiscuity and wanton living, its symptoms were often said to be caused by some other disease entirely, or someone else was blamed for the illness. At least, this was apparently done in the case of Bishop Gissur, who allegedly suffered from syphilis. This evasiveness about the disease is not unique to Iceland – quite the opposite, in fact. The term *syphilis* was first coined in Italy in the 1520s. Before that, Italians called it the French disease, a term also used in Poland and Germany. In France, however, it was known as the Italian disease. The Dutch named it the Spanish disease, and the Russians called it the Polish disease. The Turks called it the Christian disease, the English the pox, and the Tahitians the British disease. Icelanders later called it *fransós*.[119]

Several theories still flourish about the origins and spread of syphilis. The most common theory links it to the return of Christopher Columbus from America in the late fifteenth century, as that is when the first historically recorded outbreak occurred.[120] However, cases from the late fifteenth century, which indicate the rapid spread of the infection, have been found during excavations of burials at places as far flung as Trondheim in Norway, Rostov Veliky near Moscow in the northeast of European Russia, Finland, England, Denmark, and North Carolina in the United States.[121] Nonetheless, other cases from different areas of both Europe and the Americas indicate that the disease existed much earlier, even as early as the Neolithic period, although it did not become widespread until the late fifteenth and early sixteenth centuries. Consequently, most scholars regard the spread of syphilis around the end of the fifteenth century as an epidemic. In fact, it is a disease that has long infected humans and is still present today.[122]

As a result of this supposed epidemic, another well-known barber came to Iceland shortly after the Reformation. His name was Henrik Gerkens Hannesson, and he resided at the former monastic site of Þingeyraklaustur from 1569 to 1577. His presence demonstrates that syphilis continued to spread among Icelanders, just as it did among other Europeans. Still, there were other problems that required handling during the Middle Ages in Iceland, as is discussed in the following section.

Disobedience

The cases of Brother Jón in Skriðuklaustur and the nuns in Reynistaðarklaustur are certainly not the only preserved examples of religious servants – that is, monks, nuns, abbots, and abbesses – committing what may be regarded as a serious transgression against God. Such examples demonstrate clearly how eventful daily life in monastic houses in Iceland could be, as well as how differently the churchly authorities dealt with each case, perhaps because of individual desires or shifting views on the gravity of sins and crimes. For Brother Jón, it was apparently enough that he atoned for his sin – which must have been quite serious, according to canon law – by working in a monastic house, even though that house was his own place of work. Several other cases mentioned here demonstrate the diversity of the issues the episcopal authorities had to deal with and why papal dispensations were permitted in some instances but not in others.

We can recall the case when Cecilía donated her farm Skriðu to the Church as a penitence for her disobedience, but even the large gift donated to Skriðuklaustur by Einar Ormsson's family in 1494, the year it began to operate. The gift is documented in the will of Páll Brandsson and it comprised three valuable farms, plus cows, coins, a statue of Jesus Christ, two gilded candlesticks, a censer, a ring of gold, and a gilded chain.[123] It is easy to relate these two last items to the ornamental chain discovered on the land of the farmstead at Skriða in the early twentieth century and to the ring found during the excavation. However, three years later, in 1497, Halldór ríki (the rich) Brynjólfsson, a friend of Einar and Cecilía, gave the monastery the largest gift it ever received, in the form of valuable farms and other properties. In addition to the farms, the gift included coins, books, and canonical vestments.[124] Curiously enough, Halldór ríki had also been excommunicated by the Church for repeated physical attacks on a worker at Skálholt.[125] Through all these donations, the monastery was amply provided with items, furniture, and funds for its future operation, and the penitents involved were absolved of their mortal and venial sins. Further research on the establishment of Skriðuklaustur showed that Bishop Stefán personally knew all the penitents involved. He also knew the first prior he appointed, Narfi Jónsson (r. 1496–1506). He appears thus to have granted the penitent donors their absolution while simultaneously securing the operation of a new monastic institution at Skriðuklaustur, for the potential benefit of his bishopric and himself.

One interesting and indeed complicated case involving violations of canon law concerns an illegal marriage in the late fifteenth century. The case is linked to two monastic institutions, Þingeyraklaustur and Reynistaðarklaustur, but involved the leaders of both institutions, Abbot Jón Þorvaldsson (r. 1495–1514) and Abbess Agnes Jónsdóttir (r. 1461–1507). Others associated with the case were a woman named Björg, who was the daughter of Abbess Agnes's brother, Þorvaldur, who in turn was the father of Abbot Jón Þorvaldsson. Abbot Jón Þorvaldsson succeeded Abbot Ásgrímur Jónsson at Þingeyraklaustur upon Ásgrímur's death of plague in 1495, but Abbot Ásgrímur was the brother of Þorvaldur and Abbess Agnes and thus Abbot Jón's uncle.[126] His sister, Björg, married their third cousin, Jón Sigmundsson, a lawman residing at Urðir in Svarfaðardalur, in 1497. Björg and Jón had three daughters together, the eldest of whom were twin sisters born around 1500. However, in 1215, the Church had outlawed marriage between cousins within four degrees; that is, first, second, and third cousins. Consequently, Björg and Jón were excommunicated, and their daughters declared illegitimate, but this happened only when their marriage became a matter for the Church on the grounds of consanguinity.[127]

In fact, it was not until 1506 that Jón and Björg's marriage was found to be illegal, but what makes the case even more interesting is how this was discovered. The situation was exposed when an unnamed woman made public a conversation that had taken place some years before between Abbess Agnes and her brother Þorvaldur in Reynistaðarklaustur. The nuns had heard the siblings whispering inside a closed extension of the refectory of the convent, when Abbess Agnes asked Þorvaldur whether he had really given his daughter Björg to her third cousin, Jón Sigmundsson, the lawman from Svarfaðardalur. Þorvaldur answered 'yes' in a low voice, but nonetheless, he had spoken loud enough that the reply reached the ears of the nuns who were eavesdropping on the other side of the door.[128] The conversation clearly took place long before the nuns finally mentioned it because Þorvaldur died around the time his daughter was married. Abbess Agnes died in 1507, but she may still have been alive when her niece was excommunicated, as Björg's judgement was made public in a letter dated 22 January 1507.[129] At least, the abbess must have been aware of the seriousness of the case when it first came to the attention of the Church in 1506. Abbess Agnes and Þorvaldur were obviously under the impression that their conversation had been private, but in reality, the fact that it was witnessed by the nuns in Reynistaðarklaustur proved that the illegitimacy of the marriage was known from the outset. Most likely, Abbot Jón also knew from the beginning that his sister's marriage was invalid on grounds of consanguinity. What makes this case even more odd is that it was Abbot Jón Þorvaldsson himself who declared, in a letter written and signed in Þingeyraklaustur on 5 February 1497, that he had given his sister Björg in a marriage to Jón Sigmundsson, with her consent and that of her parents. In the letter it is emphasized that no one could find 'nockura meinbugi vensl edr skulldugleicka uissu æ fyrgreindra mana æ millum jóns ok bjargar' (any hindrance to this marriage, whether there were affinities or blood relation inside the forbidden degree between Jón and Björg).[130] The offence in question – that is, the illicit marriage – had clearly been committed deliberately.

The collaboration of the three siblings – Agnes, Ásgrímur, and Þorvaldur – two of whom were working within the Church, had actually begun long before Björg and Jón's marriage. This can be seen in the fact that Jón Þorvaldsson, brother of Björg and nephew of Abbess Agnes, served as a steward and a priest with his aunt in Reynistaðarklaustur during her tenure as abbess from 1461 to 1507.[131] Nevertheless, Jón Þorvaldsson needed to purify himself of having, as a priest, baptized a child that was stillborn (and thus beyond salvation) in 1483, and of having served an excommunicated man that same year.[132] Interestingly, it seems that he was assisting those who stood outside the sphere of God's grace, an unbaptized baby and an excommunicated man. The case of Jón and Björg, however, does not appear to have had any consequences for Abbot Jón, whereas the couple probably never got their marriage declared legal through dispensation – at least, there are no documents proving that they did receive a dispensation. Björg was even required to confess and pay fines to the Church because of her misconduct, but her penance was based on the grounds that she knew, better than her husband, that their marriage was illegal.[133]

At this point, several named Icelanders had already been granted papal dispensations for illegal marriages and illegitimate children, particularly in the latter part of the fifteenth century and the first part of the sixteenth.[134] This brings to mind the case of Cecilía, the founder of Skriðuklaustur. In Cecilía's case as well as Björg's, all that mattered was whether it could be proven that the illegitimacy of the marriage was known beforehand and the act itself therefore premeditated. This point is emphasized in the case of Cecilía, written by Bishop Sveinn spaki Pétursson in Skálholt on 18 May 1471:

> einar heitinn ok cecilia haufdu sin j millum bundit j saugdum meinbugum uitz vitande olaugligt ok ecki afl hafa né haft hafa. ok þeirra baurn olaugliga getin wera enn eigi skilgetin. fyrerbiodum wer stridlega under fullt forbod ok bannz pinu aullum ok sierhuerium bæde lærdum ok leikum adrgreind born skilgeten ad hallda (einar and cecilia had deliberately made illegal ties between them, without having the power to perform such [an] act. Their children are similarly illegally conceived. The couple's act was therefore strictly forbidden, so they are hereby placed under a full ban and all those who observe their children as legitimately born).[135]

As is stressed before, it was with Einar Ormsson's death and the subsequent disputes about the children's inheritance that the validity of his marriage to Cecilía was called into question. In the case of Björg Þorvaldsdóttir and Jón Sigmundsson, the nephew of Abbess Agnes at Reynistaðarklaustur, it was proven in court that the illegality of their marriage had been known before the wedding took place but that all who knew it had chosen to remain silent about it.[136]

Disobedience among the clergy was certainly not restricted to instances involving childbirth or illegal cohabitation. Cases of verbal or written transgressions are known from Þykkvabæjarklaustur, although most of the canons there became respected writers and translators. They appear to have produced many valuable books, both translations and transcriptions, such as the story of Judas, the story of Alexander, *Svínfellinga saga*, and *Hrafnkels saga*.[137] However, not all the literary works from Þykkvabæjarklaustur were received with the same enthusiasm. In 1343, three canons there, Arngrímur, Magnús, and Eysteinn, were found guilty of depravity – in poetry. Another poem composed by Eysteinn also included unpleasant verses, even about the bishop himself. These poems were considered too provocative and were thus condemned as rakish.[138]

Eysteinn was known not only for his poems, both good and bad. According to the annals, Abbot Þorlákur Loftsson had to flee his monastery because Eysteinn and two other canons, Arngrímur and Magnús, threatened him with physical violence. Abbot Þorlákur fled to Viðeyjarklaustur in 1343 and sought shelter with his fellow Augustinians.[139] It was in light of these events that Bishop Jón Sigurðsson punished Eysteinn and Arngrímur by binding their necks and feet with chains. Eysteinn subsequently moved to Norway and joined the monastery at Helgisetur in Trondheim, just as Ingimundur Skútuson had done when he left Möðruvallaklaustur after the great fire in 1316. Eysteinn died at Helgisetur in 1363.[140] The criminal acts of the canons at Þykkvabæjarklaustur prove the authority the bishops had over the monastic institutions in instances of misconduct by religious servants, but the cases also show that the perpetrators had the opportunity to leave and join another monastery if they wished to do so. Still, it must not be forgotten that in the management of their subordinates, different bishops were strict in different ways. Personal attitudes must always be considered in an examination of matters of this kind. In fact, Bishop Jón Sigurðsson was well known for his seemingly arbitrary and often disrespectful attitude towards the clergy of the diocese of Skálholt, as is highlighted in the case described in the following.

A Case of Heresy?

One even more tragic event appears to have taken place at Kirkjubæjarklaustur in the middle of the fourteenth century, although the story is based largely on rumors. It is still uncertain whether the event ever happened, even though it is documented in two annals. This event, if true, offers an indication of how harsh the episcopal authorities could become when the behavior of their religious subordinates was called into question. This single case must even have been much more shocking and devastating for the nuns than the impact of the plague fifty years later. It took place when Jón Sigurðsson was bishop of Skálholt between 1343 and 1348 and Abbess Agnes had taken over from her predecessor, Agatha, as abbess of Kirkjubæjarklaustur in 1343.

A rumor began to spread that one of her nuns, Katrín, had been in a relationship with some unknown layman, or possibly with the devil. She was also accused of having insulted the pope in writing. Bishop Jón Sigurðsson instantly ordered that she be burned to death. The annals claim that the punishment was carried out in 1343, the same year Jón took office, or possibly in 1344.[141] The execution is said to have taken place on the top of the cliff Systrastapi (Sisters' Rock), near Kirkjubæjarklaustur. In the folkloristic narratives that preserve stories of this incident, the nun's bodily remains were buried in a cairn on the top of the cliff immediately after the execution. The stories say that only thorns grow on her cairn. Some of the folkloristic tales even claim that there were two nuns, not just one, and that one of the cairns is always green, but not the other.[142]

There is a great deal of ambiguity in these accounts, making the case difficult to interpret, but through the ages it has turned into a myth rather than being considered as being based on actual events. For instance, during the excavations of the ruins of Kirkjubæjarklaustur, the archaeologists went on an expedition to Systrastapi to examine the site. First, it was very difficult to reach the top of the rock – and would have been even more difficult to carry timber and other things for the execution up there as well. Moreover, no signs of fire were found on the top of the cliff. There also appeared to be three mounds there rather than one or two.[143] This certainly lends support to the existing doubts about the veracity of the stories, although it is also possible that the execution took place elsewhere.

If true, the case from Kirkjubæjarklaustur would, in fact, be the first time an execution for this type of misconduct was carried out in Iceland. Executions were more common in cases of murder or theft. On the Continent, however, it was not unusual to burn people at the stake who had been accused of heresy or of having kept company with demons or other devils, as was the case with Sister

Katrín. Specifically, the Catholic Church had by then authorized the Inquisition, the sole purpose of which was to combat heresy and prosecute those accused of witchcraft.[144] The execution at Kirkjubæjarklaustur, where the nun is supposed to have been burnt at the stake, may thus have been influenced by the Inquisition and the ongoing witch hunts during the fifteenth century in mainland Europe. The Inquisition of the Middle Ages should however not be confused with the post-Reformation wave of witch trials conducted in Europe during the period 1560–1630. Iceland was certainly involved in this later wave of witch trials when twenty-two Icelanders, found guilty of witchcraft, were burned during the period from 1625 to 1683. Most of them were men, however, unlike the case in other European countries.[145]

The broader context of the Kirkjubæjarklaustur case is illuminating because there actually seems to have been a move by the Church during the mid-fourteenth century, to a greater degree than before, to discipline both clerics and the laity through physical punishment. During his brief tenure, Bishop Jón Sigurðsson was known mostly for extreme severity in disciplining his clerical subordinates, such as when he punished two canons at Þykkvabæjarklaustur by chaining their necks and feet for written transgressions. In another instance from 1344, Bishop Jón dismissed the abbot of Viðeyjarklaustur, Helgi Sigurðsson, and reorganized the monastery's operations, switching its allegiance from the Augustinian Order to the Benedictine without any advance warning. At the same time, he appointed his steward at Skálholt, Sigmundur Einarsson, as abbot of Viðeyjarklaustur. Bishop Jón Sigurðsson was soon removed from his post in Skálholt, however, and his successor, the Norwegian Gyrðir Ívarsson, quickly reversed Bishop Jón's decisions and returned Viðeyjarklaustur to the Augustinian Order, although Sigmundur retained his post as abbot for a while.[146] Bishop Jón Sigurðsson's harsh rule is recorded in detail in the annals, which claim that he had become so strict that it was hardly bearable for the people of the island.[147] It is thus possible that Bishop Jón Sigurðsson may have taken these various actions in an attempt to quell suspected disorder among his subordinates in Iceland by strictly enforcing ecclesiastical law. He was not the only bishop to try to enforce a stricter order; many other bishops did the same. Michael, bishop of Skálholt from 1382 to 1391, was one of them. Michael initially came from Denmark but had previously worked as a confessor for Pope Urbanus VI. He is said to have brought many interesting innovations with him to Iceland, although other decisions made by him were debated. For example, he deprived two abbesses at Kirkjubæjarklaustur of their posts without giving any advance notice or providing any clear reasons for the move. First, Þorgerður was removed from her post, even though she had respectfully served as abbess there from 1361 to 1387. Bishop Michael replaced her with Halldóra Runólfsdóttir in 1387 but removed her later that year.[148]

These actions of Bishop Michael may be interpreted as an example of pastoral care – *cura monialium* – over a female house, but it seems likely that he wanted to emphasize his episcopal authority over the nuns.[149] Michael's tenure as bishop of Skálholt ended in 1391, when he was succeeded by Bishop Vilchin, who was considered far gentler than his predecessors to all his people in the diocese of Skálholt – particularly the nuns in Kirkjubæjarklaustur. Bishop Vilchin continued to introduce ecclesiastical reforms into Icelandic society, but without using any kind of force. Moreover, he immediately reconsecrated Halldóra Runólfsdóttir as abbess of Kirkjubæjarklaustur after Bishop Michael had removed her and gave the nuns some precious gifts on the same occasion.[150]

Accordingly, ruling and administering dioceses was more likely to be successful when it was based on respect and courtesy, as Bishop Vilchin achieved, even as he continued to introduce significant reforms to the Icelandic ecclesiastical institutions. He managed to do so without forcing people into obedience. However, the examples discussed also indicate that at least some of the monasteries always depended on the bishop's governance and goodwill. Still, the assistance Þingeyraklaustur and Möðruvallaklaustur received from their local communities when they faced difficulties that were, in fact, caused by their serving bishops shows that ordinary people trusted their local monastic institution more than their bishops. Once again, the example of the battered woman who sought shelter in Kirkjubæjarklaustur proves that the abbesses retained independent control over internal matters. There were also instances in medieval England and Wales where archbishops enforced their authority over female houses; for instance, in matters regarding the nuns' clothing or the transfer of nuns (even prioresses) to other houses.[151] But no matter what other motivations may have lain behind their actions, the archbishops were most likely attempting in such cases to enforce monastic regulations and resolve a wide range of serious issues.

Notes

1 *Gottskálksannáll*, p. 321; *Konungsannáll*, p. 114.
2 *Gottskálksannáll*, p. 321; DI I, p. 193; Lagergård, 'Current knowledge on the late-medieval crisis', pp. 9–22.
3 See, for example, Grímsdóttir, 'Biskupsstóll í Skálholti', pp. 31–32.
4 *Gottskálksannálar*, p. 321; *Hungrvaka*, pp. 31–33.
5 Vigfússon, 'Rannsóknir á Vesturlandi 1891', p. 73.
6 Lucas, 'Hofstaðir in the Settlement Period', pp. 373–376.
7 *Hungrvaka*, p. 30.
8 According to *Code of Canon Law*, Chapter III, Article 4, Can 658 §1, the requirement for the validity of perpetual religious profession was if the studies were completed when the novice was at least twenty-one years of age. Still, it was possible to acquire temporary profession, but for its validity, it was required that the person who is to make it has completed it at least eighteen years of age; *Code of Canon Law*, Chapter III, Article 4, Can 655 and 656 §1.
9 Jensson, 'Íslenskar klausturreglur', pp. 30–31; Grímsdóttir, 'Biskupsstóll í Skálholti', p. 32; Þór, 'Hólabiskupa ævir', p. 405; Jakobsson, *Auðnaróðal*, p. 58.
10 Jensson, 'Íslenskar klausturreglur', p. 32; Jensson, 'Latin Hagiography in Medieval Iceland', pp. 913–918.
11 Þorláksson, 'Snorri Sturluson the Aristocrat' p. 33; Patzuk-Russell, *The Development of Education*, p. 93.
12 See, for example, Madigan, *Medieval Christianity*, pp. 24–26, 183.
13 *Jóns saga hins helga*, pp. 227–228.

14 Finnsson, *Mannfækkun af hallærum*, pp. 11–12.
15 DI III, p. 31.
16 Grímsdóttir, 'Biskupsstóll í Skálholti', p. 34; *Páls saga*, pp. 326–328.
17 Jónsson, *Historia ecclesiastica Islandiæ* IV, p. 31.
18 DI VII, p. 340.
19 See *Gottskálksannáll*, p. 339; *Lárentíus saga*, p. 242.
20 Kristjánsdóttir, *Leitin að klaustrunum*, pp. 390–392.
21 Colish, *Medieval Foundations*, p. 175–182; Madigan, *Medieval Christianity*, pp. 257–260.
22 DI IV, pp. 170–171; DI IX, pp. 305–307, 317–318; Olmer, *Boksamlingar i Island 1149–1490*, pp. 71–76; Kristjánsdóttir, *Leitin að klaustrunum*, pp. 162, 409.
23 *Gottskálksannálar*, p. 331; Sigurðsson, 'Samskipti íslenskra biskupa', pp. 508–509; Þór, 'Saga biskupsstóls á Hólum í Hjaltadal', pp. 304–305.
24 DI II, pp. 304–314.
25 *Lárentíus saga*, pp. 243, 258.
26 DI II, pp. 304–314.
27 See *Lárentíus saga*, pp. 330–331, 335–336.
28 *Lárentíus saga*, pp. 367–368.
29 *Lárentíus saga*, pp. 355–356, 367–368.
30 Jónsson, 'Um klaustrin á Íslandi', p. 256.
31 *Lárentíus saga*, pp. 391–395.
32 *Lögmannsannáll*, pp. 268.
33 *Lárentíus saga*, pp. 403–405.
34 *Lárentíus saga*, p. 418.
35 Rasmussen, 'Monastic Benefactors in England and Denmark', pp. 77–91.
36 *Lárentíus saga*, pp. 335–336.
37 *Lárentíus saga*, pp. 418–420.
38 *Lárentíus saga*, pp. 423; Þór, 'Saga biskupsstóls á Hólum í Hjaltadal', p. 412.
39 *Skálholtsannáll*, p. 224.
40 *Lögmannsannáll*, p. 295.
41 DI IV, p. 374.
42 Kristjánsdóttir, *Leitin að klaustrunum*, pp. 135–137.
43 DI IV, pp. 483–484.
44 Bos et al., 'A draft genome of Yersinia pestis', pp. 506–510; Drancourt et al., 'Yersinia pestis Orientalis', pp. 332–333.
45 Karlsson, *Iceland's 1100 years*, 112–113; Karlsson, 'Plague without rats', pp. 266–267.
46 Egilsson, 'Biskupa-annálar Jóns Egilssonar', p. 43.
47 Clark, *The Benedictines in the Middle Ages*, pp. 268–272; Ersgård, 'Change, desertion and survival', pp. 69–72; Hatcher, *Plague, Population and the English Economy*, pp. 11–20; Lagerås, 'Current knowledge on the late-medieval crisis', pp. 23–28.
48 Karlsson, 'Plague without rats', pp. 263–284.
49 Benedictow, *Plague in the Late Medieval Nordic Countries*, p. 383.
50 Júlíusson, *Landbúnaðarsaga Íslands*, pp. 175–184; Benedictow, *Plague in the Late Medieval Nordic Countries*; Þorsteinsson and Grímsdóttir, 'Enska öldin', pp. 5–12; Callow and Evans, 'The mystery of plague in medieval Iceland', pp. 254–284; Karlsson, 'Plague without rats', pp. 263–284; Karlsson, *Iceland's 1100 years*, pp. 111–117; Streeter, *Tephrochronology, landscape and population*.
51 See Steffensen, 'Rannsóknir á kirkjugarðinum í Haffjarðarey', pp. 144–162.
52 DI VII, p. 309.
53 *Vestfjarðaannáll hinn elsti*, p. 23.
54 *Nýi annáll*, pp. 9–11.
55 *Nýi annáll*, pp. 10–11.
56 Espólín, *Íslands Árbækur í söguformi* I, pp. 123–124.
57 *Lögmannsannál*, p. 286.
58 Júlíusson and Ísberg, *Íslandssagan í máli og myndum*, pp. 100–101.

59 Karlsson, *Iceland's 1100 years*, p. 112.
60 Benedictow, *Plague in the Late Medieval Nordic Countries*, pp. 342–353, 383; Ersgård, 'Change, desertion and survival', p. 81; Hatcher, *Plague, Population and the English Economy*, pp. 11–20; Prestwich, *Plantagenet England: 1225–1360*, pp. 538–546.
61 *Lögmannsannáll*, p. 286; *Nýi annáll*, pp. 10–11.
62 *Gottskálksannáll*, p. 369.
63 DI III, pp. 680–681, 682–683.
64 DI III, p. 680.
65 DI III, p. 680.
66 DI III, p. 681.
67 DI III, pp. 680–681.
68 *Alin* (ell) is a unit of measurement. One *alin* equals 114.3 cm. One *hundruð* is 120 *alin* of *vaðmál* or the same value as six cows.
69 DI III, pp. 682–683.
70 Logan, *A History of the Church*, pp. 275–287; Madigan, *Medieval Christianity*, pp. 418, 430–431.
71 See, for example, Clark, *The Benedictines in the Middle Ages*, pp. 268–272; Gilchrist, *Medieval Life*, p. 40; Logan, *A History of the Church*, pp. 275–287; Madigan, *Medieval Christianity*, pp. 418, 430–431.
72 DI III, pp. 683–684.
73 DI IV, pp. 319–320.
74 DI VIII, pp. 232–234.
75 DI VII, pp. 232–234.
76 DI VII, p. 233.
77 Arnórsdóttir, 'Gender and Donation Culture', pp. 165–175; Arnórsdóttir, 'Marital Property and Change in the Donation Culture', pp. 140–156.
78 DI II, pp. 115–116.
79 Júlíusson, *Jarðeignir kirkjunnar*, p. 35.
80 DI IV, pp. 699–700.
81 Finnsson, *Mannfækkun af hallærum*, pp. 20–33.
82 *Skálholtsannáll*, p. 224.
83 Benedictow, *Plague in the Late Medieval Nordic Countries*; Logan, *A History of the Church*, pp. 280–284; Nedkvitne, *The German Hansa and Bergen 1100–1600*, pp. 96–105, 161, 573.
84 DI III, p. 296.
85 DI III, pp. 296, 297.
86 *Lögmannsannáll*, pp. 285–286; *Nýi annáll*, p. 10–11.
87 Kristjánsdóttir, *Leitin að klaustrunum*, p. 289.
88 DI III, pp. 334, 717.
89 Kristjánsdóttir, *Leitin að klaustrunum*, p. 370.
90 *Skarðsárannáll*, p. 75; Kristjánsdóttir, *Leitin að klaustrunum*, p. 543.
91 *Lögmannsannáll*, p. 295.
92 Guðlaugsson, 'Munkaþverárklaustur', pp. 231–238.
93 DI VII, p. 340.
94 *Lögmannsannáll*, p. 286; *Nýi annáll*, pp. 10–11.
95 DI III, p. 718; DI IV, p. 700.
96 Riddell et al., 'Pollen, Plague and Protestants'.
97 Lagerås, 'Summary of conclusions', p. 160–161.
98 Gilchrist, 'Rethinking later medieval masculinity', p. 241. See even Thibodeaux, 'Introduction: Rethinking the Medieval Clergy and Masculinity', pp. 1–15; Thibodeaux, 'Man of the church, or man of the village?', pp. 380–399.
99 DI IV, p. 497.
100 Sigurðardóttir, *Allt hafði annan róm áður í páfadóm*, p. 124.
101 DI IV, pp. 456–458.

102 DI IV, pp. 456–458.
103 *Íslenskar æviskrár*, p. 520.
104 *Code of Canon Law*, Chapter III, Article 2, Can 648 §1 and §3; *Code of Canon Law*, Chapter III, Article 2, Can 653 §1.
105 *Code of Canon Law*, Chapter VI, Article 3, Can 701–704. See, also, Cohen, 'Asylums for Women in Counter-Reformation Italy', pp. 177–181; Power, *Medieval English Nunneries c. 1275 to 1535*.
106 Jónsson, *Historia ecclesiastica Islandiæ* I, p. 668.
107 DI VI, pp. 633–634.
108 See Kristjánsdóttir, 'The Poisoned Arrows of Amor', pp. 406–418.
109 Kristjánsdóttir, 'The Poisoned Arrows of Amor', pp. 406–418; Kristjánsdóttir, *Sagan af klaustrinu af Skriðu*, pp. 198–207; Walser III et al., 'Volcanoes, medicine, and monasticism', pp. 48–61.
110 Kristjánsdóttir, 'The Poisoned Arrows of Amor', pp. 406–418; Waldron, *Palaeopathology*, pp. 103, 106.
111 Hackett, *Diagnostic criteria for syphilis*; Waldron, *Palaeopathology*, pp. 103, 106.
112 Kristjánsdóttir, *Sagan af klaustrinu af Skriðu*, pp. 198–207.
113 Kristjánsdóttir, 'The Tip of the Iceberg', pp. 52–53.
114 Rasmussen et al., 'Mercury levels in Danish Medieaval human bones'; Shorter, 'Primary Care', pp. 108–109; Walser III et al., 'Volcanoes, medicine, and monasticism', pp. 48–61.
115 See, for example, Grímsdóttir, 'Biskupsstóll í Skálholti', pp. 49–50; Guðlaugsson, 'Viðeyjarklaustur', pp. 628–633.
116 Farmer, *The Oxford Dictionary of Saints*, pp. 371–372.
117 Þorláksson, 'Þjóðhagir og samfélagshópar', p. 124; Ísberg, *Líf og lækningar*, p. 162.
118 Ísberg, *Líf og lækningar*, pp. 162–163.
119 Crosby, 'The early history of syphilis', pp. 218–220; Kristjánsdóttir, 'The Poisoned Arrows of Amor', pp. 413–414.
120 Crosby, 'The early history of syphilis: a reappraisal'; Kiple, *The History of disease*, pp. 31–32; Majander et al., 'Ancient Bacterial Genomes', p. 3789; Waldron, *Palaeopathology*, pp. 104–105.
121 Anderson et al., 'Suspected endemic syphilis (Treponarid) in sixteenth-century Norway', pp. 341–350; Buzhilova, 'Medieval Examples of Syphilis from European Russia', pp. 271–276; Hutchinson and Weaver, 'Two Cases of Facial Involvement', pp. 133–143; Majander et al., 'Ancient Bacterial Genomes', pp. 3790–3791; Mays et al., 'Two Probable Cases of Treponemal Disease', pp. 133–143; Møller-Christensen, *Æbelholt kloster*, pp. 196–198.
122 Crosby, 'The early history of syphilis: a reappraisal'; Hutchinson and Weaver, 'Two Cases of Facial Involvement'; Mays et al., 'Two Probable Cases of Treponemal Disease', Majander et al., 'Ancient Bacterial Genomes', pp. 3788–3803; Waldron, *Palaeopathology*, p. 105.
123 DI VII, pp. 232–234.
124 DI VII, pp. 355–357.
125 DI VII, pp. 111–115, 117–118.
126 Guðlaugsson, 'Þingeyraklaustur', pp. 183–190.
127 DI VII, pp. 325–330, 412–413.
128 DI VIII, p. 313. See also Arnórsdóttir, *Property and Virginity*, p. 192.
129 DI VIII, pp. 133–135.
130 DI VII, p. 328. See also Arnórsdóttir, *Property and Virginity*, p. 190.
131 DI VI, pp. 499–500.
132 See, for example, DI VI, pp. 499–500 and DI VII, p. 761.
133 Arnórsdóttir, *Property and Virginity*, pp. 190–192.
134 Arnórsdóttir, *Property and Virginity*, pp. 179–195; Jørgensen et al., *Synder og pavemakt*, pp. 53–124; Salonen, 'Forbidden Marital Strategies', pp. 181–208.

135 DI V, pp. 609.
136 See also Arnórsdóttir, *Property and Virginity*, pp. 183, 190–192.
137 DI IX, p. 192.
138 *Flateyjarannáll*, p. 402.
139 *Flateyjarannáll*, p. 402; *Lögmannsannáll*, p. 274.
140 Jónsson, *Historia ecclesiastica Islandiæ* I, pp. 104, 365; Jónsson, *Historia ecclesiastica Islandiæ* II, pp. 586–588.
141 *Flateyjarannáll*, p. 402; *Lögmannsannáll*, p. 274.
142 DI II, p. 780; Kristjánsdóttir, *Leitin að klaustrunum*, p. 281.
143 Einarsson, 'Systrastapi', pp. 163–172.
144 Kallestrup, 'Reformation og trolddomsforfølgelser i Europa', pp. 248–249; Madigan, *Medieval Christianity*, pp. 201–210.
145 Kjær and Vogt, 'Straf og forvisning', p. 349; Kallestrup, 'Reformation og trolddomsforfølgelser i Europa', pp. 244–252; Þorvarðardóttir, *Brennuöldin*.
146 Grímsdóttir, 'Biskupsstóll í Skálholti', p. 38; Kristjánsdóttir, *Leitin að klaustrunum*, p. 281.
147 *Flateyjarannáll*, pp. 402–403.
148 *Gottskálksannáll*, p. 365.
149 Burton, 'Medieval Nunneries and Male Authority', pp. 123–140; Golding, 'Bishops and Nuns', pp. 97–115.
150 *Lögmannsannáll*, p. 283.
151 Burton, 'Medieval Nunneries and Male Authority', pp. 133–135.

8
THE MONASTIC COMMUNITIES

The surviving inventories of the Icelandic monasteries, presented in Chapter 6, contain a fascinating level of detail. Not only do they provide extensive information about their lodgings, but they likewise shed light on how these ecclesiastical institutions strived – through their buildings and interiors – to be honest in their operations and visible in society. However, the inventories are not the only evidence providing such a wide-ranging overview of the monastic houses in Iceland. Material remains, intertwined with other written documents, provided several interesting snapshots of the lives being lived in them. As is even described in brief in Chapter 1, the excavation at Skriðuklaustur enabled researchers to envisage a busy and bustling environment with many lay servants and visitors. This seems to have been the case for the other monastic houses as well. The sources used contained a wealth of descriptions of events and incidents involving people of all ages, classes, and sexes. Thus, to be a member of an ecclesiastical institution did not mean a quiet secluded life without any events, but rather active participation in the surrounding community. All this together debunks the myth that Icelandic monasteries were isolated, silent places or simple cells functioning principally as retirement homes for aristocrats. Moreover, the Icelandic monastic history shows clearly that the general public, no less than the clerical or secular authorities, retained a collective consciousness of monasticism, which was in turn influenced by diverse temporal motivations. The influence monasticism – male and female – had on the formation and development of Icelandic society continued steadily to increase throughout the Middle Ages. Subsequently, it became an integral part of the everyday lives of the medieval Icelander because the development was mutual. The growth of the Icelandic monasteries is noticeable, not only in the refurnishing and enlargement of their buildings after 1300, but also in the increased production of books and textiles, the growing popularity of corrody contracts, the expansion

DOI: 10.4324/9781003361077-8

of monasteries' livestock herds, and the rise in donations to them, to mention some examples that are examined further in this chapter. The saintly devotions of each monastic institution are interesting in this context because with their material and non-material aspects, they shed light on the aims and objectives of the monastic houses.

The Devotion of the Icelandic Monastic Houses

By being one of the fundamental doctrines of Roman Catholicism, the intercession of saints became a characteristic feature of medieval Europe. The saints were an all-encompassing presence in the lives of medieval Christians: they were appeared almost everywhere, in statues, likenesses, low reliefs, altarpieces, interiors, paintings, embroidered textiles, books, and even day-to-day items, with their attributes reflecting their devotional meaning. Furthermore, the saints likewise appeared in people's Christian names, votive letters, charters, testimonies, and wills. Specific masses were even held to honor the saints during the ecclesiastical year, such as Þorláksmessa, held annually in Iceland and the Faeroe Islands on 23 December at the date of Bishop Þorlákur's death.[1] Importantly, it was through the saints that people could seek help from God in matters concerning any aspect of human life, from curing specific illness to simply finding a lost tool; however, the intercession had to accord with the saint's devotional background.[2] The omnipresence of the saints encompassed sincerely the blurred boundaries between their material existence and their otherworldly nature. Body parts in shrines, as well as the corporeal appearance of saintly likenesses, were simultaneously persons and objects, emphasizing their sacredness.[3] This is highlighted, for example, in an entry in the Icelandic annals, in which it is officially announced that blood dripped from a crucifix in Þingeyraklaustur on Easter Sunday in 1273.[4]

Accordingly, in this manner, the dedication that each saint motivated is here used to shed light on the specific emphasis of the monastic houses concerned. Indeed, the ninety-four images of thirty saints and the hagiographies of sixty-six saints that were owned by them may certainly reveal some of their priorities, as will be shown hereinafter. The large number of hagiographical translations even point to a general knowledge about holy men and women in Iceland and, importantly, what they stood for on each occasion.[5] Yet, the patron saints of the Icelandic monastic churches are not known in all cases, but it is though known that the churches of Þingeyraklaustur and Munkaþverárklaustur were both dedicated to St. Nicholas,[6] the church of Helgafellsklaustur to St. John,[7] the church in Kirkjubæjarklaustur to the Virgin Mary,[8] the church in Skriðuklaustur to Virgin Mary, Jesus, and the Holy blood,[9] and finally, the monastic cell of chieftain Jón Loftsson was dedicated to St. John the Baptist.[10] Only Kirkjubæjarklaustur and Skriðuklaustur, however, appear to have owned statues of their patron saint, the Virgin Mary. The statue from Kirkjubæjarklaustur is not preserved but is mentioned in inventories, but the one Skriðuklaustur possessed may have been the one found in a barn there a century ago.

It was the bishops who had the final say in the dedication of ecclesiastical houses,[11] which were in turn supposed to be supplied with likenesses of their patron saints, respectively a vernacular version of their story. It has even been suggested that the bishops determined the dedications in accordance with what was needed than what was fitting. The presence of saints, other than the patron saints in ecclesiastical houses, is of this reason believed to have been often based on individual wishes.[12] All in all, this implies that the saints were not randomly chosen, but rather selected in response to threatening situations in the surrounding society or in accordance with personal needs. As the case of Skriðuklaustur shows, Bishop Stefán appears to have had the welfare of the founders in mind while working on the establishment of the monastery, which may indicate that bishops did, after all, prioritize principles of need when choosing patron saints or other divine saints for new ecclesiastical houses. Such decisions were though hardly made without consultation and must have been based on valid and prudent arguments. The figurine depicting St. Barbara, discovered in the monastic ruins, shows clear evidence of devotion to her in Skriðuklaustur. Primarily, St. Barbara was supposed to protect people from heat, such as that occurring during volcanic eruptions or fires, but in the fourteenth century, she was classed as one of The Fourteen Holy Helpers, the group of saints venerated together as the protectors of those suffering from fever related to the plague and other epidemics. A likeness of this saint was thus highly fitting given Skriðuklaustur's role as a hospital, inevitably, besides a likeness of the patron saint: Virgin Mary. In fact, St. Barbara appears several times in documents related to Skriðuklaustur, such as in the will of Einar Ormson's family when the monastery was established.[13] St. Barbara was also worshipped at Reynistaðarklaustur. This is demonstrated, for example, by Abbess Barbara herself, who was christened Þóra but changed her name to Barbara when she took her vows as abbess.

Nevertheless, one of the clearest examples of saintly devotion mirroring the needs is from the female convent at Kirkjubæjarklaustur. Not only was its patron saint the Virgin Mary, but the saints recorded in its possession also focus principally on women, their work, and their position in life. The likeness of Kirkjubæjarklaustur's patron saint, Virgin Mary, was listed in the inventory done in 1343, but by then it also owned a likeness of St. Catherine.[14] When Bishop Vilchin made his formal inspection of the convent in 1397, there were two new likenesses of female saints, St. Agnes and St. Cecilia, as well as the original two.[15] Still, they also had three new ones of male saints in 1397: St. Clement, probably one of the early popes; the Apostle St. Matthew; and, predictably, the founder of the convent, Bishop Þorlákur Þórhallsson, who had at that time been sanctified by popular devotion in Iceland.[16] Still, the devotional meaning of all these saints is interesting. The Virgin, in fact, was by far the most popular saint in Roman Catholic Christianity, but her veneration was associated with notions about maternal devotion, purity, and the salvation of the human soul.[17] St. Catherine was the protector of unmarried girls and schoolchildren, as well as of those working with wheels, such as spinners (Figure 8.1).[18] St. Agnes was the protector of rape victims, celibacy, and girls in general,[19] and St. Cecilia was the protector of musicians and hymns.[20]

FIGURE 8.1 From Kirkjubæjarbók. An illuminated drawing of St. Catherine (Copenhagen, Arnamagnæan Collection, AM 429 12 mo. Photograph: Suzanne Reitz. Published with permission from the Arnamagnæan Institute).

In other words, the saints present in Kirkjubæjarklaustur, in tangible and intangible forms, were venerated mostly as the protectors of women. Furthermore, one of the most precious books the nuns at Kirkjubæjarklaustur had in their library was the aforementioned *Kirkjubæjarbók*. The book deals exclusively with female saints: Saints Agatha, Agnes, Barbara, Cecilia, Dorothea, Catherine (Figure 8.1), Margaret, and finally, saints Fides, Spes, and Caritas together. It is illuminated with a number of artfully colored drawings of the saints – some containing imported indigo – along with Old Norse/Icelandic translations of their stories and prose texts.[21] The protection provided by Saints Agnes, Barbara, Cecilia, Dorothea, and Catherine has already been discussed, but St. Agatha is the protector of wet nurses and rape victims. St. Margaret is the protector of women in childbirth, pregnant women, and the dying. The last three, Saints Fides, Spes, and Caritas, are the protectors of pilgrims, the poor, and the sick, and of charity work in general, but they were all venerated together as the personification of faith, hope, and charity.[22] In this way, *Kirkjubæjarbók*, along with the monastery's saintly images, emphasized the importance of Kirkjubæjarklaustur as a place of refuge for abused women, its value for women in general, and its celebration of their profession as weavers and textile workers. In fact, it was hardly a coincidence that the female convent in Kirkjubæjarklaustur publicly acknowledged that its saintly devotion centered on women's lives. There, women could be protected and even receive an education in female professions and pursuits.

The other monastic houses display much broader and diverse aims through their saints. As has been noted, the patron saint of the monastic church in Þingeyraklaustur was St. Nicholas, the protector of sailors, fishermen, merchants, and children, although surprisingly, according to the inventories, the monastery did not own a likeness of him and, in fact, no resources support this dedication. Instead, the monastery possessed likenesses – sometimes multiple likenesses – of St. Andrew, St. Catherine, St. Clare, Bishop Jón, Jesus, James, John the Baptist, King Olaf, Paul, Peter, and St. Zita, in addition to the Virgin Mary. As in Kirkjubæjarklaustur, St. Catherine must have been the protector of spinners in Þingeyraklaustur, but St. Clare was the patron saint of tailors and those suffering from eye diseases.[23] St. Zita, whose images belonged to both Þingeyraklaustur and Munkaþverárklaustur, was the protector of lay workers.[24] Bearing in mind the two couples who had promised to undertake farming and household work for Þingeyraklaustur and Munkaþverárklaustur, both St. Catherine and St. Zita at least seem to suit the activities of their respective monasteries. St. Zita, who otherwise appears in different forms in most of the ecclesiastical institutions of the diocese of Hólar, seems to have been highly popular in that area throughout the Middle Ages.[25] The emphasis here was not exclusively on female saints, as was the case in Kirkjubæjarklaustur. However, the collection in Þingeyraklaustur is very similar those at the other monasteries, and even the female convent at Reynistaður, although there was some interesting local variation between them all. For example, Möðruvallaklaustur owned a likeness of St. Bartholomew, who protected those working at manuscript making.[26] Möðruvallaklaustur also owned the story of St. Birgit[27] of Sweden but it is not known to be found in the other monastic houses in Iceland.[28] Another unique example of devotion to a saint's cult can be detected from the figurine of St. Dorothea excavated at Viðeyjarklaustur. Her story appears in *Kirkjubæjarbók* and in one of the preserved antependia made in Reynistaðarklaustur, but a likeness of her has not been found at other monastic houses in Iceland, nor is she listed in inventories. Her attribute is a basket with vegetables and fruits, as she is the patron saint of gardeners and gardening. It is thus likely that gardening was one of the types of work carried out in the monastery at Viðey. Indeed, pollen analysis indicates that gardening on Viðey island was initiated when the monastery was in operation there.[29]

One of many other saints worth mentioning here is St. Roch. According to a charter from 1523, Þykkvabæjarklaustur owned a likeness of him – the only monastic house in Iceland that did so.[30] St. Roch was born in the Kingdom of Majorca as late as in 1348. He died a martyr's death in 1367 and was popularly regarded as a saint before being formally canonized by Pope Gregory XIV nearly two centuries later.[31] The story of St. Roch was also included in *Reykjahólabók*.[32] St. Roch's presence in Þykkvabæjarklaustur in 1523 shows that saints who might protect against illness were very popular in the fourteenth and fifteenth centuries, a time of frequent natural disasters and epidemics, with a cooling climate, periodic volcanic eruptions, and recurring outbreaks of the plague and smallpox. Most importantly, however, does the presence of St. Roch demonstrate that even in distant Iceland, Christians were adopting new ideas and the cults of new saints as they emerged on the Continent. It is truly intriguing to observe how quickly the cult of this saint was introduced into Iceland, but it highlights the ongoing and constant connection Icelanders had to their fellow Christians elsewhere.

The fact that hagiographies were translated into the vernacular Old Norse/Icelandic shows, moreover, that these must have been fundamental for the official education – vocational or academic – offered in both the episcopal and the monastic schools.[33] Further analyzation of the evidence for manuscript and textile production in the monastic houses elucidated, as we will see, important aspects of their influences, not only on society but also on nature, because all the monastic houses kept large flocks of cattle and sheep for their manufacturing. The presence of livestock on the monastic settlements does certainly hint at other uses than for manuscript and textile making, such as for dairy production, or food, for the religious, the laity, clients, and occasional visitors. In fact, quite many people must have worked with their large-scale manufacturing besides taking care of other manual tasks in the monastic houses (see Tables 8.6 and 8.7). Before their livestock and their potential residents will be discussed, an overview will be provided on the manuscript and textile work undertaken in both the male and female convents.

Textiles as Texts

The translations of the saintly stories appear to have been undertaken mostly in the monastic institutions, whose expertise in manuscript making was widely known. Þingeyraklaustur, Helgafellsklaustur, and Þykkvabæjarklaustur are some of the best known in that domain.[34] The large number of cattle owned by the monastic institutions, such as Helgafellsklaustur and Þykkvabæjarklaustur, may emphasize their focus on these pursuits. Investigations done so far on Icelandic parchment, however, show that it was generally made of calfskin, although this remains to be investigated further. Sheep and goatskin has not yet been detected in parchment from Iceland, but skin of calves, sheep, and goats were commonly used in book production in England, France, and Italy during the Middle Ages.[35] A recent study proves, moreover, that calfskin was predominant in production of parchment in Norway,[36] as appears to have been the case in Iceland too. Indeed, the livestock possessed by Reynistaðarklaustur may indicate a similar purpose as in Þingeyraklaustur, Helgafellsklaustur, and Þykkvabæjarklaustur, although nuns are generally not thought to have produced manuscripts. Intensive research on the manuscript AM 764, commonly named *Reynistaðarbók*, suggests that it was made in Reynistaðarklaustur, but specifically *for* the nuns there, rather than *by* them. *Reynistaðarbók* was written during the period from 1360 to 1380. The nuns of Kirkjubæjarklaustur are not considered to have produced either *Kirkjubæjarbók* themselves or any other book, for that matter. Instead, it has been suggested that *Kirkjubæjarbók* was compiled by the neighboring monks of Þykkvabæjarklaustur, as the nuns' occupation is usually assumed to have centered on needlework, embroidery, and weaving.[37] Unlike *Kirkjubæjarbók* that encompasses exclusively hagiographies of female saints, *Reynistaðarbók* contains vernacular translations of universal history (Lat. *aetates mundi*), annals, *Exempla*, miracles, and some hagiographies.[38] Nevertheless, a field north of the current living quarters at Reynistaðarklaustur bears a rare place name that seems to be indicative of manuscript making: Calfskin Hill (Icel. *Kálfskinnshóll*).[39] Still, this does not have to be seen as an indication that the nuns themselves participated in the writing. On the other hand, they may as well have supplied the producer with raw material for the making of *Reynistaðarbók* and possibly more books.

What may be criticized, however, is that monastic studies have too often been aimed at tracing evidence that might prove women's involvement in the male-dominated work of writing, instead of highlighting the highly skilled work the nuns carried out while making ecclesiastical cloths and even *vaðmál*. *Vaðmál* was Iceland's main export product from the eleventh to fourteenth centuries, but after that, the price of it diminished drastically. At the same time, the demand for highly valuable ecclesiastical clothes increased – most likely because of the firm foothold the Church had gained in the country and in Europe as well.[40] *Vaðmál* was otherwise used for taxation, exchange, and gifts throughout Scandinavia, but it was also accepted as currency in Shetland and Ireland. Nearly all commodities were in fact priced in *vaðmál* during the early Middle Ages in Iceland.[41] The pre-industrial textile production of *vaðmál*, furthermore, is usually believed to have taken place inside the households themselves and later in the monasteries too, but in the female convents, the more advanced ecclesiastical clothes were made.[42]

In studies, done so far, the crucial role of women in the textile making has been highlighted and thereby their important contribution to the economy of the North-Atlantic and Scandinavian societies during the Middle Ages. The women served as designers and weavers and even oversaw that the legal measurements were followed.[43] Truly, textile production was no less lucrative than manuscript making, and both seem to have occupied a very important place in the activities undertaken at Iceland's monastic houses. Textiles are, in fact, texts. Both are spun and woven fabrics, and both are commodities. Moreover, the meaning behind texts and textiles is always dependent on the observer, rather than the composer.[44] Textiles and texts even demand advanced academic and practical skills, but textiles seem nonetheless to have, during later times, ended up in the shadow of the manuscript making. It is safe to say that woven tapestries and wall-hangings were more valuable and desirable among both the clergy and the aristocracy than most other crafts, excepting perhaps the most precious metal artifacts. Embroidered chasubles, gowns, antependia, and tapestries were, similarly, extremely valuable, as were most other ecclesiastical textiles. An elaborate chasuble could have a value comparable to that of three or four farms – or a book.[45] The textile production even included making of clothes, towels, blankets, bags, and many more fabrics used by the general public, not only the Church. The inventories listed in Chapter 6 show, furthermore, that the monastic houses were furnished with different kinds of wall hangings, even embroidered with ecclesiastical motifs, but these must have been manufactured in the female convents where academic skills and the raw material were at hand. The fire in Möðruvallaklaustur in 1316 may even be mentioned in this context because, according to documents, it spread to the tapestry in the choir and became uncontrollable after that.

What is, moreover, particularly noteworthy in the inventories is that in Kirkjubæjarklaustur, there were enough chasubles for twenty-one priests in 1343 and twenty-four in 1397. This is only half of what Reynistaðarklaustur possessed in 1408, but interestingly, the number of ceremonial dresses for the male servants in Kirkjubæjarklaustur is similar to what the male monasteries had (Table 8.1). As there never seem to have been more than one or two priests serving the nuns in Kirkjubæjarklaustur at any given time, as was the case in Reynistaðarklaustur in the north, it is likely that the textiles were produced by the nuns and were meant to be given away or sold. The extra chasubles may thus have been the stock from their textile manufacturing. Regardless, both historical documents and the archaeological remains found in the ruins of the convent bear witness to its emphasis on textile work. Notably, Bishop Vilchin (r. 1391–1405) officially praised the nuns' work during his visitation in 1397. Shortly thereafter, he purchased tapestries from them for all four walls of the so-called large hall (Icel. *stóra stofa*) in Skálholt, in addition to a number of ecclesiastical garments for the cathedral.[46] The excavation of the ruins of Kirkjubæjarklaustur also revealed clear evidence of textile work, including the remains of a warp-weighted loom dating back to the fifteenth century.[47]

It is worth drawing attention again to the several precious medieval textiles, ecclesiastical and non-ecclesiastical, that are preserved today from Iceland. At least thirteen of them are believed to have been made in the Icelandic female convents, Kirkjubæjarklaustur and Reynistaðarklaustur.[48] The ones that are linked to

TABLE 8.1 Ecclesiastical textiles and garments recorded in the monastic houses in Iceland. The female monasteries are emphasized in italics.

Monastic house	*Inventory year*	*Chasuble*	*Gown*	*Robe*	*Dalmatic*	*Antependia*	*Vestment*
Skálholt							
Þykkvabæjarklaustur	1340	30	29	11	19	9	30
Helgafellsklaustur	1378	20	14	12	4	4	15
Helgafellsklaustur	1397	20	12	12	4	8	20
Viðeyjarklaustur	1367	25	21	11	7	12	16
Kirkjubæjarklaustur	1343	22	20	8	6	14	
Kirkjubæjarklaustur	1397	24	13	4	5	14	8
Hólar							
Þingeyraklaustur	1525	15	9	5	4	3	9
Munkaþverárklaustur	1429	14	18			5	4
Munkaþverárklaustur	1525	20	13	5	2	8	10
Möðruvallaklaustur	1525	2	12	7	3	3	10
Reynistaðarklaustur	1408	12	6		10	13	10
Reynistaðarklaustur	1525					7	
Total		**184**	**155**	**63**	**60**	**96**	**117**

Kirkjubæjarklaustur are a wall hanging from Hvammur, a burse from Kálfafell, and two antependia: one from Arnarbæli and another from Kálfafell. The textiles that are assumed to have been made in Reynistaðarklaustur are antependium from Reykjahlíð, Draflastaðir, Höfði, Svalbarð,[49] Grenjaðarstaður, Skarð, Vellir, and Múli, in addition to one uncertain from Hólar Cathedral.[50] Eight of these textiles are kept in the National Museum of Iceland, but five are stored or are on display in museums abroad, whereof one in Musée du Louvre in France (Figure 4.1). Interestingly enough, the name of Sólveig Hrafnsdóttir, the last abbess to serve Reynistaðarklaustur, is embroidered in the antependium from Skarð, along with images of six saints (Figure 7.1). Henceforth, what may be deduced from both documentary and archaeological sources, besides the preserved textile artifacts, is that great importance was placed on high-quality textile work in Kirkjubæjarklaustur, most likely in Reynistaðarklaustur too, in the context of both production and vocational training. The livestock there gives this expression too, as will be discussed in the following section.

The Livestock of the Monastic Houses

In the light of the evidence gained about the extensive textile production taking place in Kirkjubæjarklaustur, it should not come as a surprise that it had a significantly larger number of sheep than any other monastic house in Iceland ever had. Unfortunately, Bishop Vilchin did not count the livestock at Kirkjubæjarklaustur when he made his visitation there in 1397, only the convent's furnishings and possessions, but a massive growth in the number of sheep and, likewise, cattle can nevertheless be detected between the inventories made in 1218 and 1343. In 1218 – only two decades after its establishment – there were 290 ewes, thirty cows, and seven bulls.[51] In 1343, conversely, the home farm of Kirkjubæjarklaustur had 1,410 sheep (900 ewes, 150 rams, and 360 lambs), and 118 cattle (twenty-six calves, forty cows, and fifty-two bulls) (Tables 8.2, 8.3, and 8.4).[52]

Lambs are not listed in inventories from any other monastic house than the female convent in Kirkjubær, but the reason for this is not known. It must be underlined here that the wool differs in accordance with the age of the sheep. The best suitable wool for making textiles is of older ewes; however, twenty ewes could provide one *vætt*[53] of high-quality wool per year. Oddly enough, the high number of sheep held in Kirkjubæjarklaustur may underline increased emphasis there put on textile production as time passed, and on a larger scale than ever before. The work carried out by the nuns was certainly not *worthless* needlework and embroidery, but rather the manufacture of expensive ecclesiastical fabrics and garments, as well as textiles for the public. Still, the number of calves is also high in Kirkjubæjarklaustur compared to the other monastic houses (Tables 8.3 and 8.4). The calves may certainly have been raised there because of the skin, to be used for making parchment in the convent or perhaps for wider distribution such as to Þykkvabæjarklaustur.

TABLE 8.2 Number of cattle and sheep owned by the monastic houses.

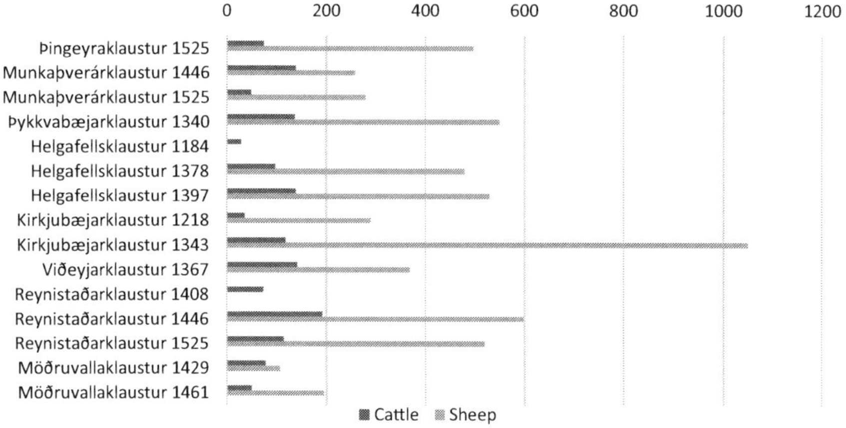

TABLE 8.3 Number of wether, lamb, rams, and ewes owned by the monastic houses.

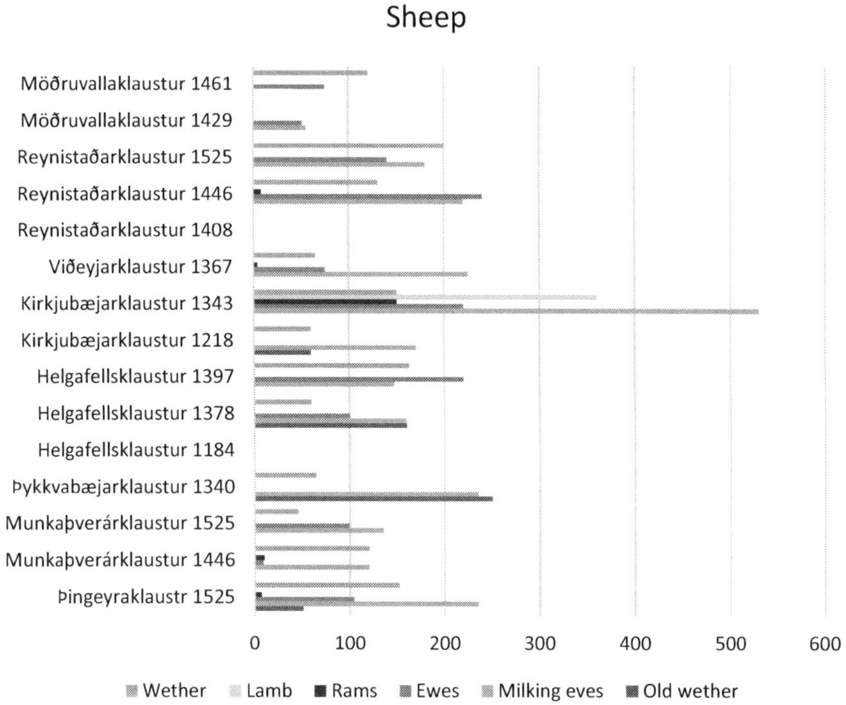

The number of livestock in the other female monastery, Reynistaðarklaustur, is also fascinating. The earliest inventory that included a count of the livestock there was made due to changes in stewardship in 1408. At that point, the livestock at the convent itself included twenty-two cows, nine old bulls, thirty-six young bulls, and seven calves. Interestingly, however, there were no sheep listed. On the other hand, on farms owned by the convent, sixty-six ewes were counted and twenty-eight cows.[54] When the livestock in Reynistaðarklaustur was counted again in 1446, it had expanded enormously. At the convent itself, there were by then no fewer than 192 head of cattle and 598 sheep (Table 8.2).[55] This is certainly large number of domestic animals on an Icelandic scale, even by today's standards. The last inventory from Reynistaðarklaustur is the one compiled by Bishop Jón Arason of Hólar in 1525. At that point, there were 114 head of cattle and 520 sheep.[56] These three inventories show that the number of sheep was highest there around the mid-fifteenth century, perhaps due to the growing demand for ecclesiastical fabrics. We can in this context call to mind the nine embroidered antependium that are believed to have been made in Reynistaðarklaustur, but these fabrics all date to the fifteenth century.[57]

The remarkably high number of cattle – notably the highest ever counted in an Icelandic monastic settlement – may even underline the nuns' overall wealth and that the nuns in Reynistaðarklaustur housed a large number of people for the inner work of the convent. Still, because there is no comparable inventory of the livestock held by all the monastic houses at the same time, it is difficult to conclude that the situation was not the same in all of them. Interestingly, nevertheless, by looking closer at the division between cows, bulls, calves, and yearlings, it is noticeable that the number of calves and yearlings are also highest ever in Reynistaðarklaustur in 1446 (Table 8.4). No other monastic house in Iceland had a livestock of similar

TABLE 8.4 Number of yearlings, calves, bulls, and cows owned by the monastic houses.

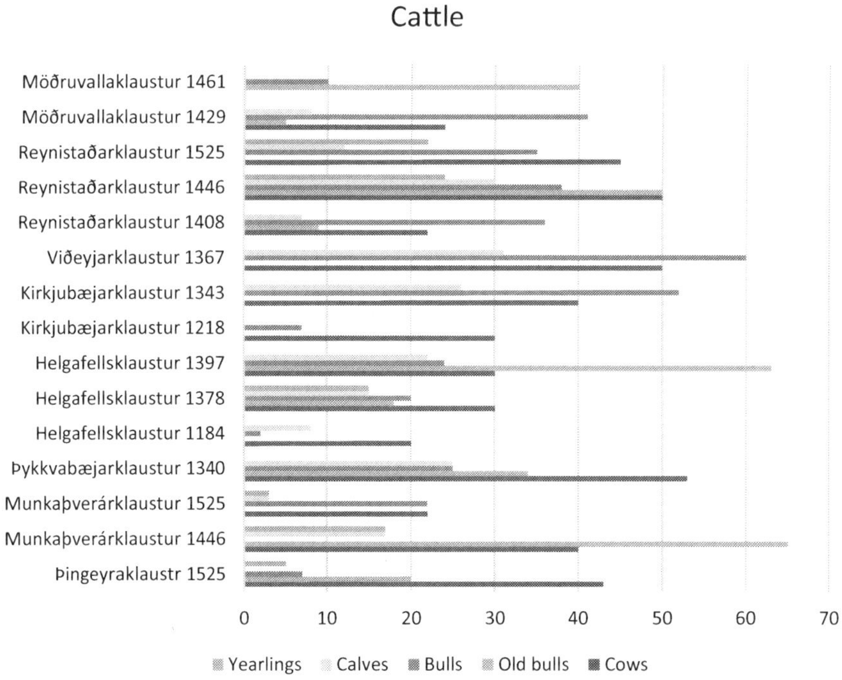

size. This may certainly underline their contribution to manuscript making, however, most likely through providing raw material for the production since the nuns appear not to have made books themselves.

As can be read in Table 8.2, even the male monastic houses ran mixed ranges of sheep and cattle, although not on the same scale as the female convents. There is no doubt that the livestock not only was meant to deliver food supplies for the residents, but also was simultaneously intended for the manuscript making and the production of *vaðmál* and other garments. However, it is hard to comprehend the generally large number of bulls the monastic houses had; some had over 100 each, but skin of fully grown cattle can't be used as parchment. It could certainly be used for making book covers, shoes, and clothes, besides the fact that the cattle provided meat and bones for making tools. Calves and yearlings are in fact relatively few in the male monastic houses, compared to the large-scale manuscript making in them. Still, the calves might have been slaughtered when the inventories were done during the winter, but according to *Jónsbók*, calves needed to be born after *Pálsmessa* (the feast of Conversion of St. Paul) on 25 January and before the end of April.[58] The approximate number of calves kept in the monasteries may perhaps only be gained through analyzing zooarchaeological material. Regardless, this important raw material that calfskin certainly may also have been distributed to the monastic houses through donations or by those who ordered a book from them.

Nevertheless, it was mainly during the fourteenth century that the male monastic houses Þingeyraklaustur, Helgafellsklaustur, and Þykkvabæjarklaustur became known for their extensive manuscript making.[59] However, Þingeyraklaustur gained a prestigious reputation for its book production – a reputation that reached far beyond Iceland itself – shortly after its establishing.[60] Not only were the Benedictine monks there involved in writing religious and historical texts in Latin and Old Norse/Icelandic for Christian kings in northern Europe, but they were also responsible for writing histories for some of the leading chieftains in Iceland, in addition to writing the bishops' saga of Jón Ögmundsson. Twenty-one manuscripts are preserved from Þingeyraklaustur, whereof the majority treasured by the manuscript collector Árni Magnússon, but it is not known how many are lost.[61] One of the most precious and famous ones made there is *Flateyjarbók*, *Codex Flateyensis*. *Flateyjarbók* is largest of all medieval Icelandic manuscripts, composed of 225 written and illustrated parchment leaves, in total 450 pages, made of approximately 100 calf's skins.[62] The making of *Flateyjarbók* begun in 1387, according to what is stated in its forewords, but there it is also indicated that it was written and made in Þingeyraklaustur. However, besides writing historical books, vernacular law books, religious texts, and translations of hagiographies, the monks in Þingeyraklaustur and the canons in Helgafellsklaustur even composed their own chivalric sagas (*Riddarasögur*) from the mid-thirteenth century and onwards.[63] The emerging of the Old Norse genre of vernacular chivalric sagas has been associated with the adaption and translation of French heroic-romantic literature at the court of Håkan the Old, King of Norway (r. 1217–1263).[64] The growing interest in translating and composing chivalric sagas in Iceland can thus likewise be linked to the transfer of the secular governing of the country to the Norwegian crown in 1262–1264. Regrettably, the only surviving inventory from Þingeyraklaustur is the one from 1525, so the number of cows and calves is not known from periods in its history when the manuscript making was at its peak. The number of livestock there at that point may thus not reveal any adequate information about manuscript making by the Benedictine monks, not at least in light of the fact that the demand for parchment at that time was decreasing, whereas printing was about to take over parchment making in Iceland (see Table 8.4).

The stock of animals on the home farm at Helgafellsklaustur was counted the first time when the monastery was moved from the island of Flatey in 1184. There were by then twenty cows, two bulls, and eight young calves.[65] When the livestock in Helgafellsklaustur was counted again in 1378, there were listed thirty cows, thirty-seven bulls, fifteen calves, the same number of yearlings, and 480 sheep.[66] Indeed, the number of animals there had grown substantially since its initial years. Still, the growth is particularly noticeable between 1378 and 1397 when an inventory was made there the third time. In 1397, eighty-seven bulls of different ages were counted, twenty-two calves, thirty cows, and 530 sheep (see Tables 8.2, 8.3, and 8.4).[67] It is worth mentioning that around this time, notably in 1363, *Skarðsbók Jónsbókar* was written in Helgafellsklaustur, but it is considered to be one of the most magnificent codices belonging to the Icelandic medieval manuscript collection, along with *Flateyjarbók*.[68] It contains a copy of the vernacular law of *Jónsbók*, written on 157 parchment leaves.[69]

Þykkvabæjarklaustur also owned quite a number of cattle, but the only official livestock count carried out there was the one done in 1340. At that point, the home farm held fifty-three cows, fifty-nine bulls, twenty-five calves and 550 sheep. *Kirkjubæjarbók* is the largest manuscript recognized from the monastery there was made at earlier point, around the year 1500. Curiously, Þykkvabæjarklaustur even owned four geese, two sows, and four piglets, but the other monastic houses were not recorded as having any of these animals.[70] The presence of the pigs and geese is unusual, but it may have stemmed from the personal wishes of the lay residents or the monks rather than the emergence of a new emphasis in monastic farming.

Preserved books from Viðeyjarklaustur, Munkaþverárklaustur, and Möðruvallaklaustur are not as well known as those from Þingeyraklaustur, Helgafellsklaustur, and Þykkvabæjarklaustur. Yet, examining the only inventory of livestock at Viðeyjarklaustur, carried out in 1367, reveals nothing surprising (see Tables 8.2, 8.3, and 8.4). There were thirty-one calves, sixty bulls, fifty cows, and 369 sheep.[71] The livestock was counted twice in Munkaþverárklaustur. In 1446 there were thirty-one calves and yearlings, forty cows, sixty-five old bulls, and 369 sheep.[72] In 1525, the number of livestock had fallen since the previous count, less than a century earlier. According to it, there were six calves and yearlings, twenty-two cows, the same number of bulls, and 280 sheep.[73] In fact, the number of domestic animals in Möðruvallaklaustur was lowest of the monastic houses in Iceland. In 1429, there were eight calves, twenty-four cows, and forty-six bulls, and 106 sheep.[74] In 1461, there were only 195 sheep and fifty bulls, but no cows (see Tables 8.2, 8.3, and 8.4).[75]

No inventory exists for Skriðuklaustur, but one letter shows that it owned some livestock. This was when Prior Þorvarður bought the farm Brekka in Fljótsdalur in 1513 and paid for it with fifteen cows and fifteen sheep, ten *hundruð* in bullocks, ten *hundruð* in calves, ten *hundruð* in butter, and twenty *hundruð* in money.[76] However, the zooarchaeological material collected during the excavation in Skriðuklaustur indicates that animal husbandry was not much practiced there, unlike at most other large monastic houses in Iceland.[77] At least, it appears to have been most common to consume only the meatiest parts of sheep and cattle there, but very few ribs and bones of the less meaty parts were found during the excavation. This pattern might suggest that instead of slaughtering animals at Skriðuklaustur, the canons purchased mainly meat and dairy food from other farms, such as Skriða. The animal bone assembly shows otherwise that mutton was the most common meat, followed by beef. Of course, the inhabitants of Skriðuklaustur also consumed fish, wild geese, seals, and whales, but fish appeared to be the second most common food eaten there.[78]

The production of manuscripts and textiles required various other natural resources than the wool of the sheep and the skin of cattle, such as for making the ink and the dye, combining the elements of nature and culture in this monastic production industry. The textile work would have ranged from collecting the wool to spinning, weaving, and dyeing, but the manuscript making involved slaughtering the animals and tanning the skin, to mention a few necessary tasks in the production process.[79] All this work demanded an extensive workforce and even specialized skills, such as in bookbinding. On the other hand, appropriate academic capacity was then needed to complete the end product through designing, and decorating, whether books or fabrics, both religious and non-religious. Altogether, on most of the monastic farms, cattle and sheep predominate, but religious servants, male or female, seem not to have been involved in caring for them or having taken part in the manual labor in general.

Household and Farm Work

The livestock owned by the monastic houses clearly indicate the breadth of non-ecclesiastical work carried out in them. However, this does not tell the whole story, because both the male and female monasteries owned properties located outside their home farms, which provide additional information on monastic activities and tasks. These farms and other assets were often received as donations from individuals seeking absolution from their sins; they were obtained through direct acquisitions and property transactions made on the initiative of the monastic houses themselves; and apparently, in some cases people donated farms or other financial assets in return for being allowed to work as official laymen or laywomen in Iceland's monastic houses. The monastic houses could also be the donators themselves. A letter written in September 1540 by Bishop Gissur in Skálholt addressed to Abbess Halldóra in Kirkjubæjarklaustur is preserved, but in it, he kindly asks her to support him with one horse, one bull, and butter because of a man he is going to accommodate in the episcopal see during the coming winter.[80]

Examples show, moreover, that the monastic houses made a substantial number of acquisitions entailing specific rights to valuable assets. These rights were often listed in written documents, showing what the monastic houses were entitled to collect from the properties in question. They included woodlands – providing firewood, charcoal, and timber – and shoreline areas with access to driftwood, fishing, seal hunting, and beached whales, among other things. In addition to this, the monastic houses were entitled to collect dairy products – such as cheese, butter, and *skyr* – from the farms they purchased or received as gifts. They also held rights to the meat of the animals and the fodder for them. This in turn required many lay servants and occasional workers to perform the various tasks all these resources demanded, besides taking care of the livestock on the home farms. Sometimes the residents of the monastic tenancies were supposed to contribute this work as a portion of their rent, in addition to transferring ownership of the valuables to the monastic houses in question.

The priors of Skriðuklaustur made numerous property acquisitions, as have been highlighted in the previous chapters, mainly to gain access to harbors and beaches. Forty-nine farms are mentioned as having been purchased or donated of different reasons to the monastery during its operation as such.[81] Some of the wealthiest monastic houses in Iceland owned up to 100 farms – Þingeyraklaustur in 1525 is a case in point[82] – while others had fewer. For example, Möðruvallaklaustur owned eighty farms by the end of the fourteenth century and Reynistaðarklaustur owned forty-four in 1446.[83] In 1378, Helgafellsklaustur owned forty-six farms, either wholly or in part, and by 1397, it owned fifty-three farms. Bishop Vilchin's inventory from 1397 states explicitly that Helgafellsklaustur had the right to collect wood, whales, and all other valuables that had washed up on the beaches beside and between specific farms that were privately owned by independent farmers.[84] This is a good example of how rights were listed, but the accessibility of the beaches varied greatly in each monastic settlement. Although nearly all the farms owned by Helgafellsklaustur, for instance, were on the Snæfellsnes peninsula, some were located in the northernmost part of the West Fjords, Strandir, and Hornstrandir,[85] an area known for its driftwood, which is abundant but very difficult to access. Particularly, gathering driftwood from such areas must have required significant manpower.

As has previously been noted, the importance of fish during periods of fasting may have been a major factor in the monasteries' need for access to the valuable farms located along Iceland's shorelines. Beached whales could also be eaten because the prohibition against meat only extended to animals with four legs. Likewise, beer was necessary for its nutritional value, particularly during fasting. No one was supposed to starve while fasting; the idea was to discipline the physical body insofar as the individual's health permitted. Exercising restraint around food was nevertheless highly important. It was not permissible, for example, to eat between organized mealtimes; however, the sick was allowed to eat whenever they wished, and as much as they wished, because food was an important part of the healing process. The excavation at Skriðuklaustur also proved that vegetables, such as turnips, kale, and even herbs, were grown and consumed there, both for flavoring food and for healing. Pollen from field garlic (*Allium oleraceum*) was even found, as were both pollen and seeds from nettles (*Urtica dioica*).[86] During a survey of surviving plants on the monastic precincts, some other specifically classified monastic plant remains were identified, such as the flixweed (*Descurainia Sophia*) in Saurbær and wild field garlic (*Allium oleraceum*) in Bær. These may have been introduced to the sites in connection with monastic activity. Interestingly, legendary stories claim that Abbot Rudolf himself imported the field garlic to Bær for cultivation at his monastery.[87]

According to inventories, as well as most other written documents and archaeological remains, the monastic buildings often appear to have been equipped with tools for brewing beer or the ingredients for making it. This should not be surprising since beer was important for fasting, as well as for celebrations, toasts, and feasts held in the monastic buildings, at the bishoprics, or in common dwellings.[88] Preserved Icelandic documents contain descriptions of feasts held, for example, when bishops were elected, during their visitations, when people gathered for Mass held in the honor of saints, or at wedding parties. Some specific and memorable occasions are known, including when the bishop's entourage in Hítardalur was killed in a fire that broke out there during a feast in 1148 (see Chapter 7). In another incident, the farm Flugumýri in Skagafjörður burned down during a wedding party in 1253. One of the guests at that party was a monk from Munkaþverárklaustur who bore the title of brewer. The fire was deliberately lit in the living quarters of the farm in order to burn it down after a fight had broken out. The brewer-monk, Þórólfur, then tried to rescue the groom, who had been so severely beaten that he had lost his leg. Þórólfur dragged him into the church, the place of sanctuary, where he died of his wounds shortly afterwards.[89] The groom, in fact, was Hallur Gissurarson, son of Gissur Þorvaldsson, to whom Ingibjörg Snorradóttir was given when their fathers, Þorvaldur Gissurarson and Snorri Sturluson, established Viðeyjarklaustur in 1226. Gissur, who belonged to the Haukdælir family clan, carried on in the same vein by marrying his son Hallur to thirteen-year-old Ingibjörg Sturludóttir, daughter of Sturlungar family chieftain Sturla Þórðarson. The marriage at Flugumýri was meant to seal an alliance between the two families in an attempt to settle the disputes of *Sturlungaöld* and prevent Iceland from being brought under the sovereignty of Norway.[90]

As has been suggested, the livestock on the monastic home farms or the monastic estates must have required many servants to feed, milk, house, and finally, slaughter the animals. The carcasses had to be worked for their meat and skin, and the bones were used for making tools. The excavation at Skriðuklaustur proved how common it was to use bones and horns to make a wide range of tools and implements, from carved shafts for knives to simpler kitchen utensils such as spoons. Even gaming pieces were made of bones and horns.[91] Skulls from large animals such as horses and cattle were usually used as stools, as was commonly done in

Iceland until twentieth century. Twenty-three stools of this kind were excavated from the ruins of Skriðuklaustur.[92] However, carved drinking horns were presumably the most valuable objects made of materials obtained from local livestock, and many of them are listed in the monastic inventories. Still, walrus tusk was undoubtedly the most valuable raw material to which Icelanders had access on the shoreline. Objects made of tusk appear several times as precious gifts in medieval documents in Iceland.

Several preserved contracts made between common workers and Iceland's monastic houses may shed further light on the work that needed to be done within the settlements. Such contracts often seem very similar to those made with corrodians, and in some cases, it is difficult to tell them apart, except that corrodians did not do any physical work for the monastic houses in which they lived. However, according to the contracts preserved from Iceland, the laity appear to have been people who carried out specific farm work or household tasks for the monastic community or even served the corrodians themselves, but in return were housed in the monastic settlements. For example, the contract signed at Þingeyraklaustur in 1394 for the couple Jón Eyjólfsson and Helga Loðinsdóttir is interesting in this regard, as both decided to move to the monastery as lay workers. Jón's responsibilities included working with the riding gear and making hay for the monastery's livestock, while Helga was to prepare meals and do all the kitchen work for the monastery. The monastic houses involved were expected to provide the couple with the cloths they needed, as was also customary for corrodians, and this was listed in the contracts. Jón and Helga's contract specifies that they received one cloth each, white and black in color, and six *alin* of linen. Furthermore, they were promised good food in the monastery – food as good as that received by corrodians. During their stay, the couple was allowed to be together during the winter but not during the summer.[93]

The contract made in 1498 with the couple Arnþrúður Árnadóttir and Jón Sigfússon at Munkaþverárklaustur is worth mentioning again here in more detail, as it is an example of a similar division of tasks. As is mentioned earlier, Jón was supposed to carry out both iron- and woodwork for the abbot, and Arnþrúður was to make garments and cloths for the abbot, whose name was Einar Benediktsson (r. 1494–1525). In other respects, the contract made with them was nearly identical to the corrody contracts made in Iceland, except for the stipulation requiring physical work. The couple's housing and food were to be paid for by the monastery, including made-up beds, *vaðmál*, and shoes. Oddly enough, Jón was allowed to take a one-month holiday per year to do his own ironwork, for which he was permitted to use fuel from the monastery.[94] What is also noteworthy is that no cottage was mentioned in the contract; instead, Jón was supposed to build his smithy at his own expense. This could well be the smithy mentioned in the inventory of 1525. As is described earlier, the smithy was also full of *vaðmál* at that point, so it can be concluded that Arnþrúður also did her weaving in her husband's smithy. This example further displays the classic sex-based division of labor during the Middle Ages, but it certainly does not indicate that women were subordinate to men. Rather, it reflects the different gendered value of their contribution to the monastery in question.[95] The preserved corrody agreements are discussed further in the following section.

Corrody Contracts

The rules governing the Benedictine and Augustinian orders assume that all classes would be able to seek service in their houses – even criminals serving their penance, as is explained earlier in this book. This seems to have been the case in the larger monastic houses in Iceland, and according to historical sources, most social groups appear to have been attracted to them in one way or another. The corrody contracts preserved from the monastic houses provide useful information in this context, as well as shedding light on the broad range of activities taking place in each of the houses. A corrody was a paid placement in a monastic institution, and corrodians were permanent paying guests residing under the institution's protection. It usually included food, drink, clothes, and housing, though this could vary according to the contract made. In return, corrodians were obliged to donate part or all of their possessions, such as farms, to the monastic house concerned.[96]

In all, there are twenty-nine corrody contracts originating from nine monastic houses in Iceland, most of them from Helgafellsklaustur and Þingeyraklaustur. The contracts contain useful information about the corrodians' lodgings, payments, duties, rights, and much more. The Icelandic corrody contracts appear otherwise to have been made with three groups of people – the leading elites, self-governing farmers, and healthy workers – and not necessarily those who wanted to withdraw from the outer world due to age. Corrodians included young people, adult men and women, and even families with children, but they were all well-to-do or came from the upper strata of society. There were also contracts that provided corrodians with burial in the monastic cemeteries. The gifts donated in exchange for such a privileged final resting place ranged from farms to money to livestock, just as the donations for a corrody placement did. In the contracts, corrodians were generally allocated separate housing or space in the monastery's lay sleeping quarters, plus food, clothing, shoes, haircuts, and beer. The oldest one, from Þingeyraklaustur, is from 1290, and the most recent, from Munkaþverárklaustur, was made in 1567, notably after its permanent closure in 1551.[97] Of course, there may have been contracts made before 1290, although none have survived. However, as may be expected, the timing of the earliest corrody contract can be linked to the beginning of the growth of Iceland's monastic institutions at the end of the thirteenth century.

The idea of donating valuable possessions to the monastic community, notably for the benefit of society, appears in most, if not all, of the corrody contracts preserved in Iceland. The principles behind donations are explained in the Rule of St. Augustine, which states that donors

> should neither be conceited if they have contributed a part of their wealth to the common life, nor take more pride in sharing their riches with the monastery than if they were enjoying them in the world.[98]

The Rule of St. Augustine contains even specific clauses about how different groups should behave while residing in a monastery or inside its precincts:

> let them not hold their heads high because they associate with people whom they would not dare to approach in the world, but rather let them lift up their hearts and not seek after what is vain and earthly. Otherwise, monasteries would become profitable to the rich and not to the poor, if there the rich become humble and the poor are puffed up.[99]

Furthermore, the rules of the Augustinians ask: 'what advantage is it to scatter one's wealth abroad by giving to the poor, even to become poor oneself, if the mind in its misery becomes prouder in despising riches than it was in possessing them?'[100] These principles can in fact be observed in the corrody contracts made with the monastic institutions in Iceland. This, of course, is in line with common practice in monastic houses outside Iceland.[101] In comparing the preserved corrody contracts from Iceland, it is at least interesting to observe that the service provided by the monastic houses was not the same for all corrodians; it varied with the fee paid for it. Thus, according to the rules of the Augustinian Order, the wealthiest were supposed to be given the best service and food available, while the less wealthy received service in accordance with what they could afford to pay for, either financially or with physical work. This may sound odd, but the ideology behind these principles was that everyone should benefit from this system, not only the rich or only the poor.

There are ten corrody contracts recorded solely from Helgafellsklaustur, the oldest from 1364 and the most recent from 1513. Two of them involved couples, one of which had a child, four were made with individual men, and three with individual women, so clearly neither gender nor marital status mattered when it came to making a contract with the monastic houses. However, gender does seem to have been a factor as regarded specific skills such as reading, giving haircuts, and making beer. Two of the most interesting and informative corrody contracts from Helgafellsklaustur were made with women. The earlier one was made in 1399 with Kristín Guðmundardóttir and the later one nearly a century later, in 1497, with Ingveldur Helgadóttir.[102] Both could choose where to build their own *stofa*, or cottage, on the monastic estate. Kristín was to provide timber for the cottage and hire a carpenter to build it at her own expense, but the monastery would cover the cost of the carpenter's food. Both Kristín and Ingveldur were also required to furnish their houses themselves with a bed and a chest for their belongings, as is specifically listed in their contracts. Furthermore, it was agreed that the monastery would inherit the cottages and their entire contents after the women's death. In addition to this, both Kristín and Ingveldur were allowed to have a personal servant with them, but they had to pay for the servant's food and accommodation as well.[103] Ingveldur's contract states explicitly that her servant could be either a man or a woman. After five years, Ingveldur was supposed to receive a placement – probably with a made-up bed – inside a certain corrodians' hall located in the monastic complex itself in Helgafellsklaustur.[104] This clause in Ingveldur's contract may indicate that care of the elderly was provided within the walls of the monastery when the time came. Ingveldur and Kristín were supposed to receive twelve *alin* of *vaðmál* and three or four *alin* of linen from the monastery each year of their stay there. The accommodation was supposed to be comparable to that received by those in the highest positions, such as the abbot and the monks. Both Ingveldur and Kristín were also supposed to receive the firewood they needed and have beer brewed for them at the monastery's expense. The donation that provided Kristín the opportunity to become a corrodian under the protection of Helgafellsklaustur comprised two farms and ready cash. Ingveldur, on the other hand, had given Helgafellsklaustur only one farm, but a highly valuable one.[105]

Although nearly 100 years separate the contracts made with Kristín and Ingveldur, they were based on the same terms in most respects. Nothing is known about who Kristín Guðmundardóttir was, but the fact that she succeeded in making a corrody contract similar to Ingveldur's and was even permitted to have a servant with her indicates that she also belonged to Iceland's elite, or at least to the middle class. It is well known that Ingveldur belonged to the Icelandic elite. She was widowed after the death of the seneschal Þorleifur Björnsson, whose father, Björn Þorleifsson, was buried in the cemetery of Helgafellsklaustur after having been slayed by English sailors in 1467.[106] Ingveldur and Þorleifur were third cousins, and their children (six by then) were therefore illegitimately born. The couple were absolved of their sins in 1471, when Bishop Sveinn in Skálholt granted them remission in exchange for a cash payment to the Church and confession before God.[107] Nevertheless, in 1474, Bishop Sveinn granted them a second remission because by then their seventh child – also illegitimate – had been born. This time they only needed to confess to be absolved.[108] But it was not enough, because Ingveldur and Þorleifur's children were still witnessed by their relatives as ineligible to inherit their parents' property, despite the absolution received from the Church. At this point, it was only the pope who could grant the couple a dispensation for their marriage – which he finally did through a royal mediation from King Christian I in 1477.[109] This was done because Þorleifur was about to be granted the honorary title of knighthood, besides a post as a seneschal, the highest royal officer in the country. His father was also both a knight and a seneschal.[110] What complicated the situation further was that Ingveldur's and Þorleifur's son-in-law, Eiríkur, was the son of the abbot of Helgafellsklaustur, Halldór Ormsson. Eiríkur also got himself into trouble, even more serious trouble than the parents of his wife had, when he slayed the sheriff Páll Jónsson in 1496.[111] This was one year before Ingveldur made her corrody contract with Abbot Halldór. Páll was married to Sólveig Björnsdóttir, the daughter of Björn Þorleifsson and Ólöf Loftsdóttir, and resided at the family estate, Skarð. Eiríkur was sent on a pilgrimage to Rome to obtain absolution, a trip from which he never returned.[112] Another interesting fact is that the wealthy woman Ingveldur Helgadóttir continued to manage her economic affairs unhindered in her cottage at Helgafellsklaustur, signing her own contracts to sell and buy farms.[113]

Examples may also be taken from three other corrody contracts from Helgafellsklaustur, these made with single men. One of these contracts was made around

1377 with a man named Snorri Andrésson, after he donated the farm Horn to the monastery for his corrody.[114] Interestingly, it has been suggested that Snorri worked as a bookbinder there when the main Helgafell's manuscripts were written, such as *Skarðsbók Jónsbókar*.[115] The book is, notably, named after the estate Skarð. Another corrody agreement was signed in 1508 but for his livelong stay in Helgafellsklaustur monastery, Árni Brandsson donated two farms to the monastery, one of them a valuable farm with specific offshore fishing rights, in addition to cash, 200 sheep, and two horses. Almost a year later, Helgafellsklaustur made a corrody contract with another man, Helgi Þorvaldsson, who had donated considerable shares in his farm to the monastery. Both contracts are based upon the idea of lifelong residence and accommodation on the monastic estate. Just like the two women, Ingveldur and Kristín, the men were required to build and furnish their own cottages at their own expense. The monastery would also inherit their cottages after their death, together with the furnishings. In return, they would receive *vaðmál* and linen from the monastery, as was customary, and would have their hair cut regularly.[116] However, there was no mention of beer, as both Kristín and Ingveldur were supposed to receive. Apparently, beer was available to some but not all; on the other hand, the women did not have their hair cut. The haircut provision in Árni's and Helgi's contracts can hardly mean that they were receiving tonsures because they did not belong to the religious community of Helgafellsklaustur. During the Middle Ages, hair and haircut did carry important symbolic meaning, not only for a monk awaiting tonsure marking that he had become the servant of God, but generally for both lay and religious as attribute of age, gender, class, and status.

Helgafellsklaustur's two surviving corrody contracts with couples are virtually identical to those made with individuals. The contract between the monastery and the couple Einar Þórólfsson and Katrín Halldórsdóttir, dating to 1493, is particularly interesting, as they were allowed to bring both their child and, at their own expense, a female servant. Like the other corrodians, they were required to build their own cottage within the monastery precinct, although later they were supposed to move into the corrodians' hall, which appears to have been located in the main monastic building. As before, the monastery was supposed to inherit their cottage and its entire contents after their death. Like many other corrodians, they had donated two farms to Helgafellsklaustur in exchange for lifelong support from the monastery.[117] The only corrody contract from Möðruvallaklaustur was also made with a couple, Oddur Þorsteinsson and Guðríður Þorgeirsdóttir, in 1431. Their contract is very nearly identical to the other ones preserved in Iceland, except that they were supposed to reside in a room called the *litla stofa* (small parlor), not in a cottage. They were, however, required to move out of it when the bishop stayed at Möðruvallaklaustur. Furthermore, the woman, Guðríður Þorgeirsdóttir, was permitted to take with her the ewes she owned and allow them to roam freely on monastery land, at the monastery's expense.[118] This sole corrody contract from Möðruvallaklaustur indicates an attempt to change the institution from a closed monastic school to an establishment more open to commoners at that point.

There are other examples of corrodians who were permitted to bring livestock with them. One of them was Elín Magnúsdóttir, who made her contract with Munkaþverárklaustur in 1519.[119] Elín was the mother of Jón Arason, who became the last Catholic bishop in Iceland. At the time of the contract, Jón was serving as a priest, but it seems he was responsible for making this contract for his mother. Bishop Jón Arason's relationship with Munkaþverárklaustur was otherwise personal and multifaceted. As a young child, he lived with his widowed mother, Elín, in a cottage called Grýta, which was owned by Munkaþverárklaustur and located near the monastic complex. Elín was the niece of Einar Ísleifsson, who was abbot of Munkaþverárklaustur for forty-eight years, from 1435 to 1487.[120] During Jón's stay at Grýta, he worked for the monastery as an errand boy. Later, Jón and Elín both moved to Laugaland in the same valley, but after that Jón received his education at Munkaþverárklaustur. Despite all these connections, Elín's corrody contract does not indicate that she received better accommodation than any of the other corrodians at that time. As regards terms and wording, her contract is very similar to the other contemporary corrody contract, particularly to include the provision of clothing and food for as long as she lived. However, Elín was not supposed to build a cottage at her own expense; instead, she was to reside in a room called the *forna stofa* (old parlor), which seems to have been a room similar to the one occupied by the couple in Möðruvallaklaustur nearly a century earlier. In addition to this, she was allowed to bring bulls, cows, and calves with her to Munkaþverárklaustur. Her son, Jón Arason, donated generously to the monastery before he signed the contract for his mother. The donation included one valuable farm and a considerable sum in cash.[121] One other interesting corrody contract, made by Abbot Einar Ísleifsson in Munkaþverárklaustur, is preserved. It was made with a couple, Magnús Jónsson and Margrét Finnbjarnardóttir, in 1466. The terms for this corrody were largely the same as for other Icelandic corrody agreements, except that the couple appears to have brought with them three children, one son and two daughters. Moreover, the abbot was supposed to provide the couple's son with clerical education and to supply the daughters with food and clothes until they would be twenty years of age. If the couple's children would die or marry before that age, this clause in the agreement would be rescinded.[122]

There are even examples of siblings making corrody contracts with monastic institutions in Iceland. In fact, the oldest surviving contract, from 1290, is one of them. It was made between Abbot Bjarni Ingimundarson in Þingeyraklaustur and the priest, Þorbjörn. The contract, for Þorbjörn and his sister Arndís, states that the siblings will receive food and clothing *in line with what the other corrodians have.*[123] Appearing as it does in the oldest preserved corrody contract made with a monastic house, this phrasing strongly suggests that such contracts had been made before then. Unfortunately, nothing specific is noted about the accommodation provided for the siblings. Another corrody contract involving siblings comes from Reynistaðarklaustur. It not only confirms that men could make such contracts with female convents but also reflects the different positions of men and women – as siblings – during the Middle Ages, at least in this convent. The man was a priest,

Jón Bjarnason, and his sister's name was Guðrún Bjarnadóttir. There is no mention of accommodation in the convent for them, as was frequently specified, nor is there any reference to whether the priest would have to undertake ecclesiastical duties for the nuns. The priest, Jón, was entitled to receive meals equivalent to those provided to a steward or the most honorable men in Reynistaður, and any other services he needed. Every year he was to receive eight *alin* of iron-grey *vaðmál*, twelve *alin* of white *vaðmál*, and another twelve *alin* of linen. In return, he was required to feed one pauper every day at the monastery's expense, most likely for his own salvation. His sister, Guðrún, on the other hand, did not receive the same benefits. For example, she was to receive only eight *alin* of *vaðmál* per year and meals that she could be well pleased with.[124] The question is whether or not Guðrún, as an unmarried woman living under the protection of her brother, was regarded as entitled to the same standard of accommodation as, for example, the two widows, Kristín and Ingveldur, received at Helgafellsklaustur.

The most recent surviving corrody contract, from 1567, is not vastly different from the older contracts, except that the corrodian seems to have received permission to move into four rooms in the old monastic complex of Munkaþverárklaustur, although the contract does not specify which rooms. The reason for this may lie in the fact that Munkaþverárklaustur had ceased operating as a monastic institution by that time, and its properties, which had been taken over by the king, were in the care of his representative in Iceland, superintendent Ormur Sturluson.[125] This last corrody contract was made with an upper class woman, Agnes Jónsdóttir, the daughter of Abbot Jón Þorvaldsson of Þingeyraklaustur, who will be discussed later in the context of an illegal marriage. Agnes Jónsdóttir was permitted to take a cow with her, much as Elín had been allowed to do by the same monastery fifty years earlier.[126] Everything else is otherwise similar to the terms listed in other corrody contracts.

It is interesting to observe how similar the corrody contracts generally are, since this suggests that they may have been standardized, either within Iceland or perhaps even across the entire archdiocese of Niðarós. The differences between the contracts are in fact minor, and most likely based on specific individual requirements. In most cases, these differences concerned accommodation. As is listed earlier, some of the contracts explicitly allow the corrodians to move into specified corrodians' halls or other rooms that seem to have been situated within the monastic complex, or into cottages. There is no reason to doubt that the terms of the corrody contracts were followed to the fullest extent possible within the social and natural environment. Indeed, the standardized contracts, the job titles, and the principles of the monastic orders underline the uniformity in the operation of monastic institutions throughout Europe.

Nonetheless, although the corrody contracts yield a considerable amount of information, questions about the appearance and design of the corrodians' cottages and their location with respect to the monastic complex remain unanswered. The cottages are not described in any detail, and the search for their remains during the MMI project was not as successful as expected. They may all have been torn down after the corrodians moved out of them, or perhaps they were demolished during the Reformation. Still, one preserved document describes a dispute that arose in 1527 concerning the exact placement of a corrodian's house within the precinct of Viðeyjarklaustur. The corrody contract itself is not preserved, only a letter describing the conclusion of the dispute. The dispute seems to have arisen from a misunderstanding concerning a cottage that the corrodian Anna Snjólfsdóttir was permitted to build there. The crux of the matter was that Abbot Ögmundur Pálsson (r. 1515–1521) had apparently allowed Anna to build her corrody cottage *wherever she wished*. His promise seems to have been given orally and not in writing, but it did not become a problem until Abbot Helgi Jónsson (r. 1521–1528) had taken over Ögmundur's post as abbot when Ögmundur became bishop of Skálholt (r. 1521–1540). The preserved document about the subsequent dispute stipulated that Anna's corrody cottage should stand in front of the church and as close to it as possible. The dispute in this case thus indicates that corrodians' cottages should be situated close to the monastic complex and could certainly not stand just anywhere.[127]

Unfortunately, this disagreement does not provide any information about how the houses of the corrodians may traditionally have been constructed. Timber is certainly mentioned in some of the contracts, but it may be that the wood was used only for furnishings. Otherwise, the term 'cottage' (Icel. *stofa*) indicates a house that was small but contained beds, at the very least, and in some cases chests as well, owned by the corrodians. Blankets are also mentioned, and one can imagine that the corrodians owned other unspecified personal objects.

Obedientiaries, Novices, and Students

Neither monks nor nuns commonly carried out farming or agricultural work, as this was in the hands of oblates. Among them were the kitchener, who took care of the cooking and the kitchen in general; the cellarer, who was responsible for the supplies; the infirmarian, who managed the infirmary; the porter, who manned the cloister gate and welcomed visitors; the sacristan, who was responsible for the maintenance and upkeep of the church, including the liturgical vessels, vestments, and relics; and the novice master, who was in charge of the novices and instructed the newcomers. Cellarer was, in fact, the most important of the servants as regards the daily administration of a monastic house, observed as the father to the whole brotherhood, but the abbot or abbess was nevertheless the superior of the monastic community and was to be obeyed in all matters and at all times.[128]

Novices included all newcomers, male and female, who wished to become members of a religious community. The novitiate period was one of instruction and testing before the novice took his or her religious vows. It was supposed to last up to two years, whereof twelve months spent in the community itself of the novitiate to be valid.[129] The studies in monastic houses took place in the schoolrooms, while the novices studied in the chapterhouse.[130] This was certainly the practice in Iceland, according to the documents preserved; at least both a schoolroom and a chapterhouse were part of the monastic building of Munkaþverárklaustur. Moreover, one of these documents pertains to a priest, Eiríkur Eiríksson, who in 1487 was supposed to undertake his novitiate in Munkaþverárklaustur prior to becoming abbot there. No contract on his novitiate is preserved, however, but his case is nonetheless known because he had a child before completing his novitiate and was then denied the expected promotion.[131] Both Bishop Guðmundur góði and Bishop Lárentíus Kálfsson were also novices at Munkaþverárklaustur, to mention some more examples.[132] Additionally, it is known that many of the Icelandic clerics received their general education at Þykkvabæjarklaustur, but they may also have served their novitiates there after finishing their studies. One of those who received his clerical education there was Bishop Árni Þorláksson (r. 1269–1298), who studied under the supervision of Abbot Brandur Jónsson. When Árni became a bishop, he even ordained three of his fellow students from Þykkvabæjarklaustur to their posts as abbots: Runólfur Ólafsson, who became abbot of Viðeyjarklaustur in 1250; Ólafur Hjörleifsson, who became abbot of Helgafellsklaustur in 1258; and Runólfur Sigmundsson, who succeeded Brandur Jónsson as abbot of Þykkvabæjarklaustur in 1262.[133] Inevitably, women also had to serve their novitiate in a monastery or an ecclesiastical institution before they took their vows as abbesses, prioresses, or nuns. One example of this is Sister Katrín who, after her vow as an anchoress in Munkaþverárklaustur, later became the first abbess of the convent at Reynistaðarklaustur.[134]

Sometimes it is difficult to determine from the sources whether the persons involved were common students or novices in the monasteries. However, the novitiate was quite different from the other general studies offered by the monastic houses. Novices were expected to learn through active participation in the canonical hours, as well as receiving instruction in the liturgical observances of their order. On the other hand, ordinary students – religious and non-religious, male and female – were commonly educated in the seven liberal arts: grammar, logic, rhetoric, arithmetic, astronomy, geometry, and music. In Iceland, the students must also have been trained in the art of writing and reading in both Latin and Old Norse/Icelandic.[135] Still, some male and female students appear to have chosen a lay life after completing their studies in a monastic house. One of them was Sigríður Sæmundardóttir, cousin of the former steward, Björgólfur Illugason. It was Björgólfur himself who, in 1413, made contracts providing for studies at Reynistaðarklaustur, both for Sigríður and for his daughter, Steinunn Björgólfsdóttir. For their education, he gave the convent fifty *hundruð* in cash, plus dried fish, meat, and three living ewes. In addition to the instruction, the convent was to provide both girls with new clothes every year. The contract states that Steinunn was allowed, if she so chose, to return to her former life again after her studies, but for some unknown reason, no such thing was specified for Sigríður.[136] At that point, Reynistaðarklaustur had been without an abbess since the plague in 1402, so new additions to the convent were accepted by serving prioress Þórunn Ormsdóttir, the former assistant of prioress Þuríður Halldórsdóttir, but all of the nuns and many other clergy and lay brothers and sisters participated in the process, as was required under canon law.[137] Apparently, Steinunn never chose to leave the convent because in 1431, Bishop Jón Craxton consecrated her and seven new nuns: Sigríður Sæmundardóttir, Þóra Finnsdóttir, Þóra Illugadóttir, Helga Bjarnadóttir, Arndís Einarsdóttir, Agnes Jónsdóttir, and Þórdís Finnsdóttir.[138] Two of these new nuns later became abbesses of Reynistaðarklaustur: the first was Þóra Finnsdóttir in 1447, who changed her name to Barbara, and the second was Agnes Jónsdóttir, who was abbess from 1461 to 1507. Sigríður Sæmundsdóttir was not mentioned among those consecrated at this later occasion. She may have become a nun immediately upon her arrival in 1413, however, because she is named as a nun there in another letter written in 1431.[139]

Once again, the record of the incident at Skriðuklaustur in 1524, when Brother Jón Jónsson lost track of the two children, gives us details about the educational function of a monastery. The episode tells us that children of both sexes were allowed to study together in the same monastic house during the last phase of monasticism in Iceland. Moreover, an interesting study contract from Skriðuklaustur documents Prior Narfi Jónsson's (r. 1496–1506) desire to acquire a share in the valuable fishing station and harbor of Borgarhöfn in Suðursveit. In return for undertaking to give a clerical education to a male relative of the owner, Ásgautur Ögmundsson, he obtained a share in the harbor.[140] In some cases, the study period is even specified in the contracts. For example, in a contract made at Viðeyjarklaustur in 1380, Valgarður Loftsson donated a farm to the monastery in return for a promise to educate his son for the next six years.[141] We can also recall here the contract made in Munkaþveráklaustur in 1466, when the abbot was required to teach the son of the corrody couple, Magnús Jónsson and Margrét Finnbjarnardóttir, so he could become a priest. Instead, the couple donated a valuable farm, Skógar in Axarfjörður, to the monastery.[142]

In other respects, the requirements for most study contracts seem to be based on terms similar to those in corrody contracts. Two study contracts made at Helgafellsklaustur in the same year, 1377, provide examples of this. In both cases, the parents had donated valuable properties to the monastery in exchange for the education of their respective sons. The value was equal to a donation for a couple's corrody.[143] In the other examples given earlier, the donations were of similar worth in all cases, regardless of whether the studies were for a boy or a girl. Still, the price for different kinds of studies does not seem to have been equal, as can be understood from two other study contracts from Helgafellsklaustur, made in 1358 and 1362, respectively. In the 1358 contract, Abbot Ásgrímur agrees to educate Loftur, son of Þorgils Guðlaugsson, as a deacon, in exchange for half of Þorgils' farm in Keflavík on the Snæfellsnes peninsula. Loftur's lodgings are included.[144] In the contract signed in 1362, Abbot Ásgrímur agrees to educate Þorbjörn, a male relative of Einar Þorláksson, as a priest. Einar pays for this with two of his farms, Botn and Þórustaðir, 500 *hundruð* in books, a vestment, and a chalice. In Þorbjörn's case, lodgings are not the only thing included in the contract; the monastery is also supposed to provide him with clothes during his period of study.[145] Another interesting study contract is preserved from Reynistaðarklaustur, but in this case for a young boy specifically training as a priest. The contract was made in 1443 between the boy's parents and Abbess Barbara. In addition to providing instruction, the convent was to provide the student with food and clothing during his studies. By then, the parents had donated two farms to it, as was customary.[146] This contract demonstrates clearly that boys could be trained in female as well as in male monasteries.

The entry fee for a novice appears thus to have been relatively high, and often it seems to have been difficult to secure admission to either a Benedictine or an Augustinian monastic house without considerable funds. At least, access to an official education was apparently restricted to those who could afford it. This does not exclude the possibility that the lowest classes, the poor, and the sick, could obtain food, shelter, and perhaps even education from the Icelandic monasteries, although no contracts survive to document such cases. As is emphasized earlier, the absence of such contracts may mean that there was nothing to make a contract about, whereas in the documented examples, the main provisions concerned the financing of accommodation. However, an education obtained at aristocratic homes such as Oddi in Rangárvellir should not be underestimated (where for instance Þorlákur Þórhallsson received his initial education), since it was possible to achieve as broad education there as in monastic houses and episcopal cathedrals.[147] It is even appropriate to reiterate here that quite a few Icelanders also went abroad for their studies, including the bishops Þorlákur Þórhallsson (r. 1178–1193), Stefán Jónsson (r. 1491–1518), Ögmundur Pálsson (r. 1521–1541), and Jón Arason (r. 1524–1550).[148]

The Number of Residents, Lay and Religious

The wide range of activities of Iceland's monastic houses, described earlier, certainly raises questions about how many people – religious and lay – may have resided in them. The names of those in charge of the Icelandic monasteries are known in nearly all instances, as are the names of the monks and nuns, but only those who were listed in connection with particular incidents. Sometimes, however, the names of monks and nuns are specified in separate lists. As we have seen, many of the corrodians who resided on the monastic estates are known by name because of the preserved contracts made with them. The stewards and priests are likewise mentioned by name on several occasions, mostly due to happenings worth documenting. One example is the incident taking place in Kirkjubæjarklaustur in 1528, when rev. Jón Jónsson attacked the carpenter, Indriði, at the church's door of the convent.[149] Jón may have been the nun's priest but Indriði working with carpentry for the nuns. Nevertheless, the names of the laity were generally not documented, making it more difficult to determine how many people lived in each monastic house for shorter or longer periods. Written documents are also silent on the exact number of residents at any given time, but it is possible to read between the lines and make estimates.

As Table 8.5 shows, there were fewer religious residents upon the establishment of the monastic houses and generally fewer again upon their dissolution in

TABLE 8.5 The number of religious inhabitants in the monastic houses, excluding the laity.

Monastic house	*Establishment*	*1316–1326*	*Plague*	*1431–1434*	*1494*	*Dissolution*
Þykkvabæjarklaustur			13			6
Helgafellsklaustur	4					5
Kirkjubæjarklaustur			14		5?	7
Viðeyjarklaustur	4					4
Reynistaðarklaustur				10?		
Möðruvallaklaustur		5				
Skriðuklaustur						4

the sixteenth century. Sometimes there were only four religious inhabitants in the monastic houses, but never more than fourteen at any time. For example, when Flateyjarklaustur moved to the mainland, there were four monks, all of whom were listed by name: the abbot, Ögmundur, and the monks Guðmundur, Ólafur, and Eyjólfur.[150] When it was closed in the mid-sixteenth century, there were again four monks: Abbot Halldór and the monks Ólafur, Jón and Gunnar (and possibly one more, Gunnlaugur, as is discussed in Chapter 9).[151]

Nevertheless, let's try to estimate further the sizes of the monastic communities from the diverse types of available information. During the first outbreak of plague in Þykkvabæjarklaustur in 1403, Abbot Runólfur Magnússon died along with six monks. Another six monks survived.[152] In Þingeyraklaustur, only a single monk survived the first wave of plague in 1402, which killed even the abbot, Sveinbjörn Sveinsson, but the total number of monks there is unknown.[153] Similarly, the number of nuns serving in Kirkjubæjarklaustur appears to have been much larger when the plague first came to Iceland in 1402 than when the convent closed. According to *Nýi Annáll*, eight of the fourteen nuns there died of the plague.[154] The Kirkjubæjarklaustur may therefore have had its heyday in the early fifteenth century, whereas by the end of the same century, there may have been only five nuns, including the abbess, if the hypothesis about the five gold rings listed in Bishop Stefán Jónsson's inventory of 1494 is correct.[155] However, the nuns continued to increase in number because fifty years later, in 1542, there were seven (Table 8.5).

According to the inventory done in 1408, Reynistaðarklaustur had seven golden rings and one silver ring,[156] which could likewise indicate the number of nuns there at that time. The ordination record from Reynistaðarklaustur in 1431 may even prove to be useful in this context. In that year, eight new nuns entered the convent.[157] But it is not known how many there were already. Furthermore, when the unnamed man who was dying of smallpox that year gave the nuns various items, six of them were named. Several other nuns may have been resident there too, since the man's will notes that gifts were to be given to 'the other nuns', and accordingly, two new names appear on the list.[158] Moreover, we should recall Margrét Bjarnadóttir, widow of the excommunicated lawman Hrafn Guðmundsson, who donated valuable properties to Reynistaðarklaustur and entered the community in 1434 as a nun.[159] This means that there were at least nine nuns at Reynistaðarklaustur in the period between 1431 and 1434, in addition to the prioress, Þórunn Ormsdóttir. It should be noted here that no information is preserved about the number of religious inhabitants in Þingeyraklaustur and Munkaþverárklaustur, but when the fire broke out in Möðruvallaklaustur in 1316, there were five brethren and the same number at the time of its rebuilding ten years later (Table 8.5).

Additionally, the number of religious inhabitants in the monastic institutions of Skálholt diocese at the time of their dissolutions is known, simply because the Danish king had them counted specifically. He had plans to re-open schools in the former monastic houses and therefore had a list of abbots, abbesses, monks, and nuns serving there compiled in 1542. At this point, there were four monks at each of the monasteries, Skriðuklaustur, Viðeyjarklaustur and Helgafellsklaustur, six in Þykkvabæjarklaustur, and seven nuns in Kirkjubæjarklaustur (including their chiefs).[160] However, no such list was made for the monastic houses in Hólar diocese at the point of their dissolution in 1551. Surviving documents indicate in this manner that the numbers of religious inhabitants increased over time and were at their highest during the peak of monasticism in Iceland in the fourteenth and fifteenth centuries.

Unfortunately, the monastic houses generally lack comparable information about the impact of the plague on other religious members of their communities or the laity the following years. Still, overall, it can be inferred that the number of monks or nuns was fairly small compared to the number of lay people, as was normal for monastic houses, even outside Iceland. In fact, it is possible to estimate roughly how many lay servants there were by making a calculation based on the number of monks or nuns. In Norway, the method for calculating the number of lay versus religious inhabitants is based on a ratio of five lay people to one religious.[161] Thus, if the average size of the monastic community was five monks or nuns, there were twenty-five lay people as well. This rule may be applicable to the Icelandic monastic institutions: for example, with fourteen nuns residing at Kirkjubæjarklaustur in 1402, there would have been seventy lay people. According to this, a total of eighty-four individuals may have lived at the convent at the time of the first outbreak of plague. This is a plausible figure, not least because of the size of the convent's livestock holdings, which must have required a sizeable workforce. Furthermore, the documents from the time of the plague highlight the problems the nuns would have faced with the loss of so many lay servants, as the nuns themselves would have lacked the skills and knowledge to undertake other work than the ecclesiastical.[162] However, at the approximate time of the convent's closure in 1542 in Kirkjubæjarklaustur, there were seven nuns, and therefore thirty-five lay workers, which gives a total of forty-two inhabitants. If such a calculation is made for Þykkvabæjarklaustur, a parallel picture appears. If there were thirteen monks, as there were at the time of the plague in 1403, there would have been sixty-five lay people, bringing the total number of inhabitants to seventy-eight. In addition to the prior, four monks seem to have lived in Skriðuklaustur in 1542, according to the list of monks and nuns in Skálholt diocese at that point (Table 8.6).[163]

TABLE 8.6 The approximate size of the monastic communities, including the laity.

Monastic house	*Establishment*	*1316–1326*	*Plague*	*1431–1434*	*Dissolution*
Þykkvabæjarklaustur			78		36
Helgafellsklaustur	24				30
Kirkjubæjarklaustur			84		42
Viðeyjarklaustur	24				24
Reynistaðarklaustur				60	
Möðruvallaklaustur		30			
Skriðuklaustur					24

Therefore, based on the Norwegian formula, the total number of Skriðuklaustur's residents, lay and religious, was twenty-four by then – which is not unlikely, so shortly before its final closure. Similarly, in Þykkvabæjarklaustur, there may have been thirty lay people in 1542, making a total of thirty-six inhabitants if the six monks are included. That same year there were five monks at Helgafellsklaustur, which indicates that there were twenty-five lay staff members and thirty inhabitants in all (Table 8.6).

There are also other ways to estimate the population of Iceland's monasteries. One method is based on the number of cattle or sheep at the monastic farm, with one cattle or six sheep assumed to be equivalent to food for one person. This method is generally used in Iceland to estimate the number of people resident at common farms.[164] Thus, for example, at Kirkjubæjarklaustur in 1343, there were 118 cattle and 1,050 sheep (excluding lambs). This suggests, according to this method, that the total number of inhabitants was around 118 if the cattle are only counted, but 175 if the sheep are used as the frame of reference. In Þykkvabæjarklaustur in 1340, there were 137 cattle and 550 sheep, meaning that there would be food for 137 people if the cattle are the reference, or ninety-one if the sheep are used. The results from such calculation can be read further in Table 8.7, but it is questionable if this method is applicable for the monastic house because of their wide-ranging manufacturing and service provided to their local surroundings, compared to what was done at common farms.

The number of plates, cups, and beds, or even chasubles can as well be used to shed light on the number of people resident on the monastic sites. In Þykkvabæjarklaustur, there were thirty chasubles and thirty-three beds in 1340, which could indicate that the monastic community was around the same number. In 1523, sixty-eight dishes are listed and thirty-four cups of various kinds. The result from this count gives a number similar to that obtained with the other calculation methods listed earlier. Furthermore, as before, a comparison of the inventories carried out at Þykkvabæjarklaustur in 1340 and 1523 indicates that the general furnishings were significantly reduced. In the latter inventory, there were only ten beds rather

TABLE 8.7 The approximate size of the monastic communities, based on the number of animals in their livestock.

Periods	*1180–1300* *cattle/sheep*	*1300–1400* *cattle/sheep*	*1400–1500* *cattle/sheep*	*1500–1525* *cattle/sheep*
Þykkvabæjarklaustur		137/91		
Helgafellsklaustur	30/0	139/88		
Kirkjubæjarklaustur	37/48	118/175		
Viðeyjarklaustur		141/61		
Þingeyraklaustur				75/81
Munkaþverárklaustur			139/43	50/46
Reynistaðarklaustur			192/100	114/86
Möðruvallaklaustur			78/17	50/32

than thirty-three, and there were just twenty chasubles instead of the previous thirty, including four in poor condition.

Notwithstanding, as regards the number of residents on the monastic estates, the clearest example may once again be taken from Skriðuklaustur, through the excavation of its cemetery. It displays quite well the relative size of the monastic community, the oblates, and the clients, who were mostly patients. All in all, nearly 300 individuals were laid to rest at Skriðuklaustur over a period of less than sixty years. As is listed earlier, 150 were patients, 130 were lay people or occasional residents, and up to twenty were benefactors or canons.[165] The monastic church at Skriðuklaustur never served as a parish church, so those who were buried there must have been inhabitants, as well as some benefactors, but the monastic institutions were also obliged to bury their clients.[166] It is difficult, however, to estimate how many of these people were actually resident in the monastery from year to year. Nevertheless, in Skriðu-klaust-ur, the monks' dormitory unearthed during the excavation may also provide useful information in this context. It measured ten meters long and nearly four meters wide, which is enough to accommodate eight beds, based on documented information on the school operated in Skálholt in 1674.[167] This indicates that there was room for eight canons there at any point in time. According to Chapter XXII in the Rule of St. Benedict – which appears not to have been radically different from the rules followed by the Augustinians in Iceland – canons should sleep alone in their separate beds, as might have been the case in Skriðuklaustur.

Lastly, perhaps the number of horses can be used as an indicator of the number of residents in the monastic houses – or be used as a marker on economical wealth. The horses were probably not kept for the meat, but rather for transport of people and commodities. Table 8.8 implies thus that Þingeyraklaustur was the wealthiest one in in 1525 or that its social connections were broad and strong. It shows, nevertheless, that the female houses kept equally many horses as the male houses, demonstrating their overall strength.

TABLE 8.8 Number of horses owned by the monastic houses in different periods.

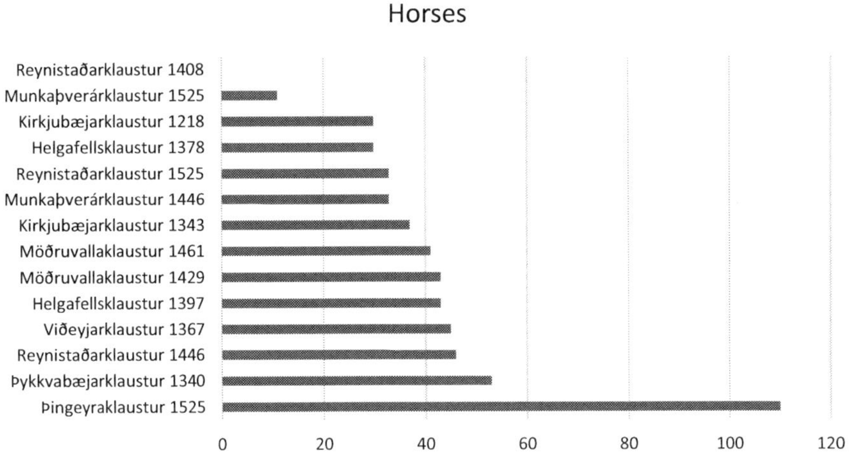

Notes

1 See, for example, Arnórsdóttir, 'Gender and Donation culture', pp. 167–169, 174; Cormack, *The saints in Iceland*, pp. 49–68; Grímsdóttir, 'Biskupsstóll í Skálholti', p. 33.
2 Bynum, *Dissimilar Similitudes*, pp. 17–27; Gilchrist, *Sacred Heritage*, pp. 110–144; Whiting, *The Blind Devotion of the People*, pp. 61–63.
3 Bynum, *Dissimilar Similitudes*, pp. 17–27; Gilchrist, *Medieval Life*, pp. 218–227; Gilchrist, *Sacred Heritage*, pp. 110–144; Kopytoff, 'The cultural biography of things', pp. 64–91; Masur, 'Symbol or Presence?', pp. 4–7.
4 *Gottskálksannáll*, p. 331.
5 Jensson, 'Latin Hagiography in Medieval Iceland', pp. 886–888.
6 DI IV, p. 374.
7 DI II, p. 115.
8 DI I, p. 394.
9 DI VII, p. 486.
10 *Þorláks saga B*, p. 180.
11 *Grágás*, pp. 11–12.
12 Cormack, 'Saints of Medieval Hólar', p. 10.
13 Wolf, *The Old Norse-Icelandic Legend of Saint Barbara*, p. 134.
14 DI II, p. 781; DI VIII, p. 5.
15 DI IV, pp. 238–239.
16 DI IV, p. 781; Grímsdóttir, 'Biskupsstóll í Skálholti', p. 33.
17 Gilchrist, *Medieval Life*, pp. 42, 155–158.
18 Wolf, *The Legends of the Saints in Old Norse-Icelandic Prose*, p. 69.
19 Farmer, *The Oxford Dictionary of Saints*, pp. 5–7; Mundal, *Legender fra mellomalderen*, p. 17.
20 Farmer, *The Oxford Dictionary of Saints*, p. 89.
21 The Arnamagnæan Collection in Copenhagen AM 429 12mo. See Wolf, *The Legends of the Saints in Old Norse-Icelandic Prose.*
22 See, for example, Egilsdóttir, 'Kvendýrlingar og kvenímynd trúarlegra bókmennta á Íslandi', pp. 91–116; Farmer, *The Oxford Dictionary of Saints*; Wolf, *The Icelandic Legend of Saint Dorothy*; Wolf, *The Legends of the Saints*; Parsons, *Good Habits*, pp. 41–42.
23 Farmer, *The Oxford Dictionary of Saints*, p. 89.
24 Farmer, *The Oxford Dictionary of Saints*, pp. 452–453.

25 Cormack, 'Saints of Medieval Hólar', pp. 33–34.
26 Farmer, *The Oxford Dictionary of Saints*, pp. 32–33.
27 Birgitta Birgisdóttir from Vadstena.
28 DI V, p. 289.
29 Riddell et al., 'Pollen, Plague and Protestants'.
30 See DI IX, pp. 190–191.
31 Chrisholm, 'Roch, St', p. 425.
32 Wolf, 'Low German Legends of the Apostles', pp. 139–181.
33 See, for example, Johansson, 'The Learned Sturlungar', pp. 343, 347–365.
34 Drechsler, *Illuminated Manuscript Production in Medieval Iceland*, pp. 45–49.
35 Ricciardi and Schmidt Patterson, 'Science of the Book', pp. 54–56.
36 Fiddyment et al., 'Parchment in medieval Norway', p. 316.
37 Arnórsdóttir, 'Cultural Memory and Gender in Iceland', pp. 385–393; Ísleifsdóttir, 'Hugleiðingar um menntun kvenna', pp. 169–182; Wolf, 'History and Provenance', p. 15; Wood, *Charity on the Fringes of the Medieval World*.
38 Óskarsdóttir, 'Universal History in Fourteenth Century Iceland'.
39 Hjartarson and Kristjánsdóttir, 'Rannsókn á örnefnum um klaustur á Íslandi', p. 23.
40 Munro, 'Three Centuries of Luxury Textile Consumption', pp. 51–53.
41 Þorláksson, *Vaðmál og verðlag*; Smith, 'Weaving Wealth', p. 21; Øye, 'Tools and Textile', pp. 245–250.
42 Guðjónsson, 'Íslensk kirkjuklæði á miðöldum', pp. 85–89; Jónsdóttir, 'Gömul krossfestingarmynd', pp. 134–145.
43 Smith, 'Weaving Wealth', pp. 24, 38; Smith, 'Thorir´s bargain', p. 732.
44 Barthes, *Image–Music–Text*, pp. 16–20, 155–164. See also '"Text" relates to "texture" and "textile" and traces back to "*texo*" – "to weave", referring to the way words and sentences are "woven" together. We speak of "weaving" a tale or "spinning a yarn." A "subtle" idea is a "finely spun" one', in 'The Relationship Between Words, Texts, Clothes, and Textiles', by Stutza and Abrudan Caciora, p. 98.
45 Jónsson, 'Dómkirkjan á Hólum í Hjaltadal', p. 234.
46 Guðmundsson, 'Íslenskt samfélag og Rómarkirkja', p. 151; *Lögmannsannáll*, pp. 287–288.
47 Mímisson and Einarsson, '"*Ora et labora*"', p. 49; see also Parsons, *Good Habits*.
48 See for example, Guðjónsson, '. . . "slitur úr eldgömlu húss-tjaldi"', pp. 9–10; Guðjónsson, 'Íslensk kirkjuklæði á miðöldum', pp. 85–89; Eldjárn, *Hundrað ár í Þjóðminjasafni*, nr. 18 and 32; Jónsdóttir, 'Gömul krossfestingarmynd', pp. 134–145; Wandel, 'Íslenzk altarisklæði', pp. 51–54.
49 The antependium from Svalbarð appears though to be a reused piece from an embroidered wall-hanging.
50 Guðjónsson, 'Íslenzkur dýrgripur í hollenzku safni', pp. 132–134; Guðjónsson, 'Íslensk kirkjuklæði á miðöldum', pp. 85–89; Jónsdóttir, 'Gömul krossfestingarmynd', pp. 134–145.
51 DI I, pp. 394–396.
52 DI II, p. 781; DI VIII, p. 5.
53 *Vætt* is a unit of measurement. One *vætt* equals 36.2 kg of wool (or thirty-four fish) (see *Jónsbók*, p. 565). Each ewe produces averagely 1.8 kg wool annually.
54 DI III, p. 718.
55 DI IV, p. 700.
56 DI IX, pp. 320–322.
57 Guðjónsson, 'Íslenzkur dýrgripur í hollenzku safni', pp. 132–134; Guðjónsson, 'Íslensk kirkjuklæði á miðöldum', pp. 85–89.
58 *Jónsbók*, pp. 212–213.
59 Drechsler, *Illuminated Manuscript Production in Medieval Iceland*, pp. 45–55.
60 Jensson, 'Latin Hagiography in Medieval Iceland', pp. 898–902; Jensson, 'Þingeyrar Abbey in Northern Iceland', pp. 152–160; Johansson, 'The Learned Sturlungar', pp. 347–353; Tómasson, 'Þingeyrar – stærsta íslenska menningarsetrið á miðöldum', pp. 19–20; Clark, *The Benedictines in the Middle Ages*, p. 246.

61 Drechsler, *Illuminated Manuscript Production in Medieval Iceland*, pp. 58–60; Jensson, 'Þingeyrar Abbey in Northern Iceland', pp. 152–160.
62 Nordal, 'Flateyjarbók', pp. 1–2.
63 Jakobsson, 'King Sverrir of Norway and the Foundations of His Power', pp. 109–135; Jensson, '**Revelaciones Thorlaci episcopi*', pp. 133–175; Jensson, 'Latin Hagiography in Medieval Iceland', pp. 875–949; Kristjánsdóttir, 'Handritalýsingar í benediktínaklaustrinu á Þingeyrum', pp. 227–311; Johansson, 'The Learned Sturlungar', pp. 347–353; Hauksson, 'Konungur af Guðs náð og blindir biskupar', pp. 113–139; Drechsler, *Illuminated Manuscript Production in Medieval Iceland*, p. 169.
64 Drechsler, *Illuminated Manuscript Production in Medieval Iceland*, p. 169; Ríkharðsdóttir, *Medieval Translations and Cultural Discourse*, pp. 18, 21–22.
65 DI I, p. 282.
66 DI III, p. 328.
67 DI IV, p. 168.
68 Drechsler, *Illuminated Manuscript Production in Medieval Iceland*, pp. 54–55, 63–116.
69 Drechsler, *Illuminated Manuscript Production in Medieval Iceland*, p. 63.
70 DI II, pp. 737–738.
71 DI III, p. 214.
72 DI VI, p. 700.
73 DI IX, p. 308.
74 DI IV, p. 373.
75 DI V, p. 291.
76 DI VIII, pp. 465–466.
77 Kristjánsdóttir, *Sagan af klaustrinu á Skriðu*, pp. 283–293.
78 Hamilton-Dyer, 'Skriðuklaustur Monastery – Animal Bones 2003–2007'.
79 De Hamel, *Making Medieval Manuscripts*; Munro, 'Three Centuries of Luxury Textile', pp. 4–7.
80 DI X, p. 562.
81 Steinsson, 'Jarðir Skriðuklausturs og efnahagur', p. 76; Kristjánsdóttir, *Sagan af klaustrinu á Skriðu*, p. 379.
82 Júlíusson, *Jarðeignir kirkjunnar og tekjur af þeim*, p. 48.
83 Júlíusson, *Jarðeignir kirkjunnar og tekjur af þeim*, pp. 64–65, 78–79.
84 DI IV, pp. 168–169.
85 DI III, pp. 325–328; DI IV, pp. 166–171.
86 Kristjánsdóttir et al., 'The Icelandic Medieval Monastic Garden', p. 573.
87 Helgadóttir, 'Laukagarðr', pp. 171–184; Kristjánsdóttir et al., 'The Icelandic Medieval Monastic Garden', pp. 565, 570; Åsen, *Norske klosterplanter*, pp. 263–267.
88 Bisgaard, 'Wine and Beer in Medieval Scandinavia', pp. 72–85; Cormack, *The Saints in Iceland*, pp. 51–53.
89 *Sturlunga saga*, pp. 639–640.
90 *Sturlunga saga*, pp. 639–640.
91 Kristjánsdóttir, *Sagan af klaustrinu á Skriðu*, pp. 286–295.
92 Kristjánsdóttir, *Sagan af klaustrinu á Skriðu*, pp. 283–290.
93 DI III, pp. 499–500.
94 DI VI, pp. 684–685.
95 Gilchrist, *Gender and Archaeology*, pp. 31–53.
96 Gilchrist, *Gender and Material Culture*, p. 107; Kerr, *Life in the Medieval Cloister*, p. 203; Luxford, *The Art and Architecture*, p. 133.
97 DI II, pp. 269–270; DI XV, pp. 27–28.
98 *The Rule of St. Augustine*, Chapter One, rule 7.
99 *The Rule of St. Augustine*, Chapter One, rule 6.
100 *The Rule of St. Augustine*, Chapter One, rule 7.
101 See, for example, Luxford, *The Art and Architecture*, p. 133; Ó Clabaigh, *The Friars in Ireland, 1224–1540*, p. 111.

102 Arnórsdóttir, *Property and Virginity*, pp. 184–187.
103 DI III, p. 445; DI VI, pp. 35–36.
104 DI VII, p. 332.
105 DI III, p. 445; DI VI, pp. 35–36.
106 Sigurjónsson, *Vestfirðingasaga 1390–1540*, pp. 114–134.
107 DI V, p. 622.
108 DI V, pp. 732–734.
109 DI VI, pp. 102–103.
110 Arnórsdóttir, *Property and Virginity*, pp. 181, 185–187; Sigurjónsson, *Vestfirðingasaga 1390–1540*, pp. 196–198.
111 Júlíusson, 'Manndráp verður að morði', pp. 86–87.
112 Sigurjónsson, *Vestfirðingasaga 1390–1540*, pp. 278–280.
113 DI VII, p. 371; DI VIII, pp. 201–202; DI VII, pp. 331–332.
114 DI III, pp. 313–314.
115 Drechsler, *Illuminated Manuscript Production in Medieval Iceland*, p. 49.
116 DI VIII, pp. 220–221.
117 DI VII, pp. 156–157.
118 DI IV, pp. 471–472.
119 DI VIII, pp. 686–687.
120 DI VIII, pp. 686–687; Espólín, *Íslands Árbækur í söguformi* II, pp. 107, 128–129; Ólason, *Menn og menntir siðskiptaaldarinnar á Íslandi*, pp. 18–21.
121 DI VIII, pp. 686–687.
122 DI V, p. 459.
123 DI II, pp. 269–270.
124 DI III, pp. 354, 357.
125 DI XII, pp. 214–215, 267.
126 DI XV, pp. 27–28.
127 DI IX, pp. 422–423.
128 *The Holy Rules of St. Benedict*, Chapter XXXI; Kerr, *Life in the Medieval Cloister*, pp. 199, 201, 205, 207, 208, 210.
129 *Code of Canon Law*, Chapter III, Article 2, Can 648 §1 and §3.
130 Clark, *The Benedictines in the Middle Ages*, pp. 77, 85; Ó Clabaigh, *The Friars in Ireland*, pp. 223–224.
131 DI VI, pp. 633–634.
132 DI I, p. 355; *Lárentíus saga*, p. 310.
133 Johansson, 'The Learned Sturlungar', pp. 354–357; Patzuk-Russell, *The Development of Education*, pp. 69–71; Kristjánsdóttir, *Leitin að klaustrunum*, pp. 196–197.
134 *Skálholtsannáll*, p. 198.
135 See, for example, Johansson, 'The Learned Sturlungar', p. 335.
136 DI III, pp. 751–752.
137 DI III, p. 752.
138 DI IV, pp. 438–439.
139 DI IV, pp. 456–458.
140 DI VII, pp. 714–715.
141 DI III, pp. 354–355.
142 DI V, p. 459.
143 DI III, pp. 312, 313–314.
144 DI VI, pp. 10–11.
145 DI VI, pp. 13–14.
146 DI IV, pp. 642–643.
147 See, for example, Johansson, 'The Learned Sturlungar', p. 343; Patzuk-Russell, *The Development of Education*.
148 Grímsdóttir, 'Biskupsstóll í Skálholti', pp. 32–33, 46–50; Þór, 'Hólabiskupa ævir', p. 418; Patzuk-Russell, *The Development of Education*, pp. 72–78.

149 DI IX, pp. 480–482.
150 DI I, pp. 281–282.
151 DI XI, p. 187.
152 Espólín, *Íslands Árbækur í söguformi* I, p. 124; *Lögmannsannáll*, p. 286; *Nýi annáll*, pp. 10–11.
153 Espólín, *Íslands Árbækur í söguformi* I, pp. 123–124.
154 *Nýi annáll*, pp. 10–11.
155 DI IV, p. 232.
156 DI III, p. 717.
157 DI IV, pp. 438–439.
158 DI IV, pp. 483–484.
159 DI IV, pp. 520–521, 551.
160 DI XI, pp. 186–187.
161 Gunnes, 'Klosteranlegg i Norge. En oversikt'.
162 *Lögmannsannáll*, p. 286; *Nýi annáll*, pp. 10–11.
163 DI XI, p. 186.
164 Júlíusson, *Landbúnaðarsaga Íslands*, p. 147.
165 Kristjánsdóttir, 'The Tip of the Iceberg', pp. 54–58; Kristjánsdóttir, 'No Society is an Island', pp. 166–167; Kristjánsdóttir, *Sagan af klaustrinu á Skriðu*, pp. 141–142.
166 See, for example, Gilchrist and Sloane, *Requiem*, pp. 63, 205–206; Harding, 'Choses and changes', pp. 386–398; Jamroziak, 'Spaces of Lay-Religious Interaction', p. 58.
167 Kristjánsdóttir, *Sagan af klaustrinu á Skriðu*, pp. 109–110.

9

ICELAND'S FIVE HUNDRED YEARS OF MONASTICISM

The End

The most commonly held view is that the Reformation in Iceland differed from that in the rest of Europe, in that the process in Iceland was comparatively smooth, taking place without any notable side effects for the Icelandic society. Accordingly, given the perceived minor status and supposed isolation of the monastic houses operated in Iceland, their dissolution has likewise been considered as having had only minor impact on the population in the country. This view should come as no surprise because it accords very well with the view that monasticism in Iceland was uninfluential and weak. The political and religious reform of the sixteenth century that culminated in the Lutheran Reformation is, on the other hand, generally considered to have caused prolonged alterations throughout Northwest Europe. Not only is the Reformation seen as having permanently changed the governing of the Church; attention has also been drawn to how it challenged people's old way of living in which Roman Catholic Christianity played an essential part. The overall governing after the Reformation was indeed not entirely religious or based on Lutheran teaching, rather it was simultaneously politically and culturally constructed in accordance with the desire of the monarchies who wanted to reformulate their societies. The bishops were stripped of their influences as the financial and political representatives of the Roman Catholic Church, and the profiles of ecclesiastical institutions were similarly altered. In most North European societies, the monastic houses stopped functioning as they had done for centuries, whereas quite many were dissolved while other were privatized and run as schools, hospices, or hospitals.[1] None of the monastic houses in Iceland survived the Reformation, and what belonged to the old monastic world there had vanished by the end of the sixteenth century. Accordingly, perhaps it was not a coincidence that the dissolution of the Icelandic monasteries started with an attack on one of the most politically influential Roman Catholic institution based there, Viðeyjarklaustur; by this act the reformulation of Icelandic society began in a symbolically noteworthy way.

DOI: 10.4324/9781003361077-9

Reforming the World

When the agents of King Christian III of Denmark attacked Viðeyjarklaustur, protestant-related unrest had been ongoing on the Continent since Martin Luther had introduced his pioneering policy in Germany in 1517. The struggle was only partly religious, however. Northwest European princes and aristocrats in, for example, Denmark, Sweden, and England were inspired by the Lutheran teaching and had participated in the then ongoing criticism of the Roman Catholic Church who had ruled their societies for centuries. One of those who was inspired by the Lutheran teaching was King Christian III who during his reign, lasting from 1534 to 1559, unveiled the initial phase of the Reformation in Denmark by establishing Lutheranism as the state church there in 1536 and by consequently forming the Lutheran Church's close ties with the Danish crown. Norway also formally adopted Lutheranism when the country became a union with Denmark in 1537. Soon thereafter, the archbishop of Niðarós, Ólafur Engelbrektsson (r. 1523–1537), was sent into exile.[2]

The Protestant-related unrest caused on the Continent appears thus not to have reached Iceland for real until King Christian III began to introduce Lutheranism to Iceland by force – notably with the attack on Viðeyjarklaustur in 1539. The reversed financial situation in Þykkvabæjarklaustur and Reynistaðarklaustur around 1523–1525 may indicate, though, that the political upheavals in Denmark had already affected their operation by then. However, in 1541, the clergy of the Skálholt bishopric officially changed their allegiance from Catholicism to Lutheranism. At the same occasion, the twenty-nine-year-old Icelander Gissur Einarsson was elected as the first Lutheran bishop in the bishopric of Skálholt.[3] The mission of the Danish king would in this way finally have been accomplished but Bishop Jón Arason remained in his office at Hólar as the representative of Catholics until 1550, when he was forcibly removed from his post. He was executed with two of his sons, one of whom he had installed in Skálholt to serve as bishop that same year.[4] Nevertheless, although Iceland's shift from Catholicism to Lutheranism, ending with the bishop's execution, is fairly well documented, the entire process has largely been approached without further acknowledgement that Icelandic society was in turmoil for a good decade beforehand and long afterwards due to the political reformulation the Reformation caused. This was not at least because all the monastic houses there were dissolved but not privatized as, for example, some of the Danish and Norwegian ones. Indeed, in an official letter written by superintendent Knut Steinsson in 1556, the Danish governmental authorities in Iceland expressed their concerns that no hospital remained in operation and that the poor and sick were wandering around the countryside.[5]

Nonetheless, under Protestant influence, scholars have claimed that only after the execution of Bishop Jón Arason did conditions emerge that allowed for the recognition of Icelandic society again after centuries of papal control. At that point, crucial reconstruction work is considered to have finally begun.[6] Later on, the Enlightenment, as an intellectual and philosophical movement in seventeenth- and eighteenth-century Europe, certainly brought about innovative visions and improvements for the Protestant world that was emerging. It appears not to have been equally kind to all classes of society. For example, the questions of what became of the labor work, such as in regard to the textile production, and the broad services the monastic houses provided have hardly been discussed, nor has what happened when everything people spiritually believed in was swept away. The former residents of the monastic houses, their religious servants and lay people alike, in most cases lost their homes, livelihood, and overall support. Very little came to replace what previously could have assisted these people in any kind of need, until much later when the service the monastic houses provided before was transferred to the state or simply to the general public. This rise in the number of homeless and ailing people may in fact have been one of many consequences of the closure of Iceland's monastic houses, which left hundreds of people with nowhere to go.

An overriding objective of the reformers appears to have been to erase as much memory of Catholicism as possible, in addition to banning its practice. In many cases, the Catholic customs were simply reused – hybridized and reformed – by those who supported ideas behind the Lutheran teaching. Moreover, as was done elsewhere in Northwest Europe, psalms, hagiographies, poetries, objects, furniture, cloths, clothes, and buildings were either recontextualized or desecrated, and sacrilege was displayed through broken likenesses and other Catholic relics that had been reformed.[7] The items of any monetary worth owned by Icelandic monastic houses appear to have been transported to Copenhagen during the initial phase of the dissolution of monastic institutions in the mid-sixteenth century, to financially support the operation of the reformed Danish state (that by then included Iceland). As will be discussed further later in this chapter, some items did remain in Iceland, such as books in Old Norse/Icelandic and hagiographies, but even a few ecclesiastical objects that could be used in the reformed, Lutheran churches.

The Reformation was certainly a gradual process. The Church shifted from being divine to human. A clearer distinction than ever before was made between the secular and the sacred. The intercession of saints had no meaning anymore, and their all-encompassing presence was symbolically removed. Moreover, the assorted iconography and ornaments that the medieval people could read and understand was classified as fine art, after having served for centuries as the agents of Catholic Christianity.[8] One could neither seek ethereal protection nor obtain benefits from God anymore by interceding with the saints through prayer or donations in wills or testimonies.[9] Such intercession was preached as idolatry and being associated with either heresy or the devil himself. Catholic images were generally banished, and the monastic buildings were in many cases torn down or altered, and their churches restructured in the aim to purify them or simply to reduce the financial cost of their needless operation. The seven sacraments were, besides this, no longer valid in the same form as before. Only three survived the Reformation: the sacrament of Baptism, Eucharist, and Penance. Marriage became non-sacramental, and this change in turn influenced the habit of gift-giving, dowries, and the inheritance practices. Consequently, celibacy was abolished and at the same time the option to escape from forced marriage by joining a monastic house.[10] The benefits of doing penance or confessing, defined in Catholicism as one of the healing sacraments, were even replaced – gradually though – by physical punishments and even with executions.[11] People's relation to death had moreover shifted when the ideas of the purgatorial fire and the Judgement Day had vanished. The practice of offering masses for deceased souls was also not valid anymore or pilgrimage to seek absolution, to mention some examples from the Catholic worldview that disappeared from the Lutheran societies in Northwest Europe due to the Reformation.[12]

Viðeyjarklaustur Attacked

Viðeyjarklaustur was attacked without warning on Whitsun in 1539, causing both terror and financial loss. The residents of the monastery seem to have had no inkling that an attack was imminent. Abbot Alexíus was not even there; he was on a visitation of his diocese. Together with the men of the Danish king, who initiated the attack, were the king's agents in the district of southern Iceland, superintendents Diðrik von Minden and Pétur Einarsson.[13] Not only did the attackers severely damage the monastic building and steal the monastery's most valuable possessions, but they also assaulted the inhabitants, beat them, and tied them up. Among the valuables stolen were chalices with a value equivalent to that of an average-sized farm, which were reportedly sold shortly afterwards in the open market.[14] This was not the end of the humiliation; those who attacked Viðeyjarklaustur also dug up the floor of the monastery's dormitory to remove all signs of the monks' presence there. Soon thereafter, Pétur Einarsson, the agent of the Danish king, instructed that a new kitchen with a joint dining room and a lavatory should be built on the spot where the monastic building had stood, and that the lavatory's drainage should flow into one of the holiest areas of the former monastery, the cemetery.[15]

There is a large amount of documented information about these houses because when the Danish superintendent Páll Hvítfeldt took over Pétur Einarsson's role in Iceland in 1553, he compiled a register of the current building at Viðey, which were then owned by the Danish king. Among the buildings were those that Pétur Einarsson had constructed on the ruins of the monastery in 1539. The inventory of 1553 also lists a milk-house, a butter-house, a cellar, a dining room, a refectory, a smithy, a tack-house, a quayside house, the church, and, oddly enough, a 'convent', which may have been what was left of the monastery itself after the attack in 1539.[16] The excavation on Viðey revealed clearly archaeological evidence from the demolition of the building of Viðeyjarklaustur. Located in the western part of the excavation area were traces of at least two connected rooms dating to the monastic period. North of them was the ruin of the monastic church, which lies beneath the present church with the adjoining cemetery.[17]

According to official documents from the time of the attack on Viðeyjarklaustur, Bishop Ögmundur Pálsson (r. 1521–1540) was immensely upset when he heard about the methods used by the king's men – and no wonder; apart from the sacrilege, it was his former place of work, as he had served as abbot there for six years, from 1515 to 1521, just before his promotion to the bishopric of Skálholt. Moreover, Bishop Ögmundur was known to be opposed to the impending change from Catholicism to Lutheranism in Iceland.[18] He continued to use what his faith had taught him and excommunicated all those involved in the attack. The official letter announcing these excommunications was signed by twelve other clerics at Skálholt.[19] However, the judicial system within which this judgement was made was about to be swept away, so the excommunications had little impact. In fact, Pétur Einarsson received the highly valuable farm Arnarstapi in Snæfellsnes and twenty *hundruð* in cash in 1540 as a reward from the Danish king for a job well done during the attack on the monastery of Viðey.[20]

Still, the attack had other more serious consequences. The superintendent Diðrik von Minden was killed along with his men in a siege at Skálholt in the autumn of 1539. It was believed, particularly by the bishop's men, that he had been on his way to attack Þykkvabæjarklaustur and Kirkjubæjarklaustur in order to destroy them as well.[21] During these killings, even more disgraceful events took place. One of Bishop Ögmundur's men-at-arms, Eyjólfur (son of Kolgrímur Koðránsson, former abbot of Þykkvabæjarklaustur), his wife, and an old friend of the bishop went so far as to rob the corpses of those killed in the attack.[22] These reprehensible events were immediately classified by the Danish king as a criminal act. At least, they were investigated as such, and the outcome was a memorable one. A new agent of the Danish king, Christopher Hvítfeldt (brother of Páll Hvítfeldt, who became superintendent in 1553), was sent to Iceland in May 1541 along with 200 soldiers to capture the former bishop, Ögmundur Pálsson, and bring him to court. Ögmundur had already agreed the year before to resign as bishop and had moved to Haukadalur in Biskupstungur. Still, he was captured as planned while on a visit to his sister's home near his own in Haukadalur. The king's intention was to transport him to Copenhagen, most likely for execution, as had already been the fate of many other Catholic bishops. However, Bishop Ögmundur died on the ship on 13 July 1541,[23] making it easy for the Danish king to succeed in his attempt to change the affiliation of Skálholt diocese from Catholicism to Lutheranism – as he had already done in his other provinces.[24]

Dissolution of Iceland's Remaining Monastic Houses

Gissur Einarsson, the first Lutheran bishop to serve in Iceland, had initially been introduced to Protestantism during his studies in Hamburg in northern Germany. He had even prepared himself for the coming election by translating the new Lutheran Church ordinance of King Christian III into the vernacular language, Icelandic. His installation was accepted at *Alþingi*, on 28 June 1541. The king's men serving in Iceland were all present, as were thirty Icelandic clerics, who all witnessed the new Lutheran ordinance. Interestingly, among them was Abbot Alexíus Pálsson, who promised on this occasion to continue running the monastery at Viðey, but only as a Latin school. This was despite the fact that the monastic building there had already been demolished and rebuilt as the dwelling for the superintendent Pétur Einarsson.[25]

The official documents from this initial stage of the Reformation in Iceland demonstrate that King Christian III may have wished for a less dramatic closure of the monasteries than that which transpired. It is possible that the situation spiraled out of control in the heat of the moment. There are letters to prove that while the king certainly had plans to close all the monastic institutions in Skálholt diocese permanently, he meant to set up schools in them instead – a mission that failed. It was for this reason that the monastic communities were counted in 1542. The list showed that, all in all, there were sixteen monks and six nuns in Skálholt diocese, two abbots, one abbess, and one prior, although there were no laity listed at all. It also showed that there was no longer an abbot at Viðey, so Abbot Alexíus must have left despite the promise he had made the year before.[26] Interestingly, the female convent at Kirkjubæjarklaustur was also included in King Christian III's plans, even though the new schools were intended solely for male students studying Lutheran rhetoric, Latin, and other related subjects. A surviving letter from King Christian III to Abbess Halldóra Sigvaldadóttir, Abbot Sigvarður Halldórsson of Þykkvabæjarklaustur, and Prior Brandur Hrafnsson of Skriðuklaustur, dated 21 November 1542, testifies to this. The same letter emphasizes, however, that the plan to open similar schools at Viðeyjarklaustur and Helgafellsklaustur had already failed to come to fruition by then.[27]

Otherwise, the course of events surrounding the dissolution of the four remaining monastic houses in the diocese of Skálholt, Skriðuklaustur, Helgafellsklaustur, Kirkjubæjarklaustur, and Þykkvabæjarklaustur appears to have been similar. They were closed one after another – for good. As has been noted previously, Prior Brandur Hrafnsson did not leave Skriðuklaustur until 1552, although the monastery there appears to have already been closed as monastic house in 1541.[28] He was at least still residing there in 1542, along with three canons, Ólafur, Magnús, and Þorsteinn.[29] Most likely, the patients and some of the lay people remained as well, either until their death or until they moved out when the former monastery was taken over by the representatives of the Danish king in 1554.[30]

When Helgafellsklaustur closed around 1544, Halldór Tyrfingsson was still serving as abbot even though the monastery was no longer in operation; at least, he was specified as such on the king's list of the ecclesiastics working in Skálholt diocese in 1542. In addition to Halldór, there were three monks listed: Ólafur, Jón, and Gunnar.[31] There had, in fact, been four monks at the time of the monastery's closure, but one of the names, Gunnlaugur, had been crossed out, as he had already left the monastery when its shutdown was imminent.[32] The remaining monks and the abbot himself also left soon afterwards. The oral tradition claims that they left both barefoot and bareheaded. The monks were even said to have cursed Helgafell in perpetuity as they left. The story also says that upon their departure, they turned their backs on the monastery and library and headed south without looking back.[33] Although this certainly appears to be based on biblical imagery, it underscores the seriousness of the closure.

Further records show on the other hand that Abbot Sigvarður Halldórsson did not leave Þykkvabæjarklaustur until as late as 1548.[34] He only left when he was unexpectedly elected to serve as a Catholic bishop of Skálholt by those who still objected to the new Lutheran Church in Iceland, which had not yet been accepted by Bishop Jón Arason in Hólar. Predictably, Abbot Sigvarður's election was not accepted in Denmark, where Catholicism had been forbidden for more than a decade.[35] Indeed, the situation was a bit confusing in any case, as Sigvarður had asked Bishop Gissur Einarsson in 1545 to teach him and his monks Lutheran doctrine, which the bishop did.[36] This document gives no information about any other residents in Þykkvabæjarklaustur at that point, but according to the king's list from 1542, there were these five canons: Jón Árnason, Jón Oddsson, Jón Grani, Magnús, and Sæmundur.[37] The last abbess of Kirkjubæjarklaustur, Halldóra Sigvaldadóttir, appears to have completed her final charity work in 1543, when she granted shelter in her convent to an unnamed woman who had escaped from her violent husband.[38] The year before, she and her six nuns – Guðríður, Oddný, Arnleif, Ástríður, Margrét, and Valgerður – were listed as in residence there.[39] They may have continued to live in the convent's building for some years after the closure, with authorization from the Danish authorities, but this is not known with any certainty. Abbess Halldóra or these nuns are not mentioned again in documents.[40]

Details about the ultimate closure of the monastic houses in Hólar diocese are on the other hand not fully known, but in 1551 their houses had all been taken over by the Danish king. Neither schools nor hospices or hospitals were run in them instead. The corrody agreement made between Munkaþverárklaustur and Agnes Jónsdóttir in 1567 may, in fact, underline that such contracts could still be made, although the monastery there had been closed down. It should be recalled here that Agnes even got the permission to use some of the old monastic rooms in her corrody.[41] However, abbess Sólveig appears to have left her post when Reynistaðarklaustur was closed in 1551, but preserved documents indicate that she stayed in her convent, along with some nuns, until her death in 1562. This means that she spent nearly seventy years of her life in Reynistaðarklaustur; she took her vow as a nun there in 1493 and was promoted to an abbess in 1508.[42] Brandur Hrafnsson the last prior of Skriðuklaustur was, interestingly enough, the blood brother of Abbess Sólveig Hrafnsdóttir.[43]

We can recall that after the Reformation, the nuns were allowed to stay in their convents at the expense of the Danish king until they died or found new work but the opportunities for single women to live spiritual lives disappeared with their closures. Inevitably, the profession of abbess also ceased to exist.[44] On the other hand, after the dissolution of the male monastic houses, the abbots and the monks were in many instances transferred to new posts as Lutheran priests.

The Execution of Bishop Jón Arason

To recapitulate, the religious and governmental shift from Catholicism to Lutheranism had not yet been implemented in Hólar diocese, when all the monastic institutions in Skálholt diocese had been permanently closed. The reason for this may lie in the fact that when Bishop Gissur Einarsson took office in Skálholt, he and Bishop Jón Arason of Hólar made an agreement to leave each other in peace. Iceland therefore remained semi-Catholic and semi-Lutheran during the period from 1541 to 1550, albeit mostly Lutheran, as Bishop Jón Arason's supporters appear to have been very few in number. However, the Protestant struggle had not yet come to an end, and the agreement between the two bishops soon vanished into thin air. When Bishop Gissur Einarsson died in 1548, Bishop Jón Arason immediately used this opportunity to attempt to resurrect the Catholic Church in Iceland. All the monastic institutions in his diocese were still active, unlike their former counterparts in the southern Icelandic diocese. In fact, Bishop Jón even managed to obtain official backing from Pope Paul III, in the form of a letter dated 8 March 1549, expressing support for Bishop Jón's plans to resist the transformation of Iceland's Catholic organizations into Lutheran ones.[45] Still, as the circumstances suggest, opposition to Catholicism had grown strong in Northwest Europe, significantly reducing the power of the papacy. Consequently, this interesting request from the last Catholic bishop in Iceland to Pope Paul III had little impact on his final struggle.

But Bishop Jón Arason had certainly not given up. When Bishop Marteinn Einarsson (r. 1549–1557), successor of Bishop Gissur Einarsson, was on his first visitation in the West Fjords in autumn 1549, he made the customary stopover in Hítardalur on Mýrar. Unexpectedly, Bishop Jón Arason and two of his illegitimate sons, Ari and Björn, took the opportunity to capture him along with the serving priest in Hítardalur, Árni Arnórsson, and held them in custody in Hólar for almost a year. Bishop Jón simultaneously took over the episcopal see in Skálholt and appointed his son Björn to replace the imprisoned Marteinn Einarsson as bishop there.[46] During the ensuing months, Bishop Jón launched his plans to resurrect the old monastic institutions in Skálholt diocese, with steadfast assistance from his son Björn. His first action was to reopen Viðeyjarklaustur early in 1550. Abbot Alexíus Pálsson returned to his old monastery and was reconsecrated as abbot. Then the bishop went to Helgafell and reopened the monastery there. He reconsecrated Narfi Ívarsson, who had served as abbot there long before, between 1512 and 1527. Apparently, both Alexíus and Narfi still sided with the Catholic bishop.[47] In any case, these actions cannot have been much more than a symbolic gesture; there were no monks left in either Helgafell or Viðey, and no monastic buildings remained. Thus, the reopening of both monasteries was utterly unsuccessful, perhaps mostly because the new bishop of Skálholt, Marteinn Einarsson, had already invalidated all past and future ecclesiastical decisions made by Bishop Jón Arason or on his behalf.[48]

In the following year, Bishop Jón, together with armed supporters, prepared for further resistance against the Danish king's agents in Iceland and their Lutheran followers. He even had a fortress built around his episcopal seat in Hólar and installed cannons there. All the while, negotiations continued between King Christian III and Bishop Jón Arason through the king's agent, magistrate Daði Guðmundsson, whom the bishop had accused of several illegal acts and even excommunicated. The negotiations achieved little, apart from bringing about Bishop Martin Einarsson's return to Skálholt in 1550, though he was not yet able to resume his old office there.[49] By the end of September 1550, Bishop Jón Arason actively initiated his final campaign against the opposition to Catholicism in Iceland. He rode with his entourage, which was not particularly large, to capture Daði at his residence in Snóksdalur in Dalir. On the way they stopped at nearby Sauðafell, where they waited for several days. In the meantime, Daði gathered his own group and managed to capture Bishop Jón and his sons, Ari and Bishop Björn. During the attack, Bishop Jón and his men tried to seek shelter in the churchyard at Sauðafell, but the Catholic concept of sanctuary was no longer valid after the acceptance of Lutheranism, and they were captured.[50] Jón, Björn, and Ari were then brought to Skálholt and beheaded there on 7 November 1550 without being tried in court. They were not even taken to Denmark for the execution, as should have been done, because King Christian III did not want to wait for a ship. On this occasion, the king said memorably that it would be impossible to have peace in Iceland as long as the three men remained alive.[51]

The conflict was not over yet, however. The final scene of the Reformation in Iceland took place in spring 1551, when supporters of Bishop Jón Arason avenged the executions by killing the five men responsible for the deed. Around that time, all the monastic houses in Hólar diocese were closed down. The first Lutheran bishop of Hólar, Ólafur Hjaltason, was elected in 1552, and Marteinn Einarsson was reinstated in Skálholt episcopate.[52] Still, even though the most brutal events of the Protestant war were over, it took a while for Icelandic society to recover and absorb the new way of life.

Valuables Transported to Denmark

One of Christopher Hvítfeldt's tasks during his tenure as a Danish superintendent in Iceland, from 1541 to 1542, was to collect portable valuables from the monastic houses in Skálholt diocese and bring them to Denmark. The king is claimed to have needed them to pay for the so-called Count's Feud, a war of succession fought in Denmark from 1534 to 1536, of which the Reformation was one end result. Most of the valuables in silver were melted, while some of the loot was sold for cash.[53] The transport of the goods from Iceland to Denmark seems to have started immediately after the affiliation of Skálholt diocese was changed from Catholicism to Lutheranism, because in a letter written in summer 1541 to Bishop Jón Arason, Bishop Gissur Einarsson announced that he had already sent the king 600 *lods*[54] of silver objects collected from his diocese. His purpose may have been to encourage Bishop Jón to do the same or, alternatively, to provoke him by demonstrating both his power and that wielded by the king. Bishop Gissur emphasized his message by saying that he knew there was a large amount of silver and gold in the monastic houses in Hólar diocese.[55] Bishop Jón should have been aware of these valuables, as he had compiled the detailed inventory of them shortly after his election in 1524.

The transport of valuables from Skálholt diocese seem to have been just beginning because Christopher Hvítfeldt announced, on 6 August 1541 that he had delivered 1380 *lods*[56] of silver to King Christian III, as well as cash and other valuables, both silver and gold.[57] It was then on Christmas Day, 25 December 1550, that the Reverend Sigurður Jónsson at Grenjaðarstaður claimed that he had also supported the Danish king with 600 *lods*[58] of silver.[59] The following year, on 17 October 1551, the representatives of the Danish king proclaimed that ecclesiastical items, relics, and silver objects from the three monasteries of Hólar diocese – Þingeyraklaustur, Munkaþverárklaustur, and Möðruvallaklaustur – as well as from Hólar cathedral itself, had arrived in Denmark. Among them there were a total of 4,226 *lods*[60] of silver, excluding coins.[61] Curiously, a few months earlier, the deceased Bishop Jón Arason's mistress, Helga Sigurðardóttir, was accused of having secretly concealed a number of precious gold and silver objects from Hólar cathedral. She was even brought before a court, accused of having mistreated the property of the king. She denied these accusations and was found innocent in a formal court on 30 September 1551.[62] It is nonetheless tempting to imagine that the bishop's official mistress was fulfilling her partner's mission by trying to prevent Catholic relics from being taken to Denmark.

As has previously been noted, a few valuable objects from the monasteries remained in Iceland after the Reformation, albeit not many, given the lengthy lists in the monastic inventories. The Danish king also demanded that some of the remaining ecclesiastical treasures from the monasteries be given to poor churches around Iceland. Now these churches served the Lutheran congregation there. This certainly happened with the chalice and paten preserved from Skriðuklaustur, which were given to the church in Loðmundarfjörður but were later transferred to the National Museum of Iceland when the church was no longer in use. Fortunately, the chalice and paten were recognized again during post-excavation work at Skriðuklaustur.[63] Still, the transports of ecclesiastical goods from Iceland – coins, silver, and other valuable items – continued annually by order of the Danish king until at least 1559.[64] The situation was similar in Norway. The most valuable single item transported from the archdiocese of Niðarós to Copenhagen was undoubtedly the shrine of St. Olaf. It was worth 5,500 *lods*[65] of silver, but parts of it were made of gold.[66] On the contrary, Bishop Gissur Einarsson chose not to send the Danes the sacred shrine of St. Þorlákur Þórhallsson, which had stood above the high altar in Skálholt cathedral since it was made in connection with Bishop Þorlákur's sanctification in Iceland around 1200. It continued to stand there despite the Reformation, though hardly because of its otherworldly meaning. Bishop Gissur namely had St. Þorlákur's shrine permanently removed from its place of honor in Skálholt cathedral. It was put into storage, where its condition deteriorated.[67] It was, however, without doubt, one of the most valuable and precious Catholic liturgical items Icelanders ever owned.

Idolatry and Heresy

According to preserved descriptions, St. Þorlákur's shrine measured over six feet long, four feet high, and two feet wide. It was house-shaped with a base made of wood, but it was covered by ornamental silver plates inlaid with diamond-like stones.[68] It had survived two major fires at Skálholt cathedral, in 1306 and 1527, and both times it had been returned to its place of honor after the cathedral had been rebuilt.[69] Interestingly, in 1405, Bishop Vilchin had the skull moved from Þorlákur's shrine for placing it in a smaller reliquary, also inlaid with silver.[70] Nothing more is known about this skull reliquary of St. Þorlákur. However, as we have seen, several shrines are mentioned in the monastic inventories, but these were most likely of the same size as two identical shrines currently preserved from Iceland (one kept in the National Museum of Denmark and the other in the National Museum of Iceland). Both shrines are known to have been made in Iceland, by the same goldsmith, around 1200. Both are in the shape of a small house, 30 cm x 19 cm x 30 cm in size, as was common for such medieval reliquaries.[71] Other large shrines known to be present in Iceland during the Middle Ages were those of Bishop Jón Ögmundsson and Bishop Guðmundur góði, both kept in Hólar cathedral. These two shrines were still there in 1550, but it is not known where they ended up after that.[72] Perhaps they were sent to Denmark along with other valuable items from Hólar cathedral on 17 October 1551, though they are not specifically listed in the cargo of that transport.

Bishop Þorlákur's shrine – the large one – was still in Skálholt in the mid-seventeenth century, but in documents from 1725, it was claimed to be dangerously linked to heresy because of the power of Bishop Þorlákur to work miracles.[73] This should not come as a surprise because a known practice in other former Catholic societies was to keep and dislocate some of the most precious relics in order to preserve, or even exaggerate, the evidence of the Protestant defeat of Catholicism as memorials of their momentous victory. Furthermore, together with a drive to profane Catholicism, this was also the reason for why saintly likenesses were deliberately demolished during the Reformation. Broken likenesses appear even to have been kept visible to people so as to demonstrate the accomplishment of the Reformation for a long time afterwards. Their veneration was predicted by the Protestants as idolatry. It appears, furthermore, that the aim of listing in inventories the broken likenesses was to underline that the popish images had been destroyed and, most importantly, the Church purified.[74]

Although the intention was to abolish the cult of saints and the veneration of images after the Reformation, the presence of Þorlákur's shrine in Skálholt cathedral may surely have been overridden by the desire to use it to commemorate the shift from Catholicism to Lutheranism. The shrine might thus have been utilized in this way – dislocated – for materially remind people about the extravagance life of the Catholic bishop and, consequently, the victory of Lutheranism. Other relics were not protected by the same urges but even so used in similar purpose however; for example, the heads of the figurines of St. Barbara, found at Skriðuklaustur, and of St. Dorothy, discovered at the site of Viðeyjarklaustur, were deliberately separated from their bodies. When the head of the figurine of St. Barbara was found, it was revealed that her eyes had been mutilated and her body broken into pieces.[75] An inventory carried out in Þykkvabæjarklaustur in 1641 noted, furthermore, that in the church were pieces of broken likenesses of alabaster.[76] The inventory done the same year in Skriðuklaustur also lists a broken likeness of some unknown female saint.[77]

The statue of the Virgin Mary, found in the wall of a barn at Skriða farm in the nineteenth century, may even have been dislocated deliberately. The dislocation of saintly images was indeed common in other Catholic societies, where they have been found immured in walls of ecclesiastical buildings.[78] In some instances, the hands were simply broken off the saintly figures, as was done with the likeness of the Virgin, originated from Möðruvallaklaustur. As said in the introduction to this book, the altarpieces from Þingeyraklaustur and Reynistaðarklaustur both became subject to iconoclasm during the Reformation. The Reynistaðarklaustur altarpiece was clearly desecrated, but some of the saintly figures on it were removed or their heads broken off. The one from Þingeyraklaustur was disfigured through removal of its two wings before being reused in the new Lutheran church in Þingeyrar. The one from Munkaþverárklaustur, however, was sent to Denmark where it still remains, undamaged. The stained glass with saintly figures found at the sites of both Kirkjubæjarklaustur and Skriðuklaustur may likewise be examples of iconoclasm, as they were found broken into pieces when they were unearthed during the excavations of their ruins. It is difficult to determine whether the breakage occurred during the Reformation or afterwards, while the sites were deteriorating. However, it is clear that no one was interested in collecting the bits until the excavations taking place there recently.

As is mentioned earlier, the Danish king did not only claimed the monasteries' possessions after the Reformation, but he also had the monastic churches scaled down, as he considered them too costly to operate. This was indeed done at Þingeyraklaustur, Þykkvabæjarklaustur, Reynistaðarklaustur, and Skriðuklaustur. The churches were also renovated in accordance with the Lutheran teaching, by removing, for example, altar curtains, choir screens, and saintly relics from them and by adding pulpits and specific seats to them for the new congregation.[79] However, the fate of the monastic buildings themselves after the dissolution, except for those at Viðeyjarklaustur and Skriðuklaustur, is not fully clear due to lack of thorough research on their ruins. Still, they appear generally to have been left to deteriorate or in some cases refurbished to accommodate the representatives of the Danish king who served as his local superintendents. This seems, for example, to have happen in Þingeyraklaustur. These superintendents were supposed to take care of the king's properties in Iceland, mainly the farms which had formerly been owned by the monastic houses.[80] There seem, however, to have been disputes about the more official documents concerning the monastic institutions' properties (Icel. *jarðabækur*) but not particularly about the use of their lodgings. After the institutions were closed, these documents appear to have been lost in larger numbers than the liturgical books and hagiographies.

It is, in fact, unsurprising that conflict should have arisen over these documents, most of which concerned valuable assets such as the farms that reverted to the Danish king after the Reformation. The conflict that arose may also be explained by the fact the many of the farms were donated to the Church as care for the deceased soul. The donators and their descendants must thus have had legal claims of protection in accordance to the Catholic doctrine, but such donations lost their meaning with the new Protestant understanding of marriage.[81] As late as May 1578, the Danish king sent a reminder to the superintendent, Johann Bockholt, ordering that all remaining documents from the Icelandic monastic institutions should immediately be sent to him, as he had *previously* requested.[82] Accordingly, the destruction of Skriðuklaustur's documents is discussed in a July 1600 register from *Alþingi*. In the register, Jón Einarsson, the steward of the monastery's properties, swore an oath confirming that he did not know what had happened to the monastic documents.[83] And when manuscript collector Árni Magnússon went to Þykkvabæjarklaustur in 1700 that he was told that the monastery's documents were long gone: they had been blown away when the steeple with the Augustini bell had collapsed in a storm.[84] Árni was told a similar story about the fate of the documents of Reynistaðarklaustur. In that instance, it was claimed that Abbess Sólveig Brandsdóttir had once laid all the documents out to dry in an open field belonging to the convent, whereupon some calves came and ate most of them.[85] Moreover, at Viðey, Árni was told that the documents had been kept in a locked chest in the church, but that only one monk had the key to it. Unfortunately, the key was long since lost – and the documents, too.[86]

It appears, on the other hand, that the furnishings and parts of monastic buildings that have survived tend to be those from monastic houses that were closed down long before the Reformation. Among these items are the church bell from Bær and the cornerstone with the face from Hítardalur (see cover image). Furthermore, the hypothesis put forward here is that the famous, intricately carved Valþjófsstaður door, which still survives, was originally the door from Keldnaklaustur. Moreover, the two identical relic shrines, made in Iceland by the same goldsmith, are in fact from Valþjófsstaður and Keldur, underlining further the close ties between these two church sites.

The Valþjófsstaður Door

Written sources demonstrate that Keldnaklaustur first shifted from being a monastic cell to a proper monastery after the founder, Jón Loftsson, chief of the Oddaverjar family clan, died in 1197. It continued to operate under the administration of his son, Sæmundur, who built up its houses and hired a prior, Sveinn. However, when Sæmundur died in 1222, his descendants were apparently not interested in keeping the monastery running, perhaps because of the ongoing civil wars in Iceland at that time. Nevertheless, Sæmundur's family decided not only to close Keldnaklaustur, but they also tore down the building and redistributed the wood to Jón Loftsson's heirs as an inheritance.[87] This wood must therefore have been considered extremely valuable and, for some reason, much more so than the wood from other houses (which was commonly reused for new buildings or as fuel). Otherwise, it would not have been officially declared their paternal inheritance. The fact that there was precious wood to share proves that a proper monastic building stood at Keldur in

1222. What possibly made it so valuable are the carvings, perhaps telling the story of the owner. This carved door, however, is known to have been used later for a church in Valþjófsstaður in Fljótsdalur valley.

The Valþjófsstaður door was carved in pine around the time Sæmundur converted his father's monastic cell, Keldnaklaustur, to a proper monastic house. The origins of the door are not known, but after having stood at the entrance of the church at Valþjófsstaður for centuries – and consequently named after it – it was sold to Denmark in 1851, in exchange for two candlesticks and a new, simpler church door. However, the Valþjófsstaður door was returned to Iceland, along with some Icelandic manuscripts and other ancient objects from the collection of Árni Magnússon, when Icelanders celebrated the 1000th anniversary of *Alþingi* in 1930 (Figure 9.1).[88] The door is unique because it is the only surviving example of a medieval Icelandic carved door. The carving depicts a church, the oldest known image of a religious building from Iceland. It also features two roundels carved in the Romanesque style. The lower carved roundel shows four dragons biting each other's tails, and the upper roundel depicts the well-known legend of the Knight of the Lion, with local modifications. The carving is usually regarded as depicting of the tale of Yvain, as well as a mixture of several vernacular chivalric sagas.[89] It shows a knight who rescues a lion from being killed by a dragon, whereupon the lion follows the knight until his death. The story ends with the lion resting on the knight's gravestone, located in front of the church. On the gravestone is a runic inscription that reads 'Sjá inn ríka konung hér grafinn er vá dreka *þenna*' (See this mighty king who slayed the dragon).

There are several links between the Valþjófsstaður door and Keldur. The first is the coat of arms of the King of Norway, Magnus Barefoot (r. 1073–1103), which appears on the shield of the knight displayed in the carving. Magnus was the grandfather of Jón Loftsson.[90] Second, one of Jón Loftsson's legal heirs was Randalín Filippusdóttir, Jón's great-granddaughter and Sæmundur's granddaughter, who was given in marriage to the chieftain Oddur Þórarinsson in Valþjófsstaður in 1249. The third link is the two identical shrines preserved from Keldur and Valþjófsstaður, which date from 1200, as does the door. The shrines are gilded (the saintly images have been removed from the one from Valþjófsstaður though), and the shrine from Keldur is one of the relics that were transferred to Denmark during the Reformation.[91] The theory is that the carved door and one of the two gilded shrines – namely, the one from Valþjófsstaður – may have been part of a dowry or inheritance that Randalín Filippusdóttir received from her father's family at Keldur when she married Oddur and moved east to Valþjófsstaður.

Matrimony, as one of the seven sacraments, was supposed to be celebrated in church, but the bride price, or dowry, soon became a necessary element of it. The bride usually brought properties belonging to her family to the marriage as a dowry, which demonstrated her family's consent to her marriage. Consequently, heirlooms were of great importance when included in a dowry because of their symbolic significance. For example, dowry items that gained the status of heirlooms were usually closely connected with a person's private or public life and were

FIGURE 9.1 The Valþjófsstaður door. It might be the only complete piece preserved from the monastic lodgings in Iceland (Þjms_11009).

often associated with transformative events in the owner's life.[92] For Randalín's father, Filippus Sæmundsson, it must have been important to include the most valuable objects in the bride's dowry when sealing the marriage alliance between two powerful families in eastern and southern Iceland – the Svínfellingar family clan, of which Oddur Þórarinsson was chieftain, and the Oddaverjar clan, to which Randalín belonged.[93]

During the MMI project, the extremely valuable wood from the monastery at Keldur and its fate aroused curiosity. It appeared that Sæmundur, who built up his father's monastic cell, had thirteen children: four sons with his wife, Ingveldur, and six daughters and three sons with three of his concubines. The heirs would have been the four sons born in wedlock: Vilhjálmur, Haraldur, Andrés, and Filippus, who was Randalín's father.[94] The story carved into the upper roundel of the door may thus depict the struggles of their grandfather, chieftain Jón Loftsson, during the earlier phase of the *Staðamál*, in which he was the central character. When the conflicts were left unresolved for decades, he was declared the winner for having fought back papal interference in internal ecclesiastical matters. The record shows that at one point, he said that neither the pope nor his cardinals would know better than the ancient Icelanders how to protect their national freedom and possessions. For this, and for violating the sacrament of matrimony, he was excommunicated by Bishop Þorlákur.[95] In 1195, just two years before his death, the 'royally born chieftain' Jón Loftsson made an indelible mark on the Icelandic Church when one of his own sons, Páll Jónsson, brother of Sæmundur, was elected to succeed Þorlákur Þórhallsson as bishop of Skálholt.

It may therefore be that Sæmundur Jónsson had his father's historical struggles carved into the door of his monastery, Keldnaklaustur, when he decided to build it up and keep it going after his father's death. Jón himself could be the knight in the carving, with the shield bearing his royal coat of arms. The lion he saves is symbolic of the Icelandic nation, and the dragon represents the evil force he defeated. The knight's gravestone demonstrates not only that he was a king but also that he had defeated an evil force. Moreover, the church that is carved on the door, behind the gravestone on which the lion is resting, may represent Jón Loftsson's monastic church, bearing in mind the memorable words he is believed to have said on his deathbed: 'Þar stendr þú, kirkja mín. Þú harmar mik, en ek harma þik' (There you are my church. You grieve for me, and I grieve for you).[96] At that time, it was well known that great chieftains, as Jón Loftsson certainly was, had their stories carved into stone or wood, and this hypothesis, although difficult to verify, could explain the value that the wood from Keldnaklaustur had for Jón Loftsson's family. The carvings on the door have been ascribed to Randalín herself,[97] but she could not have done them because the designs and the motif show that the door was made around 1200, nearly thirty years before she was born.

Interestingly, Bishop Páll Jónsson (r. 1195–1211), son of Jón Loftsson, had two servants at his episcopal seat in Skálholt, one of them a carver and the other a goldsmith, who were skilled in making shrines. They were a couple, Margrét hin haga (the skilled) and Þorsteinn skrínissmiður (the shrine-smith). In the bishops' saga of Bishop Páll, for example, Margrét hin haga is said to have carved an ivory crosier (probably a walrus tusk) that Páll gave to the archbishop in Niðarós. In the same story, Þorsteinn skrínissmiður is said to have made the precious shrine of Bishop Þorlákur in 1198, under Bishop Páll's instructions. In Páll's saga, Margrét hin haga is claimed to be the most skilled carver in Iceland at that time and Þorsteinn, her husband, the most skilled shrine maker and goldsmith.[98] Unfortunately, the skillfully carved crosier given to the archbishop in Niðarós does not survive today, but there is no reason to doubt that it was made. When the grave of Bishop Páll Jónsson, who died in 1211, was excavated at Skálholt in 1958, a crosier carved in walrus tusk was found in his stone coffin, which was made of the volcanic stone tufa. The carving of the crosier is in the Romanesque style, with zoomorphic ornaments, ending in a dragon head like the one on the door.[99] It may thus be concluded that the door and the two shrines were the work of the two servants of Skálholt, Margrét hin haga and Þorsteinn skrínissmiður, undertaken on the instructions of two of Jón Loftsson's sons, Bishop Páll and Sæmundur, for their father's monastic cell at Keldur.

The Tudor Rose and the Pomegranate

As is discussed earlier, Bishop Jón Arason's campaign against the Reformation came to nothing. It failed, as did similar resistance efforts in other Catholic societies in northern Europe. His attempt to restore Viðeyjarklaustur and Helgafellsklaustur was utterly unsuccessful, as was his attempt to re-establish the diocese of Skálholt as a Catholic see by putting his son Björn on the episcopal throne in 1550. Holding the Lutheran bishop Marteinn Einarsson in custody was likewise an act that was doomed to fail from the outset. Nevertheless, the final resistance of Bishop Jón Arason and his sons may be observed as part of a broader attempt to reinstate Catholicism, as could be witnessed in Norway, England, Scotland, and France.[100]

In fact, one preserved material artifact indicates this. It is a church bell hanging in the upper loft of the present church at Helgafell, where Helgafellsklaustur stood. Interestingly, it is engraved with the emblems of Catherine of Aragon and her husband Henry VIII, King of England (r. 1509–1547). The emblems are the Tudor rose and the pomegranate, which together were supposed to represent their marriage. Also on the bell is an image of St. Barbara and an inscription of the year 1547. The symbols of St. Barbara, the Tudor rose, and the pomegranate similarly appear together on silver armor belonging to Henry VIII and a gilded wand that belonged to one of his bodyguards.[101] Moreover, the following hymn and introit are written on the bell in Latin: 'Da pacem domine in diebvs nostris' (Give peace in our times, O Lord). They are the basis for songs used in the Catholic liturgy.

The royal couple Catherine of Aragon and Henry VIII was certainly involved in the long history of the Reformation in Britain. Their story is well known; Catherine was the first of Henry's six wives, and although King Henry VIII longed for a son, their only surviving child was their daughter, Mary. In order to be able to have a son, Henry divorced Catherine and married Anne Boleyn. However, as a Catholic he was not permitted to divorce, so he separated the Church of England from the papal authorities and founded the Anglican Church in 1534 in order to fulfil his wish. He even ordered the destruction of the monastic buildings in the realm and took over their possessions.[102] Catherine, on the other hand, always remained a faithful Catholic. She died in 1536 and King Henry VIII died in 1547, the year inscribed on the church bell. Helgafellsklaustur was closed in 1544, so the date cannot refer to that event. The only child of Catherine and Henry, Mary, used her parents' emblems – the Tudor rose and the pomegranate – as a coat of arms in her office as Queen of England. Mary I was a Catholic believer, as her mother always was, but became known as Bloody Mary because she had a number of people who opposed her burnt to death, most of them Protestants, immigrants, or those convicted of heresy. Mary I came to power in England six years after her father died and reigned from 1553 to 1558, but she actually began her campaign against the Reformation right after her father's death in 1547.[103]

Church bells engraved with these emblems, the Tudor rose and the pomegranate, soon became the best-known symbols of the resistance against the Reformation in England. The church bell preserved at the former site of Helgafellsklaustur appears to be one of them. It is not known when or how it ended up there, but it may have been meant to underscore the ongoing protests in Iceland led by Bishop Jón Arason. Specifically, its presence in Helgafell indicates that Jón was an official participant in the ongoing post-Reformation campaign to revive Catholicism in northern Europe. At least, this can be assumed in light of the support he received from Pope Paul III in his crusade in 1549.[104] After being elected bishop in 1524, Jón had even imported a new elaborate altar piece for the cathedral of Hólar and a new chasuble, dalmatic, and gown for himself, most likely from northern Germany. These are still preserved, and the chasuble is embroidered with the pomegranate.[105] Thus, it is suggested here that the bell, which now hangs in the church at Helgafell, was cast in 1547 in memory of Mary's lineage and highlights Bishop Jón's final endeavor to resist the shift from Catholicism to Lutheranism in Iceland, although the reopening of Helgafellsklaustur in 1550 was nothing more than symbolic. Additionally, it may be speculated that the hymn engraved on the bell expresses his praying for peace during the ongoing turmoil.

From its beginning to its end, Iceland's monastic history largely reflects medieval monasticism as it was practiced in mainland Europe. As has been described in this book, the consistency in the operation of the monastic houses in Iceland and elsewhere on the Continent is clear and understandable, as all of them followed a shared political, cultural, and religious agenda evolving from the framework of Roman Catholic Christianity. Accordingly, Iceland has never been an island in the sense of being cut off from social and cultural developments; it has always been part of a larger world. It is Europe.

Notes

1 See, for example, Auge, 'Monasteries and Collegiate Chapters in the Duchies of Schleswig and Holstein and the Reformation', pp. 169–193; Cameron, *The European Reformation*, pp. 294–313; Dreyer, 'Den lange danske reformationen', pp. 94–100; Ekroll, 'Thrown to the Wolves?' pp. 156–159; Gunnes, 'Klosteranlegg i Norge', pp. 74–82; Jacobsen, 'Nordic Woman and the Reformation', pp. 57–63; Kristiansen, 'Den Danske Klostre og Reformationen', pp. 228–236; Møller and Østergård, 'Lutheran Orthodoxy and Anti-Catholicism', pp. 166–171; Lausten, 'The Early Reformation in Denmark and Norway 1520–1559', pp. 29–32; Lausten, *Luther og Danmark i 500 år*, pp. 62–69; Lausten, 'Kongemagt og rigets vel', pp. 152–156.

2 Clark, *The Benedictines in the Middle Ages*, pp. 323–326, 331–332; Cameron, *The European Reformation*, pp. 272–291; Dreyer, 'Den lange danske reformationen', pp. 88–91; Kristiansen, 'Den Danske Klostre og Reformationen', pp. 223–229; Møller and Østergård, 'Lutheran Orthodoxy and Anti-Catholicism', pp. 166–171; Lausten, 'The Early Reformation in Denmark and Norway 1520–1559', pp. 12–18, 29–32; Lausten, *Luther og Danmark i 500 år*, pp. 40–68; Ekroll, 'Thrown to the Wolves?' pp. 156–157.
3 Grímsdóttir, 'Biskupsstóll í Skálholti', p. 50.
4 See, for example, Cunningham, 'Changing Fashions', pp. 65–91; Karlsson, *Iceland's 1100 Years*, pp. 132–133; Ísleifsdóttir, *Byltingin að ofan*; Lausten, *Luther og Danmark i 500 år*, pp. 69–70.
5 DI XIII, pp. 104–106.
6 Karlsson, *Iceland's 1100 years*, pp. 128–133; Guttormsson, 'Frá siðaskiptum til upplýsingar', pp. 63–65.
7 See, for example, Aston, 'Public Worship and Iconoclasm', pp. 9–25; Bach-Nielsen, 'Skriftestolen – et overset møbel i de Luterske kirker', pp. 164–191; Bisgaard, 'Senmiddelalderens Reliøse Praksis og Reformationen', pp. 7–41; Bynum, *Dissimilar Similitudes*, pp. 105–107, 130–132; Gilchrist, *Medieval Life*, pp. 223–227; Gilchrist, *Sacred Heritage*, pp. 167–169; Graves, 'From an Archaeology of Iconoclasm', pp. 36–48; Høiris and Per, 'Reformationen i Danmark', pp. 7–8.
8 Gajewski and Seeberg, 'Art in Monastic Churches of Western Europe', pp. 999–1003; Kessler, 'On the State of Medieval Art History', pp. 171–183.
9 Arnórsdóttir, 'Gender and Donation Culture in Iceland from 1300–1600', pp. 172–174; Arnórsdóttir, '"Ægtesengen skal være uden synd"', pp. 303–324; Fink-Jensen, 'Kristendom, skole og pædegogik i Danmark før 1700', pp. 369–374; Møller and Østergård, 'Lutheran Orthodoxy and Anti-Catholicism', p. 169; Petersen, 'Reformationen og ritualerna', pp. 131–150.
10 Arnórsdóttir, '"Ægtesengen skal være uden synd"', pp. 309–322; Høiris and Per, 'Reformationen i Danmark', p. 8.
11 Jónsson, *Blóðskömm á Íslandi 1270–1870*, pp. 93–112; Jónsson, *Dulsmál 1600–1900*; *Jónsbók*, pp. 319–323; Kjær and Vogt, 'Straf og forvisning', pp. 393–381; Netterstrøm, 'Reformationens betydning for kriminalisering af manddrab', pp. 413–489; Kristjánsdóttir and Hannesdóttir, 'Út yfir gröf og dauða', pp. 147–148.
12 Netterstrøm, 'Reformationens betydning for kriminalisering af manddrab', pp. 423–424; Rasmussen, 'Døden og de døde', pp. 371–381.
13 DI X, pp. 451–459; Egilsson, 'Biskupa-annálar Jóns Egilssonar', p. 82; Lockhart, *Denmark 1513–1660*, p. 75; Ísleifsdóttir, *Byltingin að ofan*, p. 181.
14 Egilsson, 'Biskupa-annálar Jóns Egilssonar', pp. 82–83.
15 Egilsson, 'Biskupa-annálar Jóns Egilssonar', pp. 82–83.
16 DI XII, pp. 595–597.
17 Kristjánsdóttir, 'Klaustureyjan á Sundum', pp. 29–52.
18 Grímsdóttir, 'Biskupsstóll í Skálholti', p. 50; Ísleifsdóttir, *Byltingin að ofan*, pp. 139–140.
19 DI X, pp. 455, 458–459.
20 DI X, pp. 534, 554–555.
21 Cunningham, 'Changing Fashions', pp. 74–75; DI X, pp. 451–459, 499–505; Grímsdóttir, 'Biskupsstóll í Skálholti', pp. 49–50.
22 Egilsson, 'Biskupa-annálar Jóns Egilssonar', pp. 71–72; *Gottskálksannáll*, p. 375.
23 Grímsdóttir, 'Biskupsstóll í Skálholti', pp. 50; Ísleifsdóttir, *Byltingin að ofan*, pp. 180–201.
24 Grímsdóttir, 'Biskupsstóll í Skálholti', pp. 49–52. Before Gissur was elected bishop, Sigmundur Eyjólfsson was consecrated as the successor of Bishop Ögmundur Pálsson by the archbishop in Niðarós in 1537, but Sigmundur passed away nineteen days later, before arriving to Iceland. He was nephew of Bishop Ögmundur (see Grímsdóttir, 'Biskupsstóll í Skálholti', p. 50).
25 See DI X, pp. 632–633, 682–683.
26 DI XI, pp. 186–187.

27 DI XI, pp. 176–178.
28 Steinsson, *Saga munklífis að Skriðu í Fljótsdal*, pp. 118–122.
29 DI XI, p. 186; Steinsson, *Saga munklífis að Skriðu í Fljótsdal*, p. 122.
30 Kristjánsdóttir, 'Lokun íslensku miðaldaklaustranna', pp. 88–89.
31 DI XI, p. 187.
32 Pálsson, *Helgafell – saga höfuðbóls og klausturs*, p. 109.
33 Hjartarson and Kristjánsdóttir, 'Rannsókn á örnefnum um klaustur á Íslandi', p. 13; Pálsson, *Helgafell – saga höfuðbóls og klausturs*, p. 113; Kristjánsdóttir, 'Lokun íslensku miðalklaustranna', p. 88.
34 Kristjánsdóttir, 'Lokun íslensku miðaldaklaustranna', pp. 87–88.
35 Þór, 'Saga biskupsstóls á Hólum í Hjaltadal', pp. 329–330.
36 DI XI, p. 450.
37 DI XI, pp. 186–187.
38 See DI XI, p. 271.
39 DI XI, p. 187.
40 Kristjánsdóttir, 'Lokun íslensku miðaldaklaustranna', p. 87.
41 See DI XII, pp. 214–215, 267.
42 *Íslenskar æviskrár*, p. 312; Steinunn Kristjánsdóttir, 'Lokun íslensku miðaldaklaustranna', pp. 88–89.
43 *Íslenskar æviskrár*, pp. 266–267; Kristjánsdóttir, *Sagan af klaustrinu á Skriðu*, pp. 47–48.
44 *Danske Kancellis Registranter 1535–1550*, p. 362; Jacobsen, 'Nordic Woman and the Reformation', p. 56; Kristiansen, 'Den Danske Klostre og Reformationen', pp. 230–231.
45 DI XI, pp. 695–698.
46 Grímsdóttir, 'Biskupsstóll í Skálholti', p. 51; Ísleifsdóttir, *Siðbreytingin á Íslandi*, pp. 244–260.
47 Ólason, *Menn og menntir siðskiptaaldarinnar á Íslandi*, pp. 328–330; Pálsson, *Helgafell*, pp. 99–117; Ísleifsdóttir, *Siðbreytingin á Íslandi*, pp. 184–187.
48 DI XI, pp. 713–716.
49 Ísleifsdóttir, *Siðbreytingin á Íslandi*, pp. 245–248.
50 DI XII, pp. 687–688. See even Lockhart, *Denmark 1513–1660*, p. 75; Ísleifsdóttir, *Siðbreytingin á Íslandi*, p. 256.
51 Cunningham, 'Changing Fashions', pp. 88–91; Lausten, *Luther og Danmark i 500 år*, pp. 69–70; Ísleifsdóttir, *Siðbreytingin á Íslandi*, pp. 255–257.
52 Grímsdóttir, 'Biskupsstóll í Skálholti', p. 51; Þór, 'Hólabiskupa ævir', p. 419.
53 Cunningham, 'Changing Fashions', pp. 76–77; Lockhart, *Denmark 1513–1660*, pp. 26, 29–35; Ísleifsdóttir, *Siðbreytingin á Íslandi*, p. 201.
54 One *lod* is 15.6 gr.; therefore, 600 *lods* equal approximately 9 kg.
55 DI X, p. 644–645.
56 *c.* 22 kg.
57 DI X, pp. 648–649.
58 *c.* 9 kg.
59 DI XI, p. 853.
60 *c.* 4220 kg.
61 *Kancelliets brevbøger vedrørende Danmarks indre forhold 1551–1555*, pp. 83–84.
62 DI XII, pp. 315–317.
63 Kristjánsdóttir, *Sagan af klaustrinu á Skriðu*, pp. 102–103.
64 DI XII, pp. 328–330, 470, 629–630; DI XIII, pp. 83, 322–323, 424–425.
65 *c.* 88 kg.
66 Ísleifsdóttir, *Siðbreytingin á Íslandi*, p. 202.
67 Cormack, 'Voru helgimyndir eyðilagðar á Íslandi?', p. 248; Harðardóttir, 'Innanbúnaður kirkna', pp. 205–206; Eldjárn, 'Þorláksskrín í Skálholti', pp. 32–39.
68 Eldjárn, 'Þorláksskrín í Skálholti', pp. 35–39.
69 Eldjárn, 'Þorláksskrín í Skálholti', pp. 26, 33–34.
70 *Nýi annáll*, pp. 12–13.
71 Eldjárn, 'Þorláksskrín í Skálholti', pp. 19–20.

72 Harðardóttir, 'Innanbúnaður kirkna', p. 207; Eldjárn, 'Þorláksskrín í Skálholti', p. 20.
73 *Biskupasögur Jóns prófasts Halldórssonar í Hítardal*, pp. 59–60.
74 Aston, 'Public Worship and Iconoclasm', pp. 9–25; Bynum, *Dissimilar Similitudes*, pp. 105–107, 130–132; Gilchrist, *Medieval Life*, pp. 223–227; Gilchrist, *Sacred Heritage*, pp. 167–169; Graves, 'From an Archaeology of Iconoclasm', pp. 36–48.
75 Kristjánsdóttir, *Leitin að klaustrunum*, p. 445.
76 Cormack, 'Voru helgimyndir eyðilagðar á Íslandi?', p. 250; Grímsdóttir, 'Heimildir í handritum um klaustrin í Skaftafellsþingi', p. 135.
77 Steinsson, *Saga munklífis á Skriðu*, p. 30.
78 Aston, 'Public worship and iconoclasm', pp. 17–19; Graves, 'From an Archaeology of Iconoclasm', pp. 36–48.
79 Harðardóttir, 'Innanbúnaður kirkna', pp. 198–204.
80 Arnórsdóttir, *Property and Virginity*, pp. 13–134.
81 Arnórsdóttir, 'Gender and Donation culture', pp. 165–166; 172–175.
82 *Kancelliets brevbøger vedrørende Danmarks indre forhold 1576–1579*, p. 353.
83 *Alþingisbækur Íslands III 1595–1603*, p. 192.
84 Magnússon, 'Um klaustrin', pp. 41, 45.
85 Magnússon, 'Um klaustrin', p. 47.
86 Magnússon, 'Um klaustrin', p. 45.
87 *Þorláks saga B*, pp. 180–181.
88 Hallgrímsson, *Fljótsdæla*, p. 271.
89 Harris, 'The Lion-Knight Legend', pp. 125–145; Ríkharðsdóttir, 'Oceanic Networks', pp. 106–107. It has also been suggested that it depicts a literary memory from some European poets' stories, but with local amendments.
90 Jensson, 'Latin Hagiography in Medieval Iceland', pp. 892–893.
91 Kristjánsdóttir, *Mynd á þili*, pp. 13–14.
92 Arnórsdóttir, *Property and Virginity*, pp. 351–373; Gilchrist, *Medieval Life*, pp. 124–125, 217, 237–242; Karras, *Unmarriages*, p. 24.
93 *Árna saga*, pp. 71–75.
94 DI I, p. 627.
95 *Þorláks saga B*, pp. 166–172. See also footnote 56.
96 *Þorláks saga B*, p. 181.
97 See, for example, Hallgrímsson, *Fljótsdæla*, p. 271.
98 Eldjárn, 'Þorláksskrín í Skálholti', pp. 19–42; *Páls saga*, pp. 310, 325.
99 Eldjárn, 'Gröf Páls biskups Jónssonar', pp. 147–158.
100 See, for example, Betteridge, *The Reformation*, pp. 123–124; Cameron, *The European Reformation*, pp. 280–291, especially pp. 285, 354–358; Clark, *The Benedictines in the Middle Ages*, pp. 337–338; Collinson, 'The English Reformation in the mid-Elizabethan period', pp. 1–2; Oldenburg, 'Toward a Multicultural Mid-Tudor England', pp. 99–100; Lausten, 'The Early Reformation in Denmark and Norway', pp. 29–32; Skovmand, 'Den engelske reformation', pp. 307–311.
101 Keily, 'Pomegranate & Rose'; Gunnarsdóttir and Kristjánsdóttir, 'Varðveittir gripir', pp. 14–16.
102 See, for example, Cameron, *The European Reformation*, pp. 281–283; Clark, *The Benedictines in the Middle Ages*, pp. 230, 322; Gaimster and Gilchrist, 'Introduction. History from Below', pp. 2–3; Lindberg, *The European Reformations*, pp. 318–319; Morris, *Europe and England in the Sixteenth Century*, pp. 36, 157, 165–166; Rosewell, The Medieval Monastery, p. 67; Skovmand, 'Den engelske reformation', pp. 307–311.
103 See, for example, Cameron, *The European Reformation*, pp. 282–285; Clark, *The Benedictines in the Middle Ages*, pp. 337–338; Morris, *Europe and England in the Sixteenth Century*, pp. 157, 226, 235–240; Oldenburg, 'Toward a Multicultural Mid-Tudor England', pp. 99–100; Skovmand, 'Den engelske reformation', pp. 311–312; Williams, 'Katherine of Aragon', pp. 36–41.
104 See again DI XI, pp. 695–698.
105 Eldjárn, *Um Hóladómkirkju*.

BIBLIOGRAPHY

Printed Primary Sources

Alþingisbækur Íslands II 1582–1594 (Reykjavík: Sögufélag, 1915–1916)

Alþingisbækur Íslands III 1595–1603 (Reykjavík: Sögufélag, 1917)

Árna saga, in Biskupasögur III. *Íslenzk fornrit* XVII, publ. by Guðrún Ása Grímsdóttir (Reykjavík: Hið íslenzka fornritafélag, 1998), pp. 3–212

Biskupasögur Jóns prófasts Halldórssonar í Hítardal (Reykjavík: Sögufélag, 1913)

Bréfabók Guðbrandar biskups Þorlákssonar, pub. by Páll Eggert Ólason (Reykjavík: Hið íslenska bókmenntafélag, 1919–1942)

Code of Canon Law. www.vatican.va/archive/cod-iuris-canonici/eng/documents/cic_lib2-cann607-709_en.html#DEPARTURE_FROM_AN_INSTITUTE [Accessed 15 March 2020]

Conciliorum Oecumenicorum Decreta, ed. by Norman P. Tanner and Giuseppe Alberigo (London: Sheed and Ward, 1990)

Danske Kancellis Registranter 1535–1550 (Copenhagen: Selskabet før Udgivelse af Kilder til dansk Historie, 1881–1882)

DI:

Diplomatarium islandicum I (Kaupmannahöfn: Hið íslenzka bókmenntafélag 1857–1876)

Diplomatarium islandicum II (Kaupmannahöfn: Hið íslenzka bókmenntafélag 1893)

Diplomatarium islandicum III (Kaupmannahöfn: Hið íslenzka bókmenntafélag 1896)

Diplomatarium islandicum IV (Kaupmannahöfn: Hið íslenzka bókmenntafélag 1897)

Diplomatarium islandicum V (Kaupmannahöfn and Reykjavík: Hið íslenzka bókmenntafélag 1899–1902)

Diplomatarium islandicum VI (Reykjavík: Hið íslenzka bókmenntafélag 1900–1904)

Diplomatarium islandicum VII (Reykjavík: Hið íslenzka bókmenntafélag 1903–1907)

Diplomatarium islandicum VIII (Reykjavík: Hið íslenzka bókmenntafélag 1906–1913)

Diplomatarium islandicum IX (Reykjavík: Hið íslenzka bókmenntafélag 1909–1913)

Diplomatarium islandicum X (Reykjavík: Hið íslenzka bókmenntafélag 1911–1921)

Diplomatarium islandicum XI (Reykjavík: Hið íslenzka bókmenntafélag 1915–1925)

Diplomatarium islandicum XII (Reykjavík: Hið íslenzka bókmenntafélag 1923–1932)

Diplomatarium islandicum XIII (Reykjavík: Hið íslenzka bókmenntafélag 1933–1939)

Diplomatarium islandicum XV (Reykjavík: Hið íslenzka bókmenntafélag 1947–1950)
Diplomatarium islandicum XVI (Reykjavík: Hið íslenzka bókmenntafélag 1952–1972)
DN:
Diplomatarium Norvegicum I, nr. 16 www.dokpro.uio.no/dipl_norv/diplom_help_eng.html#Innledning [Accessed 15 March 2021]
Diplomatarium Norvegicum V, nr. 261 www.dokpro.uio.no/cgi-bin/middelalder/diplom_vise_tekst.cgi?b=4878&s=n&str= [Accessed 15 March 2021]
Eiríks saga rauða. Grænlendinga saga, ed. by Einar Ól. Sveinsson and Matthías Þórðarson (Reykjavík: Hið íslenzka fornritafélag, 1935)
Fitjaannáll, *Annálar Íslands 1400–1800* II (Reykjavík: Félagsprentsmiðjan, 1930), pp. 1–411
Flateyjarannáll, *Islandske Annaler indtil 1578*, Gustav Storm Prepared for Publishing (Christiania: Grøndahl & Søns Bogtrykkeri, 1888), pp. 379–426
Gottskálksannáll, *Islandske Annaler indtil 1578*, Gustav Storm Prepared for Publishing (Christiania: Grøndahl & Søns Bogtrykkeri, 1888), pp. 297–378
Grágás, ed. by Gunnar Karlsson, Kristján Sveinsson and Mörður Árnason (Reykjavík: Mál og menning, 1992)
The Holy Rules of St. Benedictine www.ccel.org/ccel/b/benedict/rule/cache/rule.pdf [Accessed 15 March 2020]
Hungrvaka, in Biskupasögur II. *Íslenzk fornrit* XVI, publ. by Ásdís Egilsdóttir (Reykjavík: Hið íslenzka fornritafélag, 2002), pp. 3–43
Húnvetnskur annáll, *Annálar 1400–1800 I* (Reykjavík: Félagsprentsmiðjan, 1940), pp. 605–637
Íslands árbækur í söguformi af Jóni Espólín, sýslumann í Skagafjarðar Sysslu I (Kaupmannahöfn: Hið íslenska bókmenntafélag, 1821)
Íslendingabók, ed. by Jakob Benediktsson (Reykjavík: Hið íslenzka fornritafélag, 1968)
Íslenzkar þjóðsögur og ævintýri, recoded by Jón Árnason. Vol. i (Leipzig: Sögufélag and Oscar Brandstetter, 1928)
Íslenzkar þjóðsögur og ævintýri, recoded by Jón Árnason. Vol. ii (Reykjavík: Bókaútgáfan Þjóðsaga, 1954)
Íslenzkar þjóðsögur og sagnir, recorded by Sigfús Sigfússon. Vol. i (Reykjavík: Bókaútgáfan Þjóðsaga, 1982)
Íslenzkar þjóðsögur og sagnir, recorded by Sigfús Sigfússon. Vol. vii (Reykjavík: Bókaútgáfan Þjóðsaga, 1986)
Íslenzkar þjóðsögur og sagnir, recorded by Sigfús Sigfússon. Vol. x (Reykjavík: Bókaútgáfan Þjóðsaga, 1991)
Járnsíða og Kristinréttur Árna Þorlákssonar, pub. by Haraldur Bernharðsson, Magnús Lyngdal Magnússon and Már Jónsson (Reykjavík: Sögufélag, 2005)
Jarteinabók II, in Biskupasögur II. *Íslenzk fornrit* XVI, publ. by Ásdís Egilsdóttir (Reykjavík: Hið íslenzka fornritafélag, 2003)
Jóns saga ins helga, in Biskupasögur I. *Íslenzk fornrit* XV:2, publ. by Sigurgeir Steingrímsson, Ólafur Halldórsson and Peter Foote (Reykjavík: Hið íslenzka fornritafélag, 2002), pp. 175–316
Jónsbók, pub. by Már Jónsson (Reykjavík: Mál og Menning, 2004)
Kancelliets brevbøger vedrørende Danmarks indre forhold 1551–1555 (Copenhagen: Kommission hos C.A. Reitzel, 1885–1886)
Kancelliets brevbøger vedrørende Danmarks indre forhold 1561–1565 (Copenhagen: Kommission hos C.A. Reitzel, 1893–1895)
Kancelliets brevbøger vedrørende Danmarks indre forhold 1571–1575 (Copenhagen: Kommission hos C.A. Reitzel, 1898)
Kancelliets brevbøger vedrørende Danmarks indre forhold 1576–1579 (Copenhagen: Kommission hos C.A. Reitzel, 1900)

Ketilsstaðaannáll, *Annálar 1400–1800 IV* (Reykjavík: Hið íslenzka bókmenntafelag, 1940), pp. 403–462

Konungsannáll, *Islandske Annaler indtil 1578*, Gustav Storm Prepared for Publishing (Christiania: Grøndahl & Søns Bogtrykkeri, 1888), pp. 77–156

Kristni saga, in Biskupasögur I. *Íslenzk fornrit* XV:2, publ. by Sigurgeir Steingrímsson, Ólafur Halldórsson and Peter Foote (Reykjavík: Hið íslenzka fornritafélag, 2003), pp. 3–48

Landnámabók, ed. by Jakob Benediktsson (Reykjavík: Hið íslenzka fornritafélag, 1968)

Lárentíus saga, in Biskupasögur III. *Íslenzk fornrit* XVII, publ. by Guðrún Ása Grímsdóttir (Reykjavík: Hið íslenzka fornritafélag, 1998), pp. 215–441

Laxdæla, ed. by Einar Ól. Sveinsson. Íslenzk fornrit V (Reykjavík: Hið íslenzka fornritafélag, 1934)

Laxdæla saga, ed. by Aðalsteinn Eyþórsson og Bergljót S. Kristjánsdóttir (Reykjavík: Mál & Menning, 2017)

Lögmannsannáll, *Islandske Annaler indtil 1578*, Gustav Storm Prepared for Publishing (Christiania: Grøndahl & Søns Bogtrykkeri, 1888), pp. 231–296

Nýi annáll, *Annálar 1400–1800 I* (Reykjavík: Félagsprentsmiðjan, 1922), pp. 8–27

The Overseas Trade of Bristol in the Late Middle Ages. Vol. VII. Editors, R.B. Mowat, D. Litt and E.E. Butcher (Bristol: Bristol Record Society Publication, 1937)

Páls saga, in Biskupasögur II. *Íslenzk fornrit* XVI, publ. by Ásdís Egilsdóttir (Reykjavík: Hið íslenzka fornritafélag, 2002), pp. 297–332

The Rule of St. Augustine https://www1.villanova.edu/villanova/mission/campusministry/RegularSpiritualPractices/resources/spirituality/about/rule/chapters.html [Accessed 15 March 2020]

Sauðlauksdalsannáll. *Íslenskir annálar 1400–1800* VI (Reykjavík: Félagsprentsmiðjan, 1987), pp. 333–482

Skálholtsannáll, *Islandske Annaler indtil 1578*, Gustav Storm Prepared for Publication (Christiania: Grøndahl & Søns Bogtrykkeri, 1888), pp. 157–216

———, *Annálar 1400–1800 I* (Reykjavík: Félagsprentsmiðjan, 1922), pp. 28–272

Sturlunga saga, ed. by Örnólfur Thorsson (Reykjavík: Svart á hvítu, 1988)

Vestfjarðarannáll hinn elsti, *Annálar 1400–1800 III* (Reykjavík: Félagsprentsmiðjan, 1933), pp. 21–87

Þorláks saga A, in Biskupasögur II. *Íslenzk fornrit* XVI, publ. by Ásdís Egilsdóttir (Reykjavík: Hið íslenzka fornritafélag, 2002), pp. 47–99

Þorláks saga B, in Biskupasögur II. *Íslenzk fornrit* XVI, publ. by Ásdís Egilsdóttir (Reykjavík: Hið íslenzka fornritafélag, 2002), pp. 143–224

Þorvalds þáttr víðförla I, in Biskupasögur I. *Íslenzk fornrit* XV:2, publ. by Sigurgeir Steingrímsson, Ólafur Halldórsson and Peter Foote (Reykjavík: Hið íslenzka fornritafélag, 2003), pp. 51–89

Unpublished Theses and Reports

Ahlin Sundman, Elin, 'Osteological Analysis of the Human Remains: Skriðuklaustur 2011' (report, 2011) https://steinunn.hi.is/files/2022-09/EASHUM_2011.pdf [Accessed 15 August 2019]

Colic, Etel, 'Medieval Icelandic Pottery: The excavations at Gásir and Skriðuklaustur' (unpublished BA thesis, University of Iceland, 2006)

Collins, Cecilia, 'An Osteological Analysis of the Human Remains from the 2009 Excavation Season at Skriðuklaustur, East Iceland' (report, 2010) https://steinunn.hi.is/files/2022-09/CCHUM_2010.pdf [Accessed 15 August 2019]

———, 'An Osteological Analysis of the Human Remains from the 2010 Excavation Season at Skriðuklaustur, East Iceland' (report, 2011) https://steinunn.hi.is/files/2022-09/CCHUM_2011.pdf [Accessed 15 August 2019]
Einarsson, Bjarni F., 'Kirkjubær. Klaustur og umhverfisaðstæður' (report, 2000)
Foster, H. Megan, 'Pilgrimage Through the Pages: Pilgrim's Badges in Late Medieval Devotional Manuscripts' (unpublished thesis in Philosophy, University of Illinois, 2011)
Gunnarsdóttir, Vala and Kristjánsdóttir, Steinunn, 'Varðveittir gripir úr íslenskum miðaldaklaustrum' (report, 2016) https://steinunn.hi.is/files/2022-09/GRIP_2016.pdf [Accessed 15 August 2019]
Halldórsdóttir, Hrafnhildur Helga, 'Einsetulifnaður á Íslandi' (report, 2014) https://steinunn.hi.is/files/2022-09/EIN_2014.pdf [Accessed 15 August 2019]
Halldórsdóttir, Viktoría, 'Viðey – heimsótt á ný' (unpublished BA thesis, University of Iceland, 2014)
Hallgrímsdóttir, Margrét, 'Fornleifarannsókn í Viðey 1987' (report, 1988)
———, 'Viðey. Fornleifarannsóknir 1988–1989' (report, 1989)
———, 'Viðey. Fornleifarannsóknir 1989–1990' (report, 1991)
———, 'Húsakostur Viðeyjarklausturs. Um byggð í Viðey fram á 18. öld' (unpublished master thesis, University of Iceland, 1993)
Hamilton-Dyer, Sheila, 'Skriðuklaustur Monastery – Animal Bones 2003–2007' (report, 2009)
Hjartarson, Hermann Jakob, 'Lífsins vatn: Vatnsnotkun og vatnsöflun í íslenskum miðaldaklaustrum' (unpublished master thesis, University of Iceland, 2018)
Hjartarson, Hermann Jakob and Kristjánsdóttir, Steinunn, 'Rannsókn á örnefnum um klaustur á Íslandi' (report, 2014) https://steinunn.hi.is/files/2022-09/ORN_2014.pdf [Accessed 15 August 2019]
———, 'Jarðgöng frá fornri tíð á Íslandi. Skýrsla um jarðgöng á klausturstöðum, biskupssetrum og höfðuðbólum á miðöldum' (report, 2016) https://steinunn.hi.is/files/2022-09/JAR_HER.pdf [Accessed 15 August 2019]
Íslenzkar æviskrár frá landnámstímum til ársloka 1940, ed. by Páll Eggert Ólason, vol. I (Reykjavík: Hið íslenzka bókmenntafélag, 1948)
Íslenzkar æviskrár frá landnámstímum til ársloka 1940, ed. by Páll Eggert Ólason, vol. IV (Reykjavík: Hið íslenzka bókmenntafélag, 1950)
Íslenzkar æviskrár frá landnámstímum til ársloka 1940, ed. by Páll Eggert Ólason, vol. V (Reykjavík: Hið íslenzka bókmenntafélag, 1952)
Jónsdóttir, Guðrún Helga, 'Hjálpi mér allir heilagir. Pílagrímsgripir í íslenskum fornleifum' (unpublished BA thesis, University of Iceland, 2014)
———, 'Þjóðleiðir við klaustrin á kaþólskum tíma. Hvað geta leiðir sagt um stöðu miðaldaklaustranna í samfélaginu?' (unpublished master thesis, University of Iceland, 2016)
Jónsdóttir, Guðrún Helga and Kristjánsdóttir, Steinunn, 'Tengsl fólks í miðaldaklaustrunum á Íslandi' (report, 2014) https://steinunn.hi.is/files/2022-09/AETT_2014.pdf [Accessed 15 August 2019]
———, 'Þjóðleiðir við klausturstaði á kaþólskum tíma' (report, 2015) https://steinunn.hi.is/files/2022-09/THJO_2015.pdf [Accessed 15 August 2019]
Jónsson, Jakob Orri, 'Pots, Pipes, and Plates. An Archaeology of Consumption in 17th and 18th Century Iceland' (unpublished PhD-thesis in Archaeology, University of Iceland, 2022)
Kristjánsdóttir, Steinunn, 'Heiðnar og helgar minjar í Viðey' (report, 1995)
———, 'Viðey – trúarheimar mætast' (report, 1996)
———, 'Þingeyraverkefnið' (report, 2018) https://steinunn.hi.is/files/2022-09/THING_2018.pdf [Accessed 10 September 2019]

Kristjánsdóttir, Steinunn and Gunnarsdóttir, Vala, 'Kortlagning klaustra á Íslandi. Greinargerð um niðurstöður kolefnisaldursgreiningar I' (report, 2016) https://steinunn.hi.is/files/2022-09/KOL_I.pdf [Accessed 10 September 2019]

Kristjánsdóttir, Steinunn and Hannesdóttir, Sigrún, 'Út yfir gröf og dauða. Aftökur á þjófum á íslenskri árnýöld', *Skírnir* 1 (2020), pp. 144–176

Kristjánsdóttir, Steinunn, Hannesdóttir, Sigrún and Birgisdóttir, Magnea Dís, 'Dysjar hinna dæmdu. Áfangaskýrsla 2018' (report, 2018) https://steinunn.hi.is/files/2022-09/DYS_2018.pdf [Accessed 12 November 2019]

Lichtenberg, Emma, 'Gender Issues in the Benedictine Rule' (unpublished BA thesis in Medieval History, Trinity University, 2013)

Magnúsdóttir, Jórunn, 'Bak við veggi klaustursins. Nunnur og munkar á Kirkjubæjar- og Skriðuklaustri. Kynjafornleifafræðileg nálgun' (unpublished BA thesis, University of Iceland, 2008)

Magnúsardóttir, Lára, 'Bannfæring og kirkjuvald á Íslandi 1275–1550' (unpublished PhD-thesis in History, University of Iceland, 2007)

Mímisson, Kristján and Einarsson, Bjarni F., 'Rannsókn á rústum nunnuklaustursins á Kirkjubæ' (report, 2002)

Óskarsdóttir, Svanhildur, 'Universal History in Fourteenth Century Iceland. Studies in AM 764 4to' (unpublished PhD-thesis in Scandinavian Studies, University of London, 2000)

Pacciani, Elsa, 'Anthropological Description of Skeletons from Graves No. 4, 62, 63, 65, 66, 67, and 68 at Skriðuklaustur Friary' (report, 2006) https://steinunn.hi.is/files/2022-09/EPHUM_2006.pdf [Accessed 12 August 2020]

———, 'Anthropological Description of Skeletons from Graves No. 5, 17, 27, 34, 54, 74, 75, and 80 at Skriðuklaustur Friary' (report, 2008) https://steinunn.hi.is/files/2022-09/EPHUM_2008.pdf [Accessed 12 August 2020]

———, 'Anthropological Description of Skeletons from Graves No. 83, 84, 85, 87, 88, 95, 96, 97, and 99 at Skriðuklaustur Friary' (report, 2009) https://steinunn.hi.is/files/2022-09/EPHUM_2009.pdf [Accessed 12 August 2020]

———, 'Anthropological Description of Skeletons from Graves No. 123, 124, 125, 126, 127, 128, 129, 130, 131, 132, 133, 134, 135, 136, 141, 142, 143, 145, and 146 at Skriðuklaustur Friary' (report, 2010) https://steinunn.hi.is/files/2022-09/EPHUM_2010.pdf [Accessed 12 August 2020]

Parsons, Emily, 'Good Habits: Textile Work and the Creation of Monastic Identities at the Convent of Kirkjubæjarklaustur', (unpublished MA-thesis in Medieval Studies, University of Iceland, 2018)

Patzuk-Russell, Ryder, 'The Development of Education and Grammatica in Medieval Iceland' (unpublished PhD-thesis in Medieval History, University of Birmingham, 2016)

Pietraszek, Maria Luzia. 'The Place and Space of Donator in Late Medieval Devotional Art' (unpublished MA thesis, Bergen University, 2019)

Þórisdóttir, Kristel Björk, 'Klaustur á Íslandi. Sjúkrahús eða vistheimili á miðöldum' (unpublished BA thesis, University of Iceland, 2010)

Þormóðsson, Eiríkur, '*Möðruvallaklaustur*' (unpublished thesis, University of Iceland, 1966)

Riddel, Scott, 'Flotation sampling procedure' (report, 2014) https://steinunn.hi.is/files/2022-09/FLEY_2014.pdf [Accessed 15 August 2019]

Riddel, Scott and Erlendsson, Egill, 'Viðey Pollen analysis' (report, 2014) https://steinunn.hi.is/files/2022-09/POVEY_2014.pdf [Accessed 15 August 2019]

———, 'Bær in Borgarfjörður. Rapid Scanning for Cereals in Sample KLI-2014–51–11' (report, 2015) https://steinunn.hi.is/files/2022-09/POBAE_2015.pdf [Accessed 15 August 2019]

———, 'Helgafell pollen analysis' (report, 2015) https://steinunn.hi.is/files/2022-09/POHELG_2015.pdf [Accessed 15 August 2019]

———, 'Reynistaðir pollen analysis' (report, 2015) https://steinunn.hi.is/files/2022-09/POREY_2015.pdf [Accessed 15 August 2019]

———, 'Trumbsvalir (Þingeyrar)' (report, 2015) https://steinunn.hi.is/files/2022-09/POTHIN_2015.pdf [Accessed 15 August 2019]

———, 'Þingeyrar soil sampling' (report, 2015) https://steinunn.hi.is/files/2022-09/THISR_2014.pdf [Accessed 15 August 2019]

Steinsson, Heimir, 'Saga munklífis á Skriðu' (unpublished thesis in Theology, University of Iceland, 1965)

Stephensen, Þórir, 'Menntasetur að Viðeyjarklaustri: rannsókn á mennt og menningu í Viðeyjarklaustri með hliðsjón af öðrum klaustrum hér á landi og erlendis' (unpublished thesis in theology, University of Iceland, 2000)

Traustadóttir, Sólrún Inga, 'Skák og mát. Dægradvöl í miðaldaklaustrum á Íslandi' (unpublished BA thesis, University of Iceland, 2009)

Wood, Catherine M., 'Charity on the Fringes of the Medieval World: Skriðuklaustur, a Late-Medieval Priory-Hospital in Eastern Iceland' (unpublished master thesis, University of Iceland, 2013)

Zoëga, Guðný, 'Fornmeinafræðileg rannsókn á fimm beinagrindum úr klausturgarðinum á Skriðu No. 23, 29, 30, 33, og 43' (report, 2007)

Secondary Sources

Abrams, Lesley, 'Diaspora and Identity in the Viking Age', *Early Medieval Europe* 20 (2012), pp. 17–38

Adolf Friðriksson, *Sagas and Popular Antiquarianism in Icelandic Archaeology* (Aldershot: Avebury, 1994)

———, 'Sannfræði íslenskra fornleifa', *Skírnir* 168 (1994), pp. 347–375

Ágústsson, Hörður, 'Húsagerð á síðmiðöldum', in *Saga Íslands iv*, ed. by Sigurður Líndal (Reykjavík: Hið íslenska bókmenntafélag, 1989), pp. 261–300

Ahlin-Sundman, Elin, 'Masculinities and Diet: An Analysis of Skeletal Material from the Dominican Priory in Medieval Västerås, Sweden', *Norwegian Archaeological Review* 51 (2018), pp. 95–111

Anderson, T., Archini, C., Anda, S., Tangerud, A. and Robertsen, G., 'Suspected Endemic Syphilis (Treponarid) in Sixteenth-Century Norway', *Medical History* 30 (1986), pp. 341–350

Andrén, Anders, *Mellan Ting och Text* (Stockholm: Brutus Östlings Bokförlag Symposion, 1997)

———, *Tracing Old Norse Cosmology: The World Tree, Middle Earth and the Sun in Archaeological Perspectives* (Lund: Nordic Academic Press, 2014)

Andrén, Anders, Jennbert, Kristina and Raudvere, Catharina, 'Old Norse Religion. Some Problems and Prospects', in *Norse Religion in Long-Term Perspectives. Origins, Change and Interaction*, ed. by Anders Andrén, Kristina Jennbert and Catharina Raudvere (Stockholm: Nordic Academic Press, 2007), pp. 11–14

Anna Sigurðardóttir, *Allt hafði annan róm áður í páfadóm. Nunnuklaustrin tvö á Íslandi á miðöldum og brot úr kristnisögu* (Reykjavík: Kvennasögusafn Íslands, 1988)

Arnórsdóttir, Agnes S., *Konur og vígamenn. Staða kynjanna á Íslandi á 12. og 13. öld* (Reykjavík: Sagnfræðistofnun and Háskólaútgáfan, 1995)

———, 'Marriage in the Middle Ages. Canon Law and Nordic Family Relations', in *Norden og Europa i middelalderen*, ed. by Per Ingesman and Thomas Lindkvist (Århus: Århus Universitet, 2001), pp. 174–202

———, *Property and Virginity: The Christianization of Marriage in Medieval Iceland 1200–1600* (Aarhus: Aarhus University Press, 2010)

———, 'Cultural Memory and Gender in Iceland from Medieval to Early Modern Times', *Scandinavian Studies* 85:3 (2013), pp. 378–399

———, 'Gender and Donation Culture in Iceland from 1300–1600', in *Donations, Inheritance and Property in the Nordic and Western World from Late Antiquity Until Today*, ed. by Ole-Albert Rønning, Helle Møller Sigh and Helle Vogt (London: Routledge, 2017), pp. 165–178

———, 'Ægtesengen skal være uden synd', in *Reformationen, 1500-talets kulturrevolution*, bind 2, Danmark, ed. by Ole Høiris and Per Ingesman (Aarhus: Aarhus University Press, 2017), pp. 303–325

———, 'Marital Property and Change in the Donation Culture of Late-Sixteenth and Early Seventeenth Century in Iceland', in *Nordic Inheritance Law Through the Ages. Spaces of Action and Legal Strategies*, ed. by Marianne Holdgaard, Auður Magnúsdóttir and Bodil Selmer (Leiden and Boston: Brill, 2020), pp. 139–157

Arnórsson, Einar, 'Suðurgöngur Íslendinga', *Saga* II (1954), pp. 1–45

Åsen, Per Arvid, *Norske klosterplanter: levende kulturminner fra middelalderen* (Kristiansand: Portal, 2015)

Aston, Margaret, 'Public Worship and Iconoclasm', in *The Archaeology of Reformation 1480–1580*, ed. by David Gaimster and Roberta Gilchrist (Leeds: Maney Publishing, 2003), pp. 9–28

Aston, Mick, 'The Expansion of the Monastic and Religious Orders in Europe from the Eleventh Century', in *Monastic Archaeology*, ed. by Graham Keevill, Mick Aston and Teresa Hall (Oxford: Oxbow, 2001), pp. 9–36

Atzbach, Rainer, 'Between Representation and Eternity: The Archaeology of Praying in Late Medieval and Post-Medieval Times', *European Journal of Archaeology* 19:1 (2016), pp. 28–47

Auge, Oliver, 'Monasteries and Collegiate Chapters in the Duchies of Schleswig and Holstein and the Reformation', in *The Dissolution of Monasteries*, ed. by Per Seesko, Louise Nyholm Kallestrup and Lars Bisgaard (Odense: University Press of Southern Denmark, 2019), pp. 169–197

Bach-Nielsen, Carsten, 'Skriftestolen – et overset møbel i de Luterske kirker', in *Reformationen, 1500-talets kulturrevolution*, bind 2 Danmark, ed. by Ole Høiris and Per Ingesman (Aarhus: Aarhus University Press, 2017), pp. 164–192

Barthes, Roland, *Image–Music–Text* (London: Fontana Press, 1977)

Beach, Alison I. and Cochelin, Isabelle, 'General Introduction', in *The Cambridge History of Medieval Monasticism in the Latin West*, ed. by Alison I. Beach and Isabelle Cochelin (Cambridge: Cambridge University Press, 2020), pp. 1–15

Benedictow, Ole J., *Plague in the Late Medieval Nordic Countries, Epidemiological Studies* (Oslo: Middelalderforlaget, 1993)

Berman, Constance A., 'Later Monastic Economies', in *The Cambridge History of Medieval Monasticism in the Latin West*, ed. by Alison I. Beach and Isabelle Cochelin (Cambridge: Cambridge University Press, 2020), pp. 831–847

Bernharðsson, Haraldur, 'Kirkja, klaustur og norskublandið ritmálsviðmið á Íslandi á miðöldum', in *Íslensk klausturmenning á miðöldum*, ed. by Haraldur Bernharðsson (Reykjavík: Miðaldastofa Háskóla Íslands and Háskólaútgáfan, 2016), pp. 149–172

Betteridge, Tom, 'The Reformation', *Reformation* 10:1 (2005), pp. 123–128

Bisgaard, Lars, 'Wine and Beer in Medieval Scandinavia', in *Medieval Christianity in the North*, ed. by K. Salonen, K. Villads Jensen and T. Jørgensen (Turnhout: Brepols, 2013), pp. 67–87

———, 'Senmiddelalderens Reliøse Praksis og Reformationen', in *Reformationen, 1500-talets kulturrevolution*, bind 2 Danmark, ed. by Ole Høiris and Per Ingesman (Aarhus: Aarhus University Press, 2017), pp. 18–41

Bitel, Lisa M., 'Monastic Identity in Early Medieval Ireland', in *The Cambridge History of Medieval Monasticism in the Latin West*, ed. by Alison I. Beach and Isabelle Cochelin (Cambridge: Cambridge University Press, 2020), pp. 297–316

Björnsson, Björn T., *Íslenska teiknibókin í Árnasafni* (Reykjavík: Heimskringla, 1954)

Björnsson, Helgi, *Jöklar á Íslandi* (Reykjavík: Opna, 2009)

Boase, T.S.R., *Death in the Middle Ages. Mortality, Judgement and Remembrance* (New York: McGraw-Hill Book Company, 1972)

Bond, James, 'Monastic Water Management in Great Britain. A Review', in *Monastic Archaeology*, ed. by Graham Keevill, Mick Aston and Teresa Hall (Oxford: Oxbow Book, 2001), pp. 88–136

———, *Monastic Landscapes* [first published in 2004] (Stroud: The History Press, 2010)

Bos, K.I., Schuenemann, V.J., Golding, G.B., Burbano, H.A., Waglechner, N., Coombes, B.K., McPhee, J.B., DeWitte, S.N., Meyer, M., Schmedes, S., Wood, J., Earn, D.J., Herring, A., Bauer, P., Poinar, H.N. and Krause, J., 'A Draft Genome of Yersinia Pestis from Victims of the Black Death', *Nature* 478 (2011), pp. 506–510

Brenner, Elma, 'The Medical Role of Monasteries in the Latin West, c. 1050–1300', in *The Cambridge History of Medieval Monasticism in the Latin West*, ed. by Alison I. Beach and Isabelle Cochelin (Cambridge: Cambridge University Press, 2020), pp. 865–881

Brundage, James A., *Law, Sex, and Christian Society in Medieval Europe* (Chicago: University of Chicago Press, 1987)

Burton, Janet, 'Medieval Nunneries and Male Authority. Female Monasteries in England and Wales', in *Woman in the Medieval Monastic World*, ed. by Janet Burton and Karen Stöber (Turnhout: Brepols, 2015), pp. 123–143

Burton, Janet and Stöber, Karen, 'Introduction', in *Woman in the Medieval Monastic World*, ed. by Janet Burton and Karen Stöber (Turnhout: Brepols, 2015), pp. 1–13

Buzhilova, A., 'Medieval Examples of Syphilis from European Russia', *International Journal of Osteoarchaeology* 9 (1999), pp. 271–276

Bynum, Caroline Walker, *Dissimilar Similitudes. Devotional Objects in Late Medieval Europe* (New York: Zone Books, 2020)

Callow, Chris and Evans, Charles, 'The Mystery of Plague in Medieval Iceland', *Journal of Medieval History* 42:2 (2016), pp. 254–284

Cameron, Euan, *The European Reformation* (Oxford: Clarendon Press, 1991)

Cariboni, Guido, '*No One Can Serve Two Masters*: Abbots and Arch-abbots in the Monastic Networks at the End of the Eleventh Century', *The Journal of Medieval Monastic Studies* 2 (2013), pp. 39–74

Chrisholm, Hugh, 'Roch, St', in *Encyclopædia Britannica* 23 (11th ed.) (Cambridge: Cambridge University Press, 1911)

Clark, James G., *The Benedictines in the Middle Ages* (Woodbridge: The Boydell Press, 2011)

———, 'The Making of Nordic Monasticism, c. 1076 – c. 1350', *Religions* 12 (2021), pp. 15–22

Clay, Rotha Mary, *Hermits and Anchorites of England* (Howel: Cruachan Hill Press, 2014)

Cohen, Sherrill, 'Asylums for Women in Counter-Reformation Italy', in *Women in Reformation and Counter-Reformation Europe*, ed. by Sherrin Marshall (Bloomington and Indianapolis: Indiana University Press, 1989), pp. 167–188

Colish, Marcia L., *Medieval Foundations of the Western Intellectual Tradition 400–1400* (London: Yale University Press, 1997)

Collins, Tracy, *Female Monasticism in Medieval Ireland: An Archaeology* (Cork: Cork University Press, 2021)

Collinson, Patrick, 'The English Reformation in the Mid-Elizabethan Period', in *The Oxford Handbook of John Donne*, ed. by Dennis Flynn, M. Thomas Hester and Jeanne Shami (Oxford: Oxford University Press, 2018), pp. 1–11

Cormack, Margaret, *The Saints in Iceland: Their Veneration from the Conversion to 1400* (Bruxells: Société des Bollandistes, 1994)

———, 'Saints of Medieval Hólar: A Statistical Survey of the Veneration of Saints in the Diocese', *Peregrinations: Journal of Medieval Arts and Architecture* 3:2 (2011), pp. 7–37

———, 'Monastic Foundations and Foundation Legends', in *Íslensk klausturmenning á miðöldum*, ed. by Haraldur Bernharðsson (Reykjavík: Miðaldastofa Háskóla Íslands and Háskólaútgáfan, 2016), pp. 59–82

———, 'Monastic Foundations and Foundation Legends', in *Áhrif Lútjers. Siðaskipti, samfélag og menning í 500 ár*, ed. by Hjalti Hugason, Loftur Guttormsson and Margrét Eggertsdóttir (Reykjavík: Hið íslenska bókmenntafélag, 2017), pp. 59–82

———, 'Voru helgimyndir eyðilagðar á Íslandi? Athugun á varðveislu dýrlingamynda fyrsta áratuginn eftir siðaskipti', *Áhrif Lúthers. Siðaskipti, samfélag og menning í 500 ár*, ed. by Hjalti Hugason, Loftur Guttormsson og Margrét Eggertsdóttir (Reykjavík: Hið íslenska bókmenntafélag, 2017), pp. 243–260

Crosby, A.W., 'The Early History of Syphilis: A Reappraisal', *American Anthropologist* 71 (1969), pp. 218–227

Cunningham, Jack, 'Changing Fashions: The Coming of the Reformation to Iceland', *Reformation* 16:1 (2011), pp. 65–92

Daae, Ludvig, *Norges helgener* (Christiania: Cammermeyer, 1879)

Darwin, Francis D.S., *The English Medieval Enclosure* (London: Society for Promoting Christian Knowledge, 1934)

De Hamel, Christopher, *Making Medieval Manuscripts* (Oxford: Oxford University Press, 2018)

Deetz, John, *In Small Things Forgotten. An Archaeology of Early American Life* (New York: Double Day, 1977)

Drancourt, Michel, Signoli, Michel, La, Vu Dang, Bizot, Bruno, Roux, Véronique, Tzortzis, Stefán and Raoult, Didier, 'Yersinia Pestis Orientalis in Remains of Ancient Plague Patients', *Emerging Infectious Diseases* 13:2 (2007), pp. 332–333

Drechsler, Stefan, *Illuminated Manuscript Production in Medieval Iceland. Literary and Artistic Activities of the Monastery at Helgafell in the Fourteenth Century* (Turnhout: Brepols, 2021)

Dreyer, Rasmus H.C., 'Den lange danske reformationen', in *Reformationen, 1500-talets kulturrevolution*, bind 2 Danmark, ed. by Ole Høiris and Per Ingesman (Aarhus: Aarhus University Press, 2017), pp. 43–115

Ebenesersdóttir, Sunna, Velasco, M., Gunnarsdóttir, E.D., Jagadeesan, A., Guðmundsdóttir, V.B., Þórðardóttir, E.L., Einarsdóttir, M.S., Moore, K.H.S., Sigurðsson, Á., Magnúsdóttir, D.H., Jónsson, H., Snorradóttir, S., Hovig, E., Mattingsdal, M., Kockum, I., Olsson, T., Hansen, T.F., Cavalleri, G., Gilbert, E., Lalueza-Fox, C., Walser, J.W., Kristjánsdóttir, S., Gopalakrishnan, S., Árnadóttir, L., Magnússon, Ó.Þ., Gilbert, M.T.P., Stefánsson, Kári and Agnar Helgason, A., 'Ancient Genomes from Iceland Reveal the Making of a Human Population', *Science* 360 (2018), pp. 1028–1032

Eggertsdóttir, Margrét, 'Frómum og guðhræddum, leikum og lærðum', *Áhrif Lúthers. Siðaskipti, samfélag og menning í 500 ár*, ed. by Hjalti Hugason, Loftur Guttormsson og Margrét Eggertsdóttir (Reykjavík: Hið íslenska bókmenntafélag, 2017), pp. 145–174

Egilsdóttir, Ásdís, 'Biskupasögur', in *Medieval Scandinavia. An Encyclopedia*, ed. by Phillip Pulsiano, Kirsten Wolf, Paul Acker and Donald K. Fry (New York: Garland Publishing, 1993), pp. 45–46

———, 'Kvendýrlingar og kvenímynd trúarlegra bókmennta á Íslandi', in *Konur og kristsmenn. Þættir úr kristnisögu Íslands*, ed. by Inga Huld Hákonardóttir (Reykjavík: Háskólaútgáfan, 1996), pp. 91–116

———, 'Klerkar og samfélag', in *Kristni á Íslandi I*, ed. by Hjalti Hugason (Reykjavík: Alþingi, 2000), pp. 359–367

———, 'Páfi skrifar Íslendingum bréf', in *Kristni á Íslandi II*, ed. by Gunnar F. Guðmundsson (Reykjavík: Alþingi, 2000), pp. 42–47

———, 'Pílagrímur og píslarvottur', in *Kristni á Íslandi II*, ed. by Gunnar F. Guðmundsson (Reykjavík: Alþingi, 2000), pp. 70–74

———, 'Hjúskaparmál: Lög og reynd, in *Kristni á Íslandi II*, ed. by Gunnar F. Guðmundsson (Reykjavík: Alþingi, 2000), pp. 257–264

———, 'Biskupasögur og helgar ævisögur', in *Biskupasögur I. Íslenzk fornrit* XV:1, v–xxx, ed. by Jónas Kristjánsson (Reykjavík: Hið íslenzka fornritafélag, 2003)

———, 'St Þorlákr of Iceland: The Emergence of a Cult', *Haskins Society Journal* 12 (2003), pp. 121–131

———, 'Hrafn Sveinbjarnarson, Pilgrim and Martyr', in *Sagas, Saints and Settlements*, ed. by Gareth Williams and Paul Bibire (Leiden and Boston: Brill, 2004), pp. 29–40

———, 'Skjaldmær drottins: Frásögnin af Hildi einsetukonu í Jóns sögu helga', *Studia Theologica Islandica* 31 (2010), pp. 29–42

———, 'The Hermit and the Milkmaid. The Tale of Ásólfr in Landnámabók and Ólafs saga Tryggvasonar en mesta', in *Conversions: Looking for Ideological Change in the Early Middle Ages, Studia Medievalia Septentrionalia* 23, ed. by Leszek Slupecki and Rudolf Simek (Vienna: Fassbaender, 2013), pp. 23–32

Egilsson, Jón, 'Biskupa-annálar Jóns Egilssonar, með formála, athuga greinum og fylgiskjölum eptir Jón Sigurðsson', *Safn til sögu Íslands* I (Copenhagen: Hið íslenska bókmenntafélag, 1856), pp. 15–136

Einarsdóttir, Ólafía, *Studier i kronologisk metode i tidlig islandsk historiebeskrivning* (Stockholm: Natur och Kultur, 1964)

Einarsdóttir, Sandra Sif, 'The Ketilsstaðir burial. From the Archaeological Perspective', in *Bláklædda konan – ný rannsókn á fornu kumli/Bundled-up in blue -the re-investigation of a Viking grave*, ed. by Bryndís Sverrisdóttir (Reykjavík: National Museum of Iceland, 2015), pp. 17–24

Einarsson, Bjarni F., 'Íslenskar fornleifar: Fórnarlömb sagnahyggjunnar?' *Skírnir* 168 (1994), pp. 376–402

———, 'Systrastapi', *Dynskógar* 10 (2006), pp. 163–172

Ekroll, Øystein, 'Thrown to the Wolves? The Fate of the Norwegian Monasteries After the Reformation', in *The Dissolution of Monasteries*, ed. by Per Seesko, Louise Nyholm Kallestrup and Lars Bisgaard (Odense: University Press of Southern Denmark, 2019), pp. 151–168

Eldjárn, Kristján, *Um Hóladómkirkju. Leiðsögn um kirkju og kirkjugripi* (Reykjavík: Hólanefnd, 1963a)

———, *Hundrað ár í Þjóðminjasafni* (Reykjavík: Bókaútgáfa Menningarsjóðs, 1963b)

———, 'Þorláksskrín í Skálholti. Samtíningur um glataðan forngrip', *Árbók Hins íslenzka fornleifafélags 1973* (1974), pp. 19–42

———, 'Gröf Páls biskups Jónssonar', in *Skálholt. Fornleifarannsóknir 1954–1958*, ed. by Kristján Eldjárn, Håkan Christie and Jón Steffensen (Reykjavík: Lögberg, 1988), pp. 147–158

Elsa, E. Guðjónsson, 'Íslenzkur dýrgripur í hollenzku safni', *Andvari* 87:2 (1962), pp. 127–138

———, 'Skyldleiki erlendra prentmynda við nokkrar íslenskar helgimyndir', *Gripla* III (1979), pp. 71–84

———, '. . . "slitur úr eldgömlu húss-tjaldi"', *Breiðfirðingur* 43:1 (1985), pp. 7–14

———, 'Íslensk kirkjuklæði á miðöldum', in *Kirkja og kirkjuskrúð*, ed. by Lilja Árnadóttir and Ketil Kiran (Reykjavík: NIKU and National Museum of Iceland, 1997), pp. 85–92

Ersgård, Lars, 'Change, Desertion and Survival – An Archaeology of the Late-Medieval Crisis', in *Environment, Society and the Black Death. An Interdisciplinary Approach to the Late-Medieval Crisis in Sweden*, ed. by Per Lagerås (Oxford: Oxbow Books, 2016), pp. 69–103

Espólín, Jón, *Íslands Árbækur í söguformi* I (Copenhagen: Hið íslenska bókmenntafélag, 1821)

———, *Íslands Árbækur í söguformi* II (Copenhagen: Hið íslenska bókmenntafélag, 1823)

Farmer, D.H., *The Oxford Dictionary of Saints* (Oxford and New York: Oxford University Press, 1987)

Fiddyment, Sarah, Hesselberg-Wang, Nina, Karlsen, Espen, Östlund Nilsson, Sara, Palandri, Chirara and Weidling, Tor, 'Parchment in Medieval Norway: A Historical and Bio-Codicological Approach', *Collegium Medievale* (2021), pp. 305–330

Fink-Jensen, Morten, 'Kristendom, skole og pædegogik i Danmark før 1700', in *Reformationen i dansk kirke og kultur 1517–1700*, bind 1, ed. by Niels Hendrik Gregersen and Carsten Bach-Nielsen (Odense: Syddansk Universitetsforlag, 2017), pp. 369–389

Finlayson, Alan, 'Chapter 5: Nationalism', in *Political Ideologies: An Introduction*, ed. by Vincent Geoghegan (London: Routledge, 2014), pp. 100–102

Finnsson, Hannes, *Mannfækkun af hallærum*, pub. by Jón Eyþórsson and Jóhannes Nordal (Reykjavík: Almenna bókafélagið, 1970)

Forntida gårdar i Island: meddelanden från den nordiska arkeologiska undersökningin i Island sommaren 1939, ed. by Mårten Stenberger, Aage Roussell and Jón Steffenesen (Copenhagen: Munksgaard, 1943)

Fradenberg, L.O. Aranye, 'Making, Mourning and the Love of Idols', in *Images, Idolatry, and Iconoclasm in Late Medieval England: Textuality and the Visual Image*, ed. by Jeremy Dimmick, James Simpson and Nicolette (Oxford: Oxford University Press, 2002), pp. 25–42

Gaimster, David and Gilchrist, Roberta, 'Introduction. History from Below: The Archaeology of the English Reformation 1480–1580', in *The Archaeology of Reformation 1480–1580*, ed. by David Gaimster and Roberta Gilchrist (Leeds: Maney Publishing, 2003), pp. 1–8

Gajewski, Alexandra and Seeberg, Stefanie, 'Art in Monastic Churches of Western Europe from the Twelfth to the Fourteenth Century', in *The Cambridge History of Medieval Monasticism in the Latin West*, ed. by Alison I. Beach and Isabelle Cochelin (Cambridge: Cambridge University Press, 2020), pp. 998–1026

Galloway, Patricia, 'Material Culture and Text: Exploring the Spaces Within and Between', in *Historical Archaeology*, ed. by Martin Hall and Stephen W. Silliman (Malden: Blackwell Publishing, 2006), pp. 42–64

Gardiner, Mark and Mehler, Natascha, 'Introduction: German trade in the North Atlantic', *AmS-Skrifter* 27 (2019), pp. 9–24

Gerrard, Christopher, *Medieval Archaeology. Understanding Traditions and Contemporary Approaches* (London: Routledge, 2002)

Gestsdóttir, Margrét, 'Cecilía Þorsteinsdóttir', in *Skriðuklaustur, evrópskt miðaldaklaustur í Fljótsdal*, ed. by Hrafnkell Lárusson and Steinunn Kristjánsdóttir (Skriðuklaustur: Gunnarsstofnun, 2008), pp. 31–40

Gilchrist, Roberta, *Gender and Material Culture: The Archaeology of Religious Women* (London: Routledge, 1994)

———, *Gender and Archaeology* (London: Routledge, 1999)

———, 'Magic for the Dead? The Archaeology of Magic in Later Medieval Burials', *Medieval Archaeology* 52 (2008), pp. 119–159

———, 'Rethinking Later Medieval Masculinity: The Male Body in Death', in *Mortuary Practices and Social Identities in the Middle Ages: Essays in Burial Archaeology in Honour of Heinrich Härke*, ed. by D. Sayer and H. Williams (Exeter: University of Exeter Press, 2009), pp. 236–252

———, *Medieval Life. Archaeology and the Life Course* (Woodbridge: Boydell Press, 2012)

———, 'Monastic and Church Archaeology', *Annual Review of Anthropology* 43 (2014), pp. 235–290

———, *Sacred Heritage: Monastic Archaeology, Identities, Beliefs* (Cambridge: Cambridge University Press, 2019)

Gilchrist, Roberta and Sloane, Barney, *Requiem. The Medieval Monastic Cemetery in Britain* (London: Museum of London Archaeological Service, 2005)

Godlove, Shannon, 'Iceland's Secular Saints: Hagiographic Motifs in *Njáls saga* and *Laxdœla saga*', *Skandinavistik* 37:2 (2009), pp. 102–117

Golding, Brian, 'Bishops and Nuns: Forms of the *cura monialium* in Twelfth- and Thirteenth Century England', in *Woman in the Medieval Monastic World*, ed. by Janet Burton and Karen Stöber (Turnhout: Brepols 2015), pp. 97–122

González-Rubial, Alfredo, 'Contemporary Past, Archaeology of the', in *Encyclopaedia of Global Archaeology*, ed. by Claire Smith (New York: Springer, 2014), pp. 1683–1694

Graves, Pamela C., 'From an Archaeology of Iconoclasm to an Anthropology of the Body. Images, Punishment, and Personhood in England, 1500–1600', *Current Anthropology* 49:1 (2008), pp. 35–57

Gregersen, Niels Hendrik and Bach-Nielsen, Carsten, 'Reformationen som kirkeligt og kulturelt program', in *Reformationen i dansk kirke og kultur 1517–1700*, bind 1, ed. by Niels Hendrik Gregersen and Carsten Bach-Nielsen (Odense: Syddansk Universitetsforlag, 2017), pp. 13–31

Grell, Ole Peter, 'The Catholic Church and Its Leadership', in *The Scandinavian Reformation from Evangelical Movement to Institutionalisation of Reform*, ed. by Ole Peter Grell (Cambridge: Cambridge University Press, 1995), pp. 70–113

Grímsdóttir, Guðrún Ása, 'Afskipti erkibiskupa af íslenskum málefnum á 12. og 13. öld', *Saga* (1982), pp. 28–62

———, 'Heimildir í handritum um klaustrin í Skaftafellsþingi', *Dynskógar* 7 (1999), pp. 101–144

———, 'Biskupsstóll í Skálholti', in *Saga biskupsstólanna*, ed. by Gunnar Kristjánsson (Hólar: Bókaútgáfan Hólar, 2006), pp. 21–243

Guest, Gerald B., 'Stained Glass and Liturgy: The Uses and Limits of Analogy', *Journal of Glass Studies* 56 (2014), pp. 271–285

———, 'Handritalýsingar í benediktínaklaustrinu á Þingeyrum' in *Íslensk klausturmenning á miðöldum*, ed. by Haraldur Bernharðsson (Reykjavík: Miðaldastofa Háskóla Íslands and Háskólaútgáfan, 2016), pp. 227–311

———, 'Íslensk bókasöfn fyrir siðabyltinguna', in *Árbók Landsbókasafns Íslands 1948–1949* (Reykjavík: Landsbókasafnið, 1950), pp. 65–78

Gunnes, Erik, 'Klosteranlegg i Norge. En oversikt', *Fortidsminner* 68 (1987), pp. 49–128

Gunnlaugsson, Guðvarður Már, 'Voru scriptoria í íslenskum klaustrum?' in *Íslensk klausturmenning á miðöldum*, ed. by Haraldur Bernharðsson (Reykjavík: Miðaldastofa Háskóla Íslands and Háskólaútgáfan, 2016), pp. 173–200

Guðlaugsson, Jónas, 'Þingeyraklaustur', *Sunnudagsblaðið – Alþýðublaðið* (March 22, 1966), pp. 183–190, 299

———, 'Munkaþverárklaustur', *Sunnudagsblaðið – Alþýðublaðið* (April 10, 1966), pp. 231–238, 299

———, 'Þykkvabæjarklaustur', *Sunnudagsblaðið – Alþýðublaðið* (May 15, 1966), pp. 294–299

———, 'Helgafellsklaustur', *Sunnudagsblaðið – Alþýðublaðið* (May 29, 1966), pp. 319–322, 334–335

———, 'Kirkjubæjarklaustur', *Tíminn, sunnudagsblað* (July 16, 1967), pp. 612–616

———, 'Viðeyjarklaustur', *Tíminn, sunnudagsblað* (July 23, 1967), pp. 628–633

———, 'Reynistaðarklaustur', *Tíminn, sunnudagsblað* (August 6, 1967), pp. 665–669

———, 'Möðruvallaklaustur', *Tíminn, sunnudagsblað* (August 13, 1967), pp. 676–693, 687
———, 'Skriðuklaustur', *Tíminn, sunnudagsblað* (August 20, 1967), pp. 700–703, 718
———, 'Klaustur í Bæ, Hítardal, Saurbæ og á Keldum', *Tíminn, sunnudagsblað* (August 27, 1967), pp. 724–728
Guðmundsson, Guðmundur J., 'Tíu páfabréf frá 15. öld', *Saga* XLVI:1 (2008), pp. 56–75
Guðmundsson, Gunnar F., 'Íslenskt samfélag og Rómarkirkja', in *Kristni á Íslandi*, ed. by Hjalti Hugason (Reykjavík: Alþingi, 2000)
Guðmundsson, Helgi, *Um haf innan. Vestrænir menn og íslensk menning á miðöldum* (Reykjavík: Háskólaútgáfan, 1997)
Guttormsson, Hjörleifur, *Við rætur Vatnajökuls. Árbók Ferðafélags Íslands* (Reykjavík: Ferðafélag Íslands, 1993)
Guttormsson, Loftur, 'Frá siðaskiptum til upplýsingar', in *Kristni á Íslandi* III, ed. by Loftur Guttormsson (Reykjavík: Alþingi, 2000)
Guttormsson, Loftur and Kjartansson, Helgi Skúli, 'Siðaskiptin og fátækraframfærsla. Athugasemdir við nýjar útleggingar', *Saga* LII:1 (2014), pp. 11–43
Hackett, C.J., *Diagnostic Criteria for Syphilis, Yaws and Treponarid (Treponemastoses) and of some other Diseases in Dry Bones (for use in Osteo-Archaeology)* (Berlin: Springer, 1976)
Hákonardóttir, Inga Huld, *Fjarri hlýju hjónasængur. Öðruvísi Íslandssaga* (Reykjavík: Mál og menning, 1992)
Hálfdanarson, Guðmundur, 'Iceland: A Peaceful Secession', *Scandinavian Journal of History* 25:1–2 (2000), pp. 87–100
———, 'Severing the Ties – Iceland's Journey from a Union with Denmark to a Nation-State', *Scandinavian Journal of History* 31:3–4 (2006), pp. 237–254
———, 'Sagan og sjálfsmynd(ir) íslenskrar þjóðar', *Glíman* 7 (2010), pp. 113–135
Halldórsdóttir, Erla Dóris, *Óhreinu börnin hennar Evu* (Reykjavík: Ugla, 2020)
Halldórsson, Ólafur, 'Líkneskjusmíð', *Árbók Hins íslenzka fornleifafélags 1973* (1974), pp. 5–17
Hallgrímsdóttir, Margrét, 'Rannsóknir í Viðey. Vaxspjöld frá 15. öld finnast við uppgröft rústa Viðeyjarklausturs', *Árbók Hins íslenzka fornleifafélags 1990* (1991), pp. 91–132
———, *Þjóðminjar* (Reykjavík: Þjóðminjasafn Íslands, 2016)
Hallgrímsson, Helgi, *Fljótsdæla. Mannlíf og náttúrufar í Fljótsdalshreppi* (Reykjavík: Skrudda, 2016)
Harbison, Peter, 'The Early Irish Pilgrim Archaeology in the Dingle Peninsula', *World Archaeology* 26:1 (1994), pp. 90–103
Harding, Vanessa, 'Choices and Changes: Death, Burial and the English Reformation', in *The Archaeology of Reformation 1480–1580*, ed. by David Gaimster and Roberta Gilchrist (Leeds: Maney Publishing, 2003), pp. 386–398
Harðardóttir, Guðrún, 'Nokkrar kynslóðir kirkna og klausturhúsa á Munkaþverá', *Árbók Hins íslenska fornleifafélags 1996–1997* (1998), pp. 5–42
———, 'Vangaveltur um íslensk klausturhús – íslenskun erlendra áhrifa', *Múlaþing* 33 (2006), pp. 108–113
———, 'Myndefni íslenskra klausturinnsigla', in *Íslensk klausturmenning á miðöldum*, ed. by Haraldur Bernharðsson (Reykjavík: Miðaldastofa Háskóla Íslands and Háskólaútgáfan, 2016), pp. 201–227
———, 'Innanbúnaður kirkna frá fyrstu öldum eftir siðaskipti', in *Áhrif Lúthers. Siðaskipti, samfélag og menning í 500 ár*, ed. by Hjalti Hugason, Loftur Guttormsson og Margrét Eggertsdóttir (Reykjavík: Hið íslenska bókmenntafélag, 2017), pp. 195–214
Harðarson, Gunnar, 'Viktorsklaustrið í París og norrænar miðaldir', in *Íslensk klausturmenning á miðöldum*, ed. by Haraldur Bernharðsson (Reykjavík: Miðaldastofa Háskóla Íslands and Háskólaútgáfan, 2016), pp. 119–148

Harris, Richard L., 'The Lion-Knight Legend in Iceland and the Valþjófsstaðir Door', *Viator* 1 (1970), pp. 125–145

Hatcher, John, *Plague, Population and the English Economy* (London: Palgrave, 1977)

Haug, Eldbjørg, 'Challenges in Research of Norwegian Monastic History', *The American Benedictine Review* 29:1 (2008), pp. 64–96

———, 'Augustinian Canons and Benedictine Monks in the Medieval Stavanger Diocese', in *Monastic Culture. The Long Thirteenth Century. Essays in Honour of Brian Patrick McGuire*, ed.by Lars Bisgaard, Sigga Engsbro, Kurt Villads Jensen and Tore Nyberg (Odense: University Press of Southern Denmark, 2014), pp. 197–218

Hauksson, Þorleifur, 'Konungur af Guðs náð og blindir biskupar: tildrög og hugmyndafræði Sverris sögu', *Skírnir* 194 (2020), pp. 113–139

Hayeur Smith, Michele, 'Weaving Wealth: Cloth and Trade in Viking Age and Medieval Iceland', in *Textiles and the Medieval Economy: Production, Trade, and Consumption of Textiles, 8th-16th Centuries* 16, ed. by Angela Ling Huang and Carsten Jahnke (Oxbow: Oxbow Books, 2013), pp. 23–40

———, 'Thorir's Bargain: Gender, vaðmál and the Law', *World Archaeology* 45:5 (2014), pp. 730–746

———, 'Dress, Jewellery and Textiles', in *Bláklædda konan – ný rannsókn á fornu kumli/ Bundled-up in blue -the re-investigation of a Viking grave*, ed. by Bryndís Sverrisdóttir (Reykjavík: National Museum of Iceland, 2015), pp. 25–46

Helgadóttir, Guðrún P., 'Laukagarðr', in *Speculum Norrœnum: Norse Studies in Memory of Gabriel Turville-Petre*, ed. by Ursula Dronke, Guðrún P. Helgadóttir, Gerd Wolfgang Weber and Hans Bekker-Nielsen (Odense: Odense University Press, 1981), pp. 171–184

Helgason, Agnar, Sigurðardóttir, S., Nicholson, J., Sykes, B., Hill, E., Bradley, D.G., Bosnes, V., Gulcher, J.R., Ward, R. and Stefánsson, K., 'Estimating Scandinavian and Gaelic Ancestry in the Male Settlers of Iceland', *American Journal of Human Genetics* 67 (2000), pp. 697–717

Helgason, Jón, *Handritaspjall* (Reykjavík: Mál og menning, 1958)

Høiris, Ole and Ingesman, Per, 'Reformationen i Danmark', in *Reformationen, 1500-talets kulturrevolution*, bind 2 Danmark, ed. by (Aarhus: Aarhus University Press, 2017), pp. 7–18

Hommedal, Alf Tore, 'St Sunniva, the Seljumenn, and St Alban: The Benedictines and the Sanctuary at Selja, Norway', in *Monastic Europe. Medieval Communities, Landscapes, and Settlement*, ed. by Edel Bhreathnach, Malgorzate Krasnodebska-D'Aughton and Keith Smith (Turnhout: Brepols, 2019), pp. 44–72

Hooke, Della, 'The Sacred Nature of Rivers, Wells, and Other Wetlands in Anglo-Saxon England', in *Meanings of Water in Early Medieval England*, ed. by Carolyn Twomey and Daneil Anlezark (Turnhout: Brepols, 2021), pp. 32–57

Houts van, Elisabeth, *Married Life in the Middle Ages, 900–1300* (Oxford: Oxford University Press, 2019)

Hreinsson, Haraldur, *Force of Words. A Critical Examination of Iceland's Earliest Ecclesiastical Discourse* (Leiden: Brill, 2020)

Hugason, Hjalti, 'Frumkristni og upphaf kirkju', in *Kristni á Íslandi* I, ed. by Hjalti Hugason (Reykjavík: Alþingi, 2000)

Hughes-Edwards, Mari, *Reading Medieval Anchoritism. Ideology and Spiritual Practices* (Cardiff: University of Wales Press, 2012)

Hutchinson, D.L. and Weaver, D.S., 'Two Cases of Facial Involvement in Probable Treponemal Infection from Late Prehistoric Coastal North Carolina', *International Journal of Osteoarchaeology* 8 (1998), pp. 444–453

Ingólfsdóttir, Guðrún, *Á hverju liggja ekki okkar göfugu kerlingar?* Sýnisbók íslenskrar alþýðumenningar 20 (Reykjavík: Háskólaútgáfan, 2018)

Ingólfsson, Árni Heimir, *Tónlist liðinna alda. Íslensk handrit 1100–1800* (Reykjavík: Crymogea, 2019)

Ísberg, Jón Ólafur, *Líf og lækningar: Íslensk heilbrigðissaga* (Reykjavík: Hið íslenska bókmenntafélag, 2005)

Ísleifsdóttir, Vilborg Auður, *Siðbreytingin á Íslandi 1537–1565: byltingin að ofan* (Reykjavík: Hið íslenska bókmenntafélag, 1997)

———, *Ný heimsmynd. Siðbreyting, siðaskipti, siðbót* (Reykjavík: Nýja bókafélagið, 2000)

———, 'Öreigar og umrenningar. Um fátækraframfærslu á síðmiðöldum og hrun hennar', *Saga* XLI:2 (2003), pp. 91–126

———, 'Hugleiðingar um menntun kvenna í kaþólskum og lúterskum sið', in *Sérrit Glímunnar. Menntun og menning í Skálholtsstifti 1620–1730*, ed. by Gunnar Kristjánsson (Reykjavík: Grettisakademían, 2010), pp. 169–182

———, *Byltingin að ofan – stjórnskipunarsaga 16. aldar* (Reykjavík: Hið íslenska bókmenntafélag, 2013)

Jacobsen, Grethe, 'Nordic Woman and the Reformation', in *Women in Reformation and Counter-Reformation Europe*, ed. by Sherrin Marshall (Bloomington and Indianapolis: Indiana University Press, 1989), pp. 47–67

Jakobsen, Johnny Grandjean Gøgsig, 'A Brief History of Medieval Monasticism in Denmark (with Schleswig, Rügen and Estonia)', *Religions* 12 (2021), pp. 65–84

Jakobsson, Ármann, 'Byskupskjör á Íslandi: Stjórnmálaviðhorf byskupasagna og Sturlungu', *Studia Theologica Islandica* 14 (2000), pp. 171–182

———, 'Masculinities and Politics in *Njáls saga*', *Viator* 28 (2007), pp. 191–215

———, 'Laxdæla Dreaming: A Saga Heroine Invents Her Own Life', *Leeds Studies in English new series* 39 (2008), pp. 33–51

———, 'King Sverrir of Norway and the Foundations of his Power', *Medium Ævum* 48:1 (2015), pp. 109–135

Jakobsson, Ármann and Egilsdóttir, Ásdís, 'Abbadísin sem hvarf', in *Þúsund og eitt orð sagt Sigurgeiri Steingrímssyni fimmtugum 2. október 1993*, ed. by Guðvarður Már Gunnlaugsson and Gísli Sigurðsson (Reykjavík: Menningar- og minningarsjóður Mette Magnussen, 1993), pp. 7–9

Jakobsson, Sverrir, 'Defining a Nation: Popular and Public Identity in the Middle Ages', *Scandinavian Journal of History* 24:1 (1999), pp. 91–101

———, 'Frá Helgafellsklaustri til Stapaumboðs', in *Íslensk klausturmenning á miðöldum*, ed. by Haraldur Bernharðsson (Reykjavík: Miðaldastofa Háskóla Íslands and Háskólaútgáfan, 2016), pp. 83–102

———, *Auðnaróðal, baráttan um Ísland 1096–1281* (Reykjavík: Sögufélag, 2016)

———, 'Saints and Politicians. The Bishops of Hólar in Troubled Times', *Viking and Medieval Scandinavia* 14 (2018), pp. 193–210

———, 'Conversion and Cultural Memory in Medieval Iceland', *Church History* 88:1 (2019), pp. 1–26

Jamroziak, Emilia, 'Spaces of Lay-Religious Interaction in Cistercian Houses of Northern Europe', *Parergon* 27:2 (2010), pp. 37–58

Jasper, Kathryn and Howe, John, 'Hermitism in the Eleventh and Twelfth Centuries', in *The Cambridge History of Medieval Monasticism in the Latin West*, ed. by Alison I. Beach and Isabelle Cochelin (Cambridge: Cambridge University Press, 2020), pp. 684–696

Jensson, Gottskálk, '**Revelaciones Thorlaci episcopi* – Enn eitt glatað latínurit eftir Gunnlaug Leifsson munk á Þingeyrum', *Gripla* 23 (2012), pp. 133–175

———, 'Íslenskar klausturreglur og *libertas ecclesie* á ofanverðri 12. öld', in *Íslensk klausturmenning á miðöldum*, ed. by Haraldur Bernharðsson (Reykjavík: Miðaldastofa Háskóla Íslands and Háskólaútgáfan, 2016), pp. 9–57

———, 'Latin Hagiography in Medieval Iceland', in *Hagiographies VII. Corpus Christianorum*, ed. By Monique Gaullet (Turnhout: Brepols, 2017), pp. 875–949

———, 'Þingeyrar Abbey in Northern Iceland: A Benedictine Powerhouse of Cultural Heritage', *Religions* 12 (2021), pp. 149–164

Jóhannesson, Jón, *Íslendinga saga I. Þjóðveldisöld* (Reykjavík: Almenna bókafélagið, 1956)

Johansson, Karl G. 'The Learned Sturlungar and the Emergence of the Icelandic Literate Culture', in *Snorri Sturluson and Reykholt. The Author and Magnate, his Life, Works and Environment at Reykholt in Iceland*, ed. by Guðrún Sveinbjarnardóttir and Helgi Þorláksson (Copenhagen: Museum Tusculanum Press, 2018), pp. 333–388

Jónsdóttir, Selma, 'Gömul Krossfestingarmynd', *Skírnir* 139:1 (1965), pp. 134–147

Jónsson, Finnur, *Historia ecclesiastica Islandiæ* I (Havniae: Gerhardus Giese Salicath, 1772)

———, *Historia ecclesiastica Islandiæ* II (Havniae: Gerhardus Giese Salicath, 1774)

———, *Historia ecclesiastica Islandiæ* IV (Havniae: Gerhardus Giese Salicath, 1778)

Jónsson, Guðbrandur, 'Dómkirkjan á Hólum í Hjaltadal. Lýsing íslenskra miðaldakirkna', in *Safn til sögu Íslands og íslenskra bókmennta að fornu og nýju* V (Reykjavík: Hið íslenzka bókmenntafjelag, 1915–1929), pp. 1–418

Jónsson, Janus, 'Um klaustrin á Íslandi', *Tímarit Hins íslenska bókmenntafjelags* 8 (1887), pp. 174–265

Jónsson, Magnús, 'Áhrif klaustranna á Íslandi', *Skírnir* 88:3 (1914), pp. 283–298

Jónsson, Már, *Blóðskömm á Íslandi 1270–1870* (Reykjavík: Háskólaútgáfan, 1993)

———, *Árni Magnússon. Ævisaga* (Reykjavík: Mál og menning, 1998)

———, *Dulsmál 1600–1900* (Reykjavík: Háskólaútgáfan and Sagnfræðistofnun Háskóla Íslands, 2000)

———, 'Inngangur', in *Jónsbók*, pub. by Már Jónsson (Reykjavík: Mál og Menning, 2004)

Jørgensen, Torstein and Saletnich, Gastone, *Synder og pavemakt. Botsbrev fra Den nordiske Kirkeprovins og Suderøyene til Pavestolen 1438–1531* (Stavanger: Misjonshøjskolens forlag, 2004)

Jörundsdóttir, Sigríður H., 'Islandske straffefanger i København 1736–1830', in *København som Vestnordens hovedstad*, ed. by Andras Mortensen, Jón T. Thór and Daníel Thorleifsson (Nuuk: The Authors, 2007), pp. 79–90

Júlíusson, Árni Daníel, *Landbúnaðarsaga Íslands. Þúsund ára bændasamfélag 800–1800* I (Reykjavík: Skrudda, 2013)

———, *Jarðeignir kirkjunnar og tekjur af þeim 1000–1550* (Reykjavík: Center for Agrarian Historical Dynamics, 2014)

———, 'Manndráp verður að morði: Um mannvíg og morð á Íslandi frá fimmtándu öld til sautjándu aldar', *Saga* 57:1 (2019), pp. 87–111

Júlíusson, Árni Daníel and Ísberg, Jón Ólafur, *Íslandssagan í máli og myndum* (Reykjavík: Mál og menning, 2005)

Júníusdóttir, Ásgerður, 'Altaristafla Ólafar ríku á Skarði. Veraldlegt vald – vist á himnum' (unpublished BA thesis, University of Iceland, 2016)

Kærgård, Niels, 'Det danske samfund, økonomien og reformationen', in *Reformationen, 1500-talets kulturrevolution*, bind 2 Danmark, ed. by Ole Høiris and Per Ingesman (Aarhus: Aarhus University Press, 2017), pp. 453–465

Kalinke, Marianne E., *The Book of Reykjahólar. The Last of the Great Medieval Legendries* (Toronto: University of Toronto Press, 2000)

Kallestrup, Louise Nyholm, 'Reformation og trolddomsforfølgelser i Europa', in *Reformationen i dansk kirke og kultur 1517–1700*, bind 1, ed. by Niels Hendrik Gregersen and Carsten Bach-Nielsen (Odense: Syddansk Universitetsforlag, 2017), pp. 241–263

Karlsson, Gunnar, 'Plague Without Rats: The Case of Fifteenth-Century Iceland', *Journal of Medieval history* 22 (1996), pp. 263–284

———, *Iceland's 1100 Years. History of a Marginal Society* (London: Hurst & Company, 2000)
———, 'Stofnár Þingeyraklausturs', *Saga* XLVI:1 (2008), pp. 159–167
Karras, Ruth M., 'Marriage and the Creation of Kin in the Sagas', *Scandinavian Studies* 75 (2003), pp. 473–490
———, *Unmarriages. Women, Men, and Sexual Unions in the Middle Ages* (Philadelphia: University of Pennsylvania Press, 2012)
Keily, Jackie, 'Pomegranate & Rose: Henry VIII and Katherine of Aragon. *Museum of London* http://blog.museumoflondon.org.uk/pomegranate-rose-henry-viii-katharine-aragon/ [Accessed 16 April 2021]
Kerr, Julie, *Life in the Medieval Cloister* (London: Continuum, 2009)
Kessler-Harris, Alice, *Social History* (Washington: American Historical Association, 1990)
Kessler, Herbert L., 'On the State of Medieval Art History', *The Art Bulletin* 70:2 (1988), pp. 166–187
Kiple, K.F., 'The History of Disease', in *The Cambridge History of Medicine*, ed. by R. Porter (Cambridge: Cambridge University Press, 2006), pp. 10–46
Kjær, Mårten and Vogt, Helle, 'Straf og forvisning i det efter-reformatoriske Danmark-Norge', in *Reformationen, 1500-talets kulturrevolution*, bind 2 Danmark, ed. by Ole Høiris and Per Ingesman (Aarhus: Aarhus University Press, 2017), pp. 393–411
Kopytoff, Igor, 'The Cultural Biography of Things: Commoditization as Process', in *The Social Life of Things: Commodities in Cultural Perspective*, ed. by A. Appadurai (Cambridge: Cambridge University Press, 1986), pp. 64–91
Kress, Helga, 'Grey þykir mér Freyja', in *Fyrir dyrum fóstru. Greinar um konur og kynferði í íslenskum fornbókmenntum* (Reykjavík: Háskóli Íslands & Rannsóknarstofa í kvennafræðum, 1996)
Kristinsson, Axel, *Hnignun, hvaða hnignun? Goðsögnin um niðurlægingartímabilið í sögu Íslands* (Reykjavík: Sögufélag, 2018)
Kristjánsdóttir, Guðbjörg, *Íslenska teiknibókin* (Reykjavík: Crymogea, 2013)
Kristjánsdóttir, Steinunn, 'Klaustureyjan á Sundum', *Árbók Hins íslenska fornleifafélags 1994* (1995), pp. 29–52
———, 'The Tip of the Iceberg: The Material of Skriðuklaustur Monastery and Hospital', *NAR* 43:1 (2010), pp. 44–62
———, 'The Poisoned Arrows of Amor', *Scandinavian Journal of History* 38:4 (2011), pp. 406–418
———, *Sagan af klaustrinu á Skriðu* (Reykjavík: Sögufélag, 2012)
———, 'Becoming Christian: A Matter of Everyday Resistance and Negotiation', *Norwegian Archaeological Review* 48:1 (2015), pp. 27–45
———, 'Ankorítar og hermítar á Íslandi', *Saga* LIII:1 (2015), pp. 46–69
———, 'No Society Is an Island – Skriðuklaustur Monastery and the Fringes of Monasticism', *The Journal of Medieval Monastic Studies* 4 (2015), pp. 153–172
———, 'Introduction', in *Bláklædda konan – ný rannsókn á fornu kumli/Bundled-up in blue -the re-investigation of a Viking grave*, ed. by Bryndís Sverrisdóttir (Reykjavík: National Museum of Iceland, 2015), pp. 9–13
———, 'Lost Paths. Climate Changes and the Forgotten Route to Skriðuklaustur Monastery, Eastern Iceland', *Anthropos* 111 (2016), pp. 1–8
———, *Leitin að klaustrunum* (Reykjavík: Sögufélag, 2017)
———, 'Medieval Monasticism in Iceland and Norse Greenland', *Religions* 12 (2021), pp. 53–64
———, 'Lokun íslensku miðaldaklaustranna', *Ritröð Guðfræðistofnunar* 53 (2021), pp. 74–96

Kristjánsdóttir, Þóra, *Mynd á þili: íslenskir myndlistarmenn á 16., 17. og 18. öld* (Reykjavík: JVP and Þjóðminjasafn Íslands, 2005)

———, 'A Nocturnal Wake at Hólar. The Judgement Day Panels as a Possible Explanation for a Miracle Legend?' in *The Nordic Apocalypse*, ed. by Terry Gunnell and Annette Lassen (Turnhout: Brepols, 2013), pp. 225–228

Kristjánsdóttir, Steinunn and Collins, Cecilia, 'Cases of Hydatid Disease in Medieval Iceland', *International Journal of Osteoarchaeology* 21:4 (2011), pp. 479–486

Kristjánsdóttir, Steinunn, Larsson, Inger and Åsen, Per Arvid, 'The Icelandic Medieval Monastic Garden – Did it Exist?' *Scandinavian Journal of History* 39:5 (2014), pp. 560–579

Kristjánsson, Gunnar, 'Málverksmyndir, skurðgoð og líkneskjur', in *Áhrif Lúthers. Siðaskipti, samfélag og menning í 500 ár*, ed. by Hjalti Hugason, Loftur Guttormsson og Margrét Eggertsdóttir (Reykjavík: Hið íslenska bókmenntafélag, 2017), pp. 215–241

Krongaard Kristiansen, Hans, 'Den Danske Klostre og Reformationen', in *Reformationen, 1500-talets kulturrevolution*, bind 2 Danmark, ed. by Ole Høiris and Per Ingesman (Aarhus: Aarhus University Press, 2017), pp. 223–245

Kurmann-Schwarz, Brigitte, 'Gothic Stained Glass', in *The Art of Gothic: Architecture, Sculpture, Painting*, ed. by Rolf Thoman (Köln: Könemann, 1999)

Lagerås, Per, 'Current Knowledge on the Late-Medieval Crisis', in *Environment, Society and the Black Death. An Interdisciplinary Approach to the Late-Medieval Crisis in Sweden*, ed. by Per Lagerås (Oxford: Oxbow Books, 2016), pp. 6–22

———, 'Summary of conclusions', in *Environment, Society and the Black Death. An Interdisciplinary Approach to the Late-Medieval Crisis in Sweden*, ed. by Per Lagerås (Oxford: Oxbow Books, 2016, pp. 160–162

Lane, Paul, 'The Archaeology of Christianity in Global Perspective', in *Archaeology and World Religion*, ed. by Timothy Insoll (London and New York: Routledge, 2001), pp. 148–181

Lange, Christian, *De norske Klostres Historie i Middelalderen* (Christiania: Tönsberg Udgave, 1856)

Lauwers, Michel, 'Constructing Monastic Space in the Early and Central Medieval West (Fifth to Twelfth Century)', in *The Cambridge History of Medieval Monasticism in the Latin West*, ed. by Alison I. Beach and Isabelle Cochelin (Cambridge: Cambridge University Press, 2020), pp. 317–339

Lawrence, C.H., *Medieval Monasticism: Forms of Religious Life in Western Europe in the Middle Ages*, 3rd ed (New York: Longmans, 2001)

L'Hermite-Leclercq, Paulette, 'Reclusion in the Middle Ages', in *The Cambridge History of Medieval Monasticism in the Latin West*, ed. by Alison I. Beach and Isabelle Cochelin (Cambridge: Cambridge University Press, 2020), pp. 747–765

Lindberg, C., *The European Reformations* (Malden: Blackwell Publishers, 1996)

Lockhart, Paul Douglas, *Denmark 1513–1660. The Rise and Decline of Renaissance Monarchy* (Oxford: Oxford University Press, 2007)

Logan, Donald F., *A History of the Church in the Middle Ages* (London and New York: Routledge, 2002)

Loth, Agnete, *Reykjahólabók. Islandske Helgenlegender* (Copenhagen: Munksgaard, 1969)

Lucas, Gavin, 'Íslensk fornleifafræði í norður-evrópsku samhengi', *Ritið* (2004), pp. 11–17

———, 'Hofstaðir in the Settlement Period', in *Hofstaðir. Excavations of a Viking Age Feasting Hall in North-Eastern Iceland*, ed. by Gavin Lucas (Reykjavík: Fornleifastofnun Íslands, 2009), pp. 371–408

———, *Writing the Past. Knowledge and Literary Production in Archaeology* (London and New York: Routledge, 2019)

Lucas, Gavin and Hreiðarsdóttir, Elín, 'The Archaeology of Capitalism in Iceland: The View from Viðey', *International Journal of Historical Archaeology* 16 (2012), pp. 604–621

Luxford, Julian M., *The Art and Architecture of English Benedictine Monasteries 1300–1540* (Woodbridge: The Boydell Press, 2005)

Lyon, Jonathan R., 'Nobility and Monastic Patronage: The View from Outside the Monastery', in *The Cambridge History of Medieval Monasticism in the Latin West*, ed. by Alison I. Beach and Isabelle Cochelin (Cambridge: Cambridge University Press, 2020), pp. 848–864

Madigan, Kevin, *Medieval Christianity. A New History* (Yale: Yale University Press, 2015)

Magerøy, Ellen M., 'Islandsk hornskurd. Drikkehorn fra før "brennevinstiden"', in *Bibliotheca Arnamagnæana. Supplementum* 7 (Hafniæ: C.A. Reitzel, 2000)

Magnani, Eliana, 'Female House Ascetics from the Fourth to Twelfth Century', in *The Cambridge History of Medieval Monasticism in the Latin West*, ed. by Alison I. Beach and Isabelle Cochelin (Cambridge: Cambridge University Press, 2020), pp. 213–231

Magnúsdóttir, Auður, *Frillor och fruar. Politik och samlevnad på Island 1120–1400* (Göteborg: Göteborgs universitet, 2001)

Magnúsdóttir, Auður, 'Móðir, kona, meyja. Um karlalegar konur og kynlausar meyjar á miðöldum', in *2. íslenska söguþingið 30. maí–1. júní 2002*, ed. by Erla Hulda Halldórsdóttir (Reykjavík: Sagnfræðistofnun Háskóla Íslands, Sagnfræðingafélag Íslands and Sögufélag, 2002)

Magnúsardóttir, Lára, 'Syndin fyrir dómstólum: Um lagagildi skriftaboða og tengsl syndar og glæps í refsirétti og dómskerfi kirkjunnar á síðmiðöldum', *Saga* 45:1 (2007), pp. 131–159

Magnússon, Árni, 'Um klaustrin', *Blanda* II (1921–1923), pp. 32–47

———, *Chorographica Islandica*. Safn til sögu Íslands og íslenskra bókmennta. II fl., I.2. (Reykjavík: Hið íslenska bókmenntafélag, 1953)

Magnússon, Sigurður Gylfi, *Sjálfssögur. Minni, minningar og saga* (Reykjavík: Háskólaútgáfan, 2005)

Majander, Kerttu, Pfrengle, Saskia, Kocher, Arthur, Neukamm, Judith, du Plessis, Louis, Pla-Dı´az, Marta, Arora, Natasha, Akgu, Gulfirde, Salo, Kati, Schats, Rachel, Inskip, Sarah, Oinonen, Markku, Valk, Heiki, Malve, Martin, Kriiska, Aivar, Onkamo, Paivi, Gonzalez-Candelas, Fernando and Kuhnert, Denise, 'Ancient Bacterial Genomes Reveal a High Diversity of Treponema pallidum Strains in Early Modern Europe', *Current Biology* 30 (2020), pp. 3788–3803

Masur, Laura, 'Symbol or Presence? Archaeology and the Materiality of Catholic Devotions', *U.S. Catholic Historian* 38:2 (2020), pp. 1–21

Mays, S., Crane-Kramer, G. and Bayliss, A., 'Two Probable Cases of Treponemal Disease of Medieval Date from England', *American Journal of Physical Anthropology* 120 (2003), pp. 133–143

McClain, A., 'Theory, Disciplinary Perspectives and the Archaeology of Later Medieval England', *Medieval Archaeology* 56 (2012), pp. 131–170

McCluskey, Stephan C., 'Gregory of Tours, Monastic Timekeeping, and Early Christian Attitudes to Astronomy', *Isis* 81:1 (1990), pp. 8–22

Mehler, Natascha, Kristjánsdóttir, Steinunn and Kluttig-Altmann, Ralf, 'The Sound of Silence – A Ceramic Horn and Its Role in Monasticism in Late Medieval Iceland', *Early Music* XLVI:4 (2018), pp. 551–560

Melczer, W., *The Pilgrim's Guide to Santiago de Compostela* (New York: Italica Press, 1993)

Mímisson, Kristján and Einarsson, Bjarni F., 'Klausturlíf kvenna í Skaftárþingi. Fornleifarannsóknir á Kirkjubæjarklaustri 1995–2006', *Dynskógar* 11 (2008), pp. 151–177

———, '"*Ora et labora*". Efnisveruleiki klausturlífs á Kirkjubæjarklaustri', in *Endurfundir*, ed. by Guðmundur Ólafsson and Steinunn Kristjánsdóttir (Reykjavík: Þjóðminjasafn Íslands, 2009), pp. 44–57

Møller-Christensen, Vilhelm, *Æbelholt kloster*. First pub. 1958 (Kaupmannahöfn: Nationalmuseet, 1982)

Møller Jensen, Janus, 'Danmark og den hellige krig. En undersøgelse af korstogsbevægelsens indflydelse på Danmark ca. 1070–1169', *Historisk tidskrift* 100:1 (2013), pp. 285–328

Møller, Jes Fabricius and Østergård, Uffe, 'Lutheran Orthodoxy and Anti-Catholicism in Denmark – 1536–2011', *European Studies* 31 (2013), pp. 165–189

Morris, Alan, *Europe and England in the Sixteenth Century* (London and New York: Routledge, 1998)

Mundal, Else, *Legender fra mellomalderen: soger om heilage kvinner og menn* (Oslo: Norske samlaget, 1995)

Munro, John, 'Three Centuries of Luxury Textile Consumption in the Low Countries and England, 1330–1570: Trends and Comparisons of Real Values of Woollen Broadcloths (Then and Now)', in *The Medieval Broadcloth. Changing Fashions, Manufacturing and Consumption*, ed. by Kathrine Vestergård Pedersen and Marie-Louise B. Nosch. Ancient Textile Series vol. 6 (Oxford and Oakville: Oxbow Books, 2009), pp. 1–73

Muschiol, Gisela, 'Gender and Monastic Liturgy in the Latin West (High and Late Middle Ages)', in *The Cambridge History of Medieval Monasticism in the Latin West*, ed. by Alison I. Beach and Isabelle Cochelin (Cambridge: Cambridge University Press, 2020), pp. 803–815

Nedkvitne, Arnved, *Møte med døden i norrøn middelalder. En mentalitetshistorisk studie* (Oslo: Cappelen Akademisk Forlag, 1997)

———, *The German Hansa and Bergen 1100–1600* (Köln, Weimar, Wien: Böhlau Verlag, 2014)

Netterstrøm, Jeppe Büchert, 'Reformationens betydning for kriminalisering af manddrab', in *Reformationen, 1500-talets kulturrevolution*, bind 2 Danmark, ed. by Ole Høiris and Per Ingesman (Aarhus: Aarhus University Press, 2017), pp. 413–490

Nyberg, Tore, *Monasticism in North-Western Europe 800–1200* (London: Routledge, 2000)

Ó Clabaigh, Colmán, OSB, *The Friars in Ireland, 1224–1540* (Dublin: Four Court Press, 2012)

———, 'Monasticism, Colonization, and Ethnic Tension in Late Medieval Ireland', in *The Cambridge History of Medieval Monasticism in the Latin West*, ed. by Alison I. Beach and Isabelle Cochelin (Cambridge: Cambridge University Press, 2020), pp. 901–920

Óla, Árni, *Viðeyjarklaustur. Drög að sögu Viðeyjar* (Akureyri: Kvöldvökuútgáfan, 1969)

Ólason, Páll Eggert, *Menn og menntir siðskiptaaldarinnar á Íslandi*. Bindi I. Jón Arason (Reykjavík: Bókaverslun Guðmundar Gamalíelssonar, 1919)

———, *Menn og menntir siðskiptaaldarinnar á Íslandi*. Bindi II. Ögmundur Pálsson, Gizur Einarsson og samherjar hans (Reykjavík: Bókaverslun Guðmundar Gamalíelssonar, 1922)

———, *Menn og menntir siðskiptaaldarinnar á Íslandi*. Bindi III. Guðbrandur Þorláksson og öld hans (Reykjavík: Bókaverslun Guðmundar Gamalíelssonar, 1924)

———, *Menn og menntir siðskiptaaldarinnar á Íslandi*. Bindi IV. Rithöfundar (Reykjavík: Bókaverslun Guðmundar Gamalíelssonar, 1926)

Oldenburg, Scott, 'Toward a Multicultural Mid-Tudor England: The Queen's Royal Entry Circa 1553, *The Interlude of Wealth and Health*, and the Question of Strangers in the Reign of Mary I', *ELH* 76 (2009), pp. 99–129

Olmer, Emil, *Boksamlingar i Island 1149–1490* (Gautaborg: Wald. Zachrissons boktryckeri A. B., 1902)

Ómarsdóttir, Freyja Hlíðkvist and Walser, Joe W. III, 'The Grave Good', in *Bláklædda konan – ný rannsókn á fornu kumli/Bundled-up in blue -the re-investigation of a Viking grave*, ed. by Bryndís Sverrisdóttir (Reykjavík: National Museum of Iceland, 2015), pp. 65–70

Oulíková, Petra, 'Sphragistic Artefacts of the Benedictines', in *Open the Gates of Paradise. The Benedictines in the Heart of Europe 800–1300*, ed. by Dusan Foltýn et al. (Prague: The National Gallery in Prague, 2015), pp. 372–405

Øye, Ingvild, 'Tools and Textile Production in the North Atlantic', in *Shetland and the Viking World: Papers from the Seventeenth Viking Congress*, ed. by Turner, Owen and Vaugh (Lerwick: Shetland Heritage Publications, 2016), pp. 245–250

Pálsson, Hermann, *Helgafell – saga höfuðbóls og klausturs* (Reykjavík: Snæfellingaútgáfan, 1967)

Pasulka, Diana Walsh, *Heaven Can Wait. Purgatory in Catholic Devotional and Popular Culture* (Oxford: Oxford University Press, 2015)

Pelletier, Chloé M., 'The Pilgrim's Badge: Water, Air, and the Flow of Sacred Matter', *Postmedieval* 8:2 (2017), pp. 240–253

Petersen, Nils Holger, 'Reformationen og ritualerna', in *Reformationen, 1500-talets kulturrevolution*, bind 1 Europa, ed. by Ole Høiris and Per Ingesman (Aarhus: Aarhus University Press, 2017), pp. 131–150

Pétursdóttir, Þóra, 'Small Things Forgotten Now Included, or What Else Do Things Deserve?' *International Journal of Historical Archaeology* 16:3 (2012), pp. 577–603

Þór, Jón Þ., 'Saga biskupsstóls á Hólum í Hjaltadal', in *Saga biskupsstólanna*, ed. by Gunnar Kristjánsson (Hólar: Bókaútgáfan Hólar, 2006), pp. 245–427

———, 'Hólabiskupa ævir', in *Saga biskupsstólanna*, ed. by Gunnar Kristjánsson (Hólar: Bókaútgáfan Hólar, 2006), pp. 403–428

Þorkelsson, Jón, *Digtningen paa Island i det 15. og 16. århundrede* (Copenhagen: Höst & Sön, 1888)

Þorláksson, Helgi, *Vaðmál og verðlag: Vaðmál í utanlandsviðskiptum og búskap Íslendinga á 13. og 14. öld* (Reykjavík: Háskóli Íslands, 1991)

———, 'Þjóðhagir og samfélagshópar', in *Saga Íslands vi*, ed. by Sigurður Líndal (Reykjavík: Hið íslenska bókmenntafélag, 2003), pp. 121–162

———, 'Þorgils á Þingeyrum. Um upphaf Þingeyraklausturs', *Saga* XLVI:1 (2008), pp. 169–180

———, 'Deila um gildi fornleifa og ritheimilda', *Saga* LI:2 (2013), pp. 183–185

———, 'Snorri Sturluson the Aristocrat. Becomes *lendr maðr*', in *Snorri Sturluson and Reykholt. The Author and Magnate, His Life, Works and Environment at Reykholt in Iceland*, ed. by Guðrún Sveinbjarnardóttir and Helgi Þorláksson (Copenhagen: Museum Tusculanum Press, 2018), pp. 33–78

Þorsteinsson, Björn, *Íslenska þjóðveldið* (Reykjavík: Heimskringla, 1953)

———, *Íslensk miðaldasaga* (Reykjavík: Sögufélag, 1978)

Þorsteinsson, Björn and Grímsdóttir, Guðrún Ása, 'Enska öldin', in *Saga Íslands v*, ed. by Sigurður Líndal (Reykjavík: Hið íslenska bókmenntafélag, 1990), pp. 3–217

Þorvarðardóttir, Ólína, *Brennuöldin. Galdur og galdratrú í málskjölum og munnmælum* (Reykjavík: Háskólaútgáfan, 2000)

Power, Eileen, *Medieval English Nunneries c. 1275 to 1535* (Cambridge: Cambridge University Press, 1922)

Prestwich, M.C., *Plantagenet England: 1225–1360* (Oxford: Oxford University Press, 2005)

Raaijmakers, Janneke, 'Missions in the Northern and Eastern Frontiers c. 700–1100', in *The Cambridge History of Medieval Monasticism in the Latin West*, ed. by Alison I. Beach and Isabelle Cochelin (Cambridge: Cambridge University Press, 2020), pp. 485–501

Rasmussen, Linda, 'Monastic Benefactors in England and Denmark: Their Social Background and Gender Distributions', in *Religious and Laity in Western Europe 1000–1400*, ed. by Emilia Jamroziak and Janet Burton (Turnhout: Brepols, 2006), pp. 77–91

Rasmussen, Tarald, 'Døden og de døde', in *Reformationen, 1500-talets kulturrevolution*, bind 2 Danmark, ed. by Ole Høiris and Per Ingesman (Aarhus: Aarhus University Press, 2017), pp. 371–390

Rasmussen, K.L., Boldsen, J.L., Kristensen, H.K., Skytte, L., Hansen, K.L., Mølholm, L., Grootes, P.M., Nadeau, M-J. and Eriksen, K.M.F., 'Mercury Levels in Danish Medieval Human Bones', *Journal of Archaeological Science* 35 (2008), pp. 2295–2306

Rathje, W.L. and Murphy, C., *Rubbish! The Archaeology of Garbage* (Tucson: The University of Arizona Press, 2001)

Ricciardi, Paola and Schmidt Patterson, Catherine, 'Science of the Book. Analytical Methods for the Study of Illuminated Manuscripts', in *The Art and Science of Illuminated Manuscripts*, ed. by Panayotova, Stella (London: Harvey Miller Publishers, 2020), pp. 35–71

Riddell, Scott J., Erlendsson, Egill, Eddudóttir, Sigrún D., Gísladóttir, Guðrún and Kristjánsdóttir, Steinunn, 'Pollen, Plague and Protestants: The Medieval Monastery of Þingeyrar (Þingeyraklaustur) in Northern Iceland', *Environmental Archaeology* (2022). DOI: 10.1080/14614103.2018.1531191

Ríkharðsdóttir, Sif, *Medieval Translations and Cultural Discourse. The Movements of Texts in England, France and Scandinavia* (Cambridge: D.S. Brewer, 2012)

———, 'Oceanic Networks. Literary Production, Transmission, and Mediation Across the North', in *The Meaning of Media*, ed. by Anna Catharina Horn and Karl G. Johansson (Berlin: De Gruyter, 2021), pp. 103–124

Röckelein, 'Monastic Landscapes', in *The Cambridge History of Medieval Monasticism in the Latin West*, ed. by Alison I. Beach and Isabelle Cochelin (Cambridge: Cambridge University Press, 2020), pp. 816–830

Roffey, Simon, 'Deconstructing a Symbolic World: The Reformation and the English Medieval Parish Chantry', in *The Archaeology of Reformation 1480–1580*, ed. by David Gaimster and Roberta Gilchrist (Leeds: Maney Publishing, 2003), pp. 341–355

Romero-Raverón, Rafael and Arráes-Abyar, Luis A., 'Ole Worm (1588–1654) Anatomist and Antiquarian', *European Journal of Anatomy* 19:3 (2015), pp. 299–301

Rosewell, Roger, *The Medieval Monastery* (Oxford: Shire Publications, 2012)

Salonen, Kirsi, 'Forbidden Marital Strategies: Papal Marriage Dispensations for Scandinavian Couples in the Later Middle Ages', in *Medieval Christianity in the North*, ed. by K. Salonen, K. Villads Jensen and T. Jørgensen (Turnhout: Brepols, 2013), pp. 181–208

Schilling, Heinz, 'Discipline: The State and the Churches in Early Modern Europe', in *Social Control in Europe 1500–1800*, ed. by Hermann Roodenburg and Pieter Spierenburg (Ohio: The Ohio State University Press, 2004), pp. 25–36

Schmid, Magdalena M.E., Dugmore, Andy, Vésteinsson, Orri and Newton, Anthony J., 'Thepra Isochrons and Chronologies of Colonisation', *Quaternary Geochronology* 40 (2017), pp. 56–66

Schulte, Augustin Joseph, 'Altar Wine', in *The Catholic Encyclopaedia*, I (New York: Robert Appleton Company, 1907)

Schwarz Lausten, Martin, 'The Early Reformation in Denmark and Norway 1520–1559', in *The Scandinavian Reformation from Evangelical Movement to Institutionalisation of Reform*, ed. by Ole Peter Grell (Cambridge: Cambridge University Press, 1995), pp. 12–41

———, *Luther og Danmark i 500 år* (Copenhagen: Gads Forlag, 2017)

———, 'Kongemagt og rigets vel', in *Reformationen i dansk kirke og kultur 1517–1700*, bind 1, ed. by Niels Hendrik Gregersen and Carsten Bach-Nielsen (Odense: Syddansk Universitetsforlag, 2017), pp. 121–158

Scott, Ian R., 'Romsey Abbey: Benedictine Nunnery and Parish Church', in *Monastic Archaeology*, ed. by Graham Keevill, Mick Aston and Teresa Hall (Oxford: Oxbow, 2001), pp. 151–160

Seesko, Per, 'Between King and Congregation. Monastery Churches and Parish Organization in the Kingdom of Denmark after the Reformation', in *The Dissolution of Monasteries*, ed. by Per Seesko, Louise Nyholm Kallestrup and Lars Bisgaard (Odense: University Press of Southern Denmark, 2019), pp. 273–296

Sharp, 'Bishops, Canon Law, and the Religious, c. 1140–1350', in *The Cambridge History of Medieval Monasticism in the Latin West*, ed. by Alison I. Beach and Isabelle Cochelin (Cambridge: Cambridge University Press, 2020), pp. 1093–1108

Shoemaker, Karl, *Sanctuary and Crime in the Middle Ages 400–1500* (Bronx: Fordham University Press, 2011)

Shorter, E., 'Primary Care', in *The Cambridge History of Medicine*, ed. by R. Porter (Cambridge: Cambridge University Press, 2006), 103–135

Signori, Gabriela, 'Anchorites in German-Speaking Regions', in *Anchoritic Traditions of Medieval Europe*, ed. by Liz Herbert McAvoy (Woodbridge: The Boydell Press, 2010), pp. 43–61

Sigurdson, Erika, *The Church in Fourteenth Century Iceland: The Formation of an Elite Clerical Identity* (Leiden: Brill, 2016)

Sigurjónsson, Arnór, *Vestfirðingasaga 1390–1540* (Reykjavík: Prentsmiðjan Leiftur, 1975)

Sigurðsson, Ágúst, 'Drög að sögu Möðruvallaklausturs' (unpublished thesis, University of Iceland, 1965)

Sigurðsson, Gísli, *Gaelic Influence in Iceland. Historical and Literary Contacts* (Reykjavík: University of Iceland Press, 2000)

Sigurðsson, Jón Viðar, *Frá goðorðum til ríkja. Þróun goðavalds á 12. og 13. öld* (Reykjavík: Bókaútgáfa Menningarsjóðs, 1989)

———, 'Samskipti íslenskra biskupa við útlenda yfirboðara á öldum áður', in *Saga biskupsstólanna*, ed. by Gunnar Kristjánsson (Hólar: Bókaútgáfan Hólar, 2006), pp. 491–516

———, *Det norrøne samfunnet. Vikingen, kongen, erkebiskopen og bonden* (Oslo: Pax Forlag, 2008)

Sigurðsson, Páll, *Svipmyndir úr réttarsögu* (Reykjavík: Bókaútgáfan Skjaldborg, 1992)

Sigurðsson, Þorsteinn, 'Um Skriðuklaustur', Hannes Þorsteinsson bjó til prentunar, *Blanda* I (1918–1920), pp. 238–240

Sigurður, Nordal, 'Flateyjarbók', *Tímarit máls og menningar* 32:1 (1971), pp. 1–3

Sigurður, Vigfússon, 'Rannsóknir á Vesturlandi 1891', *Árbók Hins íslenzka fornleifafélags 1893* (1893), pp. 61–73

Simpson, James, 'The Rule of Medieval Imagination', in *Images, Idolatry, and Iconoclasm in Late Medieval England: Textuality and the Visual Image*, ed. by Jeremy Dimmick, James Simpson and Nicolette (Oxford: Oxford University Press, 2002), pp. 4–24

Skórzewska, Joanna A., *Constructing a Cult: The Life and Veneration of Guðmundr Arason (1161–1237) in the Icelandic Written Sources* (Leiden, Boston: Brill, 2011)

Skovmand, Michael, 'Den engelske Reformation', in *Reformationen i dansk kirke og kultur 1517–1700*, bind 1, ed. by Niels Hendrik Gregersen and Carsten Bach-Nielsen (Odense: Syddansk Universitetsforlag, 2017), pp. 307–320

Skúlason, Bergsveinn, *Um eyjar og annes. Ferðaþættir og minningar frá Breiðafirði* (Reykjavík: Bókaútgáfan Fróði, 1964)

Slocum, Kenneth, 'The Investiture Controversy', in *Sources in Medieval Culture and History*, ed. by Kenneth Slocum, (Boston: Prentice Hall, 2010), pp. 170–175

Spicer, Andrew, 'Iconoclasm and Adaptation: The Reformation of the Churches in Scotland and the Netherlands', in *The Archaeology of Reformation 1480–1580*, ed. by David Gaimster and Roberta Gilchrist (Leeds: Maney Publishing, 2003), pp. 29–43

Spierenburg, Pieter, *Violence and Punishment. Civilizing the Body Through Time* (Cambridge: Polity Press, 2013)

Squatriti, Paolo, *Water and Society in Early Medieval Italy, AD 400–1000, Parti 400–1000* (Cambridge: Cambridge University Press, 2002)

Stefánsson, Magnús, 'Kirkjuvald eflist', in *Saga Íslands* ii, ed. by Sigurður Líndal (Reykjavík: Hið íslenzka bókmenntafélag and Sögufélag, 1975), pp. 57–146

———, 'Frá goðakirkju til biskupskirkju', in *Saga Íslands* iii, ed. by Sigurður Líndal (Reykjavík: Hið íslenzka bókmenntafélag and Sögufélag, 1978), pp. 111–257

———, 'Um staði og staðamál', *Saga* XL:2 (2002), pp. 139–166

Steffensen, Jón, 'Rannsóknir á kirkjugarðinum í Haffjarðarey sumarið 1945', *Skírnir* CXX (1945), pp. 144–162

Steinersen, Oivind and Libaek, Ivar, *The History of Norway, From the Ice Age Until Today* (Lysaker: Dinamo Forlag, 2007)

Steinsson, Heimir, 'Jarðir Skriðuklausturs og efnahagur', *Múlaþing* 1 (1966), pp. 74–103

Stig Sørensen, Marie-Luise, *Gender Archaeology* (Cambridge: Polity Press, 2000)

Stöber, Karen, 'Bequests and Burials: Changing Attitudes of the Laity as Patrons of English and Wales Monasteries', in *Religious and Laity in Western Europe 1000–1400*, ed. by Emilia Jamroziak and Janet Burton (Turnhout: Brepols, 2006), pp. 131–146

Stopford, J., 'Some Approaches to the Archaeology of Christian Pilgrimage', *World Archaeology* 26:1 (1994), pp. 57–72

Streeter, Richard T., *Tephrochronology, Landscape and Population: Impacts of Plague on Medieval Iceland* (Edinburgh: The University of Edinburgh, 2011)

Stutza, A. and Abrudan Caciora, S. V., 'The Relationship Between Words, Texts, Clothes, and Textiles', *Annals of The University of Oradea, Fascicle of Textiles, Leatherwork* XVIII:2 (2001), pp. 95–98

Sveinbjörnsdóttir, Árný E. et al., '^{14}C Dating of the Settlement of Iceland', *Radiocarbon* 46:1 (2004), pp. 387–394

Tarlow, Sarah, 'Reformation and Transformation', in *The Archaeology of Reformation 1480–1580*, ed. by David Gaimster and Roberta Gilchrist (Leeds: Maney Publishing, 2003), pp. 108–121

Tarlow, Sarah and Lowman, Emma B., *Harnessing the Power of the Criminal Corpse* (Cham: Palgrave Macmillan, 2018)

Teitsson, Björn, 'Bjarnarfeldir í máldögum', in *Afmælisrit Björns Sigfússonar*, ed. by Björn Teitsson, Björn Þorsteinsson and Sverrir Tómasson (Reykjavík: Sögufélag, 1975), pp. 23–47

Thibodeaux, Jennifer D., 'Man of the Church, or Man of the Village? Gender and the Parish Clergy in Medieval Normandy', *Gender and History* 18:2 (2006), pp. 380–399

———, 'Introduction: Rethinking the Medieval Clergy and Masculinity', in *Negotiating Clerical Identities: Priests, Monks and Masculinity in the Middle Ages*, ed. by Jennifer D. Thibodeaux (Basingstoke: Palgrave Macmillan, 2010), pp. 1–15

Thomas, Sarah E., 'The Diocese of Sodor Between Niðarós and Avignon-Rome, 1266–1472', *Northern Studies* 41 (2009/10), pp. 22–40

———, 'Clerical Illegitimacy in the Diocese of Sodor – Exception or Rule in the Late Medieval Church?' in *Heresy and the Making of European Culture: Medieval and Modern Perspectives*, ed. by A. Roach and J. Simpson (Farnham: Ashgate, 2013), pp. 313–332

Thurlkill, Mary, *Sacred Scents in Early Christianity and Islam: Studies in Body and Religion* (Lanham: Rowman & Littlefield, 2016)

Tómasson, Sverrir, 'Þingeyrar – stærsta íslenska menningarsetrið á miðöldum', *Húnvetningar. Ársrit Húnvetningafélagsins í Reykjavík* 28 (2009), pp. 19–20
Vanherpen, Sofie, 'Remembering Unnr/Auðr djúp(a)uðga Ketilsdóttir. Construction of Cultural Memory and Female Religious Identity', *Mirator* 14/2 (2013), pp. 61–78
Vésteinsson, Orri, *The Christianisation of Iceland: Priests, Power and Social Change 1000–1300* (New York: Oxford University Press, 2000)
Vésteinsson, Orri and Gestsdóttir, Hildur, 'The Colonisation of Iceland in Light of Isotope Analyses', in *Viking Settlers of the North Atlantic: An Isotopic Approach*, ed. by Price TD, *Journal of the North Atlantic* 7 (2016), pp. 137–145
Vésteinsson, Orri, Sveinbjörnsdóttir, Árný, Gestsdóttir, Hildur, Heinemeier, Jan and Friðriksson, Adolf, 'Dating Religious Change: Pagan and Christian in Viking Age Iceland', *Journal of Social Archaeology* 19:2 (2019), pp. 162–180
Vídalín, Arngrímur, 'Ólafur Ormsson's *Leiðarvísir* and Its Context. The Fourteenth Century Text of a Supposed Twelfth Century Itinerary', *Journal of English and Germanic Philology* (2018), pp. 212–234
Walaker Nordeide, Sæbjørg, *The Viking Age as a Period of Religious Transformation* (Turnhout: Brepols, 2011)
———, 'Canonical Observance in Norway in the Middle Ages: The Observance of Dietary Regulations', in *Medieval Christianity in the North*, ed. by K. Salonen, K. Villads Jensen and T. Jørgensen (Turnhout: Brepols, 2013), pp. 41–66
Waldron, Tony, *Palaeopathology* (Cambridge: Cambridge University Press, 2009)
Walgenbach, Elizabeth, 'Church Sanctuary in the Contemporary Sagas', in *Íslensk klausturmenning á miðöldum*, ed. by Haraldur Bernharðsson (Reykjavík: Miðaldastofa Háskóla Íslands and Háskólaútgáfan, 2016), pp. 102–117
Walser, Joe Walser III, 'Reading the Bones. From the Osteological Perspective', in *Bláklædda konan – ný rannsókn á fornu kumli/Bundled-up in blue -the re-investigation of a Viking grave*, ed. by Bryndís Sverrisdóttir (Reykjavík: National Museum of Iceland, 2015), pp. 47–56
———, Kristjánsdóttir, Steinunn, Gowland, Rebecca and Desnica, Natasa, 'Volcanoes, Medicine, and Monasticism: Investigating Mercury Q1 Exposure in Medieval Iceland', *International Journal of Osteoarchaeology* 29 (2019), pp. 48–61
Walser, J.W. III, Kristjánsdóttir, S., Gröcke, D., Gowland, R., Jakob, T., Nowell, G., Ottley, C., and Montgomery, J., 'At the World's Edge: Reconstructing Diet and Geographic Origins in Medieval Iceland Using Isotope and Trace Element Analyses', *American Journal of Physical Anthropology* 171 (2020), pp. 142–163
Wandel, Gertie, 'Íslenzk altarisklæði í erlendum söfnum', *Melkorka* 3 (1952), pp. 51–54
Whiting, Robert, *The Blind Devotion of the People* (Cambridge: Cambridge University Press, 1989)
Williams, Patrick, 'Katherine of Aragon', *History of Review* 69 (2011), pp. 36–41
Winroth, Anders, *The Conversion of Scandinavia. Vikings, Merchants, and Missionaries in the Remaking of Northern Europe* (New Heaven and London: Yale University Press, 2012)
Wolf, Kirsten, *The Book of Reykjahólar. The Last of the Great Medieval Legendries* (Urbana, IL: University of Illinois Press, 1996)
———, *The Icelandic Legend of Saint Dorothy. Studies and Texts 130* (Toronto: Pontifical Institute of Medieval Studies, 1997)
———, *The Old Norse-Icelandic Legend of Saint Barbara. Studies and Texts 134* (Toronto: Pontifical Institute of Medieval Studies, 2000)
———, *A Female Legendary from Iceland*, ed. by Kirsten Wolf (Copenhagen: Museum Tusculanum Press, 2011)

———, *The Legends of the Saints in Old Norse-Icelandic Prose* (Toronto, Buffalo and London: University of Toronto Press, 2013)

———, 'Low German Legends of the Apostles in Icelandic Translations', *Gripla* XXVI (2015), pp. 139–183

Wood, Susan, *The Proprietary Church in the Medieval West* (Oxford: Oxford University Press, 2013)

Woolf, A., 'The diocese of Sudreyar' in *Ecclesia Nidrosiensis 1153–1537 Søkelys på Nidaroskirkens og Nidarosprovinsens historie*, ed. by S. Imsen (Trondheim: Fagbokforlaget, 2003)

INDEX

Made in the USA
Las Vegas, NV
29 October 2024

c6789b8d-213a-4e34-b744-cc3ac98f9b2bR01